# Thinking Straight about Being Gay

# Thinking Straight about Being Gay

Why It Matters if We're Born That Way

*by*

T. M. MURRAY, PHD

authorHOUSE

*AuthorHouse™ UK*
*1663 Liberty Drive*
*Bloomington, IN 47403 USA*
*www.authorhouse.co.uk*
*Phone: 0800.197.4150*

*Published by AuthorHouse  08/11/2015*

*ISBN: 978-1-5049-4396-3 (sc)*
*ISBN: 978-1-5049-4395-6 (hc)*
*ISBN: 978-1-5049-4397-0 (e)*

*Print information available on the last page.*

# CONTENTS

# ACKNOWLEDGMENTS

I am deeply indebted to Dr. Beverley Clack of The Westminister Institute of Education, Oxford Brookes University, for her patient guidance and advice at key stages in the production of this manuscript. She also deserves credit for teaching me to mind my manners when writing. I am also gratefully indebted to Dr. Bernard Hoose for the time and careful attention he gave to reading drafts. His helpful feedback and constructive criticism were always given in a gentle and encouraging spirit. I would also like to thank the members of my family, who have, in various ways and at different times, spurred me on in my quest to reconcile my personal experiences and inquisitive nature to the religious tradition we share. Their unwavering love and acceptance have strengthened my belief in the overriding importance of our common humanity and given me hope for the possibility of a truly inclusive and progressive Christian faith. Without their living examples, my parents' teachings about the Christian faith would have had a hollow ring. I would also like to thank the Rev. Lara Ellen Dose for sharing with me many interesting and amusing moments along my adult journey to comprehend Christian ethics. Though we differ a great deal in how we experience and practice spirituality, her insights have provided both nourishment for my soul and challenges for my intellect. I would be remiss not to mention the personal encouragement and support I received from Maxine Altman, a fellow traveler with whom I have shared many doubts along the journey to this book's final publication. I am very grateful for her constant faith in me and in the worth of my projects. Finally, I would like to thank Estelle Asselin de Beauville for her long patience and tolerance during the production of this book. Her constant companionship and understanding have been a priceless gift.

# FOREWORD

Nowhere in this book do I assert that being 'born that way' is a necessary condition for granting full social and legal acceptance of homosexual behavior. In a liberal democracy, bisexuals and people not born with a predisposition to be attracted to the same sex ought to be allowed to participate in homoerotic (or any) sexual behavior, so long as it is consenting and between adults. Nor do I suggest that all people who identify as 'homosexual' were born that way. What I do claim is that the outdated religious arguments that are still used to demoralize homosexual activity are rendered obsolete by certain facts about human nature, and human sexuality in particular.

Homosexuality (and the kinds of sexual behavior it entails) is not a disease, not an addiction, not an aberration of nature, and not a 'sin', except when seen from within a particular religious worldview that is arguably quite flawed. Homosexuals and homosexual behavior have existed since the beginning of recorded history. The best available evidence suggests that homosexuality is a naturally occurring variant of human (and animal) sexuality. Nevertheless, homophobic attitudes have pervaded some religions and this has impacted cultural perceptions of homosexual behavior throughout history up until the present day. This book traces the historical demoralization of homosexual activity as it developed in Christian naturalist ethics from the beginnings of Christianity until now. My aim is not to provide an exhaustive study of all variants of Christian prohibitionist attitudes towards homosexual activity. Rather, I am looking at the predominant role played by natural law ethical reasoning in Christian homophobia and at how this approach to ethics has failed to evolve alongside our changing understanding of human biology and human sexual behavior.

A variety of anthropological archetypes have held sway at various times in the history of Western thought, each with different answers to the question of how human nature relates to the rest of the natural world and the causal laws that govern it. Behind the faith-based polemics surrounding sexual activity, there is a broader and equally longstanding controversy over whether a human ethical ideal can rest upon a biological understanding of our nature, or whether moral ideals must rest upon voluntary aspects of behavior. Misrepresentations of 'nature' and the relationship between the 'natural' and the normative have resulted in much ethical confusion. The purpose of this book is to dismantle the longstanding constructs that have distorted this relationship and been deployed in Christian discourses to stigmatize homosexual persons and/or demoralize homosexual behavior.

I will begin by examining a very specific instance of how misinterpreting 'nature' functioned within Christian teaching. St. Paul, in his letter to the Romans, Chapter 1, established a particularly pernicious precedent. He was not merely arguing *from* ignorance of homosexual orientation, but establishing a form of theological naturalism that actively *promoted* it. In spite of this, Paul's reasoning did not prevent the Roman Catholic Church from adapting its doctrine in 1975 to new empirical research findings in sexology and psychology. While the Vatican's encyclical *Persona Humana* tentatively accepted the distinction between homosexuality as transitory behavior and homosexuality as definitive of the person, it pathologized the homosexual's innate sexual orientation in the same stroke, calling it "incurable" and "intrinsically disordered". The church's reasoning was that non-procreative sexual *activity* represents a misuse of the sexual faculty and act. This book follows revisionist Catholic theologians Charles Curran, Josef Fuchs, Richard McCormick and others in arguing that the Roman Catholic doctrine on sexual ethics has placed disproportionate weight on involuntary biological functions in the moral assessment of sexual conduct. It also presents a range of arguments to demonstrate that the 'new natural law' approach to Christian sexual ethics (advanced by Germain Grisez, John Finnis and their followers) not only fails to overcome the problems that beset the traditional Roman Catholic natural law approach to sexual ethics, but adds several more of its own. Both the traditional Catholic approach to natural law and the 'new natural law' are attempts to ground positive law or normative ethics in a selective, theological interpretation of human nature -- one in which unchanging principles of divine law are presupposed and then given an ontological status. This amounts to a reification of theological *ideas about* nature rather than an empirical study of human nature.

In the 1990's, as research methods improved, a new 'gay science' emerged, strengthening the case for homosexual essentialism (i.e. the theory that some people are born homosexual). Geneticists even suggested the possibility of a so-called 'gay gene'. This set the Christian prohibitionist's assertions that the homosexual orientation is an 'objective disorder' in tension with traditional understandings of 'health' as acting in accordance with one's given nature (unless there are good ethical reasons not to). It seemed the new 'gay science' of the late twentieth century threatened to destabilize the Christian prohibitionist stance towards homosexual activity. The 'preceptive' natural law ethic that had long been entrenched in Church doctrine had exhorted Christians to 'read the language of the body in truth'. With the genetic code being metaphorically described as 'the book of life' and with scientists implying that homosexuality might be found hidden in one of its chapters, the preceptive model appeared to fail on its own terms. If reading the language of the body in truth would mean reading even the biological substructure, down to the genes and chromosomes, then Christians might find things there that would clash with their traditional wisdom that homosexuality is 'not natural'. Knowing this, the Christian homophobes changed their tack. Since there is nothing "unnatural" about the homosexually orientated person, Christian ethicists needed, but failed, to explain why homosexuality is 'disordered' in terms *extrinsic* to the homosexual person (i.e. in terms of the 'harmful' behavior to which it leads). This book outlines the ways in which they attempted to make a case against homosexuality in terms of extrinsic harms. Their failure to do so makes the moral case against homosexual activity so weak as to be redundant in modern liberal democracies.

The recent convergence of reproductive technology and genetic research makes the demand to decide the role that biology ought to play within a proper understanding of the human subject ever more urgent. Constructionists (i.e. those who claim homosexual attraction is socially conditioned, not inherent in nature) cannot deny that there has been ample discussion, even if misguided or fantastical, about whether gay identity can be 'mapped' onto a set of genetic or biological markers. This book provides an unprecedented survey of Christian bioethicists' responses to this possibility, showing how Christian ethical thinking developed and abandoned some of its basic principles alongside the new 'gay science'. Suddenly, instead of describing the 'given' aspects of natural creation as the very benchmark of God's design and plan, Christian bioethicists began emphasizing how biotechnology might facilitate human interventions into creation in order to 'restore' it to 'its full glory'. I maintain that this tacit reversal of the 'preceptive' natural law approach has not been openly acknowledged, nor critically assessed. The authors I examine not only suggest, implicitly or explicitly, that homosexuality represents the kind of pathology that would be an acceptable target for reprogenetic[1] modification, but they also play influential roles in shaping public policy on these issues, in both the United States and the UK.

Christian conservatives have laid the discursive groundwork for a eugenic age. This book explains how they anticipate a future in which they will have at their disposal a means of avoiding the dilemma between the desire to promote their own theological versions of public morality and the dominant liberal injunction to protect the sovereignty and liberty of the individual. This new situation urgently necessitates a public discussion of so-called 'liberal eugenics'. This is because liberal eugenics, though not a Christian invention, provides the ideological Trojan horse by which Christian (or any) eugenics can get a legitimate foothold in a liberal democracy. In the past, liberals worried about the intrusion of the state into the private lives of individuals. Today, they may have to worry more about the opposite: personal reproductive decisions made in the privacy of a consultant's office could have an irreversible impact on public life and future generations. 'Liberal eugenics' leaves eugenic decisions to the market, driven by the demands of consumers and regulated only by the discretion of parents. This book builds upon and expands existing arguments against liberal eugenics (eg. by Jürgen Habermas, Michael Sandel and Francis Fukuyama). It also goes beyond the existing critics by explaining exactly how 'liberal eugenics' diverges from J. S. Mill's classic liberal values in several important respects. It further offers an outline for how a principled line can and should be drawn between beneficial therapeutic uses of biotechnology and insidious eugenic ones.

Homosexuality falls on the illegitimate eugenic side of that line, as do any biological targets perceived to influence the behavioral patterns of the subject/patient. Like the salvation doctrines derived from Pauline Christianity, a eugenics aimed at correcting or improving human behavior from the outside threatens to demolish the modern concept of human beings as autonomous agents, possessing both biological urges *and* the ability to learn, choose and assume responsibility for their actions. Should we fail to safeguard our collective belief in human beings' autonomy and responsibility, we stand to lose the human rights that are their logical corollary.

---

[1] The term 'reprogenetics' was coined by molecular biologist Lee Silver of Princeton University. The term refers to the merging of reproductive and genetic technologies. Silver distinguishes reprogenetics from eugenics in that the former would be voluntarily pursued by individual parents with an aim to improve their children (a policy of which Silver approves) whereas the latter were compulsory and imposed upon citizens by governments for particular ultimate goals.

# INTRODUCTION

The point of departure for this book is a concrete historical situation: namely, that lesbians and gay men worldwide experience social discrimination and human rights violations on the basis of their sexual orientation. In the vast majority of cases, the hatred and violence directed against lesbians and gay men is motivated by religious beliefs about what is or is not natural, according to God's purposes. Amnesty International has documented some of the known abuses[1] but countless others go unreported. After the end of World War II, when the United Nations drafted the *Universal Declaration of Human Rights*, gay men and lesbians were left unprotected by its international framework for the protection of human rights. Lesbians and gay men (as well as bisexuals and transgendered persons) have historically been persecuted and oppressed by means of laws that criminalize sexual acts between consenting adults of the same sex, even when such behavior occurs in private. More than seventy countries continue to outlaw homosexual behavior, with penalties ranging from one year to life imprisonment. Six Islamist states impose the death penalty, and in provinces of other countries gay and lesbian acts are punished under Sharia law by stoning. In June 2011 The United Nations Human Rights Council narrowly passed a resolution to research and document acts of violence and discrimination, in all parts of the world, committed against individuals because of their sexual orientation and gender identity.

Proponents of gay and lesbian human rights argue that, in theory, homosexuals should enjoy the protection of general human rights treatises, which are intended to secure "all rights for all people." For centuries, however, homosexuality has been looked upon not as a natural variant of human sexuality, but as something immoral that people *do*. In the context of a modern western liberal society, the classification of homosexuality with other forms of immoral behavior has been particularly difficult to conceptualize and analogies with other crimes or harmful behaviors remain unpersuasive.[2]

This book traces the stigmatization and demoralization of the homosexual across a history of 'naturalist' ethical reasoning that has treated homosexuality first as a pattern of behaviour involving the wilful (and sinful) rejection of nature (or 'creation') and later as a pathological condition rooted in the biological nature of the homosexual person. In particular, this book interrogates specific inconsistencies in the application of naturalist methodology in Christian sexual ethics, especially as it has developed in the 20th century, both in Roman Catholic doctrine and evangelical Christian discourses in the United States.

There are two basic accounts of what it is to be gay: essentialist and constructionist. Essentialists argue that homosexuality is a naturally occurring trait genetically (or otherwise) encoded as a basic substrate of some people's essential identity, just like red hair, left-handedness or indeed heterosexuality. Constructionists attribute homosexuality to social or psychological conditioning, which implies that homosexual orientation is not 'essential' or 'natural' but is the product of external influences on an individual's behavior. This implies that homosexual orientation is *learned* or chosen, and can be unlearned or changed. Of course, with new developments in biotechnology, we may find that homosexuality can be changed even if the constructionist account of its origins is mistaken. But the question I am posing here is not just whether it *can* be changed, but whether it *ought* to be, and by whom. Unless it can be established that homosexuality is inherently undesirable or harmful there can be no good reason to seek to change or prevent it. The question of *how* to do so arises only after this condition is met. Since arguments for changing or preventing homosexual behavior have arisen primarily within religious ethical frameworks, I have made these arguments the focus of my research.

This book is an argument about the *implications* of gay essentialism. I do not treat homosexual essentialism as a fact but as a hypothesis about why some people seem to be naturally attracted to members of the same sex. Nowhere do I purport to be a scientist, nor do I claim to understand the biological or genetic factors that may or may not explain same sex attraction in humans. There is an existing Christian discourse around the hypothesis that some people are born gay, not made that way. Insofar as this theological discourse has addressed the ethical implications of the new "gay essentialism", it is the subject of my book.

Until the late 20th century, social and religious taboos that stigmatized or criminalised homosexuality were based on a corresponding form of 'naturalism'. In the West, Christian versions of natural law have grounded political and legal policies that left homosexuals vulnerable to discrimination. These naturalist ethical theories have exhibited a common structure no longer philosophically tenable in a modern liberal context. They start from the premise that homosexuality is not in accord with God's intention or God's will as manifest in creation. They then conclude that homosexual behaviour is morally bad because it is tantamount to rejecting the 'natural' or one's own nature (and so the Creator of nature) in favour of what is 'unnatural' (against God's intention). In all versions of this argument, 'God's will' is disclosed by the workings of nature, while at the same time 'nature' is correctly comprehended only by perceiving God's will. God's intention is known through religious and metaphysical speculation (deductively). The test by which Christians have assessed homosexual behaviour is whether the act accords with 'God's will' as perceived in nature. Within this religious context, the criterion by which morally responsible agency may be judged is by its 'responsiveness' (i.e. obedience) to God's intention (as inscribed in nature). Ordinarily, freedom is a presupposition of moral responsibility. But if the agent is not free to dissent from the religious view of nature without being punished for disobedience or stigmatized for his 'sinful' disagreement, then ultimately this reduces to a kind of divine command ethic.[3] In the theological contexts I examine, 'freedom' presupposes a set of religious truths to which the agent either freely conforms or from which he freely chooses to dissent ('sin'). Since the choice to express any honest intellectual disagreement with the Christian interpretation of the natural order is pictured as an act of 'revolt' against God or against one's own created nature, this formula effectively demoralizes any honest intellectual disagreement about matters of fact, or about the workings or order of nature. This form of religious intolerance towards other views on matters beyond the scope of its legitimate authority has characterised a wide-ranging set of Catholic and evangelical homophobic discourses. This book provides a survey and critique of those Christian versions of natural law that have grounded the prohibitionist stance vis-à-vis homosexual behaviour.

There are also two quasi-eugenic strains of thinking that have arisen in response to the gay essentialist hypothesis – one theological and the other secular (and ostensibly liberal). In certain respects, these two outlooks could be mutually beneficial and share ideological presuppositions that contribute to the erosion of social diversity and (genuinely) liberal values. I explain why both of these responses to gay essentialism have failed. They neither cohere with widely accepted liberal ethical principles, nor, in the case of the theological arguments, with their own past reasoning about sexual ethics.

Informing the discourses about the hypothetical 'gay gene' is a more generalized conceptual set that presupposes that character traits are less the products of individual choice than of the individual's biological inheritance. Accordingly, it is assumed that a criminal typology or anti-social pre-disposition can be identified within involuntary aspects of human nature. The purpose of this book is to suggest how homosexual identity is conceptualized within a broader (and problematic) ideological framework that reifies categories of human *behavior* by describing them as biological properties or propensities located in the brain or gene(s). Consequently, a pattern of free choices is re-described as the inevitable outcome of a biological aspect of the individual's body. For this reason, I want to begin by emphasizing my broader concern that, if we accept the premise that biology makes us morally good or bad, conservative or liberal, rational or emotional, our attitudes towards crime and methods of law enforcement will become more deeply enmeshed with medicine and biotechnology. According to our current thinking, the very concept of **morally** bad behaviour depends upon the *voluntary* aspects of human behaviour or what might be called human agency. And this freedom, plus whatever harm is caused to significant others by our choices, ought to continue to be the locus of public or private efforts to prevent illegal or immoral behaviour. Most post-enlightenment ethicists eschew any suggestion that enhancing human biology can improve human behaviour in anything other than a pre-moral sense. The belief that enhancements in human biology can prevent human immorality seriously undermines our longstanding belief in both personal and social responsibility. As I explain in chapters 5 and 6, the opposing discourses with which I engage have considered the possibility and permissibility of modifying the biological causes of sexual attraction in order to prevent or reduce the corresponding behaviour. I approach these quasi-eugenic arguments from a broadly liberal standpoint, assuming that many of my readers in Western Europe and the United States will share my acceptance of the nexus between agency, moral responsibility and rights in the domains of law and medicine, although I acknowledge that liberalism is a complex and fractured political ideology with many variants and internal tensions (particularly with regard to economic policy). However, I am assuming that liberals generally agree that interference in an individual's liberty must be justified by showing what harm such interference prevents to others; that the burden of proof is on the state to justify any new interference in the private sphere; that human beings have basic dignity and should never be treated as mere instruments or objects; and that the purpose of the state is not to promote any particular vision of the 'good life' (religious or otherwise).

Today, the scientific establishment and its institutions possess a perceived infallibility and exert a powerful social influence in America and Western Europe that was once the preserve of the church. It should not be too surprising that there are points of ideological intersection between the Christian theocracy of the past and the newly emerging 'science' of human immorality, with its technocratic solutions to human imperfection. History cautions against the unquestioning acceptance of ideologies that buttress social hierarchies. When institutional authorities place one set of humans permanently above others, or dictate to individuals what is in their best interests based on a conception of psychological 'health' that is socially constructed by an elite set of 'experts', we need to beware.

The arguments I will examine and critique share my premises about homosexual essentialism. We agree that biological factors explain homosexual *attraction* but do not determine homosexual *behavior*, as human biology does not override free will. Yet my opponents reject the seemingly obvious conclusion that homosexual behavior *per se* is morally neutral, just like heterosexual behavior. Their reluctance to draw parallel conclusions from parallel cases suggests a deeply rooted homophobia that appears to be in the process of dismantling a key premise of the liberal moral and legal framework (namely, the nexus between morality and intentional behavior, or what ethicists call *agency*). Worse, it seems they would prefer to dismantle the very foundations of liberal ethics than to incorporate new discoveries about human sexuality into the existing liberal ethical framework, since this would mean relaxing their prohibition of homosexual behavior. It is as though they are so loathe to be corrected by the evidence – even on their own terms -- that they have decided it would be better to change the rules of the game.

Scientists, theologians and academics continue to research and debate the ontology of the elusive "gay gene". In this climate there is a looming expectation that the heterosexual paradigm may be on the verge of a major shift. If this shift takes place, changes will logically follow in ethics as well. Many people, whether conservative religious moralists or leftist queer activists, are unsure exactly what impact a "gay gene" would have on traditional moral attitudes towards homosexual activity.

The discovery of a so-called "gay gene" (or any biological substrate that causes homosexuality) could have a dramatic impact on social institutions such as marriage, sex education and law. The existence of an underlying biological cause for homosexual attraction and the behavioral choices related to it may call into question the seemingly 'natural' bond between sex and gender and might suggest that universal heterosexual complementarity is a fragile social construct, not a natural fact. Gender stereotypes based around oppositions between characteristically female and male attributes *could* rest more on precarious social myths than on nature or divine design. The Western Christian model of heterosexual complementarity and gender oppositionality (i.e. the predominant blueprint around which romantic partnership is structured) may cease to hinge primarily and exclusively on the reproductive potential of the partners' genitalia. Homosexuality may cease to be construed as a deviation from 'nature,' and so homosexual *behavior* may cease to be regarded as 'unnatural', deviant or immoral.

Social and religious taboos that stigmatize or criminalize homosexuals or homosexual acts unanimously rest on a corresponding type of 'naturalism.' Whether couched in the form of Biblical exhortations or appeals to deductive philosophical reasoning, naturalist theories form the only basis for the Christian view that homosexuality is morally wrong. Where they exist, legal prohibitions against homosexual acts are rationalized and defended with reference to a type of natural law thinking that reduces human sexual nature to its reproductive aspects[4] and gives only secondary importance to sexual attraction, psychological and emotional health and self-determination. Not all Christians agree on the interpretation of natural law that has dominated the Christian view of sexuality, as we will see. Nevertheless traditional Christian religious precepts have been used repeatedly to justify the political and legal policies that leave homosexuals vulnerable to discrimination or human rights abuses.

My task, then, will be to engage with the Christian discourses around homosexuality - moral, religious, pseudo-medical and bioethical – and to chronicle how the rationale of homophobia is being reinvented alongside new developments in genetics and biotechnology, and in response to the essentialist hypothesis.

Conceptualizing socially 'problematic' or unacceptable behaviors as objects within the biology of the individual that can be controlled by medical intervention is seductive. This mindset signals a gradual attenuation of the post-Enlightenment nexus between morality and autonomy. As such, it is politically attractive to religious conservatives who are shaping the discourse on homosexual essentialism and labeling it a 'disorder' in need of a therapeutic response. The aim of this book is to illustrate and interrogate the ways in which these discourses are being developed.

1   See <u>Breaking the Silence</u> :<u>Human Rights Abuses Based on Sexual Orientation</u>, Amnesty International United Kingdom, 1997. For copies of this report write to : AIUK at 99-119 Rosebery Avenue, London EC1R 4RE. See also, Carroll, Aengus and Itaborahy, Lucas P., <u>State-Sponsored Homophobia, A World Survey of Laws: criminalization, protection and recognition of same-sex love</u>, May 2015, 10th Edition, (www.ilga.org)

2   I address these analogies explicitly in chapters 2, 5 and 6.

3   Divine Command Theory is the meta-ethical position that the authority or truth of moral statements depends upon God, and that moral obligation consists in obedience to God's commands.

4   Even where this is the case, the definition of embodiment is very narrow, with the sensuous, psychological, social or emotional aspects of biological human nature given relatively little weight in comparison to its reproductive aspects.

# CHAPTER 1

# Behavioral Essentialism:
## Past and Present

Ethics is the discipline in which we attempt to answer questions such as "What is good?" or "How ought we to live?" We seek and measure the value of our behavior and of our lives in many ways. However different their methodologies may be, all theories of ethics are attempts to say something about human beings and how human fulfillment is best achieved. Ethics presuppose that certain things can be said about human beings in general, about the kind of beings we are and about the kinds of goals we ought to pursue. Behind the question posed by ethics -- how ought we to live? -- lurks the more basic question: who or what are **we**?

## Naturalist Methodology

Broadly speaking, naturalist ethical theories rest on the assumption that it is possible to arrive at true moral statements from premises that are not about morality. The natural law approach to ethics involves a serious and disinterested search for what is truly human, and uses the answers as a guide to how humans should behave. Natural law, however, is not a single monolithic theory but a generic methodology that has been interpreted and applied in a wide variety of ways. Since the basis of natural law theories is non-moral knowledge, which is abundant, it is difficult to decide which part of that knowledge ought to be emphasized.

Theories of human nature offer comprehensive accounts of human beings' most essential or distinctive characteristics. Such theories purport to furnish an anthropological archetype that holds for all people in all places at all times. These accounts are central to ethics because they reflect the perennial human endeavor to comprehend our relation to God, to nature, and to each other; and to disclose the possibilities and purposes of human life.

Ethics rest upon a model of human nature, or an anthropological archetype. The truth about human nature is not something we tend to search for with the kind of objective detachment of a scientist. It is the peculiar nature of philosophical anthropology that we are the subjects of our own 'discoveries' in a way that other objects cannot be. Consequently, the self-image, interests, and worldview of the group most responsible for conducting them will often taint the outcome of investigations into human nature. The guardians of social institutions often have vested interests that may make their supporting anthropological theories less than completely objective. Precisely because anthropological constructs have such a profound bearing on other human institutions, (e.g. religion, politics, law, psychology, and medicine) the stakes are high when the predominant model of man alters.

Anthropology can appear to be a strictly objective, scientific discipline, when it is limited to *descriptive* accounts of human nature. That is, it tells us how we organize our societies, what we in fact do, and how we do it. However, even descriptive terms can be imbued with evaluative content. The language in which descriptions are couched can tend to add evaluative connotations to terms that may otherwise appear morally neutral or 'scientific'. Descriptive accounts of anthropological facts do not tell us *why* we do what we do, or what we *ought to* wish to become by means of our choices and creativity. These are questions of *value*. These questions belong to the realm of moral philosophy. They do not merely describe human nature; they also recommend to us how to measure the value or worth of human life.

Theories of human nature, like all theories, are constructed within specific historical contexts by particular interest groups, and may therefore reflect the scientific, moral or political preoccupations of the time, place or group. One reason that theories of human nature are not entirely objective is that they are present as presuppositions of empirical research, structuring the conceptual framework within which it is conducted. Anthropological constructs are not merely conclusions of empirical research but also influence the purposes, methods, priorities and standards that both direct and inform empirical investigations.

There are many possible ways to conceptualize human nature and society's ethical rules hinge on them. For example, lawyers assume that people are responsible for their actions, whereas psychologists, doctors or social anthropologists may suggest that an individual's behavior is determined by subconscious urges, chemicals, genes, socialization, conditioning or other factors outside of her direct control. However, in Western liberal democracies even experts in these disciplines tend to accept that human beings have enough self-control to respond in a variety of ways to these various influences.

## The rationalist dualist paradigm

Theories of human nature typically perform a regulatory function, legitimizing some methodological approaches while de-legitimating others.[1] The Western philosophical tradition has tended to conceptualize human nature as both universal and trans-historical. It might be tempting to say that the emphasis until the nineteenth century was rationalist and dualist. This tradition stressed the dichotomy between body and soul, matter and form. Those features humans share with the animal species were thought to constitute only a part of human nature. Human beings were seen as distinct from the other animal species, rather than as belonging entirely to the kingdom of non-human animals. Human nature was conceptualized as having a reflective, transcendental dimension. Under the influence of philosophers like Plato, Augustine and Descartes, human nature was distinguished by the possession of something incorporeal, usually understood as a 'soul' but also closely identified with the capacity to reason.

The 'good life' was envisioned as the fulfillment of rational potential, but it was not always clear exactly what this meant. In some cases, man's rational potential was given relatively less emphasis than the biological aspects of his nature. Giving one's intellectual assent to the paramount importance of a select set of biological facts, and then allowing these facts to guide behavior, is hardly the only means of fulfilling one's rational potential.

However, it is not entirely accurate to over-generalize the predominant model of man before the nineteenth century as fitting the rationalist and dualist mould. In the Stoic cosmology, and in parts of Aristotle's philosophy, human nature and the physical universe were regarded as belonging to a single physical substance. For Seneca, reason is not understood as that which transcends the body and the physical universe; rather, it is that which characterizes the *natural* human life.[2]

But even where the relationship between the physical and the metaphysical did conform to the rationalist dualist model, there were dramatic variations in interpretation. The teleological theories of Aristotle and Aquinas measured the value of human life relative to its end or purpose. But it is uncertain whether this purpose (or '*telos*') was to be understood as integral to the *individual's intentions* (as a rational agent's motivating reason for action) or as an intrinsic 'function' generic to the species irrespective of rational agency. If understood as the latter, then personal liberty and self-determination would be less important than obedience to external authorities whose role is to ensure that individuals fulfill their generic functions. While a traditional Catholic rendering of Aquinas's ethics emphasized a generic '*telos*' (end or ultimate purpose) for all humans as such, Descartes' (1596-1650) anthropology placed the emphasis on the thinking subject -- an entity connected to, but ultimately independent of, its body. There is much debate over whether the Catholic interpretation of Thomas Aquinas's approach to natural law is faithful to Thomas's own intended meaning. Thomas combined the conviction that what one ought to do rests upon an understanding of what is good for human beings *as such* with his belief (perhaps borrowed from Aristotle's *Nichomacean Ethics*) that human fulfillment involves more than health, sleep, nourishment, etc. but also intellectual understanding and social engagement. While basic physical needs can generally be understood as uniform and universal, the same cannot be said for what humans make of their lives through personal development and social intercourse. Here there is no formulaic or generic recipe for human fulfillment, as there might be for, say, human health. Human persons seem to require sufficient liberty for personal discovery, development, achievement and experimentation in order to find personal fulfillment.

## St. Paul's cosmic dualist paradigm

Long before Descartes, in the early Christian tradition St. Paul's epistles established a dualism of flesh (*sarx*) and spirit (*pneumos*). For centuries afterwards, Paul's theology perpetuated the notion that human will is subordinate to flesh (and rendered ineffectual by the power of its 'sinful' desires). In Paul's blueprint of human nature, the flesh made man's will 'captive' to its desires in a deterministic sense, and the only freedom man could attain came from a Spirit that had its source **outside** of man, in God.[3]

What was implicit in Paul, St. Augustine made explicit. In Augustinian theology, Pauline dualism (with its emphasis on the dominance of the flesh over the will) became the basis for a pessimistic stance towards nature, the world and mankind that shaped the character of medieval Western Christianity.[4] If mankind and the physical realm were dominated by carnal vices of the flesh then the only salvation for humanity must come from a source outside of human nature -- God. Augustine followed Paul, who had already established a cosmic dualism between God and nature, or divinity and humanity. The only avenue open to human virtue was through obedient submission to the mediating authorities representing the transcendent God. Human destiny could never be entrusted to individual humans, or to mere human reason. This pessimistic anthropological model legitimated a theocratic political model.

Today, biological determinist theories are beginning to arise as modern, secular counterparts to the Pauline/Augustinian anthropology. The paternalistic authority formerly wielded by the church is today being transposed to parents and medical experts, who may soon be given the legal power to use biotechnology to make undesired aspects of their children's natures conform to preferred social norms. In America, a Christian majority view homosexuality as an unhealthy behavioral tendency. I will explain in chapter 6 how medicine appears to be on the brink of a transformation from a therapeutic to a eugenic discipline involving active social participation in the evolutionary process of human design. This will herald a significant break from the modern model of human agency that dominated the nineteenth and twentieth centuries.

At the level of popular discourse, there is a prevalent 'gene myth' that reduces the self to its genetic determinants. Joseph Altpher and Jonathan Beckwith refer to this myth as "genetic fatalism".[5] The ancient Pauline-Augustinian model of the agent's flesh (*sarx*) dominating his will converges with the modern scientific concept of genetic determinism to consolidate conservative Christianity and segments of the scientific left into a single ideological force – one that is, even if not deliberately, mutually supporting. The ideology of the religious right creates a potentially lucrative market for the scientific left's products. And the legitimacy of the scientific methodology lends credibility to the Christian right's illiberal moralizing aims. Both undermine the modern model of the individual as an autonomous, morally responsible agent. Central to this new narrative is the transition from a modern, agent-centered concept of crime or immorality to a deterministic, biological model of the 'criminal type'. The pseudo-medical stigmatizing of biological difference is one conceptual set through which the scientific discoveries are being framed. The Human Genome Project's worldwide multi-billion dollar effort to sequence the 3164.7 million chemical nucleotide bases on the DNA and map the estimated 30,000 genes was at the same time a search for 'defective genes'. In determining what constitutes a 'defect', a normative conceptual set must be employed. It can only be fully understood in light of a particular definition of what constitutes the norm, or the optimally 'healthy' human person.

Descartes' mind-body dualism was a throwback to a pre-Christian, Platonic notion that there were divisions *within* human nature, not *between* the human and the divine. Descartes' dualism shifted the Pauline emphasis by giving the rational side of human nature its due. The Cartesian picture of human nature made a significant separation between mind (or 'soul') and body by granting the mind autonomy. The two aspects of human nature were conceptualized as subject to different causal laws: the laws of morality (or God) governed the mind/soul and the laws of science governed the physical, material world. It wasn't until the modern era (and especially the philosophical Enlightenment of the 18th century) that the practical and political implications of the Cartesian rationalist anthropological model were followed through to full effect. Descartes' assertion that all humans were potentially equal in their capacity to reason set the tone for more egalitarian political and ethical norms. The mind or soul of the human person was not only the seat of contemplation; it was also the seat of freedom and responsibility. It was in a person's volitional life that he or she could be distinguished from abstract 'humanity' and conceived as an individual.

Following Nazi atrocities that led to World War II, Jean-Paul Sartre reflected on the implications of human autonomy for the individual's moral responsibility. We can reflect upon our immediate feelings and instincts. This self-conscious reflection can change the way we feel and act. For Sartre, this freedom, once acknowledged, dispelled the myth that human beings were endowed with an essence to which their behavior would inevitably conform. Instead of a generic human essence determining the individual's behavior, the individual's conscious choices determine his essence; his character as a human person. The nature that we possess is the one that we have *chosen to make* of ourselves.

## Towards a post-Darwinian anthropology: behaviorism

Not all modern models of human nature share this dualistic view of man as an autonomous agent, subject to the laws of nature but also capable of deliberation and self-determination. Gilbert Ryle accused Descartes of a 'category mistake' in thinking that the complex operations of the human brain constituted a separate, incorporeal entity. Modern philosophers follow Ryle, ridiculing the Cartesian *cogito* as a 'ghost in the machine'. Where, they ask, would this 'mind' reside? And how could it conceivably interact with the body to bring about the bodily movements associated with human acts?

The post-Darwinian concept of human nature stresses evolutionary continuity between human and non-human animals. In the seventeenth century the English philosopher Thomas Hobbes had compared individual behavior and politics to the laws of mechanics, and explained all human motivation as driven entirely by self-interest. In similar fashion, Julien Offray de La Mettrie's *L'Homme Machine* (1748) popularized the notion that human beings are simply the playthings of causal forces, their actions compelled either by biology or social conditioning. In section IX of his *Enquiry Concerning Human Understanding* David Hume claimed,

> "any theory, by which we explain the operations of the understanding, or the origin and connexion of the passions in man, will acquire additional authority, if we find, that the same theory is requisite to explain the same phenomena in all other animals."[6]

In like fashion, British Utilitarians such as Jeremy Bentham focused new emphasis on the similarities rather than the differences between humans and animals. Darwinism reinforced these theories with scientific plausibility by showing that the distinctive features of human nature were the outcome of natural selection over thousands of years. This made room for the theory that the distinguishing characteristics of human nature are differences in degree rather than in kind. In contrast to the dualism of the Cartesian anthropological model, human beings (and the mind) were seen as one with the physical, material universe (the brain). Even the ancient Roman Stoic philosopher Seneca believed that mind and the ability to reason do not transcend the physical universe and the body. Rather, thinking characterizes the natural human life.

But unlike the Stoic vision of integrated reason and nature, some post-Darwinian models of human nature explained all human behavior as determined, ultimately, by biological forces beyond human control. Darwin's demonstration of evolutionary continuity between humans and other animals brought in its wake a renewed interest in biological causality, which in many cases was applied to human behavior in a reductionist manner. The Freudian model of the human 'mind' reduced all human motivation to two basic drives -- the sexual drive, or libido, and the aggressive drive. For Freud,

> ". . . the individual of his culture represented 'man', and those passions and anxieties that are characteristic for man in modern society were looked upon as eternal forces rooted in the biological constitution of man."[7]

In section I of his *Enquiry* ('Of Liberty and Necessity', Part 1, 8-9) David Hume explained that we cannot generalise from our experience of the world to a necessary connection between events. We believe that certain effects *necessarily* follow from certain causes because of the regularity with which we have observed events of type B (shattering glass) following events of type A (brick thrown at window). But causality itself is not something of which we have any experience, apart from the constant conjunction of events in the world. For Hume, causes do not **compel** effects; they are just descriptions of the uniformity and regularity with which we have come to expect the world to behave. In this narrow sense at least, our decisions and actions are not necessitated or compelled. In Hume's empiricist account of causality, he emphasises "uniformity": "*We acknowledge a uniformity in human motives as well as in the operations of the body.*"[8] He provides various examples of predictability in human behaviour. Workers take their goods to market, sure that they will sell them. Prison guards act with a determination as fixed as the walls of the prison itself. Hume pictured physical events and human desires as belonging to the same universal pattern. Our human thoughts are part of a connected chain, just like the principles of variation in the weather. Physical events affect mental events and vice versa. However, Hume thought it would not be contradictory to claim that a person could have acted otherwise. For Hume, possessing free will simply meant that we are free to act on our desires without coercion or constraint. In this sense we are free and responsible because we do what we want to do without external constraint. So freedom means that we can do what we desire; it does not mean we can choose what we desire.

Post-Darwinian views of human nature tend towards a psychological model rooted in behaviorism and generally lack the concept of free will. Harvard biologist Edward O. Wilson is one of the most renowned and prolific contemporary proponents of the materialist, monist view. Wilson argues for the unity of the human and nonhuman worlds.[9] He envisions a future in which all of our social behavior will be fully explicable by brain science, which in turn can be translated into biology, and finally, particle physics. What Wilson calls "the consilience worldview" is centered around the idea that "all tangible phenomena, from the birth of stars to the workings of social institutions, are based on material processes that are ultimately reducible, however long and tortuous the sequences, to the laws of physics."[10] Wilson contends that a truly scientific study of humankind must link human behavior to biologically encoded networks of causation. In other words, individual human beings follow the "epigenetic rules" coded in their chromosomes. These rules direct them to respond in ways most likely to ensure survival and reproduction. Wilson regards territoriality, tribalism, and xenophobia as behaviors built in to the human genetic constitution by millions of years of evolution.[11]

Nobel laureate biochemist Walter Gilbert is co-founder of the biotech start-up companies **Biogen** and **Myriad Genetics.** He identifies our ability to "see more and more clearly how connected all life really is" as an important consequence of the "data base of the human genome, coupled with our knowledge of the genetic makeup of model organisms."[12] Indeed, Gilbert's deterministic affinities are revealed when he claims that we not only see ourselves as having tremendous variation, but we,

> "look upon ourselves as having an infinite potential. To recognize that we are determined, in a certain sense, by a finite collection of information that is knowable will change our view of ourselves. It is the closing of an intellectual frontier, with which we will have to come to terms...."[13]

Determinist theories flourish in scientific journals such as *Nature,* but they also seem to have wide appeal in popular culture. In recent years biological determinist theories have routinely cropped up in novel cultural contexts as loose explanations of individual or group behavior.

With homosexual behavior still viewed by some as "undesirable" or a "sin" deserving punishment, the new theological discourse makes the genetic propensity for this behavior into a 'disease' or 'defect' in need of 'therapy'. This shift in the description of homosexuality from a rejection of one's own nature to a defect *within* one's nature coincided with a trend in the early nineties to widen the deterministic net to include an ever-expanding range of behaviors. The underlying presupposition of this perspective was that the root cause of many human behaviors is not the agent's voluntary will, but her involuntary predisposition. Robert Kennedy Jr., son of the senator murdered in 1968, said that alcohol problems are "in the genes" of the Kennedy clan. In an interview broadcast on CBS television in the US, Mr. Kennedy said that he feels he was "born alcoholic" and that "it wasn't something I became."

During the 1990's, essentialist theories of behavior increasingly cropped up in legal contexts to show that criminal *behavior* is a hereditary or innate trait. In the summer of 1993 the journal **Science** carried the headline *"evidence found for a possible 'aggression' gene"* and **Time** magazine followed with *"Born to Raise Hell?"* (Feb. 21, 1994). In the United States, the Department of Health and Human Services initiated a program called the *Violence Initiative* that conducted research to discover biological markers that could be used to distinguish violence-prone children as early as age five.[14] The underlying philosophy of this trend was captured in the 1995 court case of murder defendant Steven Mobley, who was on death row for shooting a pizza parlor manager twice in the back of the neck after robbing the till. Mobley's lawyers attempted to introduce genetic evidence in the Georgia Supreme Court for his defense. Mobley's family background and economic status did not fit those stereotypically associated with such behavior. He came from an ordinary middle-class family that did not abuse him as a child. His lawyers, however, unearthed violent and criminal behavior over the last four generations of his family. The antisocial behavior of his relatives was enlisted as a mitigating factor in his defense. Although genes have been found which it is claimed cause violence and alcoholism, the deterministic implications tend to undermine social responsibility. As *Guardian* newspaper columnist Suzanne Moore commented:

"Cause is a key word here. If primacy is given to genes as causal mechanisms then we can forget environmental or experiential factors. In other words, we begin to believe that some people are just born bad, and nothing much can be done about it. . . . In such a scenario, we are relieved of our duty to alleviate the stresses that poverty and unemployment and homelessness cause, whereas the one fact that most geneticists agree on is that if there is any predisposition towards destructive behaviour it will be activated by such conditions."[15]

In another egregious example of how patterns of culturally conditioned behavior become re-defined as biological aspects of human nature, John Gray's 1992 bestselling book ***Men are From Mars Women are From Venus*** explained virtually all communication problems in heterosexual relationships as a 'natural' product of inherent sexual differences. Gray says that he does not directly address the question of *why* men and women are different. To be sure, he does not treat this as a question at all, because his book is premised on the *assumption* that certain personality attributes are inherently 'feminine' while others are distinctively 'masculine'. His book popularized an essentialist view of sexual difference by stereotypically describing "loving and nurturing" as intrinsically "feminine" attributes, while these may have to be given up "in order to earn a living in a work force that rewards masculine attributes."[16] Implicitly masculine attributes include competition and something opposite to "loving and nurturing" behavior. Gray admits that he makes many generalizations about men and women in his book and that men and women in his seminars do not necessarily identify with the roles that Gray associates with their sex. Rather, they sometimes identify with the roles typically assigned to the opposite sex. If he were using a scientific methodology, these observations would seem to render his premise (that each sex has intrinsic 'natural' gender roles) suspect. But Gray simply describes the counter-evidence as "role-reversal" rather than treating it as evidence against this theory that men and women *naturally* have different gender roles. This shows that his theory was formed *prior to* the evidence rather than as a result of it. Since his whole theory starts from abstract, *a priori*, deductive grounds, it is more accurate to view it as pseudo-science re-interpreting *learned* gender roles and *socialized* behavior patterns as innate 'nature'. Gray says of his book,

"It reveals how men and women differ *in all areas of their lives*. Not only do men and women communicate differently but *they think, feel, perceive, react, respond, love, need, and appreciate differently*. They almost seem to be from different planets, speaking different languages and needing different nourishment."[17] [my emphasis] This is a premise of this 'research', however, not an outcome. As such, it provides the interpretative framework for all of the 'evidence' presented, while the premise itself is never actually proved, except by 'evidence' which in many cases is culturally manufactured. There is a vicious circle of question begging which apparently goes unnoticed by the millions of readers who subscribe to Gray's theory. Gray identifies the *cause* of miscommunication as sexual differences, when these apparent differences may in fact be an *effect* or symptom of miscommunication between two social groups who are alienated from one another by cultural myths, stereotypes, traditions, customs and gender roles. If our individual and social preconceptions, rather than 'nature', cause the miscommunication problem, then it is one that we have the potential to change by social means. So, rather than adapt our language to conform to a naturalistic explanation of gender difference, we might instead de-mythologize the naturalistic explanations of gender oppositions by taking responsibility for their social perpetuation. By acknowledging that our own constructions cause communication problems that divide and alienate the sexes, we empower ourselves to change them more than if we define them as intrinsic in human nature.

Essentialist theories of gender are just one instance of the biological reductionism that today seems to permeate Western culture, at the popular level as well as in scientific institutions. A study of Manchester University students showed that males with larger testicles and a higher sperm count were more promiscuous and more likely to be unfaithful to their long-term partner.[18] Conversely, men with smaller gonads and lower sperm counts engaged in sexual intercourse less frequently. Dr. Robin Baker, who headed the study, says these findings suggest men are genetically disposed towards one of two sexual strategies thrown up by millions of years of evolution. The well-endowed subconsciously incline towards promiscuity, while the little men lean towards fidelity and staying close to their partners. But such studies are descriptive, not prescriptive. That is, they explain our behavior rather than recommending or making a value judgment about it. Yet it is tempting to turn an explanation into an evaluation with respect to the moral significance of findings about biological differences. What do such studies tell us about human behavior? May we measure a man's guilt, say, for adultery, against the size of his testicles? While this may seem ridiculous, religious laws have deployed a similar biological rationale to justify double standards for punishing male and female infidelity differently. Religious traditions have also stigmatized female promiscuity while tacitly accepting male promiscuity.[19]

Another study led by British scientists attributed behavioral differences between the sexes to genetic differences. Their theory is that "feminine intuition", or the capacity to observe and read non-verbal behavior, stems from a single location on the X chromosome. Though both sexes have the "intuition" gene, located somewhere near the middle of the X chromosome, it only *functions* in women.[20] Professor David Skuse, who led the research at the Institute of Child Health, emphasized that the gene may explain why boys can more easily be persuaded to behave badly: they are less able to see that their behavior is errant. Women more easily recognize social norms without prompting. Skuse pointed out that such a definite sexual split in the allocation of a gene would have to have an evolutionary advantage for both genders. One theory is that being less empathetic makes it easier to go out and kill somebody, which makes males better warriors and hunters. But it is all too easy to mistake an explanation for a justification. May we also conclude that men make 'better' murderers than their female counterparts, in the sense that men are less morally responsible (hence less blameworthy) for their violent behavior than females who behave in the same way? Should the law treat female murderers differently than it treats male murderers?

All of the above theories attribute an individual's behavior to biological causes that subconsciously influence her choices, preferences, and goals. Together, such theories suggest that human behavior is less free than we think and that much of what motivates our apparent choices is beneath the conscious level of reflection. Similar theories could offer a biological explanation for behavior that is anti-social, self-destructive, or harmful.

Biological determinist theories often downplay the more polemical social causes of crime and other socially disruptive behaviors. Too often they are wheeled in to rationalize, or divert attention from, existing inequalities and power structures in society. In addition,

> "...they are often inspired by the same motivation of discovering universal and unchanging social values. Typically, they describe as 'natural' aspects of behaviour thought to be biologically determined; though few would assert that natural behaviour is always to be encouraged or even permitted, characterizing some behavioural tendencies as natural provides a certain legitimation for them."[21]

Whether an innate predisposition to behave in a particular manner is described as 'natural' or as 'pathological' depends entirely on the socio-political context or perspective from which that behavior is described.

The phenomena of human existence and experience are always simultaneously biological *and* social and an adequate explanation must involve both. As an example, consider the supposition that pre-born babies may carry anti-social genes. The claim has an anachronistic ring to it, since one has to be social before one can be anti-social. Whereas an autistic child does not have a fully functional capacity to be sociable in the first place, an anti-social child would have to have a potential for, and experience of, healthy social interaction that she then rejects or rebels against. One could aim similar criticisms at the notion that alcoholism is an innate tendency, since one has to develop a habit of drinking too much alcohol before one can be 'alcoholic', making it difficult to see how a pre-born baby could have **genes** for such a tendency. Biological determinist theories not only downplay the social and environmental factors that contribute to crime and anti-social behavior. They also tend to diminish the individual's responsibility for his or her choices.

If human behavior is not really free then we will need to re-think the entire modern concept of morality, which presupposes that adult human beings are autonomous agents and are ordinarily responsible for their own actions, except in rare cases, such as where a mental illness inhibits the capacity to reason. Behavioral determinist theories make it very difficult to distinguish the kleptomaniac from the thief or the person with Tourette Syndrome from the person who is just rude.

Natural law theories appear in some ways to cohere with aspects of modern science. They rest on empirical fact, and relate ethics to observation, evidence and scientific knowledge about human nature. However, the method of defining *morality* in terms of biological nature and function glosses the important distinction between facts and values. Some natural law ethicists have treated particular biological facts as though they disclose values in an automatic way, without considering arguments as to why a select set of facts are given emphasis or relevance to a given moral question. The method of deriving moral norms from observations of nature (or from facts about certain aspects of nature) continues to influence twenty-first century ethics. In general this approach is not problematic. However, it can lead to a narrow physicalism, premised on the belief that human nature is static and primarily to be understood in biological and chemical terms. This ignores the conscious, rational, and creative aspects of human personhood. Where 'deviant' or 'sinful' behaviors were once rooted in the individual's will, today biotechnological advances hold out the promise of preventing bad behaviors by neutralizing the genetic mutations allegedly responsible for them.

## Criticisms of the behaviorist model

Our putatively 'modern' concept of morality has a long pedigree traceable to the ancient annals of human history, and seems almost intuitive to most of us. Ordinarily, we acknowledge that various internal and external influences shape our desires and inclinations: biology, parents, cultural totem and taboo, and personal idiosyncrasies. But many of us also acknowledge that none of these is so powerful that it can compel us to behave against our will. In other words, we remain free and capable of making our own choices and decisions, even if there are biological inclinations or social pressures to behave differently than we wish to. In this sense, we think of our*selves* as the incontestable authors of our lives.

'Physicalism' describes mental states as physical events – causal responses to physical stimuli that lead to movements in the body. But we ordinarily think of human actions as having meaning and importance. If you are walking along and someone suddenly shoves you, this is not just a physical event; it is an action, with purpose and meaning. Libertarians make a distinction between **events** and **actions**. Events may be random or caused, but they only tell us *what* happened. We can demand to know of actions *why* they were performed, and this links them to agency and responsibility. The presupposition that individuals are responsible moral agents takes us into the realm of reasons rather than causes. From this perspective we can praise or blame someone when we know *why* he performed an action. We distinguish between bodily movements and their meaning. Depending on the context and the individual's intention, shoving someone can be a charitable means of pushing him out of harm's way, or a vicious act intended to push him into the tracks.

Libertarians acknowledge that the physical world is subject to the causal laws of nature, determined through cause and effect. But they claim that the mental world is free from deterministic causation. In the mental world decisions are made which relate to goals and social values, and these are not just the outcome of passive desires but of reflection and choice, and can be justified with reference to reasons. Causes are backward-looking while reasons are aimed at goals and require looking forward. Reasoning creatures are creative. They produce new situations for specific reasons; they act upon and transform their environment, rather than merely responding to environmental stimuli.

As our capacity for self-reflection develops we become active decision makers. We construct values and ideals. When Socrates said it was only the 'examined life' that was worth living, he was alluding to the fact that values are decided, purposes are expressed and responsibility is assigned. As we become more reflective, we develop attitudes to our desires, sometimes called 'second-order desires'. I may have a desire to eat lots of sweets, but I have a second order desire to maintain a healthy body. My second-order desire is the attitude I express towards my first-order desire to eat lots of sugary foods.

Morality concerns itself with that portion of our behavior that we have the freedom to control. All of this may seem painfully obvious to the modern reader, but my point is simply that morality is premised on that part of human nature that transcends individual biological differences. Western norms of crime and punishment rest on the assumption that human beings share a common potential for choice and responsibility. This potential is conceived as almost universal, and it sets the boundaries of our moral responsibility, by determining which aspects of character are under our control, while acknowledging that we also have biological needs that are not. The assumption that we each have some degree of free will is the universal human foundation upon which our most authentic and fulfilling interpersonal relationships rest. This is not to deny that we express our relationship to others as incarnate creatures, through sexuality and the body. The accepted model of the human person that has prevailed in Western civilization pictures the brain as

> "the locus of the mind; but somehow the mind transcends the physio-chemical activity of the brain and the neurosensory system of the body. This transcendence is palpably demonstrated by the voluntary exercise of the will in making decisions and directing the actions of the body."[22]

The challenge posed to this model of the human person by DNA is serious and inescapable. It must be met. It is the challenge of genetic determinism.[23]

One of the greatest historical testimonials to the extent of human freedom is the Christian image of Jesus hanging on the cross. The quality and meaning of Jesus's life was clearly more important to him than his powerful instinct for biological survival. It was this conviction that allowed him to sacrifice his physical safety for a higher principle. Many may view a phenomenon like self-sacrifice as 'inhuman' insofar as it elevates abstract ideals or the common good above all practical biological values and self-interested motives. Many regard such an act of courage as too extreme to be taken seriously by ordinary men and women or even as disparaging 'embodiment'. But others would argue that such an act, just like the act of suicide, is the practical outcome of the conviction that life without self-determination (i.e. without a higher purpose than mere biological survival) is not worthy of being called a human life, and is not worth living. Martin Luther King Jr. once said, "Until a man has found something for which he is willing to die, he is not fit to live."[24] King lost his life in the struggle for civil rights in America, proving his own commitment to this view. That many of those who have subscribed to this view of life have been held up as models of human achievement and moral virtue is testimony to its enduring significance. I am not arguing that any expression of freedom short of self-sacrifice is worthless. Rather, these examples show that being human is more than a biological set of functions. Humans have the potential to "make something" of themselves, by means of their choices and achievements. This notion of a human life as a project, rather than a product, is central to the Western worldview and has arguably led to human flourishing and social progress in a way that is impossible in its absence.

## Postmodernism: a rejection of essentialist models

Since the 1970's the whole project of developing a comprehensive model of human nature has been subjected to the criticisms of poststructuralist and postmodern philosophers such as the French writers Michel Foucault and Jacques Derrida. These authors reject as political propaganda claims to universal truths. They argue that truth is relative to historically contingent and self-perpetuating discourses and that there can be no genuinely objective "master" discourse that might serve as a neutral basis for other more specific ones. Variations in the human condition allegedly rooted in biology were reinterpreted as mere 'labels' reflecting disparities in human relationships of power. Foucault's privileging of cultural determinism ('labeling') over biology emerged out of his ethnology of sexual 'types'. He chronicled the history of sexual norms by concentrating on the fluid notion of "homosexuality". He decried heteronormativity as a mere social mythology fashioned by psychoanalysts and what he called "Freud's conformism."[25] This does not mean that Foucault ruled out any biological dimension in the formation of sexuality, but rather that he emphasized the role of institutions and discourses in the conceptualization of sexuality. He did not comment explicitly on the causes of same sex desires.[26]

Nevertheless, while Foucault may have focused his emphasis on how 'sexuality' functions conceptually within social contexts, rather than on what sexuality *is*, this does not in itself prove that there are no true facts about sexuality. It simply suggests that the production of knowledge *about* sexuality takes place within social relationships of power, and that this too is something about which facts can be discovered and knowledge generated. Down the centuries, anthropological theories have shifted and evolved with our growing knowledge of the cosmos. In large part, 'master discourses' have achieved pre-eminence due to what Foucault called 'knowledge-power', by which he meant access to, or authority in, accepted methodologies for the discovery, and use of, facts. Foucault disclosed the relationship between knowledge and the institutions that deploy it within social contexts of power. Our moral evaluations of actions or events often hinge on our beliefs about the facts. For example, until the discovery of the female ovary in the 1820's the belief that women were by nature inferior to men was supported by the popular scientific belief that men supplied the genetic seed for new life, while women contributed incubation but no genetic material of their own. The notion that abortion is morally wrong is related to underlying beliefs about the ontological status of the fetus. This issue is problematic precisely because the empirical evidence is inconclusive. On one view fetuses are potential children who do not have a definitive claim to moral rights. A different view is that fetuses are "pre-born children" with all of the rights of born children. Those who differentiate morally between fetuses and children will have different attitudes to the notion of "fetal rights" than those who do not. The root of the disagreement is a lack of consensus on the question of when a truly "human" life begins. Then we must ask the related question of what makes us truly human. Biologists and scientists are inclined to look upon ethical judgments as expressions of sentiment *about* certain biological or social facts. We have nothing to ground our disputes about sentiment or social policy unless we make reference to facts. Facts are descriptive but they have importance because they ground normative judgments.

The Catholic Church teaches that abortion is always wrong because "ensoulment" occurs at the moment of conception. However, this was not always the predominant Catholic theory. St. Thomas Aquinas maintained the ancients' view that the fetus did not have a soul until it assumed human form: "The conception of the male finishes on the fortieth day and that of the woman on the ninetieth, as Aristotle says in the *IX Book of the Animals*" (**Aquinas**, *Commentary on III Sentences* 3:5:2). We now know that there was no substantial evidence for that theory, but one has to remember that what counts as knowledge is also subject to change.

Around the middle of the last century, Alfred Kinsey's studies in sexology and later studies by Masters and Johnson and Shere Hite dispelled many myths pertaining to human sexuality.[27] In the early years of the twentieth century sex research ceased being a concern with pathologies and became part of a crusade for sexual liberation. The work of Havistock Ellis, in being descriptive rather than normative in intent, epitomized the new "sexology". Ellis's work aimed at a universal appreciation of human sexuality in all its aspects, including its formerly taboo manifestations in masturbation and homosexuality.[28] The more society has become open about the facts of sexual experience and its diversity, the more we have tended to view traditional taboos as superfluous or obsolete. Some attribute the more tolerant modern attitudes towards sexuality to the 'permissiveness' of the 1960's, which they view as a time when sacred traditional values were eroded by feminism, 'secular' disciplines (including sexology and sociology), and an entertainment industry that reflected, and in some cases shaped, the prevailing sexual ideology.

In spite of these changes, some conservative Christians maintain that the only authoritative source of ethics (including sexual ethics) is the Bible, understood as the infallible word of God. For many, the Bible is regarded as the only authoritative source of anthropological theories. Creationism and original sin co-exist alongside modern secular theories of evolution and personal moral responsibility.

The German theologian Helmut Thielicke has made several relevant observations in his critique of the Roman Catholic view of Natural Law. The first of his criticisms is directed at what he calls an "inconstancy in the view of man."[29] Norms of human behavior generally rest on a corresponding anthropological archetype. This implies that there is one enduring archetype for all places and all times. Historically this has not been the case. Aristotle's view of natural law, for example, was used to justify slavery because Aristotle's idea of man is identical with the idea of the citizen, the *civis*. According to Theilicke, this particular association "means that the idea of humanity arises only within a very definite 'political' relation, which is itself conditioned by the contingency of the social order as it existed at that time. Accordingly, ethics itself is politically determined. The political relation . . . constitutes the nerve of the value system of natural law."[30] Thielicke highlights the potential conflict between socially defined ideas of human nature and new empirical discoveries about human nature. Just as Michel Foucault argued that sexuality is less an essential or constitutive part of our nature than a product of cultural knowledge that contributes to the maintenance of specific power relations, Thielicke argues that 'human nature' is less an empirical discovery than an institutional invention.

Poststructuralist and postmodern philosophers have made us aware that research and its outcomes do not take place in a political vacuum. The language in which discoveries or knowledge are couched as well as the uses to which it is put take place within institutions and relationships of power. For this reason, many homosexuals, queer rights activists and their liberal allies refuse to view any genetic research into biological homosexuality as other than genocidally motivated. However, I urge homophile skeptics of the new 'gay gene' science not to dismiss as irrelevant the profound impact empirical discoveries may, and *ought,* to have on traditional beliefs and moral attitudes. Though there is tentative evidence of a relationship between our biological endowments and our actions, it is still assumed by most of us that we are free to act on our inclinations, to weigh the value of so doing, and to direct our lives through conscious, reflective decisions. This belief grounds both our rights and our responsibilities. My greatest hope is to enable my readers on both sides of the aisle to accept the consequences that homosexual essentialism (if true) ought to have on moral evaluations of homosexual behavior. The danger in the quasi-eugenic discourses I examine lies in the contradictory logic of locating some subset of human beings for which moral autonomy and responsibility are rendered impossible by aspects of their biology. What we risk losing in a 'eugenic age' is far more than biodiversity (or homosexuals). What is at stake is our longstanding belief that human individuals are moral agents responsible for defining themselves through the choices they make in the project of living.

Perhaps a wholesale rejection of the 'morally responsible agent' will be welcomed in some quarters, and hailed as a paradigm shift long overdue. What should not be welcomed is an unreflective dismantling of the anthropological paradigm that has been more effective than any previous one in establishing human rights for all people, including women, ethnic minorities and homosexuals.

1    Jaggar, Alison M. and Struhl, Karsten J., 'Nature' in <u>Encyclopedia of Bioethics</u>, Vol. 2, Warren T. Reich, ed. (New York: Simon & Schuster), 1995, p. 1172-3.

2    Clack, Beverley, <u>Sex and Death: a reappraisal of human mortality</u>, Polity Press in association with Blackwell Publishers, Ltd., 2002, p. 111.

3    "Let not sin dwell in your mortal bodies to make you obey their passions." (Romans 6:12) "Nothing good dwells in me, that is, in my flesh. I can will what is right but I cannot do it." (Romans 7:18) "I see in my members another law at war with the law of my mind and making me captive to the law of sin which dwells in my members, wretched man that I am!" (Romans 7:21-24)

4    Augustine of Hippo, <u>Letter to Valentinus</u>, Chapter 1 [I.], accessed online at NewAdvent.org/fathers on 15 January, 2012. See also Miles, Margaret Ruth, <u>The Word Made Flesh: a history of Christian thought</u>, Malden, MA: Wiley-Blackwell, 2005, pp. 101-2 and <u>The Confessions of Saint Augustine</u>, Book VIII, translated by Edward Bouverie Pusey, [1909-14], at sacred-texts.com.

5    Alper, Joseph S. and Beckwith, Jonathan, 'Genetic Fatalism and Social Policy: The Implications of Behavior Genetics Research', *Yale Journal of Biology and Medicine* 66 (1993), pp. 511-524.

6    Hume, David, <u>An Enquiry Concerning Human Understanding</u>, Harvard Classics Volume 37, Copyright 1910 P.F. Collier & Son, public domain released August 1993.

7    Erich Fromm, <u>The Fear of Freedom</u>, Edited by Karl Mannheim, (London: Keegan Paul, 1942), p. 8.

8    Hume, David, <u>An Enquiry Concerning Human Understanding</u>, 'Of Freedom and Necessity', Part 1, 8-9.

9    Wilson, Edward, O., <u>Consilience: The Unity of Knowledge</u> (New York: Knopf: Distributed by Random House, 1998).

10    Spayde, John, 'The Theory of Everything' in *Utne Reader*, August 98, No. 88, p. 96.

11    Rose, Steven, Lewontin, R.C. and Kamin, Leon J., <u>Not in Our Genes: Biology, Ideology and Human Nature</u>, (London: Penguin Books, 1990), p. 27.

12    O'Neill, Terry, Ed., <u>Biomedical Ethics: Opposing Viewpoints Series</u>, (San Diego: Greenhaven Press, 1994), p. 264.

13    Ibid.

14    Sellers-Diamond, Alfreda A., <u>Disposable Children in Black Faces: The Violence Initiative as Inner-City Containment Policy</u>, 62, University of Missouri Kansas Law Review 423, Spring 1994.

15    Suzanne Moore, 'Genetic Scientists Lost in Inner Space', *The Guardian*, Thurs. February 16, 1995.

16    Gray, John, <u>Men are From Mars Women are From Venus</u>, (New York: Harper Collins, 1992), p. 7.

17    Ibid, p. 5.

18  Aaronovitch, David, 'Tell-tale Signs of the Adulterer: is it all a load of gonads?', Sat. 4 October, 1997, *The Independent*.

19  See, for example, Gil, Rosa Maria and Vazquez, Carmen Inoa, <u>The Maria Paradox: How Latinas Can Merge Old World Traditions with New World Self-Esteem</u>, New York, G.P. Putnam Sons, 1996.

20  Arthur, Charles, 'Revealed at Last: Why boys will be boys and girls will be girls' Thursday, 12 June, *The Independent*.

21  Jaggar, Alison M. & Struhl, Karsten J., 'Human Nature' in Warren T. Reich, Ed., <u>Encyclopedia of Bioethics</u>, Vol. 2., New York: Simon & Schuster, 1995, p. 1177.

22  Nelson, Robert J., 'What is Life?', Christian Social Action, in <u>Biomedical Ethics</u>, Bender and Leone, Eds., 1991, p. 266.

23  O'Neill, Terry, Ed., <u>Biomedical Ethics: Opposing Viewpoints Series</u>, (San Diego: Greenhaven Press, 1994), p. 267.

24  23 June 1963, Speech at the Great March on Detroit

25  Foucault, Michel, <u>The History of Sexuality, Vol. 1: An Introduction</u> (Vintage Books Edition, 1990), pp. 5, 53, 56, 119, 150,151.

26  Spargo, Tamsin, <u>Postmodern Encounters: Foucault and Queer Theory</u>, (Icon Books, Duxford, Cambridge: 1999), p. 13.

27  A.C. Kinsey, W.B. Pomery, and C.E. Martin, *Sexual Behaviour in the Human Male* (Saunders, 1948); A.C. Kinsey, W.B. Pomeroy, C.E. Martin and P.H. Gebhard, *Sexual Behaviour in the Human Female* (Saunders, 1953); W.H. Masters and V.E. Johnson, *Human Sexual Response* (Little Brown, 1966); S. Hite, *The Hite Report on Female Sexuality* (Knopf, 1979) and *The Hite Report on Male Sexuality* (Knopf, 1981).

28  Lewontin, R. C., 'Sex, Lies and Social Science', *The New York Review of Books*, April, 20, 1995, p. 24.

29  Thielicke, Helmut, <u>Theological Ethics, Foundations, Vol. 1</u>, William H. Lazareth, Ed. (Philadelphia: Fortress, 1966), pp. 420-430.

30  Ibid, p. 420.

# CHAPTER 2

# *St Paul and Natural Law*

In the previous chapter I suggested several reasons why most natural law thinking about homosexuality has been problematic. First, the reasoning deployed was sometimes circular: 'God's will' is disclosed by the workings of nature, while at the same time 'nature' is correctly comprehended only by first perceiving God's will. On the latter view, dissent from the 'correct' or 'Godly' comprehension of nature was not tolerated as an honest intellectual disagreement about matters of fact, but was stigmatized or even punished as 'sin'. Second, natural law ethics have sometimes glossed the distinction between facts and values. Instead of using facts as a *basis* for *arguments* about why moral conclusions should follow from those particular facts and not others, they have simply slid from facts to values without the linking arguments.

The aim of this chapter is to demonstrate that the blueprint for the first of these problems can be traced back to its earliest Christian proponent: St. Paul. I will not analyse Paul's approach through a systematic biblical exegesis but through the use of Pauline scripture in more recent theological discussion of 'the natural' as it relates to Christian sexual ethics. Since the Pauline epistles are the only sources of moral wisdom dealing with homosexuality in the New Testament (and hence, strictly speaking, in the *Christian* scriptures) we do well to pay attention to the reasons given within them for declaring homosexual acts sinful. If Paul's prohibition of homosexual acts ultimately flows from a version of natural law reasoning then, by entailment, we may conclude that natural law is the *only* method

Christians ever use to justify their traditional prohibitionist stance towards homosexual activity.

In making recommendations as to the view Christians should take of homosexuality, the traditional arguments have tended to fall into two broad categories: those based on scripture and those based on natural law. While most contemporary Biblical scholars agree that the appeal to scripture provides us with a rather narrow and somewhat ambiguous basis for contemporary Christian teaching, nevertheless it is also argued that the Old and New Testament passages that prohibit homosexual practices contain an underlying assumption, which cannot be entirely dismissed, that such practices represent a departure from human nature as ordained by God. How or why this should be so is not made fully explicit. One way in which the Roman Catholic Church has made this assumption explicit, without direct appeals to scripture, is through the natural law approach. But even in the Christian scriptures, the most salient condemnation of homosexual acts -- St. Paul's letter to the Romans, Chapter 1.18-32[1] -- appears to draw its authoritative force from a version of natural law reasoning.

The section begins with a primitive natural law argument ("Ever since the creation of the world, God's invisible nature has been clearly perceived in the things that have been made." – vv. 20-23) and becomes progressively more specific as Paul goes on to compare homogenital activity[2] to idol worship, impurity, lust and untruth. He appears to equate heterosexuality and God, or "God's invisible nature" and contrasts this nature with "dishonorable passions" and "unnatural relations." Paul concludes with a reminder of "God's decree": that those who do such things [homogenital acts] deserve to die. This final warning refers to Leviticus 20:13 which says, "If a man lies with a male as with a woman, both of them have committed an abomination; they shall be put to death, their blood is upon them." Some Biblical exegetes have challenged the ethical significance of this passage. They claim that the stipulations in the Levitical Holiness Code do not translate into contemporary ethical prohibitions, because the context of their use was very different; the code was intended to set the identifying boundaries of cultic purity, not to ascertain guilt and innocence.

L. William Countryman has helped to illuminate the deep connection between cultural identity and concrete rules of behavior. With their external pressures and internal conflicts, the purity rules enabled the Jewish people to be clear about their own identity.[3] This was not just a matter of belief; it was a matter of obedience to rules, manifest in conventional forms of behavior. Purity rules about sex quite possibly functioned to distinguish the people of Israel from the Canaanites.[4] But additionally, these laws literally defined or established the organization of the family; to infringe them was to confuse role-assignments thought to be definitive, in this case not just of the culture but of humanity universally. Within ancient Jewish purity rules, condemnation is typically unrelated to actual harm caused by the acts in question, but relates solely to the act's symbolic significance.[5] The 'sin' is to be found in the offense caused by breaking convention, not in any concrete damage done. Purity-based ethics tend to concern what goes in and out of bodily orifices. "Defilement" is seen as something automatic, independent of any conscious intentions. For example, accidentally touching a corpse or a man having a nocturnal emission or female menstruation were all forms of 'impurity.' Impurity was attached to what, from a modern perspective, are 'pre-moral' facts. Those who observe purity rules cannot generally give empirical reasons for them apart from references to "values" or ideas of the "sacred" prevalent in the culture to which they belong. From within this context, religious institutions perform the auxiliary function of legitimating social customs and taboos.

Countryman has argued that, if we view Paul's condemnation of homogenital activity in Romans 1 in the wider context of the letter, it is evident that Paul no longer endorses the validity of the purity system. In Romans 14 we read: "I know and am persuaded in the Lord Jesus that nothing is unclean of itself." Paul is here speaking of food, but Countryman argues that, by implication, this rationale extends to sexual purity as well.

There is wide scholarly consensus that, for Paul, the legalistic inheritance of the Mosaic law is not binding on Christians, who are made righteous by their faith in Jesus Christ. The crucial question on which the debate centers is whether this radical newness in the gospel of Jesus does, in Paul's thinking, apply to sexuality as to circumcision and dietary stipulations in the ritual law. Countryman argues that since purity rules about sex in the Old Testament come into the category of ritual purity, they must logically be entailed in Paul's general relaxation of those distinctive observances that separate Jews from Gentiles. According to Countryman, the reference to homosexuality in the first chapter is not an instance of Paul stating his own opinion, but an allusion to a specific example of Jewish prejudice that will "set up" the Jewish segment of his audience for the next chapter, where he will chastise them for judging according to the law, and argue that man is justified by faith rather than by works of law.[6] On this view, homosexuality is merely employed as a specific example of something that, while it is repulsive or "unclean" *to Jews* (not to Paul), carries no such stigma in the Gentile world. Consequently when Paul describes homosexuality as 'unclean' he does not mean to state **his** opinion that it is morally wrong or 'sinful' (i.e. that it violates the moral requirements in the *justice* system). Rather, he is alluding to a Jewish purity way of thinking for the sake of argument -- one that he will subsequently set aside (in Chapter 2) in light of the further revelation of God's purposes found in the gospel of Jesus, who claimed a higher authority than the Jewish Law.[7]

Like Countryman, Rev. Walter Houston[8] has helped to illuminate the deep connection between cultural identity and concrete rules of behavior. Houston has observed that the relationship between behavioral norms and culture was an intimate one in Judaism. So intimate, in fact, that some describe the relationship as one of literal identity between the two: a Jew was one who, among other things, would not eat pork. It was typical of purity thinking to maintain that particular acts were wrong in themselves. One of the important functions that purity rules performed in ancient Judaism was to reinforce the external boundaries of the community in a situation where the people were politically vulnerable and geographically mixed up with other people.[9]

Houston is one of several scholars who have demonstrated that the weight of evidence is against Countryman's theory (that Paul is *not* describing *his own* opinion when identifying homosexuality as violating moral requirements in the justice system's purity rules about sex). As Houston has pointed out,

"If Paul accepts the verdict of Leviticus he must be reprobating same-sex intercourse as such, regardless of circumstances and attitudes; and that is an essential characteristic of purity thinking."[10] Countryman's theory fails to explain Paul's strong pejorative language in Romans 1:24-27:

> "Therefore God gave them up in the lusts of their hearts to impurity, to the dishonouring of their bodies among themselves, because they exchanged the truth about God for a lie and worshipped and served the creature rather than the Creator, who is blessed forever! Amen. For this reason God gave them up to dishonourable passions. Their women exchanged natural relations for unnatural, and the men likewise gave up natural relations with women and were consumed with passion for one another, men committing shameless acts with men and receiving in their own persons the due penalty for their error."

Countryman's interpretation of Paul also conflicts with the unexceptional use of purity language in which Paul more generally couches his disapproval of certain types of sexual conduct, including homoerotic acts. According to Houston, Paul continued to speak of sex in purity terms, even though, where food is concerned, "nothing is unclean in itself." It would seem that in Paul's thinking there are many things in the sexual field which *are* taken to be "unclean in themselves" and should be avoided for that reason.

Houston's conclusion concurs with the report of the Church of England's 1978 *Working Party on the Theological, Social, Pastoral and Legal Aspects of Homosexuality*. In section 114. of their report, its authors state:

> ". . .the New Israel has abandoned many of the things which the Old Israel saw as vital for the preservation of its distinctive religion and society and to which it ascribed the status of divine commands. . . . . many of these, for example, circumcision, are set aside in the New Testament because of the further revelation of God's nature and purposes found in the Gospel of Jesus . . . However, as we have also noted, this is not the case with homosexuality, where the attitude of the Old Testament is reinforced by Paul . . ." [11]

Whereas the food laws were cultic conventions distinctive of Judaism, the laws and ethical perceptions about sex in Judaism "were generally held by Jews to apply to all human beings; for they *defined* the cultural features of marriage and the family which were seen as common to humanity. . . It is clear that Paul shared this view. . . . therefore he includes men who engage in such acts in a list of people who are excluded from the Kingdom of God (I Cor. 6:9-11)."[12] Houston accepts that Countryman has raised an important question, for, even if Countryman is mistaken in thinking that the New Testament abandons purity thinking in relation to sex, we might still ask whether purity as understood by Paul and ancient Jewish culture is relevant today and whether it is consistent with the Gospel's more general relaxation of purity thinking.

One of the nuances in this debate focuses on the fact that Paul is condemning only what he sees as a perversion of one's natural (heterosexual) orientation. Robin Scroggs[13] and John Boswell[14] contend that the only kind of homosexual relations Paul would have been familiar with were those typical of Greek pederasty, which were often brief, exploitative or commercial. When Paul speaks of people 'giving up'[15] or 'leaving' or 'exchanging'[16] heterosexual relations, he certainly seems to be describing the whimsical, promiscuous behavior of people who are really heterosexually orientated -- not the actions of the true homosexual. It is unlikely that Paul would have made anything like our modern distinction between homosexual *orientation* (which was unacknowledged within his historical context) and homogenital *acts*. Since Paul did not recognize constitutive or immutable homosexual orientation, he views *all* homogenital acts as a deliberate departure from the person's true (heterosexual) nature. Boswell and Scroggs have argued that Paul's objections to "unnatural relations" should be understood not as moral condemnations of homogenital acts *per se*, but aim at the exploitative nature of the only types of homogenital relationships that Paul would have been familiar with – those typical of Greek pederasty.

Houston argues against this view that Paul is not condemning homosexual acts on the grounds that Scroggs and others would like him to: "He is not objecting to the asymmetry or to the exploitative nature of the relationship, but to the simple fact that males lie with males, just as Leviticus does."[17] This brings us back to Houston's essential point -- that Paul presents the issue from a purity point of view in which it is the act of same-sex intercourse *as such* that is condemned, regardless of circumstances, intention or harm. The Rome of Paul's time operated by a simple, brutal rule: that a free male "may satisfy his sexual desires by subjugating women and boys without distinction."[18] It is reasonable to think that the practice of pederasty amongst heterosexual males would have been familiar to Paul. However, it appears that Paul's purpose in Romans 1 & 2 was to condemn homoerotic acts *per se*, not merely their exploitative character, but the mere fact that they are 'impure' because they represent a transgression of "God's invisible nature" as it is expressed in His creation. As Thomas E. Schmidt points out, Paul's disapproval of homoerotic acts of *any* kind seems evident from the fact that his first reference in Romans 1:26-27 is to relations between females. This makes it implausible to limit the application of Paul's words to pederasty.[19]

Schmidt has located several major flaws in Countryman's argument. For present purposes, I will mention only those that do not require entering into arcane exegetical debates requiring specialist familiarity with Greek or Hebrew. The first problem is chronological. Countryman argues that Paul uses homosexuality as a prime example of something Gentiles accept as morally neutral (like eating bacon) but which the Gentiles know is repulsive to Jews. Homosexuality was simply a fact within Gentile culture, and not particularly taboo. According to Countryman, the Gentile segment of Paul's audience already understand that Paul does not associate impurity with sin (immorality), so they will not associate his words in Romans 1: 26-27[20] with sin, but only with *Jewish* impurity. This will effectively convey Hellenic Jewish thought about impurity to prepare the readers for his attack on Jewish hypocrisy in the next chapter. Paul wants to expose the hypocrisy of legalists among his audience in Chapter 2, so he finds an example of behavior that distinguishes Jews from Gentiles, so that he can then replace these distinctions with his real message: "nothing is unclean in itself".[21] Countryman says that Paul is careful here not to use the language of 'sin' (*hamartia*).[22] However, Schmidt reminds us that Paul writes from Corinth after settling a few problems there. He had not visited Rome prior to this letter. According to Schmidt, there is little reason to suppose (as Countryman does) that Gentile Christians in Rome were aware that Paul does not associate impurity with sin. "It is inconceivable", says Schmidt, "that Paul would simply assume that the Romans had such information."[23] In fact, Paul's lengthy comments about ritual purity in Romans 14 indicate that he assumes *no* prior knowledge of this position amongst Gentiles in Rome.

We may still ask, however, why Paul continues to see Jewish purity rules related to sex as binding on Christians, who are made righteous by their faith in Jesus Christ (Romans 14:14). There seems to be an inconsistency between Paul's application of purity thinking about sexuality as opposed to its application to circumcision and dietary stipulations in the ritual law. Perhaps this could be explained by analyzing the *basis* of Paul's condemnation of same-sex relations. Rather than seeing same-sex relations as taboo or unconventional, he seems to see them as a transgression of "nature", which is universal for humans everywhere (not particular to Jewish law). Paul does not explicitly quote Genesis, but Romans 1 is filled with tacit allusions to humanity's creation and fall. "Ever since the creation," verse 20 begins, God's power has been evident in "the things he has made." Verses 26-27 do not use the usual Greek words for "women" and "men" but instead use females and males, as in Genesis 1:27, "male and female he created them".[24] These observations strengthen the association in Paul's thinking between "natural" and the creation account of sexual differentiation. It is quite unusual that Paul begins his account of unnatural relations in Romans with a reference to women (v. 26).[25] Ancient authors did not ordinarily link male and female same-sex acts into a single category. By doing so, and by using terminology denoting mutual desire (they were "consumed with passion for one another") he apparently alludes neither to exploitative pederasty nor to prostitution. As Schmidt points out, Paul understands that "male and female were created for each other with complementary sexualities grounded in the distinctive constitutions of their sexual organs.[26] It appears clear that, for Paul, the desire of female for female or of male for male dishonours this 'natural' arrangement by substituting untruth for truth.

Further evidence that Paul takes a moral position against homogenital acts *per se* comes from the surrounding paragraph. Paul certainly seems to equate same-sex relations with other forms of improper conduct (wickedness, evil, covetousness, malice, murder, strife, deceit, etc.) that he mentions in verses 18-32, which is clearly a unit. These verses are introduced by a reference to "the wrath of God ... against all ungodliness and wickedness." While Schmidt concedes Countryman's (and Boswell's) point that Paul does not use the word 'sin' (*hamartia*) anywhere in the first two chapters of Romans, the description of sin (immoral conduct) is clearly their primary subject. Similarly, Rabbi David Novak claims that the list of vices destructive of human relationships in vv. 24-32 are intended to exhibit "the inherent connection between idolatry as the lie about one's created status, sexual immorality -- especially homosexuality -- as the lie about one's relationship with his or her own body, and murder as the lie about one's relationship with the life of another human body."[27] 'Unnatural relations' are portrayed by Paul as the first symptom of worshipping something other than the true God.

Paul's rationale is taken over from earlier polemics against pagan society: that the widespread practice of homogenital sex was an appropriate reward for idolatry. His thinking seems to be that those who "exchanged the glory of the immortal God for images" found themselves exchanging natural intercourse for unnatural; or to put it another way, *failing to recognize* the Creator, they found themselves abandoned to the misuse of creation.

The strength of Schmidt's argument comes from its relative simplicity, compared to the complex and protracted explanations that interpret Romans 1 as an exception to Paul's horror of sin. The overall structure of the argument about homoerotic acts in Romans 1 is more easily explained when viewed as a prime and specific example of sin, even if Paul does not explicitly use that word. Richard B. Hays agrees with Schmidt that same-sex relations are singled out because Paul seeks "a vivid image of humanity's primal rejection of the sovereignty of God the Creator."[28]

Schmidt points out that in vv. 18-32 Paul is describing not individual actions but the *corporate* rebellion of humanity against God and the *kinds* of behavior that result:

"The point is that same-sex relations are a *specific* falsification
of right behaviour, made possible by the general falsification of
right thinking about God (idolatry). Paul's concern is not with
individuals who deny their true selves but with humanity that first
generally and now specifically (and sexually) has replaced truth
with a falsehood."[29]

Paul's first concern, claims Schmidt, is not motivation but practice. In this
regard Schmidt is in agreement with Houston's conclusion that Paul was
condemning homosexual acts *per se*, as a violation of the purity law, which
in this case, he sees as applying to humanity generally.

However, this does not settle the issue of whether Paul had in mind
anything like homosexuality in the modern sense. Today we know that a
minority of human beings is very likely born with a homosexual orientation.
If so, we cannot morally assess homogenital acts *per se* as simply a stubborn
rejection of 'nature' or Creation. And anyway, modern ethicists do not
evaluate sexual acts prior to consideration of the agent's intention and the
impact of his acts on the wellbeing of morally significant others. Schmidt's
analysis is problematic only because he assumes without explanation that
homogenital acts *per se* are, because relatively less common, "unnatural"
and so immoral. Despite this, he is careful to stress that moral norms of
behavior depend upon the *will*, or motive, of the agent. Schmidt provides a
clear and succinct explanation of what is most pressing in the contemporary
homosexuality debate:

"Moral questions have to do with the rightness or wrongness of
my actions, regardless of **the source** or strength of my desires.
Whatever I may attribute to my genes, or to my parents, or to my
culture, none of them can force me, at the crucial moment, to
turn a glance into a fantasy, or a flirtation into a sexual act. At that
moment my *will* is involved, and precisely such moments define
my obedience and growth as a Christian."[30]

While it is probably true that all of us have free will and our moral
responsibility depends upon it, this does not explain why Christians have
treated homogenital acts as a prime example of immoral behavior. To
participate in consenting homogenital acts is viewed not as a matter of

biological difference, which might be regarded as morally neutral, but as a 'sin' or a deliberate departure from a moral good. Upon reflection, most heterosexuals do not view conforming to their own nature as a moral good. Attraction to the opposite sex *per se* is not deliberate behavior. Their will *is not involved* except in how they choose to *express* this attraction. In acts where the will *is* involved, a moral assessment of an act has nothing to do with the sex of the people involved and everything to do with the intentions that motivate the act and how it impacts on *others*. Otherwise every heterosexual act would be morally good just because it involves persons of the opposite sex. Just as with heterosexual acts, the moral description of homosexual acts as 'sins' ought to reference the motives of the act and the harm it does to the victim(s), if any.

Schmidt admits that Paul's first concern, however, is *not motivation* (or actual harm to others) but the practice *per se*. Therefore, it is odd that Schmidt supports Paul's condemnation of homosexual acts, since Schmidt himself says "it is not the **source** of my desires that makes my actions morally praiseworthy or blameworthy, but my *will*". Even if the *source* of my sexual desire is my subconscious sex drive, my actions in the world are conscious and voluntary. This is true whether the agent is heterosexual or homosexual. Schmidt seems to agree with the modern view that there is nothing about involuntary heterosexual orientation that is necessarily morally good. He would very likely agree that whether a heterosexual act is morally good is determined not by the unintentional attraction, but by the interpersonal effects of his actions. He says that while it is *unnatural* for him (and presumably any heterosexual man) to be faithful to one woman, this is not a *justification* for unfaithfulness. While it might *explain* his involuntary urge to be unfaithful, it does not by itself furnish a good reason why he *ought* to act this way. Infidelity is done with the awareness and intention of deceiving another person from whom one presumably receives certain benefits, including love and support. Infidelity is potentially harmful, insofar as it breaches the trust between intimate partners. Schmidt offers no comparable reason why homogenital acts should be morally illicit.

Like Paul, Schmidt describes homogenital acts *in themselves* as a form of *moral* evil, irrespective of the agent's motives and irrespective of any harm to others. On Schmidt's own reasoning, we can assume that marriage is not natural (since it involves male fidelity to one woman). Therefore, it cannot be the "naturalness" of heterosexual marriage or heterosexual intercourse that makes deviations from it wrong. Schmidt implies but fails to explain why there is something morally wrong with voluntary homogenital acts. His negative evaluation of such acts, like Paul's, is rendered prior to any assessment of the homosexual person's motives and prior to any harm done to others. Instead, the form of the act itself (in its biological structure) is defined as a 'sin' on cultic, religious or scriptural grounds. This is analogous to purity thinking, in which particular actions are wrong in themselves, prior to any evaluation of the harm they do. Their harm is only explicable in terms of non-conformity to the theoretical or symbolic 'goodness' of heterosexual acts. In other words, such acts are simply unconventional or taboo when viewed from within a particular cultic form of life.

Schmidt follows Paul in equivocating on the word 'natural'. Both Paul and Schmidt shift from the pre-moral sense of 'natural' (i.e. observed to occur in nature) to another (theological) sense of 'natural' to morally condemn homogenital acts. Schmidt says Paul is using 'natural' as referring to something that is in accord with God's intention. "Natural" means "conforms to God's will". But if God's will is discerned by observing how nature works, then it is a mystery why *some* things that regularly occur in nature (like homosexuality) contravene God's will. Effectively, the argument is circular in asserting both (a.) that God's will is disclosed by how nature works *and* (b.) that the true meaning of 'nature' is discerned by comprehending God's will.

When describing why heterosexuality is 'natural' both Paul and Schmidt refer to a selection of pre-moral facts. They identify as 'natural' the more common pattern of sexual expression observed in nature, classifying it as "God's creation". Schmidt acknowledges that homosexuality may be just as 'natural' (intrinsic to the person) as heterosexuality. He then claims that the "naturalness" of homosexuality or heterosexual male promiscuity (infidelity?) cannot *of itself* make these acts morally good. Yet he continues to assume that the "naturalness" of heterosexual behavior is what makes willful deviations from it morally wrong. Never does he offer any other explanation why they are 'sinful'. He seems to assume that the naturalistic fallacy[31] does not apply to his own logic concerning the intrinsic *moral* goodness of all heterosexual acts even though he explicitly acknowledges that it poses a problem. He seems to want a half-baked natural law ethic in which the facts of nature do not automatically disclose moral imperatives, but they do reveal moral prohibitions.

When he talks about the will as being decisive in moral questions, Schmidt refers only to the agent's *willingness* to conform to pre-defined conventional (cultic) modes of action (discernible as 'good' with reference to their exterior structure). The real emphasis of Schmidt's understanding of moral questions falls on the "rightness or wrongness of my actions". On Schmidt's account, it is the performance of certain types of exterior acts *in themselves* that makes my will morally good or evil, not the intention with which I perform them. Accordingly, homogenital acts are not 'sins' because of my intent to harm another human being, but because they conflict with a conventional Christian definition of 'nature' – one that portrays heterosexuality as the only form of human sexual expression in which 'God's will' is manifest. As Schmidt says: *"But as a moral category natural refers to something that is in accord with God's intention."*[32] Schmidt's only reason for describing homosexuality as a "fundamental falsehood" is his accepted definition of 'nature', which he claims has its source in God. According to Schmidt, what distinguishes 'nature' as a specifically moral category, as opposed to merely referring to things observed to happen with regularity in the world, is that it has God as its source. For Schmidt, it is not *my* will that makes heterosexual acts morally superior to homosexual ones, but my obedience to *God's* will, which is the source of (hetero) sexual nature in general. This leaves unanswered how we are to distinguish which aspects of the natural world uniquely disclose God's intentions. Schmidt gives us no clear means of detecting the natural events in which the will of God is manifest as opposed to those from which his will is absent. Perhaps he assumes that we can determine this by reference to the authority of St. Paul. If this is the case, we are forced to the conclusion, along with St. Paul, that heterosexuality's source in nature (here equated with created biology) makes it morally good. In that case, it is not the *will* of the human agent that makes sexual acts morally good, as Schmidt's comments would lead us to believe, but their heterogenital complementarity.

Instead of focusing on the procreative function of the organs, Paul alludes to the creation account in Genesis to establish that heterosexual complementarity was God's intention from time immemorial (Romans 1:20). However, as Schmidt explicitly points out, Paul's understanding of sexual complementarity is grounded in the distinctive constitutions of sexual organs -- or 'creation' as he understood it at the time.[33] Schmidt draws a parallel between the ideal human biology and an advertisement for a beverage with "all natural ingredients." He claims that we do not analyze the ingredients but simply acknowledge that the manufacturer wants us to think the drink is good for us. So with the ultimate Manufacturer (God) -- who proclaims human sexuality as "the best stuff on earth" (Gen. 1:31).

In response to this, it should be made clear that critics of Paul's sexual ethics do not object to the (pre-moral) goodness of heterosexuality. They only take issue with the notion that human sexuality has *only one* kind of 'natural' manifestation. Rather than viewing homosexuality as a 'perversion' of, or 'substitute' for, heterosexuality, more recent sexologists argue that it is another natural variant of human sexuality. Instead of seeing homosexuality as futile to the survival of the species, one could regard it as a natural means of preventing over-population, especially where resources are scarce. Just as being female is not a perversion of the one and only male sexual category, but is another kind of human sexual variation, so too is homosexuality not a perversion of the one and only heterosexual category, but another category of human sexuality. Whether homosexuality is a 'natural' variant of human sexuality or a 'falsehood' or 'lie' (as Paul's language suggests) is an empirical question, not a theological/moral one. Today, scientific and sociological research promises the best means of solving this riddle.

Like Paul, Schmidt vacillates between treating homosexuality as a moral issue and treating it as a mistake about a matter of fact. Depending as they do upon ancient Scriptures for their understanding of the empirical world, neither is in an ideal place to judge matters of fact. If biology is the only relevant matter of fact, as the view of 'creation' (above) seems to imply, then Paul should have reached the conclusion that rape is more 'natural' (ie. genitally complementary) and consequently less evil, than masturbation or consenting homosexual acts. Given the ancient view of women, this is not entirely unlikely. Nevertheless, if he had taken consent, or the will of the agent, or the harm done, to be important criteria for moral evaluations of human acts, he might have concluded, as we do now, that what makes sexual acts good or evil is the agent's intention and the benefit or harm done within an inter-personal context. Cruel intentions, harm, humiliation and lack of reciprocity make rape an act of violence rather than a healthy form of sexual expression. Yet, following Paul's rationale, we could not rule out the notion that rape is 'natural' in the moral sense of expressing "God's invisible nature". Modern commentators like Schmidt rest their condemnation of homosexual expression not on the *will* of the agent in performing such acts, but on the agent's deliberate deviation from Paul's limited and unscientific definition of 'nature'. The homosexual is condemned for disagreeing about the facts of nature (and behaving accordingly), not for willing to do anyone harm.

In I Corinthians 6: 9-10 Paul includes sexual perversion in a list of vices rampant in the licentious pagan society of first century Rome. In 1 Timothy 1: 9-10 Paul, or one of his followers, reminds us that the Law is not intended for those who are good but for such people as criminals, liars, the wicked, irreligious, and those who practice patricide, matricide, and "those who are immoral with boys or men." In both of these texts the meaning of the Greek words *malakoi, arsenokoitai, pornoi* and *andrapodistai* are a matter of dispute. But without getting into the nuanced exegetical debate, it seems safe to infer from *all* of the New Testament passages dealing with the issue that homogenital sex is regarded as comparable to sins involving deliberate disobedience to God, as well as harm to others. Paul's language and his inclusion of sexual perversion (or its cognates) within lists of moral vices assumes a volitional aspect to such behavior that necessitates legal or social regulation of such forms of sexual expression. The implication is that punishment or social stigma of the kind sanctioned by God is required because some human beings do not use their freedom to the glorification of God, but rather as an opportunity to rebel against His will (as manifest in the natural order). Homosexual behavior is "revolting" because it epitomizes in sexual terms a more general *revolt* against God.[34] Paul consistently invokes a negative evaluation of homosexual *behavior*, not of homosexual *people*. He treats homosexuality as a *moral* issue (i.e. one involving a deliberate abuse of freedom). This suggests that he believed that all people are equally free to choose heterosexuality without thereby forfeiting their authentic ('God given') nature.

In comparing homosexual behavior with paganism's failure to recognize the Creator, Paul's attitude is somewhat equivocal. He seems to attribute the falsehood of such acts to some kind of *moral* turpitude. As such, the sexual error is less analogous to paganism than it is to heresy or blasphemy. The pagans, after all, simply did not recognize the one Jewish God. This is quite different from rejecting or betraying a God whose existence one *does* recognize. Nevertheless Paul's language is *moralistic* -- it contains a presumption that there is a deliberate betrayal of a God whom the sinner does acknowledge, but whom he stubbornly rejects.[35] When Paul speaks of people "giving up" or "leaving" or "exchanging" heterosexual relations, he seems to be describing not an inherent lack of 'recognition' but a denial or disowning of what one does really recognize. This might explain why Paul's posture generally tends towards *moral* condemnation. Moral reproach presupposes that the subject is blameworthy, not just mistaken or ignorant of the truth. Paul seems to want to condemn people who fail (he thinks willingly) to recognize the truth about creation. He simply cannot countenance the possibility that homosexual people *cannot* recognize the 'facts' about their nature because the facts are false.

Paul's moralistic rebukes about 'recognition' seem to presuppose that the morally wayward agents have the potential to acknowledge the universal truth of heterosexuality in nature (i.e. "God's creation"), but simply refuse to do so. The moral goodness of 'recognition' belongs, then, to human agents, who are free and responsible for their decision to 'recognize' or assent to, "God's invisible nature" that "has been clearly perceived in the things that have been made." Yet in contrast to this, Paul also attributes intrinsic moral value to human sexual nature (in his thinking, heterosexuality) because it reflects God's design. As Schmidt says, "as a moral category *natural* refers to something that is in accord with God's intention". Schmidt too seems to think that agreement with "God's intention" as inscribed in biology is the key to moral goodness. And since the Creator has inscribed heterosexuality into human nature itself, constitutive homosexuality is ruled out *a priori* with no consideration of the evidence. Paul's theology simply labels some aspects of creation 'natural' (good) and others 'unnatural' (evil).

In 1 Cor. 7 Paul extols the virtue of celibacy and insinuates that its practice requires a degree of moral fortitude that is not possible for everyone. This tells us two things about how Paul viewed sexuality. First, his declared personal preference for celibacy implies that there is nothing moral to be gained by the expression of one's heterosexual nature *per se*. What makes such acts 'natural' (or, in Paul's thinking, 'good' in the moral sense) is not that we ***practice them at all***, but that we 'recognize' them (i.e assent to the proposition that human sexuality is inherently directed towards members of the opposite sex).

Secondly, 1 Corinthians 7 reveals that Paul views (hetero)sexual expression as so basic to human nature and well-being that for most people it is not even possible to practice abstinence. We might infer that Paul views heterosexual behavior more like eating and drinking or as 'need fulfillment' than as intentional behavior. Heterosexual behavior may be biologically driven like the drive to eat or sleep. Specific intentional activities (such as having intercourse with my neighbor's wife, or having intercourse with my wife, or having intercourse with someone for money, or having intercourse with a minor) are, as it were, layered over the non-intentional aspect of sexual nature. Sex drive appears to be relevantly like such biological needs as eating and sleep, in that it exists independently of one's intentional acts. Just as my basic pre-conscious drive to eat does not dictate that I eat a Big Mac right now, nor does my basic sex drive compel any one of my sexual actions. I still have free will and moral responsibility. So, for example, a heterosexual male will have a basic unintentional drive to have sex with females but this does not dictate that he must have sexual intercourse with every female he meets, nor even that he must have sexual intercourse with any particular female at any given time. His actions are ultimately free, and he may choose never to engage in sex with *any* female if he has sufficient reason to choose celibacy. Even when we do not act on our basic drives they are there, as healthy aspects of our nature. They are not "addictions" which we must act upon; they are a precondition of any possible addiction. For example, over-eating may become psychologically addictive, but this is unrelated to a person's basic need to eat, otherwise everyone would be prone to over-eating, which is not the case.

However, if we return to the first chapter of Paul's letter to the Romans, we find a contemptuous moralizing posture there that is altogether inexplicable given his understanding of human sexual nature. Paul does not address his readers as biological automatons, but as free, rational, conscious human agents whose sexual behavior is a product of their conscious choices. His moralistic approach signals his underlying belief that it *is possible* for those who indulge in "dishonorable passions" and "unnatural relations" to recognize (assent to) the heterosexual norm. The problem is that Paul's posture towards the issue presupposes that it *is not* humanly possible to *fail to* recognize this heterosexual ideal, and hence it is amazing that Paul is able to find anyone to disagree with him. His supposition that heterosexuality is universally inherent in human nature itself makes anyone who does not recognize this less than fully human. Yet his style of argument never contains the assertion that it is the sub-human status or mere difference of those who indulge in "dishonorable passions" that makes them contemptible. Paul is not some sort of racist. Instead it is their willful *behavior* that is *disobedient.* Instead of attacking what might be viewed as an ***innate inability*** to 'recognize' the heterosexual ideal, Paul attacks his opponents for their ***willful refusal*** to 'recognize' it. While Paul never officially recognized a 'natural' homosexual orientation (biologically determined), he nevertheless condemns homosexual behavior on the grounds that heterosexual behavior is the only kind that is conceivable, given human nature. But if this were true there would be no one to condemn, except the sub-human disobedient creatures who, though heterosexual, for some odd reason stubbornly refuse to assent to the obvious truth about their own nature.

The moralistic thrust of his argument weakens Paul's premise about "nature" because, by his own account, 'recognition' is a given, inscribed in nature itself. ("For what can be known about God is plain to them, because God has shown it to them. Ever since the creation of the world, his invisible nature, namely, his eternal power and deity, have been clearly perceived in the things that have been made. So they are without excuse; for although they knew God they did not honor him as God or give thanks to him, but they became futile in their thinking and their senseless minds were darkened.") It is certainly possible that what is "plain" to heterosexuals is simply not plain to homosexuals. Paul may think it is "plain" from the biological function of the reproductive organs that human sexuality is exclusively heterosexual, but he must have been aware of homosexual attraction since he is condemning those who act upon it. He seems to think such a thing is inconceivable (or, if conceivable, *inadmissible*).

To discern the way that nature works requires openness to all aspects of nature, from the brain to the body to the genes. Paul's lack of scientific sophistication may be forgiven as a product of its time. Nature does not always disclose its variations to us in the simple ways we assumed it did in the past. Nevertheless, we can ask whether it is appropriate, in the twenty-first century, to cling to Paul's ancient and limited understanding of human sexuality.

Paul's empiricism is limited to a narrow 'biological fundamentalism' that excludes all psychological, social, and experiential evidence as irrelevant to an understanding of human nature. In this respect, Paul set a particularly pernicious precedent. While Houston may be correct that purity thinking in regard to sex was taken to be applicable to humankind universally -- and therefore is a natural law theory -- it is the kind of theory that rests on definitions rather than on a balanced examination of the evidence. This is why some contemporary theologians[36], myself included, hold Paul's views to be outdated and inapplicable today.

Countryman's theory -- that it is not Paul's own opinion that homosexual behavior is morally wrong -- appears to be a stretch. Houston and Schmidt are probably correct to deny that Paul's intended meaning in Romans 1 is other than what it seems. If Houston is correct, Paul invoked the purity code to render homosexual acts *per se* inherently unclean. This would suggest that other types of acts might be intrinsically pure or clean, insofar as they did not deviate from "God's invisible nature".

> If it were reasonable, the moralistic argument against human sexual actions would be based on an assumption that human agents are responsible for all of their actions, good and bad alike. The Catholic Magisterium, following Paul's rationale, condemns homosexual behavior. . . even though, unlike Paul, the Catholic Church now formally recognizes a homosexual orientation so basic as to be unintentional. The Church's present authority, however, is largely indebted to Paul's theology, around which the institution and its subsequent traditions developed.

There are two possibilities as to why Paul addresses the perpetrators in Romans 1 as failed moral agents: either (**1**) he makes no distinction between social convention and moral obligation (Romans 13 certainly implies this!) or (**2**) he does not think that it is *humanly* possible sincerely not to recognize the Creator and 'the truth' about creation. A closer examination of his argument shows that these two possibilities probably were complementary in Paul's thinking: because he does not allow that it is humanly possible authentically to be homosexual by nature, it is equally wrong (morally) to deny the definition of nature on which positive laws pertaining to sex are based. As we know from his attitudes towards circumcision and dietary rules pertaining to table fellowship, Paul does see a distinction in general between purity codes/conventional rules and moral obligation, but refuses to extend the applicability of this distinction to rules within the sexual domain. In Paul's natural law ethic, to dispute the premise (that human nature is universally heterosexual) amounts to "lying". As I suggested above, Paul vacillates between treating homosexuality as a moral issue and treating it as a mistake about a matter of fact. It seems he morally condemned a sub-set of people who simply couldn't agree with him about the facts. One of the problems of starting a theory with a definition rather than with empirical observations is that the definition colors the interpretation of subsequent observations. In this case, the observation that many people did not agree with Paul's definition of nature was not taken as a reason to question his own understanding of the "natural facts". Rather, it was proof of the obstinacy of those who disagreed. It signified their revolt against God's natural order (or **his** interpretation of it, the truth of which he took for granted).

Berger and Luckmann's findings in the sociology of knowledge offer a useful framework through which Paul's claims may be assessed:

> "The symbolic universe assigns ranks . . . to different types of men, and it frequently happens that broad categories of such types (sometimes everyone outside the collectivity in question) are defined as 'other' or less than human. This is commonly expressed linguistically (in the extreme case, with the name of the collectivity being equivalent to the term 'human')."[37]

From this perspective, it is tacitly the homosexual's status, not his behavior, which is condemned. His denial that heterosexuality is normative or 'natural' to all human sexuality automatically disqualifies him from the moral community. Ordinarily this would not lead to any moral condemnation, since it is not his behavior to which the stigma attaches, unless, of course, the denial itself is viewed as a piece of deliberate falsehood, like telling a lie. This may explain why Paul's language seems to equate homogenital desire and acts with "falsehood" and untruth. At many points Paul's language does betray more than a hint of incredulity. Paul may have regarded the 'evil' of homosexuality not as a harmful intention of the kind that can be measured by reference to harm, but rather as any rejection of the absolute truth of his definition of human nature. What is peculiar about Paul's interpretation of natural law is that he does seem to equate it with the positive laws that define the religious (moral) community as distinct from the "wicked, irreligious" (1 Cor. 6:10) people who voluntarily "exchange the truth about God for a lie" (Rom. 1:25) and "did not see fit to acknowledge God" (Rom. 1: 28). It seems Paul cannot seriously entertain the notion that someone could *in good faith* dissent from his definition of 'nature.'

Purity thinking is frequently deeply embedded in a worldview that informs all of the subject's subsequent beliefs. Those who thought in terms of purity did not view their norms as relative to their culture, they saw them as self-evidently true for everyone. Purity rules are not ordinary rules, but industrial-strength conventions. Houston's thesis (above) is that Paul understood the difference between convention and ethics, that he did not equate moral law with cultic rituals and taboos, at least not where dietary matters and circumcision were concerned. In the domain of sexuality, however, the notion that there could be a 'good' act that contravenes the conventional religious rules is rejected. Homosexual behavior is treated as a 'sin' because it subverts the definition of what is sexually acceptable within the entire human community. The meaning of Paul's terms is related to the way of life practiced within the Spiritual community and can have no valid source of meaning independently of it. Positive laws (or conventional rules) are equated with the natural moral law, hence there can be no morally motivated dissent.

Paul's attitude towards outsiders, in some places, does seem excessively intolerant (e.g. 1 Cor. 5:9,11: "I wrote to you in my last letter not to associate with immoral men... not even to eat with such a one..." ; 1 Cor.5:13: "Drive out the wicked person from among you." ; 2 Cor. 6:14-15: "Do not be mismated with unbelievers. For what partnership have righteousness and iniquity? ... Or what has a believer in common with an unbeliever?"). Nevertheless legal positivism is incompatible with Paul's salvation theology, which attributes truth and goodness to a universally valid source in Jesus Christ, and which puts faith in Christ above cultic purity rituals (though, again, this contradicts his message in Romans 13). Everywhere but in relation to "sexual impurity" (and in Romans 13) Paul seems to acknowledge a distinction between morality and conventional definitions of 'good' and 'evil'. Generally speaking, Paul adheres to the view that faith in Christ transcends parochial cultic purity laws (just not in sexual matters).

Berger and Luckmann's studies in the social legitimization of institutions and symbolic universes provide a perspective from which it is conceivable that Paul's demonization of 'those who do such things' is motivated less by faith in Jesus Christ than by the appearance of an alternative symbolic universe, which ". . . poses a threat because its very existence demonstrates empirically that one's own is less than inevitable."[38] The purity rules concerning sex that were prevalent in Paul's milieu were cultural identity markers. To infringe them was not to palpably harm anyone; it was merely to transgress role assignments or to break convention. As Countryman has shown, their significance was for the maintenance of a symbolic universe whose internal meanings, in the case of sexual codes, were thought to extend to humanity universally. According to Berger and Luckmann, it is through the process of *reification* (the bestowal of an ontological status on institutions; a status which is claimed to be independent of human activity and significance) that "the world of institutions appears to merge with the world of nature. It becomes necessity and fate . . ."[39]

Schmidt's observation that Paul sees the homosexual offenders as literally "revolting" against God is consistent with Berger and Luckmann's sociological observation that "the deviant probably stands as a living insult to the gods . . .", and hence "there must be a theory of deviance (a 'pathology') that accounts for this shocking condition (say by positing demonic possession)."[40] This description of the deviant in pathological or demonic terms seems somewhat applicable to Paul's treatment (in Romans 1) of "those who do such things" as the embodiments of *all* varieties of evil, not just sexual misconduct. Berger and Luckmann describe the predicament of those who deny the dominant anthropological or cosmological theory as follows:

> ". . . by virtue of being possessed by demons or simply because they are barbarians, [they] are denying their own nature. Deep down within themselves they know that this is so. One need, therefore, only search their statements carefully to discover the defensiveness and bad faith of their position. Whatever they say in this matter can thus be translated into an affirmation of the [dominant] universe, which they ostensibly negate. In a theological frame of reference, the same procedure demonstrates that the devil unwittingly glorifies God, that all unbelief is but unconscious dishonesty, even that the atheist is <u>really</u> a believer."[41]

This description of defensiveness and bad faith is entirely consistent with Paul's attitude towards "the wicked" in Romans 1 when he says God's wrath is revealed against all ungodliness and wickedness of "men who by their wickedness suppress the truth" (v. 18) and later claims they are "without excuse" because, "...although they knew God, they did not honor him as God or give thanks to him, but became futile in their minds and their senseless minds were darkened." (v. 21) Paul concludes Chapter 1 with a reminder that "Though they know God's decree that those who do such things deserve to die, they not only do them but approve those who practice them." (v. 32) It seems reasonable to conclude that Paul had a vested interest in the legitimization and defense of laws pertaining to the social organization of sexuality typical of purity thinking. However, we have no mandate to cling to these ancient categories today.

It may be argued that in principle it is possible for a person who does not 'naturally' recognize a heterosexual nature within himself to assent to the proposition that heterosexual nature is definitive of human sexuality. This seems to be what Schmidt and other Christian prohibitionists recommend -- a good will is an *obedient* will[42]. But whether it is humanly *possible* for a person to capitulate to the norms prescribed by his/her religion or culture is a separate issue to whether it is morally good or right that he do so. Certainly it is not *impossible* for a person who does not naturally possess a heterosexual orientation to capitulate to a Christian definition of human sexuality as normatively heterosexual. Nor is it impossible for a Jewish person to capitulate to an anti-Semitic ideology, or for women to subscribe to misogynist constructions of 'womanhood'. The relevant issue is not whether it is *possible* for a person to outwardly 'recognize' (or pay homage to) a particular definition but whether it is morally good to expect people to capitulate to conventional definitions of which they are not genuinely convinced.

The following statement from the Second Vatican Council affirms the dignity and inviolability of conscience over and above positive law: "For man has in his heart a law written by God. To obey it is the very dignity of man; according to it he will be judged."[43] Christian existentialist Gabriel Marcel makes an important distinction between outward 'acts' characteristic of a theatrical performance and the kind of action characteristic of human moral agency. He locates the moral character of an act in the degree to which it is "impossible to repudiate it without completely denying oneself."[44] There is no act, he says, without responsibility. The degree to which we are willing to assume personal responsibility for our behavior, or to which we can honestly claim it as our own is, for Marcel, the meaning of true action.

In a similar way, Sulpician priest Richard Gula stresses the important distinction between moral conscience and the superego, a psychological notion of conscience: "The moral conscience is the key to responsible freedom of wanting to do what we do because we value what we are seeking. Whereas the 'shoulds' and 'have-tos' of the superego look to authority, the 'wants' of the moral conscience look to personalized and internalized values."[45] Sometimes, however, it is difficult to distinguish the superego from the moral conscience, because the superego installs itself within the psyche from early childhood:

> "We fear punishment as children not for its physical pain only, but more because it represents a withdrawal of love. So we regulate our behaviour so as not to lose love and approval. We absorb the standards and regulations of our parents, or anyone who has authority over us, as a matter of self-protection. The authority figure takes up a place within us to become a source of commands and prohibitions."[46]

In contrast to the obedient child, who conforms to authority out of self-interest, the morally mature person "must be able to perceive, choose, and identify the self with what one does. On the moral level we perceive every choice as a choice between being an authentic or an inauthentic person. In short, we give our lives meaning by committing our freedom. The morally mature person is called to commit his or her freedom, not to submit it. As long as we do not direct our own activity, we are not yet free, morally mature persons."[47]

The demands of the superego are learned social conventions. Richard Mohr describes conventions as "industrial strength" rules.[48] These rules are so strong, says Mohr, that they are actually treated as different in kind from ordinary rules: it is a rule one breaks only if one wants to destroy the rule itself:

> ". . . consider the rule-breaking that is involved in desegregating lunch counters in the segregated South. If I am black and sit at the 'whites only' section of the lunch counter, I am not breaking the rule for some self-interested end, to get some advantage just for me, thinking the while that others really should obey the ban. No, when I sit down, what I am trying to do is to destroy the 'whites only' rule, and the only people who do consciously break the rule are those who want to destroy it. This rule -- 'whites only' --- is a convention, not a mere rule. . . . To break such a community-defining rule is to appear to be a traitor to the community. But what appears as treason to some can actually be social reform . . . one hopes thereby to establish a morally improved community."[49]

Breaking conventions is a way of challenging the absolute value of society's community-defining rules. Dissent of this kind is aimed at exposing the myth that a society's rules are necessarily or supremely valuable for the *human* community as a whole.

In supposing that there exist universal human principles that can justify breaking community-defining conventions, we are appealing to natural law. Natural law theories presuppose the existence of facts about human nature in general. These facts are taken to be relevant to the formation of ethical standards for the human community and interpersonal interactions within it. Natural law ethics presuppose that moral values should be grounded in objective facts. This places natural law morality in strict opposition to legal positivism.[50] An accurate appeal to natural law must depend on discovering what being human really means. According to Vincent Macnamara, the most basic concern of natural law theory is that there is a moral basis to life that can be established, not just for believers, but for all men and women, by reflecting on what it means to be a human person and ideally this should be respected by positive law (conventional moral rules).[51] The difficulty of such theories is that people do not always agree on what it means to be a human person. They may differ especially on what is most essential or distinctive of human beings.

What makes conventions so powerful is that, while they are based on tentative, often limited, knowledge, they are *treated as though* they were absolute rules. Mohr's extract (above) illustrates that a "failure to recognize" specific public conceptions of 'human nature' or 'human welfare' is not tantamount to a deliberate choice not to acknowledge what one does, in good conscience, recognize to be true or right.

To the extent that it acknowledges constitutive homosexual orientation, Catholic doctrine represents an advance beyond Paul's thinking. On the other hand, there *is* a personal choice in sexual expression and in this case magisterial teaching judges all homogenital expression to be objectively immoral because it falls short of the unitive and procreative norms for sexual expression. These norms are still derived in part from the creation accounts in Genesis and Catholic doctrine still references Paul to supplement the more sophisticated Thomistic account of sexual ethics. As with Paul, it is the free choice involved in moral agency that makes certain acts 'sins'. But unlike Paul, Catholic doctrine today also holds that the choice to express one's innate *homosexual nature* is sinful.

Many Christian theologians now acknowledge that homogenital acts are, of themselves, morally neutral. The preponderance of evidence suggests that Paul simply ignored the available evidence that pointed to the existence of homosexual *people*. In light of modern scientific research, the best available evidence now suggests that homosexuality is 'natural' for a minority of human beings. If true, it would follow that it is as natural for the homosexual person to behave in accordance with his homosexual nature as it is for the heterosexual person to behave heterosexually. Prohibition of homogenital acts is groundless, however, only insofar as it is aimed at homogenital expression *per se*, without reference to the human motives and inter-personal effects of such actions. No positive moral value can attach to homogenital acts *per se* prior to an evaluation of the intentions of the agent(s), the circumstances in which the acts take place, and the consequences. This makes the moral evaluation of homosexual acts no different from that of heterosexual acts. If Paul's reasoning seems obsolete we should not be surprised given the limited understanding of human sexuality typical of his milieu. In order to understand why Christian opposition to homosexual activity persists within Catholic and evangelical teaching today, we need to turn to the naturalist reasoning behind more recent versions of Christian prohibitionism.

1   For the purposes of this chapter I am using the Revised New Standard Version of the Bible, containing the Old and New Testaments with the Apocrypha/ Deuterocanonical Books (Expanded Edition). New York: Collins, 1973.

2   Paul identifies "dishonorable passions" with the actions of women who "exchanged natural relations for unnatural" and of men who "gave up natural relations with women and were consumed with passion for one another." (vv. 26-7) There is much debate about whether Paul regarded these behaviors as acts of the constitutive homosexual, or as homogenital behavior between persons who were essentially heterosexual, but I address this debate later in the chapter.

3   Countryman, L. William, _Dirt, Greed & Sex : Sexual Ethics in the New Testament and Their Implications for Today_, London: SCM Press, 1988, pp. 45-65.

4   Ibid.

5   Ibid, p. 18.

6   Countryman, pp. 98-123. See especially pp. 122-23 on the appropriateness of homosexuality as an example.

7   This argument -- that Paul is careful not to use the vocabulary of sin with reference to homosexual behavior -- was first advanced by John Boswell in Christianity, Social Tolerance and Homosexuality (New Haven, Conn.: Yale University Press, 1980), pp. 112-13 n. 72.

8   Houston, Rev. Walter, 'Homosexuality and the Bible' in Homosexuality: A Christian View, The Homosexuality Working Party of the United Reformed Church, Ed., 1991.

9   Ibid, p.13.

10  Ibid., p. 16.

11  Homosexual Relations: A Contribution to Discussion, The Working Party of The Church of England, 1978, p. 36.

12  Houston, Op Cit., p.17

13  Scroggs, Robin, The New Testament and Homosexuality, Fortress Press, 1993.

14  Boswell, John. Christianity, Social Tolerance, and Homosexuality: gay people in Western Europe from the beginning of the Christian Era to the fourteenth century. Chicago / London: The University of Chicago Press, 1980.

15  Romans 1: 27

16  Romans 1: 23, 25 & 26

17  Houston, Op. Cit., pp. 15-16.

18  E. Cantrella, Bisexuality in the Ancient World (New Haven, Conn.: Yale University Press, 1972), p. 137.

19  Schmidt, Thomas E., Straight and Narrow? : Compassion and Clarity in the Homosexuality Debate (Leicester, England: Inter-Varsity Press, 1995), p. 66.

20  "For this reason God gave them up to dishonourable passions. Their women exchanged natural relations for unnatural, and the men likewise gave up natural relations with women were consumed with passion for one another,

men committing shameless acts with men and receiving in their own persons the due penalty for their error." Excerpted from The Holy Bible, Revised New Standard Version (London: Collins, 1973).

21  Romans 14:14

22  Countryman extends Boswell's thesis, first introduced in <u>Christianity, Social Tolerance and Homosexuality</u> (New Haven, Conn.: Yale Univeristy Press, 1980), pp. 112-13.

23  Schmidt, p. 66.

24  Ibid, p. 81.

25  Ibid.

26  Ibid., pp. 81-2.

27  D. Novak, 'Before Revelation: The Rabbis, Paul and Karl Barth,' *Journal of Religion* 71 (January 1991), p. 62.

28  Richard B. Hays, 'Relations Natural and Unnatural: A Response to John Boswell's Exegesis of Romans 1,' *Journal of Religious Ethics* 14, 1986, p. 191.

29  Schmidt, Op. Cit., p. 78.

30  Schmidt, pp. 131-32.

31  The logical fallacy of moving from the premise, that something is natural to the conclusion that, therefore, it must be good.

32  Schmidt, p. 133.

33  Schmidt, pp. 81-2.

34  Ibid., p. 85

35  See, for example, Romans 1:18-32, 1 Cor 6: 9-10, and 1 Timothy 1:9-10

36  E.g. Bailey, Boswell, Countryman, Helminiak, Nissinen, Petersen, Scroggs

37  Berger P. and Luckmann T., <u>The Social Construction of Reality: a treatise on the sociology of knowledge</u>, New York: Anchor Books/ Doubleday, 1966, p. 102.

38  Ibid, p. 108.

39  Ibid., p. 90.

40  Ibid, p. 113.

41  Ibid., p. 116.

42  Schmidt explains the relationship between the individual's nature and his will thus: "Whatever I may attribute to my genes, or to my parents, or to my culture, none of them can force me, at the crucial moment, to turn a glance into a fantasy, or a fantasy into a flirtation, or a flirtation into a sexual act. At that moment my *will* is involved, and precisely such moments define my obedience and growth as a Christian." (pp. 131-2) Notably, the good will here is defined not in terms of intention primarily, except insofar as my intention is **to obey** Christian doctrines or teachings about what is "natural" in God's creation.

43  *Pastoral Constitution on the Church in the Modern World, Gaudium et Spes, n. 16.*, promulgated by Pope Paul VI on December 7, 1965.

44    Marcel, Gabriel, <u>Creative Fidelity</u>, Trans. Robert Rosthal, New York: Crossroad, 1982, p. 109.

45    Gula, Richard, M., <u>*Reason Informed By Faith: Foundations of Catholic Morality*</u>, Paulist Press, Mahwah, N.J., 1989, p. 126.

46    Ibid., p. 125.

47    Ibid., p. 124.

48    Mohr, Richard, <u>Gay Ideas</u>, Boston: Beacon Press, 1992, pp. 28-29.

49    Ibid., p. 28-29.

50    Gula, Op. Cit., p. 241.

51    Macnamara, Vincent, <u>The Truth in Love: Reflections on Christian Morality</u>, Dublin, Gill & Macmillan, 1988, pp. 98-99.

# CHAPTER 3

# *The Natural Law: Catholic Tradition and Homosexuality*

Naturalist theories of ethics start from a basic consideration of what can be known about the nature of human beings. This approach to ethics involves searching for what is truly human, and using the answers as a guide to how we should behave. In the traditional Catholic application of this approach to sexual ethics, "natural law is understood to be the summary of precepts based on the given and unvarying nature of man as such and which can be deduced from it."[1]

The natural law approach to sexual ethics that was accepted as normative within Western Christianity and was passed down through the Roman Catholic tradition has its roots in Augustine and Aristotle. However St. Thomas Aquinas's adaptation of Aristotle's naturalism has formed a significant basis for Catholic teaching on sexual and interpersonal ethics. Thomas's development and adaptation of Aristotelian reasoning exerted a lasting influence on contemporary natural law theory. Shortly before Aquinas took up his post at the University of Paris in 1256, many volumes of Aristotle's writings had been re-imported into Western Europe from Persia, where they had been preserved in centers of Islamic learning. St. Thomas is credited with synthesizing Greek philosophy (Aristotle in particular) and Christian moral teaching.

His was not, however, the first natural law argument that had been used in Christian circles to proscribe homogenital acts. In the previous chapter

I discussed how St. Paul's moral exhortations against homosexual behavior not only presupposed universal heterosexual essentialism but stigmatized any attempt to argue differently. The Vatican's documents draw heavily on St. Thomas's natural law approach to ethics, but also reference St. Paul's scriptural passages in support of their prohibition of homogenital behavior. *Persona Humana* (1975) draws on Romans 1:24-27, 1 Corinthians 6:10, and 1 Timothy 1:10. *Universal Catechism of the Catholic Church* (French,1992/ English, 1994) makes reference to Genesis 19:1-29, Romans 1: 24-27, I Corinthians 6:10, and 1 Timothy 1:10. *Considerations Regarding Proposals to Give Recognition to Unions between Homosexual Persons* (2003) appeals to Romans 1:24-27, 1 Corinthians 6:10, and I Timothy 1:10.

However, natural law ethicists generally maintain the existence of some ethical wisdom apart from the explicit revelation of God in the Christian scriptures. The basic claim of natural law theorists is that there is a moral basis to life that can be established, not just for believers, but for all men and women, by reflecting on what it means to be a human person. The Catholic debate between Catholic traditionalists and revisionists reflects ongoing attempts to use reason as a standard for natural law and at the same time to remain historically conscious and open to experience, development and change.

From St. Paul through St. Thomas to our own day and the 1975 Vatican *Declaration on Certain Questions Concerning Sexual Ethics (Persona Humana)*, Catholic tradition has consistently judged all homosexual acts as against nature and hence sinful. The version of natural law that dominated nineteenth and twentieth century manuals of Catholic theology and was the official teaching of the church pictured homosexual behavior (and all non-procreative sex acts) as a willful rejection of nature, and therefore a rejection of God's purposeful design within one's own person. *Rerum Novarum,*[2] the encyclical of Pope Leo XIII (15 May, 1891) enmeshes the rights of individuals within their 'social and domestic obligations'. Whilst not condemning homosexuality *per se*, it conspicuously excludes same sex relationships. "In choosing a state of life" two options are available -- virginity and marriage. The principle purpose of marriage is procreation:

*12. The rights here spoken of, belonging to each individual man, are seen in much stronger light when considered in relation to man's social and domestic obligations. In choosing a state of life, it is indisputable that all are at full liberty to follow the counsel of Jesus Christ as to observing virginity, or to bind themselves by the marriage tie. **No human law can abolish the natural and original right of marriage, nor in any way limit the chief and principal purpose of marriage ordained by God's authority from the beginning: "Increase and multiply."** (3) Hence we have the family, the "society" of a man's house - a society very small, one must admit, but none the less a true society, and one older than any State. Consequently, it has rights and duties peculiar to itself which are quite independent of the State.* [my bold]*

The Vatican's traditional position on all aspects of sexuality, including homogenital activity, can be studied in eight documents published between 1968 and 2004. In 1968 the church's position, stated in *Humanae Vitae*,[3] was that marriage is "the wise and provident institution of God the creator." (II, 8) The document's author further alleges that the inseparable connection between the unitive and procreative aspects of conjugal love is "established by God". Consequently, acts intended to interfere with the procreative capacity "frustrate His design which constitutes the norm of marriage, and contradicts the will of the Author of life" (II, 13)

In this encyclical, the Vatican maintained that each and every marital act must of necessity retain its intrinsic relationship to the procreation of human life. This teaching is based on the inseparable connection "established by God ... between the unitive and the procreative significance which are both inherent to the marriage act." (I, 4) In effect the Church maintained that the procreative aspect, while perhaps not sufficient to the "marital act", is a necessary condition for it.

Since one of the two ends of sexual intercourse is procreation (the other being unity of husband and wife, *Humanae Vitae* 12), engaging in sex while deliberately frustrating the procreative act is, as Pope John Paul II has repeatedly called it, "a lie in the language of the body." "The body, and it alone," John Paul says, "is capable of making visible what is invisible, the spiritual and divine. It was created to transfer into the visible reality of the world, the invisible mystery hidden in God from time immemorial, and thus to be a sign of it" (general audience address, February 20, 1980). The language here is reminiscent of Paul's argument in Romans 1:20: "Ever since the creation of the world his invisible nature, namely his external power and deity, has been clearly perceived in the things that have been made."

Over a period of five years from September 5, 1979 to November 28, 1984, Pope John Paul II gave a series of short homilies at his Weekly Audience in Rome on Marriage, Family and Celibacy based on passages in scripture. In his catechesis on the 'Redemption of the Body and the Sacramentality of Marriage' he said marital intercourse combines within itself both the unitive and procreative dimensions. The truth of the language of the body must be sought, not just in the act itself, but in the nature of the persons who perform it. The spouses themselves must read the language of the body in truth.

The significance of the psychological dimension here seems to be that it passively conforms to, or correctly 'reads', what is given in the language of the body. In her critical study, *The Natural Law Yesterday and Today*,[4] E. Chiavacci describes this approach as 'preceptive.' According to this outlook, 'immutable' nature discloses to the man, who 'reads' and 'understands' her, what right behavior can and must be once and for all in the different areas of reality. This perspective apparently validates the notion that the homosexual agent is willfully opposing his/her own God-given biological functions, in a posture of deliberate rejection of embodied nature. As such, he or she is at cross-purposes with his or her own sexual faculties and with the immutable principles of divine law inscribed therein.

This model seems to presuppose universal heterosexual essentialism. However the 1975 *Declaration on Certain Questions Regarding Sexual Ethics* (*Persona Humana*) took the step of recognizing irreversible homosexuality, or what is more commonly called a "homosexual orientation". In this document the church acknowledged that involuntary homosexuality exists in some cases "because of some kind of innate instinct or a pathological constitution judged to be incurable." (VII, para. 2) While this properly makes a distinction between homosexuality as transitory behavior and homosexuality as definitive of the person it pathologizes (as 'incurable') the homosexual's innate sexual orientation in the same stroke. The document's authors hasten to add that, for the definitive homosexual, homosexual acts can never be justified as right (par. n. 8). *Persona Humana* asserts that the true meaning and value of human sexuality is to be found in two sources – revelation and the essential 'order of nature' where one finds the immutable principles of divine law. From this, absolute norms are extrapolated based on the function and nature of the sexual faculty and act (par. n. 1-5).

While *Persona Humana* expresses the church's tentative acknowledgment of constitutive homosexuality (i.e. homosexual orientation) it nevertheless defines homosexual **acts** as "intrinsically disordered", immoral and unworthy of approval (VIII, para. 4). "Disorder" necessarily carries negative connotations and so operates as a prejudicial label. Because of its clinical connotations, it appears to give credibility to a bias that one may already have against gay and lesbian people.[5] "Disorder" in the context of such theological proclamations is not a medical term at all but a theological one. It can only be understood relative to a preconceived theological idea of what constitutes 'order'. One can infer from the Catholic and Thomistic literature that 'order' in this context is the 'order of nature' that can be 'read' directly from the biological functions of organs. It is significant to note that this represents a shift of emphasis away from condemnation of the homosexual **person** and towards condemnation of homosexual **acts.** This move forms the basis for the popular slogan: "Love the sinner, hate the sin," a phrase widely adapted and deployed by American evangelical spokespersons as well as Catholics, especially in the 1990's.

The view that homosexuality is an 'objective disorder' is maintained in subsequent Vatican documents: *Letter to the Bishops* (1986), 3. Para. 2 & 3, 7 para. 2, 8, para. 2, 10, para. 2; *Some Considerations* (1992), II, para. 10 & 12; *Universal Cachetism* (1992/1994), 2359; *Considerations Regarding Proposals* (2003), I, 4, para. 1 & 3.
In July 2013 Pope Francis made a brief remark that many took as a significant sign that the Vatican is ready to relax its stance on homosexuality. Francis struck a more compassionate tone when he said, "If someone is gay

and he searches for the Lord and has good will, who am I to judge?" but Vatican officials were quick to point out that Francis was not suggesting that anyone should act on their homosexual tendencies. *Persona Humana* rests its proscription of homosexual acts on the Christian doctrine that every genital act must be within the framework of marriage and must be open to the possibility of procreation. It is because homosexual acts lack the marital and teleological procreative purpose that they are "intrinsically disordered" (VIII). In a 1992 document, even the homosexual *inclination* itself "must be seen as an objective disorder."[6] The Catholic Church's moral stance is not grounded in universal heterosexual essentialism, then, but rather in the reproductive function of the human genitalia. On this model of natural law ethics, all human sexual behavior (whether the individual is essentially heterosexual or homosexual) should conform to nature's biological 'designs' or functions. Genital 'design' or function is apparently more important than the diverse 'designs' within human sexual orientation.

This emphasis on genitals and their complementary reproductive function need not be identified with natural law ethics in general. One of the major weaknesses of traditional natural law methodology was its supposition that natural law is a monolithic philosophical system, the content of which commands unanimous consent. The broad basis of natural law theory is that what is morally right action is in some way indicated by what we are, by what one calls human nature.[7] Natural law thinkers, says Bernard Hoose, "arrive at knowledge of values by reflecting upon what it is to be a human person and upon what makes human persons flourish."[8] Knowledge of what it is to be human changes over time, and must therefore be open to revision.

Modern theologians have frequently criticized the traditional Catholic interpretation of natural law as applied to sexual ethics for its narrow physicalism. So-called 'revisionist' theologians (including Charles E. Curran, Josef Fuchs, Richard M. Gula, Edward A. Malloy, Louis Janssens, Kevin T. Kelly, Richard McCormick, and Vincent Macnamara) have disparaged the tendency to emphasize a particular physical, biological aspect of sexual actions to the exclusion of psychological, intentional, and emotional attributes of the same acts. The result of such a narrow 'physicalism' is that sexual actions are regarded in a manner very different from the way in which other human actions are perceived.

Charles E. Curran's criticisms furnish a particularly thorough and representative set of revisionist arguments.[9] In 1968 Curran was amongst some 600 Catholic theologians who authored a response to *Humanae Vitae*. Throughout the following two decades Curran gained prominence for his disagreement with official church teachings on subjects such as contraception, homosexuality, divorce, abortion, moral norms, and the proper role of the hierarchical teaching office in moral matters. The Congregation for the Doctrine of the Faith, headed by then-Cardinal Josef Ratzinger, decided that Curran was neither suitable nor eligible to be a professor of Catholic theology. As a result of that Vatican condemnation, he was removed from the faculty of the Catholic University of America in 1986 and, since then, no Catholic university has been willing to hire him. Today he is Elizabeth Scurlock Professor of Human Values at Southern Methodist University. This whole affair suggests that magisterial teaching on ethical issues is too fragile to tolerate the rigors of critical analysis.

Curran's critique of methodology begins with preliminary observations about the procedure by which the 1986 *Letter to the Bishops of the Catholic Church on the Pastoral Concerns of Homosexual Persons* was produced. He notes that bishops around the world were neither consulted nor asked for contributions. Curran believes that this undermines its credibility and internal authority, especially given the many suggestions and comments that arose in response to it. For example, a British Catholic journal characterized the document as "violently hostile" to Catholic groups ministering to lesbian and gay people and noted that, "not a word of appreciation is offered".[10] A Jesuit periodical editorialized that the "letter explicitly aims at 'pastoral care' for homosexuals, but it is doubtful they will feel especially cared for. Despite the stated intention of the letter's title, it makes a series of decidedly unpastoral missteps".[11] In an interview, Cardinal Basil Hume said that "[Vatican pronouncements on homosexuality] lacked a true pastoral compassion. They did not, he suggested, reflect the face of the always empathetic Jesus".[12] For his part, Curran concluded that the

Church's position on homosexuality was not representative of the best of Catholic thought. He further noted that Catholic encyclicals on sexuality place much emphasis on norms, criteria and laws almost to the exclusion of any prior affirmation of the goodness of sexuality and its development in terms of openness to another human being.[13]

Curran's criticisms were consonant with those of other revisionist thinkers. Their critique of methodology in *Persona Humana* applies equally to the Vatican's methodology in sexual ethics elsewhere. The revisionists' arguments can be divided into three general categories, each of which will be examined in turn. These are: (1) defects in the anthropological model employed, (2) too little reference to empirical realities, and (3) selective use of empirical evidence and the naturalistic fallacy.

### i. Defects in the anthropological model employed in the natural law methodology

The Vatican's documents employ a limited and partial anthropological model – one that gives too little emphasis to the intentional, rational and interpersonal aspects of human nature and behavior. The traditional use of natural law typical of Vatican encyclicals dealing with human sexuality has been described as a 'physicalist' approach to ethics because it defines the nature of a particular act primarily in terms of its biological, exterior and/or material aspects. This way of interpreting natural law allows moral positions to be taken without ambiguity in every instance where the same kind of physical action occurs. This allows physical acts that have an exterior resemblance to be categorized as identical 'types' of acts, irrespective of the agent's motives and/or the beneficial or harmful impact of the act on others. The main objection to the anthropological model that results from this is that it smacks of natural determinism inconsistent with the experiences of human subjects. Although we are embodied, and must pay attention to the material aspects of our humanity, these do not alone determine the shape of our moral lives. They do not *dictate* how we are to behave or to use our bodies in interacting with others. A more modern approach to natural law grounds moral evaluations of actions in their concrete interpersonal context, as well as giving emphasis to the intentions of the moral agent.

The Vatican's 1975 *Declaration on Certain Questions Regarding Sexual Ethics* (*Persona Humana*) emphasizes the certitude of laws and obedience to the exclusion of relationships and responsibility. Curran believes that the document is dismissive of certain values innate in human nature, such as dignity, intelligence and maturity. Ironically the document begins by mentioning these human qualities as important values, only to then treat them rather dismissively relative to laws. The Declaration inverts the proper relationship between laws and the human values they are intended to protect and preserve. It envisions humans in the service of eternal and immutable laws rather than laws as protecting and preserving eternal human goods. The Declaration envisages laws as absolute when it should appeal to social and individual human needs and values to establish laws and norms. Here Curran appeals to Thomas Aquinas, who recognized that, as one draws close to particular questions, the laws more readily admit of exceptions and uncertainty.[14]

Nevertheless, it is common for traditional natural law moralists to claim that there are right and wrong acts or rules of behavior that are binding independently of circumstances, intentions and consequences. Accordingly, moral good or evil attaches to certain kinds of acts. Once you know that an action falls under a particular description, or fits into a category, you can say with certainty that it is wrong; you do not need to take into account further consequences, circumstances or intentions in formulating a moral evaluation of the action.[15] The method of giving the biological/physical structures of the human action (*actus exterior*) priority over the rational, intentional aspect of the action has resulted in the subordination of 'personalism' to 'physicalism' in natural law thinking.

Critics of the Church's teaching claim that physicalist approaches do not give sufficient importance to the personal aspect of sexuality and instead identify the problem as trying to discover the true "use of the sexual faculty" (*Persona Humana*, par. n. 5). In response, Curran explains that sexual acts and faculties "can never be viewed only in themselves but must be seen in terms of the person and the individual person's relationship to other persons."[16] The Vatican's model of sexuality is dehumanizing to the extent that it views sex primarily in terms of physical functions. Curran accuses the Declaration of physicalism, "since it understands sexuality primarily, if not exclusively, in the light of the physical structure of the act itself."[17] The interpersonal, psychological and emotional aspects of human sexuality are missing. The Declaration "sees meaning as something embedded in human nature, which the intellect in a somewhat passive way discovers as already being there."[18]

This has led to debate about the proper place of human reason in the evaluation of human actions. Critics of Catholic tradition ask whether human reason is not more like a an *active* faculty that allows us to judge the value of material forms of human life in terms of the human purposes and values we bring to them. Josef Fuchs has pointed out that man with his evaluating *ratio* forms moral judgment either at the moment of action and in reference to it or in advance and not with reference to the actual event as such.[19] Fuchs is interested in the ongoing, *participatory* aspect of moral responsibility. Moral agency implies the free, conscious and active exercise of rational potential. Each new situation presents the moral agent with a different set of information, and that new data is relevant to moral judgment. One cannot have a moral responsibility to act in a particular manner in advance of knowing things like circumstances and purpose. Knowing is not just a matter of having psychological access to foregone conclusions, nor to a wholly exterior reality. It is also to take some responsibility for what that reality is, for what it means. This model of man treats human intentions, will, behavior, language and symbols as moral agency - as chosen acts with human consequences. This view of agency allows for a distinction between actions and bodily movements. Bodily movements can be explained with reference to muscular reflexes, skeletal structure and the laws of physics. But to describe human actions without reference to conscious thought and motives would be odd. Events tell us only *what* happened. We can demand to know why an action happened because it was performed by a human agent. Explanations are backward looking, while reasons are goal-oriented and forward looking.

On this modern anthropological model, human agency in its conscious aspect is both 'natural' and morally relevant. Because the pre-modern traditionalist model treats ethics as unreflective obedience to a static set of rules that apply in an unchanging way to types of physical actions, Charles E. Curran has remarked that the 1975 *Declaration on Certain Questions Regarding Sexual Ethics (Persona Humana)* does not give adequate recognition to "ongoing human creativity."[20]

Fuchs objects to the practice of formulating our moral judgments in advance of any particular conscious interpretation of the event because the underlying anthropology is too simplistic. Fuchs claims "a moral judgment of an action may not be made in anticipation of the agent's intention, since it would not be the judgment of a 'human' act."[21] Events are not human events at all, and have no moral meaning, until they are related through consciousness to the total personal situation, or to what Richard McCormick calls 'the whole hierarchy of values.'[22]

In a similar way, Louis Janssens supplies a personalistic criterion -- "the human person adequately considered" -- in which he seeks to express this important shift from human nature (conceived in purely biological terms) to the human person (for whom active reasoning is an integral part of his 'nature').[23] Janssens begins with a thorough analysis of the structure and the moral quality of the human act. He observes two aspects in human actions: the *intention* and the *act-in-itself*. For Janssens, the 'act-in-itself' refers to the *means* to the end intended. Janssens points out that in St. Thomas the starting point for evaluating human action is the person, especially the 'end of the inner act of the will', i.e. the intention. The subject or the interior act of the will is the 'form' of the act – the determining and decisive factor, and the "basis of [Thomas's] description of the structure of the human act."[24]

Janssens identifies two distinct currents of thought about the structure and morality of human actions in the medieval Catholic tradition. The first stresses the importance of the object (*finis operas*) within the framework of the action. The second (which had already been put forward by Anselm of Canturbury and was later elaborated by Abelardus and his followers) was adopted and systematized by St. Thomas. "It ties the definition of the structure of the morality of the human action to the agent."[25] "To the mind of Thomas there is no end without the inner act of the will of the subject and vice-versa..... In other words, the good, which is the appropriate object of the will, can only be termed an end insofar as it is aimed at by the subject and through his action; it is always a ***finis operantis***."[26]

Janssens further argues that Thomas understood means and ends as a unity. Means (even if they involve ontic evils[27]) are not to be evaluated as discreet actions if they form part of a single whole. A composite act is defined by the end. The act of the will is a single dynamic event of which the end is the formal and defining element. Thomas illustrates this with his example of taking a remedy (means) to recover from an illness (end). Since the end is the reason that I want the means, it involves only one act of the will, even though Thomas does distinguish the structural elements (means and ends) of the complex whole.

However, the action cannot **only** be an inner act of the will (*interior actus voluntatis*) since it must be **done** in order to effect the end. Hence our action is both an inner act of the will and an exterior event that brings us into touch with external reality.[28] However, in Thomas the end of the act of the will is the determining and decisive factor. It is the human purpose, the intended reason for the action being done. It is the agency or the interior act of the will that Thomas takes as the basis for moral evaluation of acts.

Thomas addressed the question of whether the interior act of the will and the exterior means to that end are one act or two. He concluded that the intention ('interior act of the will') is the formal element and the exterior act is the matter ('material element') of a single act. The inner act of the will (end) and the exterior act (means) must be treated as one from the moral viewpoint. The far-reaching significance of this view is that situating the agent/subject in the activity "makes it possible to consider our actions not as a succession of separate and disjointed actions but as the integrated moments of a life history in which unity and wholeness can be realised by virtue of the ends of the agent."[29]

Thomas states in his *De Lege Aeterna* (Ia IIae, q.93) and *De Lege Naturali* (Ia IIae, q. 94) that reason is the measure of morality. The moral goodness of the human act depends upon its consonance with reason. Reason is closely tied to Thomas's understanding of virtue. Whether or not the human agent takes the moral good as the end of his action depends on his inner disposition. The moral virtues direct us toward the moral good as the end, even when we do not act. Purity of motive defines the virtuous person. In Thomas's doctrine on the virtues he stresses that they allow us to discern the concrete actions by which the love of the moral good can be expressed. Janssens insists that Thomas rejected the opinion that the material event of an act can be evaluated morally without consideration of the subject, or the inner act of the will. The exterior action considered as nothing but the material event is an abstraction to which moral evaluation cannot be applied. Thomas was clear that moral evaluations of human actions must rest primarily on the agent's intention. Actions that may have the same external features could nevertheless fall into very different categories, depending upon the human purpose or intention directing the material event. The implications of this approach come into focus if we reflect on the fact that Jesus was betrayed by means of a kiss, an act that conventionally signifies tenderness towards a fellow human being. The same point is evident in Jesus' teaching about giving alms (an act that is conventionally virtuous) for vainglory. When we judge such acts by their exterior aspects alone, we may miss their true (interior) significance.

Janssens concludes that concrete material norms are relative and not absolute. It is humanly impossible to do away with all forms of material/ontic evil, because doing so would impede us from realising moral objectives, which sometimes necessitate ontic evils as means, as when we cauterize a wound to prevent infection. Concrete material norms are relative: they only forbid that we cause or tolerate more suffering or damage than is necessary to bring about the actualization of good ends.[30]

Janssens interprets this outlook as consistent with Thomas Aquinas. He maintains that Thomas understood rational discernment of proportionate human values as *essential* to moral action, whereas concrete material norms are *relative*. Doing material/ontic evil is not forbidden where a moral agent can reasonably judge that it is a necessary means to the preservation of a greater good. Thomas illustrated this with an example from Book I of Plato's *Republic*. The norm that one should return borrowed property to its owner in good faith is generally a reliable guide to right behavior. However, when we know that the owner is demanding we return a weapon that he intends to use to commit murder, we can suspend this general norm because it conflicts with the greater good of protecting human life. The action would be morally interpreted as a single act – protecting innocent human life from unjust harm, not as stealing borrowed property (a vicious act) ***and*** protecting human life (a virtuous act). Thomas apparently understands the formal definition of an act in terms of the subject's purpose in doing it. A moral evaluation of the agent's action looks to his motives – this is what is meant by saying he should act with 'good reason'.

The development of human technology and progress, says Janssens, reduces the amount of material/ontic evil we have to suffer, tolerate or inflict as means to morally good ends. Our essential human values – life, human integrity, truthfulness in social relations – remain valid over time. But the means to the fulfillment of these ends change and evolve. The concrete norms must adapt to each new state of affairs because our moral obligations will be fulfilled in new concrete material forms that may not have been available in the past.

While this emphasis on moral agency may have influenced many of Thomas's moral teachings, it is not clear whether it was primary in his understanding of the purposes of human sexuality. As with Pauline sexual ethics, there is a question mark over whether Thomas extended his general approach to the moral evaluation of acts to those in the sexual sphere. In the 1975 Vatican *Declaration on Certain Questions Regarding Sexual Ethics*, the 'order of nature' comes more directly from God than the 'order of reason', over which human agents exercise responsible control. Richard M. Gula, himself a revisionist, has argued that the Vatican's interpretation is consistent with St. Thomas's position in the *Summa* when dealing with the morality of sexual matters. The scholastic conception of natural law developed by Thomas Aquinas has been the traditional Catholic point of reference for sexual ethics.

Thomas's thinking can be viewed as a synthesis of two strains of interpretation that dominated the history of natural law ethics: the 'order of reason' and the 'order of nature'. In the *Summa* Thomas expressed his most fundamental understanding of natural law: the human person's participation in eternal law through the use of reason. An accurate appeal to the Thomistic conception of natural law must not lose sight of the fact that its aim is to discover what being 'human' really means. This is the work of reason reflecting on the totality of human experience and not only on one aspect of it, such as the physical or biological.[31] Reason in the Thomistic sense of *recta ratio* entails the human tendency to want to know the whole of reality and to come to truth.

Thomas' view in the *Summa* is that law is the means of returning to God. All creatures participate in the eternal law according to their nature -- the animal world by instinct and humans by reason. In the *Summa* Aquinas situates natural law in the treatise on law (I, II, qq.90 – 97) where it is described as a means of returning to God. All things in creation come from God and return to God. Everything participates in the eternal law according to its nature. Thomas follows Aristotle in identifying reason as the unique human faculty: humans participate in eternal law through the use of reason (cf. I, II, q.91, a.2; and q. 93). Here there seems to be a clear distinction between humans and the animal world.[32]

However, in his discussion of sexual matters (cf. II –II, q. 154, aa. 11,12) Thomas makes no such distinction. He appeals to the order of nature or "generic natural law" and retains the *biological* sense of natural law for humans just as Ulpian (Domitius Ulpianus, d. 228) had done before him. Particularly in relation to sexual matters, Thomas is influenced by Ulpian's definition of *Jus Naturale (i.e.* what nature has taught all animals). Ulpian held that natural law -- *Jus Naturale* -- is not peculiar to humans but is the generic rule of action common to humans and animals.[33] Here Thomas reasons (in a manner reminiscent of St. Paul) that since the order of nature comes directly from God as its author, it assumes a priority over the order of reason, which comes more immediately from the human person:

"Reason presupposes things as determined by nature . . . so in matters of action it is most grave and shameful to act against things as determined by nature." (II-II, q. 154, a. 12)

St. Thomas goes on to say in II-II, q. 154, a. 12 that in matters of chastity, the most serious offences are those against the order of nature, i.e. those actions which do not fulfill the finality written by God into biological nature.[34] This seems to conform to the 'preceptive' model whereby immutable principles of divine law are inscribed in the body or nature, and can simply be "read off" or discerned by reason.

Revisionists such as Richard Gula and Louis Janssens have criticized the implications of this reasoning because it would lead us to conclude that masturbation, oral or anal stimulation or consenting adult homogenital sexual acts are more serious violations of chastity than incest, rape, adultery, or fornication. This Thomistic model encourages moral evaluation of actions prior to considerations of consent, harm, circumstance and intention. The agent's purposes, circumstances and relationships are rendered morally irrelevant. This seems decidedly counterintuitive and certainly conflicts with what we now know about the psychological, emotional and interpersonal damage done by acts such as rape, pedophilia, incest and adultery. It seems that a moral evaluation of these actions cannot rest exclusively on biological factors.

Nevertheless, there seems little doubt that Thomas was influenced by Ulpian's definition of *Jus Naturale* -- what nature has taught all animals. But it is difficult to explain why Thomas, who in the treatise on law is strongly inclined to prioritize the rational aspect of human nature, should, in the *Summa*, retain the notion that humans are more like animals than unlike them. If this were correct, then our sexual actions, unlike our other actions, would conveniently not be subject to the dictates of reason and consciousness, but instead would have a 'reason' of their own, independent of the reflective intervention of the human *ratio*. On this model of human nature, sexual actions would be very different from other forms of intentional behavior; it seems they would not require reflection or active agency. While the sex drive itself may be involuntary or pre-reflective, we are nevertheless capable of controlling our particular sexual acts, which are intentional. We choose whether and how to express this naturally occurring aspect of our nature.

According to the Thomistic interpretation of human nature in the *Summa*, matter is not merely subordinated to mind, it is treated as disconnected from it, as a separate and autonomous 'law' unto itself. Nature follows its own rules and reason's only function is to observe the rules and accept them, not to modify them to human ends. This interpretation of natural law *identifies* the natural order with the moral order. Practical reason perceives the natural inclinations in human persons in the form of moral imperatives.[35] But this does not tell us which natural inclinations we ought to obey. Homosexuality may be a strong natural inclination in the homosexual person. Thomas's approach seems to require that the biological functions of reproductive organs should provide a natural inclination in all humans to use them for reproduction. The result is a 'physicalist' theory of natural law in which moral evaluations of acts are based on their biological purpose apart from the totality of the person.

The adoption of Ulpian's definition of *Jus Naturale* by later thinkers has had a lasting impact on the Church's natural law tradition. In addition to exercising an influence on Thomas Aquinas, it was also given longevity by Justinian, who incorporated it into the *Corpus Juris Civilis* -- the most authoritative source of Roman Law.[36] The manner of deriving a moral position by privileging the 'order of nature' over the 'order of reason' in sexual ethics and pronouncing specific moral judgments on *acts in themselves* has been continually employed in magisterial documents on sexual and medical reproductive matters. Aquinas's perspective on matters of sex and gender is quite limited by his social setting and, says Lisa Cahill, "by his tendency to forget that the most distinctive human capacities are intellect and will. He is predisposed to focus the 'natural' on physiological function."[37] Consequently, he takes for granted that sex has above all a reproductive purpose and that woman's existence is explained primarily in relation to this purpose.

By contrast, the 'personalist' interpretation of natural law adopted by Catholic revisionists acknowledges that God has given us much else besides our physical and biological functions -- in particular our intelligence and creativity. The work of ethics is to discover what it is that enables us to be human and to become more authentically human.

Catholic doctrine has not made explicit the implications of its reasoning - namely, that procreative potential is an absolute moral requirement for *all* sexual intercourse. The natural law argument in its classical form *implicitly* ruled out any intercourse, even in marriage, which will not lead to conception, whether on account of age, pregnancy, or permanent or temporary infertility. The latter applies to most of the female's monthly cycle. One may be forgiven for wondering why this procreative requirement has become the basis for saying that all homogenital acts are unnatural and hence objectively wrong and immoral. Given what we now know about the nature and irreversibility of homosexuality, the Catholic position seems selective in emphasizing the procreative function of sexual organs over the 'given' (i.e. natural) physical, emotional and psychological facts about sexual attraction. Why the emphasis must remain on reproduction has never been made clear.

To be fair, Aquinas did make a distinction between those deprivations of procreative potential which *essentially* lack such potential and those that only *accidentally* lack it. In the **Summa Contra Gentiles**, Thomas stipulates that any genital activity that allows for no possibility of insemination (the depositing of semen in the vagina) is regarded as *essentially* non-procreative and hence unnatural. While heterosexual infertility is deemed only 'accidentally' non-procreative, homogenital acts or contraceptive acts are 'essentially' non-procreative. This distinction appears somewhat academic, however. For instance, few would claim that insemination continues to have the same 'essentially' procreative potential after the female partner is post-menopausal, or between a married couple when one partner is infertile. Yet there is no suggestion from the Vatican that post-menopausal intercourse, or intercourse between a fertile and an infertile spouse is in any sense immoral. The *essential-accidental* distinction of St. Thomas is unconvincing and casts doubt on whether his conception of natural law provides an adequate basis for the condemnation of homogenital acts as such.

Official magisterial teaching judges all homogenital *expression* to be objectively immoral because it falls short of the unitive and procreative sexual norms suggested by the creation accounts in Genesis. It was only with Vatican II's ***Gaudium et Spes***[38] (1965) that the unitive aspect of human sexuality was put on a par with the procreative aspect. This document officially recognized that while procreation was a *necessary* component of the sexual act, it was not *sufficient* to describe its human meaning and value.

It could be argued, however, that the necessity of the procreative aspect of the sexual act has not been adequately established, and that the essentially human meaning of sexual acts is to be found not in their procreative potential but in their unitive aspect. **The English Quakers** put forward just such a view in 1963.[39] According to this document, homogenital acts *per se* are morally neutral. Genital acts are to be judged not by their physical aspect, nor in isolation from the personal relationship in which they occur. Rather, it is the quality and nature of the relationship that matters in a moral evaluation of sexual acts.

A reasonable, modern way to evaluate an action or behavior might be to ask whether it preserves and promotes our humanity or fails to do so. The difficulty for reaching a clear-cut system by this means is that not everyone agrees on what is most essential to being a human person. They may differ especially over what is most distinctive of human beings or which aspects of humanity are most relevant to a particular ethical question. With respect to homosexuality, serious doubts remain as to whether human sexuality *is* universally heterosexual and so it is difficult to judge whether homosexual expression preserves or corrupts some peoples' nature.

In Thomas's doctrine on the virtues he stresses that they help us to discern the concrete actions that can embody the love of the moral good. This seems to suggest that particular acts can disclose the virtuous intentions of the morally good agent. But again, this leaves open the question of how Thomas defines particular actions (how he defines the 'object' of an act, and whether he favors the 'order of nature' or the 'order of reason' in defining human sexual nature). Defenders of the physicalist natural law model (Robert P. George, Germain Grisez, John Finnis, Kevin Flannery, S.J., William E. May, Patrick Lee) have defended their anthropology and have demonstrated how aspects of it have been misrepresented. In the next chapter I will consider their arguments and look at them in more detail.

## ii. Too little reference to empirical realities and the use, instead, of an outdated, deductive, *a priori* classicist worldview and methodology

A second criticism of the Vatican's methodology in sexual ethics is that it's encyclicals make little or no reference to empirical realities and instead employ a deductive, classicist worldview. The inadequacies of the classicist worldview provide the backdrop against which Thomas wrote but they also form the context in which his writings were interpreted and applied by others. Revisionists point out that the classicist worldview speaks in terms of substances and essences. Applied to human nature, change and history are seen as irrelevant 'accidents' and do not alter the constitution of reality itself. The classicist methodology tended to begin from abstract, *a priori* premises.

Curran claims that *Persona Humana* (1975) represents no substantial development on the approach taken in the encyclical *Humanae Vitae* (1968). As in the earlier document, the meaning of human sexuality is to be found in the essential order of human nature. But this "essential order of sexual nature" is reduced to "the finality and structure of the sexual act." Respect for its finality insures the moral goodness of the act (par. N. 5). The first defect in this approach is that insufficient emphasis is given to developing, historical and cultural realities.[40] Evaluations of sexual acts are based more on classical natural law definitions of the 'intrinsic' meaning and purpose of physical actions than on an empirical analysis of human actions based on interdisciplinary observations.

The Declaration gives insufficient emphasis to experience. "Without any supportive data the Vatican Declaration appeals to the magisterium and to the moral sense of the Christian people to support the contention that homosexual relations cannot be judged indulgently or even excused (par. n. 8) and that masturbation is an intrinsically and gravely disordered act."[41]

The 'personalist' account of natural law acknowledges that our moral responsibility is connected to our potential as meaning-makers, but it also acknowledges the biological, historical and circumstantial limits imposed on our attempt at meaning-making. Ethical theories that use an inductive methodology and a vision of the human person as embodied, rational and social are consistent with a 'naturalistic' approach that relates moral knowledge to features of the real word. The entire pertinent reality has to be taken into account, says Josef Fuchs, "if behavioral norms are to be operative."[42] This connection between behavior and the concrete human reality is not relativism but the very standard for objectivity and truth. The non-historical, deductive ethical methodology that stands opposed to this, and that provides norms in advance for every interpersonal situation, sacrifices objectivity by ignoring relevant facts. Fuchs argues that objectivity or the "truth" of ethical behavior can only conform to the whole concrete reality of man (or society).

Some interpretations of naturalism depend more on definitions than on evidence. To be precise, some evidence may be regarded as *definitive*, relevant, or more 'normative' than other kinds of evidence, for determining the truth of ethical statements. The selection of partial evidence for emphasis is not objective. Selectivity narrows the criterion for truth to whether it 'fits' a particular cultic worldview. When a single system of meaningfulness involving a set of internally interdependent beliefs becomes more important than a balanced, interdisciplinary study of the evidence, the demands of truth become secondary.

To take one example, the Church has deployed an ideological framework that rejects all evolutionary theories that offer alternative explanations for sexual drives, pleasures, practices and mating patterns. One exception to this ideological framework was the Jesuit Teilhard de Chardin's explanations. Fr. Teilhard de Chardin, a French paleonotologist and philosopher, attempted a synthesis of Darwinian evolution and Catholic theology. At times, however, he openly expressed his belief that evolution was superior to the Deposit of the Faith. He wrote: 'Is evolution a theory, a system, or a hypothesis? It is much more: it is the general condition to which all theories, all hypotheses, all systems must bow and which they must satisfy henceforward if they are to be *thinkable* and *true*. Evolution is a light illuminating all facts, a curve that all lines must follow.'[43] The Holy See suppressed de Chardin's works, first, during his lifetime, by sending him to China, and later, after his death, by issuing official warnings against his teaching. The Church issued this monitum [*i.e.*, a solemn warning] after his death:

> "Several works of Fr. Pierre Teilhard de Chardin, some of which were posthumously published, are being edited and are gaining a good deal of success.
>
> Precinding from a judgement about those points that concern the positive sciences, it is sufficiently clear that the above-mentioned works abound in such ambiguities and indeed even serious errors, as to offend Catholic doctrine.
>
> For this reason, the most eminent and most revered Fathers of the Holy Office exhort all Ordinaires as well as the superiors of religious institutes, rectors of seminaries and presidents of universities, effectively to protect the minds, particularly of the youth, against the dangers presented by the works of Fr. Teilhard de Chardin and of his followers.
>
> [Given at Rome, from the palace of the Holy Office, on the thirtieth day of June, 1962. Sebastianus Masala, Notarius.]"[44]

In 1963 the Vicariate of Rome, in a decree, required that Catholic bookshops in Rome should withdraw from circulation the works of Fr. Teilhard de Chardin, and also any books favorable to his allegedly erroneous doctrines. However, at the Second Vatican Council, Paul VI, and other liturgical 'reformers' including Cardinal Agostino Casaroli (1914-1998) were influenced by Teilhard de Chardin's teachings. Paul VI, said that 'Fr. Teilhard is an indispensable man for our times; his expression of faith is necessary for us.'[45] Fr. Teilhard de Chardin was often quoted on the floor of the Council. In the opinion of some observers these references to his work influenced the outcome of the council almost as much as Pope John XXIII.

In a letter re-printed in *L'Osservatore Romano,* John Paul ll's Secretary of State, Cardinal Agostino Casaroli, wrote*:*

> In [Teilhard de Chardin], a powerful poetic intuition of nature's profound value, a sharp perception of creation's dynamism, and a broad vision of the world's future join together with an incontestable religious fervor. Similarly, his unremitting desire to dialogue with the science of his time and his bold optimism about the evolution of the world have given his intuitions - through the rich variety of his words and the magic of his images - considerable influence. . . . the complexity of the problems he analyzed and the variety of approaches he adopted raised difficulties that understandably called for a calm, critical study - in the scientific, philosophical and theological realms - of his extraordinary work.

> (Cardinal Agostino Cardinal Casaroli, L'Osservatore Romano, June 10, 1981)

However, a group of cardinals of the Roman Curia soon protested against Teilhard's allegedly undeserved praise. Consequently, the apparent attempt at rehabilitating the Jesuit paleontologist suffered a fresh setback. On July 22, 1981, a press release from the Holy See hastened to proclaim that Cardinal Casaroli's letter, written "in the Holy Father's name", was not at all meant

> ...to constitute a revision of the previous stand taken by the Holy See vis-a-vis that author (Teilhard), and especially with reference to the Monitum of the Holy Office (of June 30, 1962) warning the faithful that that author's works were teeming with ambiguities and grave doctrinal errors.[46]

This drawn out affair shows how, by suppressing alternative, testable, theories about the evolution of the human species and human sexual behaviour, the Church has at times privileged its own un-testable theological views on the matter.

In a similar vein, Pope Pius XII condemned polygenism (a theory which holds that the origins of humanity are multiple, rather than of a single lineage traceable to Adam and Eve) in his encyclical *Humani Generis*:

'The faithful cannot embrace that opinion which maintains either that after Adam there existed on this earth true men who did not take their origin through natural generation through him as from the first parent of all, nor that Adam represents a certain number of first parents. Now it is no way apparent how such an opinion can be reconciled with that which the sources of revealed truth and the documents of the Teaching Authority of the Church propose with regard to original sin, which proceeds from a sin actually committed by an individual Adam and which through generation is passed on to all and is in everyone as his own.' (*Humani Generis*, 1950, Paragraph No. 37)

Here the argument put forward is simply that the faithful shouldn't accept what contradicts church teaching. No argument (i.e. a conclusion supported by reasons) is put forward except that the theory is impossible to reconcile with the dogma and authority of the church, here identified as 'revealed truth' and the 'Teaching Authority of the Church'. Yet Pius' stance on polygenism is no longer official Catholic teaching.

At various times the Vatican has claimed that homosexuality undermines a person's fulfillment and happiness (*Letter to the Bishops*, 1986, point 7, para 3), is detrimental to health (*Letter to the Bishops*, 1986, point 9, para. 2), is a threat to marriage and the family (*Letter to the Bishops*, 1986, point 9, para. 3), corrupts the minds of the young (*Considerations Regarding Proposals*, 2003, Section III, point 6, para. 3 & *Letter to the Bishops*, 1986, point 17, para. 9), constitutes a bad influence on children in same-sex families (*Considerations Regarding Proposals*, 2003, point 7, para 3), and has detrimental consequences for the common good (*Considerations Regarding Proposals*, 2003, point 8, para1). I have to concur with Donald Cochrane, when he says that these assertions "can easily be refuted on the basis of empirical evidence."[47] But lack of evidence has not diminished the persuasive effect of such claims on those who might be susceptible to them.

Robert Nugent has noted that, until recently, all ecclesiastical statements described the homosexual orientation in terms indicating its "inadequacy" or lack as a desirable form of sexual identity.

"This evaluation is based more on the classical natural law understanding of the normative meaning and purpose of human sexuality than on a descriptive analysis of what is the actual present reality from an empirical scientific understanding of the development of various kinds of human sexual identity. Thus, in the empirical sciences the homosexual orientation is generally accepted as well within the range for healthy, human sexual identity."[48]

Nugent concludes that the logical inference from the empirical data is that a valid description of the homosexual orientation is that of a "natural form of human sexual development at least for a standard percentage of the human race in a majority of cultures studied and in many periods of human history."[49] While scientists claim that the homosexual orientation is a natural variation of human sexuality, moralists draw on other sources (Scripture, natural law, tradition, etc.), for their definition of human sexuality.[50]

In the nineteenth century the name Charles Darwin came to symbolize the historicization of human nature and the natural sciences.[51] _On The Origin of Species_ (1859) heralded the abandonment of the idea of a static nature. As Kevin Kelly has noted, "We now know that what we call our 'nature' is the result of historical evolution over billions of years. So if we are to speak of the 'givenness' of human nature we must include its historicity as part of its givenness. To make human nature static would be to interfere with it, since our nature is essentially historical."[52] Understanding man as a historical being is not tantamount to a rejection of nature. Even if nature is the Creator's manifestation of what He willed to exist, it is not His Manifesto of how he wills the human person to use this existing reality. The given physical and biological orders do not dictate moral obligations; they provide the raw data and possibilities for the person to use towards the fulfillment of authentic human ends.

Whereas the classicist methodology worked from the abstract and universal towards the more concrete and particular, the starting point for a consideration of the human person in the context of historical consciousness is quite different. Whereas theology was once understood as a deductive science, it is now largely empirical. The personalist interpretation of natural law relies on modern methodology, which is concrete, *a posteriori*, and inductive. Some modern theologians take into account the fact that we experience human life subjectively. We perform intentional acts and recognize ourselves as agents. Edward Schillebeeckx contributes an important point:

> "This fundamental characteristic of being human, namely, the ability creatively to participate in historical process, shifts the category for understanding what is paramount in the human person from human nature to subjectivity. Human nature is a static, because abstract, concept; subjectivity is a center of intelligence, decision, and action, and so presupposes change, growth and development." [53]

Existentialists, both Christian and atheist, stress the importance of agency and subjectivity to our sense of personal moral responsibility. 'Humanity' is not just an abstract concept; it is what we do, and what we make of our selves by means of our choices. Essence does not determine a person's nature; rather, a person's 'nature' (character) is a by-product of her actions, choices and culture. From this perspective, our natures may be regarded as works-in-progress.

### iii. When the church's documents *do* make reference to empirical realities, or employ an inductive, *a posteriori* methodology, they do so too selectively and commit the naturalistic fallacy.

A third criticism of the traditional Catholic approach to sexual ethics is that references to observable features of the world are partial or selective. The Church's documents place too much emphasis on a narrow set of empirical facts and exclude other relevant ones. To equate 'natural' with a limited set of predictable patterns in the created order leads to what some critics call 'natural fundamentalism' and yields a 'blueprint' or 'maker's instructions' theory of the natural law. Such an approach has little room for the distinctively human, experiential, creative aspects of moral knowledge and freedom. In particular it tends to over-state the classical Greek distinction between natural and artificial. The ancients contrasted nature (*physis*) and art (*techne*). In general 'natural fundamentalism' places human ingenuity and creativity outside of the 'natural order' by over-stressing the difference between those features of the world that are as they are *independently* of human activity and those features of the world that are as they are *because* of human activity.[54] Human beings interact with their environment and each other in many ways. One way we relate to our environment is based on a rational understanding of nature, which is used to produce human values that the operation of natural processes alone would not. We might ask, for example, whether human flight is 'natural'. It defies the laws of gravity to which humans are naturally subject. Human beings were not born with wings. Yet few would say that it is inconsistent with human nature to fly. Some would argue that the urge to exceed the 'givens' of our material conditions *is* quintessentially human.

Naturalist theories of ethics maintain that it is possible to arrive at true moral statements from factual premises, established *a posteriori*. Accordingly, we can have knowledge relevant to ethics just as we have knowledge in other disciplines. Gerard Hughes interprets natural law ethics as a version of naturalism:

> ". . . ethics is at root an empirical study, something we *find out* about, in the way that we might find out about astronomy or physics or psychology or medicine. And just as further information will as a matter of course call in question previously accepted conclusions in these sciences, so too further information about human nature and its environment can call in question previously accepted conclusions in ethics. Ethics is inevitably provisional, revisable, for the same kinds of reason that our beliefs about astronomy, physics, or medicine are revisable."[55]

In Hughes's view, the quest for *moral* truth is related to the quest for truth about other facts, which can be tested against empirical evidence. The facts are revisable in ethics, then, for exactly the same reason that they are revisable in other disciplines -- because our knowledge of ourselves and of the world is constantly evolving. Therefore, our conclusions in ethics will be provisional at best. Hughes argues that it is implicit in a natural law ethic that our view of what is ethical will change over time as our knowledge of human nature develops.

This kind of naturalism is quite different from Magisterial naturalist theories that maintain that certain given patterns in nature have *intrinsic value* that dictate or disclose human purposes in an unchangeable way. Hughes' understanding of natural law differs dramatically from theories that define value judgments as *implicit in* matters of fact. In some modern writings about ethics, 'naturalism' is used in a narrow sense to refer to theories that *equate* or *reduce* ethics (values) to a selected set of observed facts, or slide from descriptions to prescriptions, as though moral imperatives were 'inscribed' in nature and could be 'read off' as precepts.

In *Principia Ethica* (1903) G.E. Moore argued that this kind of naturalism committed what he called *the naturalistic fallacy*.[56] Later Moore made an important refinement when he said that a value term like 'good' is not **identical with** any natural or metaphysical property. This was a significant modification, for Moore was not saying that 'good' was *unrelated* to our knowledge of natural properties, but only that moral value could not be automatically *identified* with or revealed in those properties. Commenting on what he had said about the naturalistic fallacy in *Principia Ethica*, Moore clarified that committing the 'naturalistic fallacy' means *either* confusing Good with a natural or metaphysical property *or* holding it to be identical with such a property *or* making an inference based upon such a confusion.' Moore's revised way of understanding the naturalistic fallacy also excludes what David Hume thought suspect: the attempt to derive an *ought* directly, and without further explanation, from an *is*. The move from propositions containing *is* to others containing *ought*, says Hum,

> ". . . is of the least consequence. For as this *ought,* or *ought not,* expresses some new relation or affirmation, 'tis necessary that it should be observed and explain'd; and at the same time, that a reason should be given, for what seems altogether inconceivable, how this new relation can be a deduction from others, which are entirely different from it." [57]

To say that ethics should be *related* to non-moral knowledge (i.e. empirical facts) is not the same as saying that ethics should be patently dictated by, or equated with, this knowledge. One of the main difficulties, as Hughes points out, is that there is an enormous amount of non-moral knowledge and there is no self-evident way to discern which part of that knowledge ought to be relevant to a particular ethical question. The choice to give emphasis to one set of facts over others is a matter of values, not of 'objective' truth or 'revealed' wisdom.

Facts alone do not dictate moral values, but they do set the boundaries within which moral responsibility can be assigned to human agents. In this respect, facts do matter, and they matter quite a bit. According to Lisa Sowell Cahill, the consistency and frequency of homosexuality as a human phenomenon, while having implications for moral judgments, are not sufficient to establish whether a certain constitution or behavior is psychologically healthy or pathological.[58] Even less, she says, does the mere recurrence of "certain biological or psychological conditions" in human societies establish whether those conditions are right or wrong. What, then, would be sufficient to ground normative judgments – like Cahill's own – that homosexual orientation is "less than fully human"?[59] Cahill admits that her own (and the Church's) use of both scriptural and non-scriptural sources is "not without equivocation."[60] I have already explained how St. Paul and other moralists have equivocated on 'natural'. Some Catholic theologians seem to recognize this.

My objection, like that of revisionists, is not that the physicalist interpretation of natural law valued the connection between fact and value. Facts *should* influence value judgements. Rather, my objection is to the way that physicalist approaches to sexual ethics selected such a narrow set of facts to emphasize. In particular they gave some physical aspects of human nature disproportionate weight in comparison to the other physical, emotive, affective, and rational aspects. It treated us less as persons than as bodies, and even as such, selected a narrow set of functions for which our bodies may be used. I do not in any way disparage embodiment. To expect that sexual acts ought to involve the kind of sexual attraction and arousal of which homosexuals, no less than heterosexuals, are physically and psychologically capable seems to me the essence of 'embodiment'. And to expect that a homosexual person will behave in accordance with her own given sexual orientation (unless there are good reasons not to) also seems consistent with an integral understanding of human nature as both mind and body.

It seems that what is distinctive of human nature, or what is universal to all of us in distinction from animals, is not our particular biological capacities, but conscious freedom to direct our lives within the limits set for us. Conscious freedom, or the ability to act for reasons of our own making, appears to be the most common basis of our human nature.

In a sense, natural law is neither 'natural' nor is it 'law.' It is not natural in the sense that the moral law cannot be identified with physical, chemical, or biological laws of nature which purport to express the way the natural world works.[61] Thomas Schmidt has observed that, "*Natural* may refer to something that happens repeatedly in nature -- that is, in the world -- in which case we assign no moral judgment to it. Events occur in nature: for example, spiders kill and eat other spiders, including their mates."[62] Schmidt makes the important distinction between this sense of 'natural', which is an *explanation* of behavior, and the putatively moral sense of 'natural', which purports to be a *justification* for behavior.

Natural law is not *law* in the way that forensic laws function as absolute commands, directly disclosing to us our duties. The connotations of the word 'law' seem to imply that given physical and biological orders *dictate* moral obligation. The human concept of law would appear to suggest that natural law simultaneously describes how things are and prescribes how they should be. How we choose to define our nature is important because the descriptive informs the prescriptive; what we prescribe or think we ought to do depends upon what we describe as 'good' or 'healthy' or 'natural' for beings such as us. Unfortunately, it is impossible to deploy these terms without presuppositions about 'health' or 'nature' and so to separate them from value judgments.

While description is an attempt to explain what 'is,' not to evaluate what 'ought' to be, some terms actually do both. Synthetic terms, according to Janssens, are "words which refer to the material content of an action but at the same time formulate a moral judgment."[63] When considering how synthetic terms are applied to particular sexual acts in Christian parlance (e.g. "adultery", "fornication", "perversion", "sin"), it is important to bear in mind that symbols, linguistic conventions or definitions can actually 'construct' a reality while seeming merely to explain or describe it. As Peter Berger and Thomas Luckmann have argued, apparently 'scientific' theories have a tendency to shape the reality they claim only to interpret -- especially when they achieve dominance in a culture.[64] The description given to a particular act will, if we accept its relevance, color our moral evaluation of it. By our conventions of reference we impute meaning to the raw data, which in turn reflects human purposes -- our own or those of the group to which we belong. These meanings become "common sense" and provide the community with its identity. To break such community-defining conventions is to appear to be a traitor to the community.

Laws, in the human juridical sense, are prescriptive and conventional. Laws of nature, by contrast, are descriptive. One of the clearest explanations of the modern distinction between descriptive and prescriptive laws comes from Bryan Macgee:

> "The word 'law' is ambiguous, and anyone who talks of a natural or scientific law being 'broken' is confusing the two main uses of the word. A law of society prescribes what we may or may not do. It can be broken --- indeed, if we could not break it there would be no need to have it: society does not legislate against a citizen's being in two places at once. A law of nature, on the other hand, is not prescriptive but descriptive. It tells us what happens --- for instance that water boils at 100° Centigrade. As such, it purports to be nothing more than a statement of what, given certain initial conditions, such as that there is a body of water and that it is heated, occurs. It may be true or false, but it cannot be 'broken', for it is not a command: water is not being ordered to boil at 100° Centigrade . . . nowadays no one would dispute that [laws of nature] are not prescriptions of any kind, to be 'kept' or 'obeyed' or 'broken', but explanatory statements of a general character

which purport to be factual and must therefore be modified or abandoned if found to be inaccurate."[65]

The Catholic arguments to demoralize those who engage in homosexual behavior have exploited the ambiguity in terms like 'law' and 'natural' to full advantage. As a result the documents produced have been fraught with confusion about the relationship between the empirical and the moral. A typical example appears in Considerations Regarding Proposals to Give Legal Recognition to Unions Between Homosexual Persons, where it is stated that *"the natural truth about marriage was confirmed by the Revelation contained in the biblical accounts of creation, an expression also of the original human wisdom, in which the voice of nature itself is heard."* The Vatican's teaching has wavered between two extremes: *a priori* pronouncements that give too little attention to observable features of the real world, or over-emphasis on some features of the real world to the exclusion of others. Critics propose an *a posteriori* methodology that takes into its scope the most universal and distinctive features of our humanity (i.e. our capacity to reflect, learn, grow, relate and choose). They recommend that we use these features as a basis for moral judgments about human behavior. Critics also realize that moral judgment is not appropriate where there is no possibility of choice. For example, few heterosexuals would claim to merit moral praise for what is not in their power to control. Heterosexuals have never, to my knowledge, suggested that being attracted to the opposite sex, and behaving accordingly is, in itself, a moral virtue. This is because they recognize that no one deserves praise for involuntary urges, or doing what comes naturally to oneself. It is not heterosexuality, *per se*, that might be considered a moral good, but the ways in which the human agent responds to the fact of his heterosexuality (or homosexuality) within an interpersonal context. One response to heterosexual impulses might be to act on every sexual impulse one feels. A heterosexual male might be womanizing, exploitative, or even violent. Any wanton expression of his 'natural' impulses might be regarded as a moral virtue, were we to view natural biological inclinations as key criteria for measuring moral virtue. But we do not. It is not his heterosexuality, nor the procreative potential of his actions, that might make a heterosexual's sexual behavior good (in the moral sense). Rather, we must evaluate his acts relative to the ways in which they impact others.

Grounding sexual morality in the will of the agent in his interpersonal situation (and not in the biology of his genitalia) illuminates the reasons why homosexuality *per se* is not a tendency towards moral vice. This is not to say that homosexuals could not act in morally vicious ways, for example, if they chose to express their given sexuality in exploitative or abusive ways. But this would be equally true of heterosexuals. Homosexuals have never claimed that their sexual orientation extinguishes their free will, thus making their sexual behavior immune from moral evaluation. They simply argue for the adoption of ***a single standard*** *for evaluating the morality of **all** sexual behavior.* Anything short of this single standard constitutes discrimination, as it demoralizes one group on the basis of innate biological differences. In this sense homophobia is tantamount to racism or sexism.

Thomas Schmidt has observed that, to many people today, homophobia *is* viewed as tantamount to racism. He correctly notes that many now see homosexuality as a civil rights issue, not a moral issue.[66] But Schmidt misrepresents the reasoning behind this shift, calling it "confusion between what is legal and what is moral".[67]

The shift away from seeing homosexual behavior *per se* as immoral is underpinned by natural law methodology, which relates ethics to a holistic understanding of human nature. It aims to rest conventional laws on features of humanity common to all of us. Like most Christian versions of ethics, natural law theory presupposes that conventional laws can, and should, be measured against the natural law that aims to protect what is essential to human flourishing.

Thomas Schmidt says the incorporation of gay rights into the wider civil rights movement is the symptom of a society that has made tolerance the supreme virtue, where "a foolish majority" turn liberty into license.[68] Schmidt claims homosexual behavior is seen as a 'right', as opposed to immoral behaviors like adultery, polygamy, or incest. This, he observes, is because homosexuality is seen as something that people *are* rather than as something that people *do*. Schmidt is correct to say that many people today look upon homosexuality the same way they look at heterosexuality: as something that people are, such that a particular set of activities (including sex) will 'naturally' flow from this fact. Those who think homosexuality is a matter of civil rights would regard homosexual adultery, paedophelia, rape, exploitation, or polygamy no differently than they would regard heterosexual versions of these acts. Homophiles understand that liberty to express one's sexuality with other consenting adults is not license to abuse others. Homosexuals have never suggested that their sexual orientation gives them license to perform abusive, or any, immoral acts. Homosexuals merely demand that they be permitted to engage in consenting sex with a partner of their choice (in keeping with their given biological nature), just as heterosexuals are permitted to do. The difference between their demand for civil rights and the demands of other people with inclinations to engage in unconventional sexual behaviors is that the latter behaviors listed by Schmidt (adultery, polygamy, or incest) are illegal or taboo *for a good reason* – namely, they harm others or tend to be unilaterally applied in exploitative ways. In the case of homosexuality, no such harm exists. The 'harm' done is purely theoretical. It is really just *offence* to a traditional set of religious definitions and beliefs. Consenting adult homosexual behavior only harms the sensibilities, tastes or values of those who cling to theological definitions of nature not grounded in empirical fact. In this sense, the 'harm' it causes is comparable to the harm done by any unconventional belief or behavior. Many unorthodox beliefs are seen in hindsight as progressive and enlightened in comparison to the relative narrowness of their contemporary milieu.

The drive to proscribe behaviors that are merely offensive, but not harmful, presupposes the infallibility of the predominant or powerful group's worldview. It also undermines what most people today agree to be definitive of an immoral act: namely, that it willfully **harms others** without justification. Schmidt himself says, "The New Testament frees believers from the constraints of ritual purity (Mk. 7; Acts 10) and redefines sin as "intent to harm".[69]

Human rights activists argue that positive laws ought to reflect, and protect, fundamental aspects of our humanity. While there is room for debate about which features of human nature are most important, the methodology used to discover truths about human nature cannot be so limited as to exclude the intellectual, creative, *active* aspects of human reason. Nor should it eschew a broad base of empirical evidence, and the vast experience of human individuals. A description of 'nature' that rests entirely upon the beliefs or doctrine of a particular religion is today widely regarded as furnishing only the most biased and limited of definitions. Thomas Schmidt's arguments are exemplary of what is wrong with contemporary Christian arguments against homosexual civil rights in his insistence that the basis for positive law must be a religious one. He admits that, "as a moral category *natural* refers to something that is in accord with God's intention . . . . In summary, that which is *natural* to human experience or human desire is not necessarily *natural* in God's moral design."[70] But Schmidt himself often uses the prescriptive sense of *natural* as though it were more than a synthetic term used by a community of fallible religious believers. Although he is clear about his moral judgment against homosexual behavior, he justifies his position by referring back to the specifically religious category of 'unnatural' even while reluctantly acknowledging that homosexuality may well be 'natural' in the descriptive sense that it is found to occur in many species (including homo sapiens) and may even have genetic causes. This refusal to move beyond narrow religious categories that describe nature without reference to empirical evidence and vast human experience supplants natural law ethics with a cultic version of positive law.

********

In addition to the three weaknesses outlined above, Charles Curran suggests one final weakness in the traditional Catholic teachings on sex, unrelated to the others. The use of Scripture is open to question. "At the very least", says Curran, "one must do more than cite scriptural texts to prove that 'sexual intercourse outside marriage is formally condemned.' (*Persona Humana*, note 16)."[71] Here Curran alludes to the scholarly arguments I mentioned in Chapter 1 that have investigated whether Paul's letter to the Romans 1:24-27 must be interpreted as a condemnation of *all* homosexual actions for *all* people (as opposed to condemning cases in which the 'deviant' heterosexual 'leaves' his own given heterosexual nature to practice homosexuality). While it is certainly acceptable for Catholics to choose to believe the teachings of their own authorities, the demand of a natural law theory of ethics is that sources of ethical wisdom apart from the explicit revelation of God in the Christian scriptures can be drawn upon to support 'revealed' wisdom. As I said at the beginning of the chapter, natural law theorists claim there is a moral basis to life that can be established, not just for believers, but for all men and women, by reflecting on what it means to be a human person.

As I argued in the previous chapter, the precedent for natural law thinking in Christian tradition can be traced to sources that antedate Aquinas. The Protestant tradition has relied more heavily on Biblical passages to argue that homosexuality is morally wrong. I attempted to demonstrate some of the difficulties in interpretation that form part of the Christian legacy – beginning with the earliest Christian proponent of natural law, St. Paul. If we accept both the presumption of responsible agency implicit in Paul's moral exhortations and the presumption of active agency in human nature, (as forming morally relevant aspects of universal human nature), then it seems to me we will come closer to understanding which aspects of homogenital behavior could rightly be called 'sins'. To condemn consenting homosexual activity as such, in the absence of an evaluation of interpersonal agency, seems to me discriminatory. It departs from ordinary ethical norms generally deployed to evaluate human behavior.

In the next chapter I will turn to contemporary Christian discourses on sexual ethics in order to discern how they have attempted to rectify or defend the stated weaknesses in traditional Catholic natural law methodology. I will also consider how they have adapted to new empirical data that indicate homosexual orientation may have a biological basis.

1    Fuchs, Josef, 'The Absoluteness of Behavioural Moral Norms' in <u>An</u> <u>Introduction</u> <u>to Christian Ethics, A Reader</u>, Ronald P. Hamel and Kenneth R. Himes, Eds., New York, Paulist Press, 1989, p. 495. Fuchs himself does not see the nature of man as 'given and unvarying' in this way.

2    English translation: 'Of New Things'

3    English translation: 'Of Human Life'

4    in F. Festorazzi et al., <u>Nuove prospettive di morale coniugale</u>, Brecia, 1969, p. 75.

5    Cochrane, Donald B., 'Christian Opposition to Homosexuality', in James McNinch and Mary Cronin, (Eds.), <u>I Could Not Speak My Heart: Education and Social Justice for LGBT Youth,</u> Regina, Saskatchewan Canadian Plains Research Centre, 2004, p. 5.

6    SCDF, *Some Considerations Concerning the Response to Legislative Proposals on the Non-Discrimination of Homosexual Persons,* I, para. 2.

7    Macnamara, Vincent, <u>The Truth in Love: Reflections on Catholic Morality,</u> Dublin: Gill & Macmillan, Ltd., 1988, p 99.

8    Hoose, Bernard, 'Proportionalism: a Right Relationship Among Values', *Louvain Studies* 24,1991, p. 50.

9    See esp. Curran, Charles E., 'Sexual Ethics: A Critique' in <u>Issues in Sexual and Medical Ethics</u>, University of Notre Dame Press, Notre Dame/London, 1978, pp. 30-49.

10    *The Tablet*, Nov. 8, 1986.

11    *America*, Nov. 22, 1986.

12    Monsignor James Lisante, *The Long Island Catholic*, Aug. 26, 1992.

13    Curran, Op. Cit., p. 37.

14    see Janssens, Louis, 'Ontic Evil and Moral Evil' in <u>Readings in Moral Theology, No. 1</u> (Curran & McCormick Eds.), pp. 40-93, esp. pg. 86 and Curran, Charles, 'Sexual Ethics: A Critique' in <u>Issues in Sexual and Medical Ethics</u>, University of Notre Dame Press, Notre Dame/London,1978, pg. 41.

15    Macnamara, Vincent, Op. Cit., p. 97.

16    Curran, Op. Cit., p. 39.

17    Ibid., p. 40.

18    Ibid., p. 39.

19    Fuchs, Josef, 'The Absoluteness of Behavioural Moral Norms' in <u>An</u> <u>Introduction</u> <u>to Christian Ethics, A Reader</u>, Ronald P. Hamel and Kenneth R. Himes, Eds., New York, Paulist Press, 1989, p. 497.

20    Curran, Op. Cit., p. 39.

21    Fuchs, Josef, 'The Absoluteness of Moral Terms,' *Gregorianum* 52, 1971, p. 121.

22    McCormick, Richard A., <u>Notes on Moral Theology 1965 - 1980</u>, Washington, D.C., University Press of America,1981, p. 123.

23   Janssens, Louis, 'Norms and Priorities in a Love Ethics,' in *Louvain Studies* 4, Spring 1977, p. 214.

24   Janssens, Louis, '*Ontic Evil and Moral Evil*,' in <u>Readings in Moral Theology, No. 1</u>, Curran & McCormick, Eds., New York: Paulist Press, 1975, p. 47.

25   Janssens, Louis, '*Ontic Evil and Moral Evil*,' in Curran, Charles E. and Richard A. McCormick, S.J., Eds., <u>Readings in Moral Theology No. 1. Moral Norms and Catholic Tradition</u>, New York, Paulist Press 1975, p. 40.

26   Ibid., p. 43.

27   Ontic evils are those that are not immoral but that merely cause pain or suffering (e.g. damage, injury, death or destruction caused by childbirth, disease, accidents or natural disasters).

28   Ibid., p 46.

29   Janssens, Op. Cit., pp. 43-44.

30   Curran and McCormick, Op. Cit., p. 86.

31   Gula, Richard M., <u>Reason Informed By Faith: Foundations of Catholic Morality</u>, New York, Paulist Press, 1989, p. 224.

32   Aquinas draws on Aristotle's *Nichomachean Ethics*. Aristotle begins from the premise that any useful knowledge must be a generalisation from experience. Nevertheless he thinks it is reasonable to take for granted that human action aims at its own good (a teleological approach). *Eudaimonia* is the ultimate end for humans, but Aristotle does not identify human *eudaimonia* with a hedonistic understanding of happiness. Rather he sees human flourishing in terms of fulfilment, and in particular of the fulfilment of our unique human faculty: reason. This is what separates us from other living creatures. Therefore the good life for humans, and the one that will bring us true *eudaimonia*, is a life well-lived according to reason.

33   Gula, Op. Cit., p. 222.

34   Ibid., p. 228.

35   Gula, Op. Cit., p. 225.

36   Ibid., p. 223.

37   Cahill, Lisa Sowle, <u>Sex, Gender and Christian Ethics</u>, Cambridge University Press, 1996, p. 50.

38   English translation: 'Joy and Hope'

39   *Towards a Quaker View of Sex*, Friends Home Service Committee, London, revised edition, 1964.

40   Curran, Charles E., 'Sexual Ethics: A Critique' in <u>Issues in Sexual and Medical Ethics</u>, University of Notre Dame Press, Notre Dame/London, 1978Curran, p. 38.

41   Ibid, p. 42.

42  Fuchs, Josef, 'The Absoluteness of Behavioural Moral Norms' in An Introduction to Christian Ethics, A Reader, Ronald P. Hamel and Kenneth R. Himes, Eds., New York, Paulist Press, 1989, p. 500.

43  Teilhard de Chardin, Pierre, Human Energy, New York: Harcourt, Brace, Jovanovich, Inc., 1969, p. 96.

44  This admonition is from a re-print in a Communiqué of the Press Office of the Holy See (appearing in the English edition of L'Osservatore Romano, July 20, 1981).

45  Kraft, R. Wayne, The Relevance of Teilhard, Fides Publishers, Inc., Notre Dame, Ind., 1968, p. 29.

46  Cf. Si Si No No, June 15, 1981, pp.1 sq. and Sept. 15, 1981 pp.5 sq.

47  Cochrane, Donald B., 'Christian Opposition to Homosexuality', in James McNinch and Mary Cronin, Eds., I Could Not Speak My Heart: Education and Social Justice for LGBT Youth, Regina, Saskatchewan Canadian Plains Research Centre, 2004. p.5.

48  Nugent, Robert, 'Homosexuality and Magisterial Teaching', Irish Theological Quarterly 53, 1987, p. 71.

49  Ibid.

50  Ibid, p. 72.

51  Jaggar, Alison M. & Struhl, Karsten J., 'Human Nature' in Warren T. Reich, Ed., Encyclopedia of Bioethics, Vol. 2., New York: Simon & Schuster, 1995, p. 1175 ff.

52  Kelly, Kevin T., New Directions in Moral Theology: The Challenge of Being Human, London: Geoffrey Chapman,1992, p. 70.

53  Schillebeeckx, Edward, 'The Human Person in Contemporary Theology: From Human Nature to Authentic Subjectivity' in Hamel and Himes, Eds., An Introduction to Christian Ethics, A Reader (New York: Paulist Press, 1989), p. 59.

54  Lennox, James G., 'Nature' in Warren T. Reich, ed. Encyclopedia of Bioethics, Vol. 4, New York: Simon & Schuster, 1995, p. 1816 ff.

55  Hughes, Gerard, 'Natural Law Ethics and Moral Theology' in The Month, March 1987, pp. 100-101.

56  Baldwin, Thomas Ed., Principia Ethica: Revised Edition, Cambridge University Press, 1993, esp. pp. 89-90. Moore's discussion of the naturalistic fallacy appears in Chapter II, section 24, paragraphs 2 and 3.

57  Hume, David, A Treatise of Human Nature (1739), III .i.i ., reprinted from the Original Edition and edited by L.A. Selby-Bigge, Oxford, Clarendon Press, 1896.

58  Cahill, Lisa, Between the Sexes: Foundations for a Christian Ethics of Sexuality, New York: Paulist Press, 1985, p. 147.

59    Cahill, Lisa, 'Moral Methodology: a Case Study' in R. Nugent Ed., <u>A Challenge to Love: Gay and Lesbian Catholics in the Church</u>, New York: Crossroad, 1983, p. 88.

60    Ibid., p. 88.

61    Gula, Richard M., <u>Reason Informed By Faith: Foundations of Catholic Morality</u>, New York, Paulist Press, 1989, pp. 220-21.

62    Schmidt, Thomas E., <u>Straight *and* Narrow? : Compassion and Clarity in the Homosexuality Debate</u>, Downers Grove, Illinois: InterVarsity Press, 1995, p.133.

63    Janssens, Louis, 'Norms and Priorities in a Love Ethics,' in *Louvain Studies* 4, Spring 1977, p. 216.

64    Berger, Peter and Luckmann, Thomas, <u>The Social Construction of Reality</u>, New York, Doubleday, 1966.

65    Magee, Bryan, <u>Popper</u>, Fontana Paperbacks, 1973, p. 18.

66    Schmidt, Op. Cit., p. 25.

67    Ibid., p. 26.

68    Ibid.

69    Ibid., p. 35.

70    Schmidt, Op. Cit., p. 133.

71    Curran, Charles E., 'Sexual Ethics: A Critique' in <u>Issues in Sexual and Medical Ethics</u>, University of Notre Dame Press, Notre Dame/London, 1978, pp. 42-3.

## CHAPTER 4

# *A New Approach to Natural Law Ethics: Basic Goods Theory*

*And I must beg of you to persevere, that the true rule of human life may become manifest. Tell me, then: -- you say, do you not, that in the rightly developed man the passions ought not to be controlled, but that we should let them grow to the utmost, and somehow or other satisfy them, and that this is virtue?*

-- Socrates [in Plato's *Gorgias*]

Before embarking on this chapter, a warning to the reader: much of what follows requires elaborate exposition of what amounts to a breathtakingly unfathomable exercise in Catholic casuistry. Anyone who does not have patience for long drawn out theoretical explanations that use abstruse terminology intended only for initiates or academics should skip this chapter.

The difficulties that plague the pre-modern natural law theory of ethics may explain the impetus behind what has been labeled a 'new natural law theory'. Germain Grisez and John Finnis have been the chief architects of this new approach to natural law, but other proponents and defenders include Robert P. George, Joseph M. Boyle and William E. May. Grisez and Finnis claim their work constitutes a reclamation of 'natural law' that is free of the problems that beset Aquinas's natural law theory.[1] Grisez understands his own project as that of providing a post-Vatican II system of ethics that avoids the problems inherent in the classic (scholastic) natural law position and provides an alternative to proportionalism. Proportionalist theories hold that *"it is never right to go against a principle unless there is a proportionate reason which would justify it"*.[2] At least two senses of proportionality are commonly encountered in moral theology: (1) means will be disproportionate if choosing them causes the end in view to be undermined, and (2) we should take into account all of the goods and evils involved to check that there is due proportion [or 'correct relation'] among them. The second sense of proportionality is the one most commonly adopted by proportionalists. Interestingly, Peter Knauer, whose writings are often described as the beginning of the debate on proportionalism, does not adopt this second sense.

Russell Hittinger locates the Grisez/Finnis system of natural law within a trend that started in the mid-sixties towards recovering what could be called a "pre-modern" ethics. In this recoverist movement Hittinger also includes Elizabeth Anscombe and Alaisdair MacIntyre. The Grisez/Finnis project is perhaps the most ambitious of the recoverist arguments for several reasons. The New Natural Law approach, says Hittinger, represents a systematic and comprehensive position that its advocates place on a par with Kantian ethics. They also purport to have saved the core of the classic natural law theory in a way that makes it persuasive to contemporary philosophers. Their project aims to shift the center of gravity for pre-modern ethics from its traditional locus in the Catholic Church to the secular academy, where proponents defend it by reason alone.[3]

I will start by outlining the purposes and methodology of the Grisez/Finnis school's approach to natural law (also sometimes referred to as the Basic Goods Theory or BGT), saving critical reflection on its merits for later. I will attempt to give only a concise overview of the theory first, followed by a more detailed account of aspects of the theory that yield norms in sexual ethics. Grisez wants to progress beyond both Kantian and Utilitarian theories of ethics because neither "considers material goods to be intrinsically related to the ultimate good of man".[4] He seeks to distinguish, within practical reason, between the (pre-moral) ***first principle of practical reason*** (that the goods ought to be pursued) and the *first principle of morality* (that they should be chosen in a way that respects the integrity of human well-being).

According to Grisez, Finnis and Boyle the most basic practical principles prescribe actions which people have reasons to perform because they constitute opportunities to realise for themselves and/or others benefits whose intelligible value is not merely instrumental.[5] The Grisez/Finnis view is that people can have non-instrumental reasons for action and "practical reason can determine the target."[6] Finnis has referred to reasons for action as 'rational motives'. These motives are distinguished from feelings, desires and other sub-rational motives.[7] Reasons for action can give positive moral guidance in ethics. The claim of Basic Good theorists (hereafter 'BGT') is that people can be motivated to pursue certain ends because of reasons constituted by the ends themselves. Accordingly, some ends are intrinsically and invariably worthy of pursuit, for any human being *as such* and in any situation. This is what they suppose gives us both reasons and (if we are clearheaded) desire to act for those ends.

George asserts that ethics begins from the question: What is human nature like? He then says this question concerns the human '*telos*'. He assumes that the answer this question seeks is knowledge of the **natural ends** constitutive of human fulfillment. [my bold] 'Good' in this formulation simply refers to those actions that conform to properly human ends; 'evil' refers to those actions that fail to so conform. "Once we acquire this knowledge", says George, "we can judge proposed actions according to their conformity, or lack of conformity, to these ends."[8] Accordingly, 'sound practical thinking' depends upon a methodologically prior anthropological inquiry. This yields the philosophy of human nature upon which moral philosophy rests. To the extent that we derive moral norms from speculative knowledge of human nature, nature is indeed normative.[9] As Grisez interprets him, Aquinas believed that ultimately any choice has its intelligibility by reference to the intelligible end(s) for which it is done.

The relevant issue for moral norms is their grounding in human nature, and theological and metaphysical inquiry yields the philosophy of human nature upon which moral philosophy rests.[10] George says that, far from being a kind of 'justice of nature,' the knowledge of human nature discovered by the inquiring intellect in the discipline of metaphysical anthropology is normative in the sense that it provides moral norms for free human choosing.[11]

Specific moral norms are not self-evident (in the natural order) but derived. So they must be derived from 'first principles' that **are** self-evident. The first principle of practical reason (**fppr**) and the first principle of morality (**fpm**) provide the foundations of moral arguments. Presumably these foundations about the pre-moral 'goods' that are relevant to deriving ethics, help us to progress beyond the old classicist version of natural law by narrowing the field of ethically relevant empirical facts to those that are 'good for us' to preserve and protect[12]. These foundations are not inferred from other beliefs but are self-evident and practical judgment can affirm them without the need for a derivation. George says, "one cannot argue one's way to them."[13]

The determinations of the **fppr** are the intrinsic goods that render human choices intelligible. The intrinsic goods to which they refer are called 'basic human goods' in the Grisez/Finnis system and they include anything that can be intelligibly chosen as an end-in-itself. In *Natural Law and Natural Rights* (1980), Finnis categorizes them as: Life (and health); knowledge; play; aesthetic experience; sociability (friendship); practical reasonableness; and 'religion'. In *Christian Moral Principles* (1983), Grisez lists these seven: self-integration; practical reasonableness; justice and friendship; religion or holiness; life and health; knowledge and aesthetic appreciation; and activities of skilful work and play, "which in their very performance, enrich those who do them."[14]

A similar sevenfold list to this last occurs, in reverse order, in *Practical Principles* (1991),[15] the main difference in the latter list is that "practical reasonableness" seems to have been replaced by a reference to "peace of conscience and consistency between one's self and its expression", which is intended to play the same general role in the theory as practical reasonableness (and "authenticity") did in the earlier lists. Grisez later added an eighth basic good to the previous seven – that of marriage.[16]

The basic goods are supposed to be regress-ending in that they require no further explanation. They provide the data needed to make a person's decision intelligible (i.e. rational, insofar as it has a point). So, how do we get from **fppr**'s to *moral* norms? George concedes that the basic goods are 'pre-moral' (or 'ontic') goods as opposed to moral goods. We need to have a way to distinguish morally upright decisions from those that are merely 'rational' *qua* intelligible. A rational egoist can be described as 'rational' insofar as he chooses means conducive to self-interested ends. But most people distinguish between morality and selfishness. And it is difficult to see how selfishness could provide a universal, law-like ground for ethics, since not even a rational egoist would wish to universalize an ethic based on selfishness.

It would seem that only if the BGT can get beyond mere rational egoism to rational *ethics* can their theory represent a legitimate rival to proportionalism.[17] To this end, Grisez and Finnis present their own set of general moral principles that structure and guide human choosing between merely **intelligible** human goods (ends). In *Natural Law and Natural Rights*, Finnis called these principles for choosing 'requirements of practical reasonableness'. Grisez and Finnis later labeled them 'modes of responsibility'. George notes that the Grisez/Finnis natural law theory resembles consequentialist ethical theories in certain ways.[18] In classic consequentialist ethics, the agent is directed to act in the way that is likely to produce the best proportion of good to bad consequences. But the consequentialist calculation requires that the desired ends of our actions are somehow commensurable, and so can be weighted against one another in order to calculate which choice will bring about the highest proportionate good. By contrast, Grisez and Finnis reject the commensurability of the human goods. They deny the existence of an objective hierarchy for choosing among the basic goods. Proportionalists do not argue for an 'objective' hierarchy but they do allow that we sometimes need to weigh different goods according to the total human situation we are striving to produce.

The 'modes of responsibility' are a set of general norms that form the criteria by which unreasonableness in human choosing can be identified.[19] The modes of responsibility provide guidelines for choosing between rationally-grounded possibilities. Roughly, the modes of responsibility connect the first principle of morality ('do good, avoid evil'), which is too vague to provide practical guidance in specific instances of choice, to specific norms for choosing in particular situations. The modes constrain choice to those actions alone that do not "involve willing in certain specific ways inconsistent with a will towards human fulfillment".[20] One of these modes forbids acting directly against a basic good, i.e. 'doing evil that good may come of it' (CMP, Ch. 26., question k). According to George, 'the first principle of morality' enjoins persons to "choose and otherwise will those and only those possibilities whose willing is compatible with integral human fulfillment." This is given more specific content: they exclude as practically **unreasonable (i.e. immoral)** various types of willing that are inconsistent with (or not 'open to') *all* of the human goods.[21]

George is quick to point out that no set of humanly possible choices *can* bring about overall integral human fulfillment. No human choice or set of choices can realize anything more than aspects of complete human well-being. As Finnis and Grisez put it, "[e]thics cannot be an architectonic art in that way; there can be no plan to bring about integral human fulfillment."[22] For Grisez and Finnis, the 'principle of integral human fulfillment' is an ideal that provides the standards by which choices may reasonably be guided. To choose with a will that another good be sacrificed or damaged is to seek a goal 'at the expense of reason, part of whose directiveness will have been ignored by choice.'[23] This choosing is the mark of immorality, not because the end willed is bad, but because it responds to the good imperfectly[24] (i.e. it does not respond to all of the goods in every act of choosing).

## The 'new natural law' theory and sexual ethics

Having outlined the 'new natural law' theory let us now turn to the specific ways in which this theory has treated sexual ethics. Only then will we see why it has arrived at the conclusion that homosexual behavior is morally wrong. As I explained above, Grisez added marriage to the list of basic goods in 1993, and his followers also include marriage among the basic human goods. Their definition of 'marriage' is the complementary union of man and woman as "two in one flesh".[25] They maintain that biologically, every animal, whether male or female, is a complete individual with the sole exception of reproduction, where each one is "only a potential part of the mated pair, which is the complete organism that is capable of reproducing sexually."[26] The union of opposite sexes (specifically their sexual organs), irrespective of any *actual* capability of reproducing, defines the complementary union as 'marriage'.

Grisez is careful to expunge the notion of human agency from his definition of "one flesh union" so that sub-voluntary functioning of glands and organs, not the intentions of the partners, are what 'make' the union exclusive and indissoluble:

> Even if couples planning to marry understand and accept that the good they desire calls for a truly mutual and entirely dependable relationship, they will realize, if they are clearheaded, that they themselves cannot make their marital union exclusive and indissoluble. If the union they are about to form is to have these properties, they will see, *it cannot be by their own wills but must be by virtue of something about one-flesh union itself which they must accept*, so that once they enter into that union, *nothing they subsequently choose or do* will be able to divide them from each other and/or unite them simultaneously in a similar union with someone else.[27] [my emphasis]

Basic Goods theorists derive sexual ethics from their (theological and metaphysical) definition of marriage. Accordingly, any non-marital sexual act violates the basic good of marriage and is therefore inappropriate and to be avoided.[28] A married couple's union depends upon mutual consent and must allow for the formal, but not actual, possibility of procreation.[29]

This outlook is consonant with Pope Paul VI's encyclical *Humanae Vitae* (1968). The encyclical reaffirmed that man may not on his own initiative break the inseparable connection "between the unitive significance and the procreative significance which are both inherent to the marriage act."

(*Humanae Vitae*, n. 12) The necessity of formal procreative potential was retained, while conceding that this could not be sufficient for sexual ethics. Procreative acts lacking interpersonal intimacy (eg. marital or non-marital rape) could be morally condemned, while the absolute necessity of formal procreative potential could be maintained. This move also ruled out any suggestion that the unitive aspect of the 'marital act' (ie. of sexual intercourse) could alone be sufficient to justify it. It followed that contraception and homosexuality were still disparaged. Consequently, all sexual activity outside the communion of marriage and all non-loving and necessarily non-procreative sexual activity within the communion of marriage were to be avoided. (*Humanae Vitae*, n. 11 & 12)

Robert George and Gerard V. Bradley follow the same reasoning, arguing that marriage, understood as a two-in-one flesh union of persons that is consummated in sexual acts of the reproductive type, is an intrinsic human good. As such, marriage provides a non-instrumental reason for spouses, whether or not they are capable of conceiving children in their acts of genital union, to perform such acts.[30] Accordingly, in choosing to perform non-marital orgasmic acts, persons necessarily treat their bodies and those of their sexual partners as instruments in ways that damage their personal (and interpersonal) integrity. Thus, regard for the basic human good of integrity provides a conclusive moral reason **not to** engage in non-marital sex acts.[31]

John Finnis, consistent with Grisez and George, claims that non-marital sex acts cannot realise any intrinsic common good. As such, homosexual acts cannot but be willed for instrumental reasons (i.e. reasons such as to express love or to give or receive pleasure). Finnis claims that in such willing, "the partners treat their bodies as instruments to be used *in service of their consciously experiencing selves*; their choice to engage in such conduct thus dis-integrates each of them precisely as acting persons."[32] [my emphasis]

## A critical assessment of the 'new natural law theory'

Having outlined the 'new natural law theory' and its approach to sexual ethics, let us now turn to the question of its success. For the purposes of this book, I will not present a full examination of the merits of this general approach to ethics, but will focus my assessment on aspects of this approach that directly impinge on sexual ethics.

The theory is haunted by the questionable assumption that a "theological and metaphysical" inquiry into human nature can yield an objective ground for ethics. Critics Jeffrey Goldsworthy, Nicholas Bamforth and David A.J. Richards claim the new natural law thus rests on a confused non-cognitivism.[33] Any natural law ethicist would agree with Robert George's claim that 'sound practical thinking' in ethics depends upon a methodologically prior anthropological inquiry. But for the new natural law proponents a speculative inquiry (which is theological and metaphysical) yields the philosophy of human nature upon which moral philosophy rests. "To the extent that we derive moral norms from speculative knowledge of human nature," says George, "nature is indeed normative."[34]

Critics[35] have attacked the methodology by which BGT defenders reach their conclusions about human nature. By their own admission, the BGT's anthropology is grounded not primarily in a broad range of empirical evidence, but in a speculative inquiry that is metaphysical and theological. This suggests that the New Natural Law methodology has not moved beyond that of the 'old' natural law methodology by incorporating a balanced set of references to empirical realities. Instead it tends to employ an abstract, deductive, *a priori* classicist worldview and methodology. I outlined some of the problems associated with this approach in Ch. 3 (ii.). Evaluations produced by this classicist methodology are based more on classical natural law definitions of the 'intrinsic' meaning and purpose of physical (and sexual) actions than on an empirical analysis of human actions based on vast human experience and interdisciplinary observations.

In Grisez's view, God's will for us is made manifest by the basic goods we rather mysteriously prescribe when we are ethical. As he puts it, the basic goods depend upon "the requirements which arise from the meanings and values God has embodied in his creation."[36] This resembles the 'preceptive' model of traditional Catholic natural law, in which immutable principles of divine law are 'inscribed' in nature and can simply be 'read' in truth by the discerning observer (see above, Ch. 3). Bamforth and Richards argue that such a form of alleged 'cognitivism' can only reasonably be understood as resting on a confused non-cognitivism, based ultimately upon faith in magisterial authority "that immunizes these views from any kind of accountability to rational assessment of relevant matters of fact bearing on the issues."[37] Bamforth and Richards point out that Grisez denies his views are noncognitivist while also denying they are naturalistic or intuitionistic. Consequently, Grisez needs another kind of "cognitivism" that grounds his moral imperatives not in facts, but in the creative action-guiding will, yet which also grounds the will in something more objective than the will itself. Cognitivism requires an objective ground from which ethical propositions can be verified or falsified. But since Grisez does not have the kind of objective grounds typical of moral cognitivism, he has to resort to rather mysteriously introducing his idea of basic goods. The basic goods, while not the naturalistic object of our rational desires, and not based in intuition, are nonetheless the goods in terms of which the creative will gives or makes ethical sense.[38] Since we can only make sense of Grisez's argument if we think of the BGT school as grounding it in the magisterium of Papal religious and moral authority, Bamforth and Richards conclude that the "cognitivism" of the new natural law ultimately depends upon a divine command theory of ethics.[39]

Similarly, Todd A. Salzman points out that both reason and experience have equal status within creation and within human experience – both provide knowledge from which moral truth can be discerned. He says there is a "curious tension" in the BGT's use of these two sources. Experience is a questionable source of moral knowledge, according to the BGT, especially if it leads to dissent from 'a constant and very firm moral teaching of the Church'.[40] If Salzman is correct, the BGT deploys a curiously selective form of empiricism that hasn't really progressed beyond the traditional 'classicist' natural law methodology.

Homosexuals can insist that prohibitionists follow John Paul II's imperative to seek the truth of the language of the body not in acts themselves but in the nature of the persons who perform them. (In his catechesis on the *Redemption of the Body and the Sacramentality of Marriage*, His Holiness said "marital intercourse combines within itself both the unitive and procreative dimensions" and that "the truth of the language of the body must be sought, not just in the act itself, but in the nature of the persons who perform it. The spouses themselves must read the language of the body in truth.") It seems to be the case, as *Persona Humana* (1975) acknowledged, that a proportion of the human species may be intrinsically homosexually orientated. If it turns out that homosexuality is a naturally occurring variant of human sexuality, this might lead to the conclusion that the procreative significance of the sexual act is *naturally and intrinsically* 'severed' from the unitive significance of sex for homosexual persons, and that consequently they *do* 'read the language of the body in truth' when choosing to engage in unitive, but non-procreative, sexual acts.

In the 1975 *Declaration on Certain Questions Regarding Sexual Ethics* (*Persona Humana*), the church took the step of recognizing irreversible homosexuality, or a homosexual orientation. In the same document, the church deployed medical language to promote a theological position, calling the variation "pathological" and "incurable" (VII, para. 2). While the declaration properly made a distinction between homosexuality as transitory behavior and homosexuality as definitive of the person, it used medical terminology in a non-medical context to stigmatize the variation. It also added a demoralizing message, claiming that, for the definitive homosexual, homosexual acts can never be justified as right (par. n. 8). *Persona Humana* asserts that the true meaning and value of human sexuality is to be found in two sources – revelation and the essential 'order of nature' where one finds the immutable principles of divine law. From this, absolute norms are extrapolated based on the function and nature of the sexual faculty and act (par. n. 1-5). Neither of these sources (revelation or the religiously discerned 'order of nature') is 'objective' in any scientific or medical sense. Both deploy theological definitions and criteria. Homophiles should demand to know why DNA or one's given sexual orientation, whatever its biological cause, is selectively excluded from the 'order of nature'. It may be that, if we read the language of the body in truth, we will discover that nature is simply less uniform than we supposed, or than we wish it to be. There is simply no reason to privilege the reproductive functions of the sexual organs over the given and naturally inscribed sexual orientation (whatever its biological origin). Nature has purposes that we do not always understand. Biodiversity is a fact of life, and not a 'disorder' vis-à-vis an anthropocentric concept such as the 'order of nature'. Instead of reading 'our' (theological or merely narcissistic) order into the natural facts, we should remain open to possible benefits or reasons for biodiversity – reasons possibly as beneficial as preventing over-population on a planet where resources are scarce.

It would seem that 'moral norms' are presupposed in the metaphysical and theological "inquiry", such that a particular set of anthropological facts is selected for emphasis and given the status of 'normativity' (by the appropriate Catholic authorities). This appears to be at odds with more universally accepted, empirical methods of inquiry into nature and anthropology. The imperative to adopt this particular theological 'knowledge' of the natural order yields a particular set of moral norms for choosing and this seems inconsistent with the kind of intellectual freedom we typically associate with intellectual objectivity. While Robert George maintains that the meaning and value of the 'natural order' is that it provides moral norms "for free human choosing", he also assumes there is only one choice/option that (prior to taking it) accords with divine intelligence. Thus his definition of 'freedom' is reminiscent of St. Paul's. The agent is 'free' to dissent from the theological view of moral norms and to take the punishment that rightfully comes with it. The "free choice" George describes is the freedom to *conform to* right action (as defined by a theological and metaphysical inquiry) or to dissent from it and therefore to do wrong.[41] The morally good agent is not free to express genuine intellectual dissent from the 'facts' as supplied by the appropriate theological authorities. George explains that one cannot affirm the proposition that 'there are no free choices' within a political context unless one chooses between either freely submitting to the authority's prescriptions of the norms of rationality on the one hand, or refusing to adhere to their prescriptions. This choosing is itself an instance of free choice, so any argument that this kind of legal positivism eliminates free choice is self-defeating.[42] George himself is a professor of jurisprudence, not theology. His understanding of the role of BGT natural law ethics is that the legislator makes this understanding of natural law effective for his community by deriving positive laws from it. This is little more than a recipe for authoritarian theocracy.

The "theological and metaphysical"[43] perspective may add to the natural facts some moral meaning or value, but there is no reason, other than faith, that non-initiates ought to subscribe to this perspective. I have to agree, therefore, with Bamforth and Richards, that this approach to sexual ethics resembles a divine command theory of ethics more than a natural law approach.

To the extent that ethics depend upon a philosophy of human nature, nature is normative.[44] Thus a great deal hinges on how 'nature' (or the 'natural end') is defined and understood within the theory. But the term 'nature' is notoriously difficult to define.[45] George describes this speculative inquiry into human nature as "theological and metaphysical". Other contemporary philosophers and revisionists see the inquiry as primarily empirical and existential.

Another problem with Basic Goods Theory is that human beings may not have a generic 'essence' of the kind its ethics presupposes. George distinguishes between possible actions that are mere 'possibilities' and those that are 'opportunities' – the latter are worth doing precisely because they have an intelligible point, i.e. promise some intelligible benefit for the class 'humans'. When Grisez, Finnis and Boyle refer to the basic human goods that provide non-instrumental reasons for action as the goods of 'particular persons,' they mean the genuine wellbeing and fulfillment of members of a generic class (*qua* human beings). This presupposes a class concept of human nature as an abstract, static and uniform set of traits. As such, it seems to revert back to the static anthropology found in traditional Catholic interpretations of Aquinas.

It is essential to notice that there is a metaphysical anthropology informing this new natural law theory according to which human flourishing ('integral human fulfillment') is synonymous with remaining open, in all of my actions, to **all** of the basic goods without suppressing **any** of them. This rules out any choosing in which one of the basic goods is suppressed or sacrificed to another. This is intended as a corrective to proportionalism. "Integral human fulfillment" provides the guiding behavioral norms that fulfill our human essence in *any* situation, and so provide for each individual person a blueprint for action that will ensure a fulfilled 'human' life. On this model, the abstract, *a priori*, definition of human nature comes first and furnishes the moral blueprint according to which individual human beings must choose if they are to fulfill themselves *qua* human beings.

This approach could be criticized for failing to reflect upon, and remain open to, experience. In reflecting upon what it means to be a human person, many Catholic and non-Catholic philosophers have favored an *a posteriori*, empirical methodology, beginning with particular human beings and observations about what fulfils them, and then moving from this inquiry to generalizations about human nature. When anthropological inquiry proceeds in this manner, the particulars of the situation are needed in order to understand the reasons (motives) for human choices, since even the description of the 'ends' of the action requires understanding the individual's motives in context. Yet neither the freedom necessary for this understanding of human agency nor the personal responsibility that flows from it is found amongst the 'basic goods' of the new natural law theory.

The very way in which the BGT authors describe these basic goods as 'self-evident' and as constituting non-instrumental goods, makes them appear very much as though they must be recognized as intrinsically valuable by 'any sane human being' just because it is in the nature of humans to recognize their value.[46] George never explains *how or why* these 'reasons for action' are anything other than the basic human instincts that we share with other species. Ralph McInerny explains:

> "Clearly there is no need of a precept commanding us to pursue goods to which we are naturally inclined. We do not require direction as far as the ends of natural inclinations are concerned. Such ends are givens of human nature: we do not choose to hunger or to thirst or to be attracted by the opposite sex. Yet Grisez's

understanding of determinations of the first practical principle, which he calls the natural law precepts, is precisely the judgment that the ends of natural inclinations are to be pursued, protected, etc. If that is what natural law precepts said, they would be otiose. We do not need to be told to hunger and thirst."[47]

As basic animal instincts, the basic goods seem to furnish a generic rule of action similar to Ulpian's *Jus Natural* – what nature has taught all animals. As such, they are open to same criticisms leveled against the putatively Thomistic model, namely that it failed (specifically in sexual ethics) to distinguish humans from other species of animals.[48]

There are also problems with the incommensurability of the basic goods. Living within the material realities of the world, we sometimes have intelligible reasons to instantiate both values and disvalues in a single action. Salzman uses the example of a therapeutic amputation to illustrate the way in which a moral agent might accomplish a pre-moral value (saving a person's life) while violating the integrity of the corporeal subject (pre-moral disvalue). According to revisionists, a conflict between competing pre-moral values and disvalues is resolved by using proportionate reason. Making a moral judgment requires actively weighing the basic goods in concrete situations. This, of course, depends upon the commensurability of values that the BGT denies. Janssens's "personalist" criterion allows for the fact that concrete situations frequently constrain our ability to realize all of the basic goods, and in some cases, we must sacrifice one for another to bring about the best possible situation for human persons. For example, circumstances might demand that we choose between life and friendship, and it would not be too difficult to work out that saving a life ought to be prioritized over saving a friendship, if confronted with a conflict between them.

While BGT defenders deny that the basic goods can be weighed in this way, they are not entirely consistent on this point when it does not furnish their desired conclusions in applied ethics. In order to generate their traditional conclusions in sexual ethics, they need to introduce an ever more complex set of terms, such as the seemingly arbitrary distinction between 'direct' and 'indirect' acts of killing.

George writes:

> "The modes thus provide premises for the often complex moral
> analysis by which persons can reason their way to specific moral
> norms. While our grasp of the modes gets moral argument off
> the ground, it does not always make such arguments easy. Often,
> extremely careful and insightful analysis is required to determine
> whether a proposed act of, say, killing is direct and therefore
> impermissible; or, where an act of killing is clearly indirect, it
> sometimes takes equally subtle analysis to establish the fairness or
> unfairness (forbidding unfairness is one of the modes) of the act."[49]

The BGT theorists *generally* reject any definitive connection between act
and intention. That is, the agent's end goal is not what 'characterizes' the
act as, say, an act of 'justice' or of 'sadism' or of 'self-defense'. However, in
the case of a woman who shoots a would-be rapist in self-defense, the BGT
theorists argue that the death of the rapist is neither willed as an end nor
chosen as a means; it is completely unintended. The act that she intended
was self-defense.[50] The agent's aim in acting can be described solely by
reference to the good *end* she seeks. Here it does not seem to matter that
she neglects the basic good of "life" in choosing this end. Her act can be
described with reference to the ultimate good she seeks (her end goal)
rather than with reference to the bad means by which it is accomplished, as
when Finnis (though not Grisez) describes capital punishment as 'justice'.

But this just is to define the act by reference to the agent's purpose in
acting within the entire human situation, which makes the method of
defining it indistinguishable from that of proportionalism. As a rule, BGT
defines the moral status of an act according to whether it successfully
includes *all* of the basic goods (and neglects none), except in these most
contentious cases where we find BGT defenders resorting to another
(proportionalist) methodology to define the act. In these, but only these,
exceptional cases the fact that the act involves neglecting a 'basic good'
is treated as unimportant to its definition and hence unimportant to its
moral status. It is a mystery why the homosexual act, or the decision to
terminate a pregnancy in some instances, could not likewise be defined
according to this 'special' standard. It seems that where BGT defenders

want to reserve the right to kill, they depart from their own reasoning (and use proportionalist ethics) to generate the desired conclusions.

BGT proponents insist there is a necessary connection between contraception and a will that directly attacks the good of life. Grisez and Boyle write, 'contraceptors necessarily foresee that a baby might come to be, they want that foreseen baby not to come to be, and they choose to do something to make it less likely that he or she will be.' This would seem to foreclose the possibility that the contraceptor may will another good (eg. prevention of AIDS or other diseases) by means of practicing contraception. Salzman asks why is it that, in the case of self-defence, there is no necessary relationship between the act of wounding/killing the assailant and the intention to defend oneself, while in the case of contraception there *is* a necessary relationship between artificial birth control and a contralife will?[51]

Grisez says it is necessary that contraception be seen as a single, indivisible act (quite apart from the sexual act). He offers two arguments for why this must be so. (1) One can practice contraception independently of a sexual act. (2) A couple considering whether to fornicate has two distinct choices to make: whether or not to fornicate and/or to contracept.

There are several replies to this. Edward Vacek, S.J.[52] argues that contraception certainly is intended as part of a sexual act, otherwise it would be an act of self-mutilation (Grisez's example was a man who gets sterilized and then cannot find a sexual partner). Second, as Porter and Vacek have argued, there is no necessary logical relationship between a contraceptive act and a contralife will.[53] Depending upon the will of the agent, contracepting can have many purposes, and preventing fatal diseases like AIDS could be one of them. In addition, preventing a new life from beginning is not the same as willing an existing life to end. Contracepting cannot be contra-life unless there is some life towards which it is 'contra'. Anyway, from the wider perspective of current Catholic doctrine, infertility does not render heterosexual intercourse 'contra-life', and indeed constitutes 'marriage'. So if contracepting is 'contra-life' the reason why it is so must be explained in other terms not related to infertility.

"According to BGT, contraception, understood accurately in terms of the intention involved, is always contralife."[54] Certainly, says Salzman, "when the act or corresponding will or motives are *defined in this way*, the act and the norm forbidding it are absolute."[55] The significant question is whether or not, by definition, certain motives are necessarily entailed in certain acts. As Salzman puts it, "the question is whether or not, by definition, certain motives necessarily correspond, logically or causally, to certain acts."[56] BGT does not allow for the possibility that one could practice contraception with a will directed immediately towards responsible parenthood, AIDS prevention or anything else. Nor does it allow that an act of capital punishment might be undertaken with a sadistic will for revenge. The causal arrow in terms of characterizing the act *as an act of a particular kind* seems to point backwards from the material effect or the means ("life ended") to the agent's will ("therefore his will was contralife"). In the case of contraception, no actual life even has to end in order for the act to earn the stigma attached to the "contralife will". For the contraceptor, it is enough that the agent neglected to bring new life into existence when she had the opportunity. With respect to homosexual activity the claim is that such acts "disintegrate" the agent or damage his personal integrity. For sexually active homosexuals, this choosing is the mark of immorality, not because the end willed is bad, but because it responds to the good imperfectly. To choose with a will that another good ("marriage") be sacrificed or damaged is to seek a goal "at the expense of reason, part of whose directiveness will have been ignored by choice."[57] Yet in the case of capital punishment, the general rule of defining an act according to its openness to the sum of basic goods ("life, a basic good, was violated") does not even apply.[58]

The BGT posits a necessary connection between certain acts and the orientation of the will that chooses those acts. With other, equally controversial, acts (capital punishment) it leaves interpretation of the orientation of the will open to "extremely careful and insightful analysis". This may be convincing to those who already share the conclusions generated by such analysis. To others, it is not.

Salzman's criticism - that BGT theorists diverge from modern moralists by denying the role of human will/intention in discerning the objective definition of an action – seems generally correct, except in some "complex" cases, such as capital punishment, where BGT proponents don't like the conclusions furnished by their own reasoning, and so have to adopt a more modern outlook. Without any consistent criterion for defining an act of killing as "justice" as opposed to "anti-life", it is difficult to see how to distinguish (morally) between an act of contraception, an act of abortion, an act of capital punishment, or an act of self-defense. Robert George says the **fpm** helps us to clarify the standard by which we 'characterize' the act. He says that the modes help us to get "moral argument off the ground", but do "not always make such arguments easy. Often, extremely careful and insightful analysis is required to determine whether a proposed act of, say, killing is direct and therefore impermissible; or, where an act of killing is clearly indirect . . ."[59] George ultimately concedes that the only method by which we might decide the matter is "extremely careful and insightful analysis". This leaves unanswered how we can judge whether the analysis is 'insightful'. In respect of what should it be 'careful'? Even Basic Goods Theory (BGT) sympathizer Timothy Chappell is troubled by the over-easy progress from the **fpm** to ethical norms. He concedes that this could lead to the cynical conclusion that the modes of responsibility have simply been generated *ad hoc* to produce certain conclusions in applied ethics.[60] Proportionalism furnishes a more consistent ethical guideline, by defining the agent's act, with reference to the proportionate good sought by means of the act, i.e. by reference to the object of the agent's will.

The will of a homosexual agent in engaging in consenting homogenital sex acts cannot properly be defined by reference to the act's procreative potential or lack thereof. Rather, it must be defined by reference to its interpersonal aspects, or the total personal situation – the proportionate good sought. Nothing about procreation (or "marriage") is so essential to human nature that it ought to be a requirement of every human act. Nothing about the possibility of bringing new life into existence makes an act that does not participate in it tantamount to murder or a "contra-life" will. If so, then cooking dinner or doing laundry or choosing to watch television instead of having heterosexual intercourse would be acts undertaken with a "contra-life" will.

George says we need to have a way to distinguish morally upright decisions from those that are merely rational/intelligible. He points out that the basic human goods are "in a sense" pre-moral. He says: "...the general prescription to act for the sake of health grounds the **rationality** of [an agent's] decision, it says nothing about whether that decision was **morally** required or even permissible."[61] If it is true that the **rationality** (i.e. 'reasonableness') of acting to fulfill pre-moral goods (like health) **says nothing about what is *morally required/right*,** then the converse is also true, i.e. the **irrationality** of failing to protect/preserve those pre-moral goods **says nothing about what is *morally wrong.*** If the mere 'intelligibility' of a choice isn't enough to make it morally good, then the absence of the 'intelligibility' of a choice cannot make it morally bad.

George is quick to point out that no set of humanly possible choices *can* bring about overall fulfillment (i.e. "integral" human fulfillment). Yet this is precisely what is needed in order to conclude that neglecting part of the set is a moral failure. No human choice or set of choices *can* realize anything more than aspects of complete human well-being. As Finnis and Grisez put it, "[e]thics cannot be an architectonic art in that way; there can be no plan to bring about integral human fulfillment." Nevertheless, for Grisez and Finnis, **the 'principle of integral human fulfillment' is an ideal that provides the standards by which choices may reasonably be guided.** [my bold] But, if this standard does not require that humans realize *all* of its ideals in order to be moral (since this is admittedly humanly impossible), then nor can a human's failure to realize *any one of them* constitute immorality. "In an immoral choice," says George, "the failure to respond to the first principles taken as a whole may be judged 'imperfect' in a way that morally upright choices may not."[62] But this cannot be seen as a 'failure' or as 'imperfect' form of human choosing if, as they admit, it is *impossible* for humans to respond perfectly to the first principles "taken as a whole". Imperfect choosing is, by their own logic, the *only* kind of choosing of which humans are capable. The BGT theorists seem to both accept and deny that 'ought implies can'.

The key dispute in Catholic sexual ethics is with the narrowness and selectivity of the facts the Vatican has averted to when reaching conclusions in sexual ethics. What seems common to the experience of all human beings of any sexual orientation is that we experience ourselves as the authors of our own lives, as beings who make choices, and conceive of ourselves as responsible agents. We are conscious of our subjective will guiding our behavior. We are aware of our ability to decide whether and when to act upon our instinctive urges and natural inclinations. We can, and do, curb our appetites and control and direct our natural inclinations, according to a social awareness of ourselves as members of a human community. We feel it just that we should take credit for our virtues and take blame for injustices we may visit upon others. We experience our achievements as the products of our efforts and we measure our failures only against potentials we actually possess. Experiencing ourselves as responsible agents is essential to the *moral* evaluation of human sexual acts.

As we have seen, Grisez and his followers include marriage amongst the basic human goods. Their definition of 'marriage' is the complementary biological union of man and woman as "two in one flesh".[63] In reproduction, each single animal is "only a potential part of the mated pair, which is the complete organism."[64] It is the union of biologically opposite sexual organs, irrespective of any *actual* capability of reproducing sexually, which exclusively defines this kind of complementary union as 'marriage'.

Gareth Moore O.P. has argued that this approach to the definition of marriage conflates the sub-voluntary functioning of glands and organs and the voluntary (hence specifically personal, morally relevant) activity of an animal.[65] Moore argues that a mating pair is not a single complete organism as Grisez supposes, but two organisms participating in a joint activity of mating. This may appear to be a rather pedantic point, but Grisez's definition of "one flesh unity" plays a pivotal role in his later claims about sexual ethics. Unless the premise about "one flesh unity" is coherent, the conclusions it generates will be vitiated.

Central to Grisez's argument is the idea that what makes the one flesh union a 'marriage' (and indissoluble) is not human agency, since, "it cannot be by their own wills but must be by virtue of something about one-flesh union itself."[66] As in Catholic teaching, the prospective couple will see, if they are clearheaded, that procreative potential (the biological union of male and female) is a *necessary,* even if not sufficient, element of any morally upright sexual activity ('marriage'). But as Moore points out, clearheaded couples *do* make their relationships so that they either have, or do not have, the qualities of exclusivity and/or permanence. There is nothing about the biological union itself that renders the human relationship "exclusive" or "indissoluble". If the union they are about to form is to be exclusive and permanent, then it will be so because they work/choose to make it so. It will not be by virtue of the nature of the one-flesh union as such.[67] If people thought that they could not make (i.e. be responsible for constructing) exclusive and permanent relationships then they would never attempt to enter into such relationships. But they do. Arguably, the unitive aspect is more essential to making them "exclusive and indissoluable" than the reproductive aspect, as evidenced by happy, monogamous couples who either cannot or choose not to reproduce.

Experience has taught us that our present intentions and desires to form lasting relationships are not always sufficient to make it so, but this is no reason to disparage the voluntary nature of human relationships. In this respect marriage is no different from any other human project. All human undertakings are fallible, and to ritualize and fetishize biological aspects of a human endeavor in an attempt to guarantee its success is to resort to superstition and tokenism. According to Grisez, once a couple enters into this one-flesh union, nothing they subsequently do will separate them from each other. But the alleged "one-flesh union" cannot give couples anything but an abstract, metaphysical definition of permanent 'unity,' and this is not what human persons understand by 'unity'. It seems the guarantee of permanence offered by Grisez's metaphysical and theological definition of 'unity' is little more than wishful thinking.

The BGT derives sexual ethics from their (theological and metaphysical) definition of marriage. Any non-marital (ie. essentially non-procreative) sexual act violates the basic good of marriage and is therefore inappropriate and to be avoided.[68] A married couple's union depends upon mutual consent *and must allow for the possibility of procreation.*[69]

There are two problematic assertions within BGT's approach to sexual morality. First is the claim that essentially non-procreative sexual activity is necessarily non-marital. Grisez makes reproductive capacity an element of mutual love in the sexual acts of married partners:

> A marital act expresses and fosters the couple's marital communion precisely because, when they willingly and lovingly cooperate with each other in an act itself suited to procreating, their mutual self-giving actualizes their one-flesh unity. If one or both spouses engage in a sexual act which does not realize one-flesh unity in this way, that act is not marital.[70]

A good deal hinges on Grisez's definition of "one-flesh unity". We have seen Gareth Moore's argument (above) that the married couple do not have this kind of unity and hence such unity is not actualized by any act of theirs, sexual or otherwise. We might choose to agree with Moore and simply reject the premise that a mating pair is a single complete organism as Grisez supposes.

The contention that any non-marital sexual activity violates the good of marriage is equally troublesome. The difficulty lies in the assumption that an act's inherent procreative potential is essential to its ability to foster 'marital' communion and that an act must foster marital communion in order to be a 'marital act'. Surely any voluntary and loving joint activity (hanging shelves, dancing together, sharing a joke, preparing a meal together) would, like procreative sexual intercourse, strengthen marital communion. These other joint activities do not make a union marital, but they do strengthen personal communion, whether marital or not. It is difficult to see why a joint sexual non-procreative sexual act should not achieve the same effect. Grisez's answer is to say that such non-procreative sexual acts are undertaken for motives which are "at odds" with the marital communion. Hence any non-procreative sex act, whether between married partners or non-married partners (whether homosexual or heterosexual)

> . . . cannot be an act of conjugal love, that is, the reciprocal self-giving which brings about one-flesh unity. So, their actions must have other motives, which, even if they include mutual affectionate feelings, are unintegrated with conjugal love and more or less at odds with it.[71]

The sexual act in question is held to be non-marital by its form taken apart from the end goals of the couple. With reference to homosexual intercourse Grisez says, "The coupling of two bodies of the same sex cannot form one complete organism and so cannot contribute to a bodily communion of persons."[72] This lack of 'one flesh union' is what makes such acts wrong.

As with other non-marital forms of sexual activity the *moral* deficiency of homosexual acts is not in the act performed but in the agent's *will* or *choice* to perform the wrong action. To participate in such non-marital sexual acts is, Grisez claims, "to choose a specific kind of self-disintegrity".[73] To choose self-disintegrity is always morally bad, because it damages the basic good of self-integration, which violates the eighth mode of responsibility (*do no evil that good might come of it*).[74] But again, choosing to be a sexually active homosexual could only be to choose with a will to self-disintegrity if one accepted Grisez's apparent presupposition that one's given sexual orientation is not as 'basic' or integral to the self as 'one flesh union'. Most homosexuals do not accept this premise. Their sexual acts say nothing obvious about their will. We can't just assume that *Grisez's interpretation* of the object (end purpose) of their will is the same as their own in choosing it. This would imply that Grisez's interpretations of other people's motives can infallibly be 'read off' from the structure of the sexual act. This is what he has to prove.

Robert George and Gerard V. Bradley follow the same reasoning in arguing that, in choosing to perform non-marital orgasmic acts, persons necessarily treat their bodies and those of their sexual partners as instruments in ways that damage their personal (and interpersonal) integrity. George and Bradley identify "regard for the basic human good of integrity" as a conclusive moral reason **not to** engage in non-marital sex acts.[75] Again, this begs the question as to whether homosexual attraction and the corresponding forms of behavior are integral to some persons' bodies and persons.

Gareth Moore says that this neglects the 'intentional' element in choice. The intentional aspect relates to my understanding of the object of my choice. Moore explains:

> In choosing to drink from the cup I may end up drinking strychnine, but to choose to drink from the cup is not to choose to drink strychnine. It becomes a choice to drink strychnine only if I know that the cup contains strychnine. If I do not know that, . . . this shows nothing about my will; it will not be a choice to commit suicide.

Likewise,

> my choice to masturbate is a choice to fall into self-disintegrity only if I know that masturbating has this effect. It may be that my choice to masturbate is an unfortunate one, since I will end up damaging my self-integrity, but again this shows nothing about my will; if I masturbate, it will not be morally reprehensible or violate any modes of responsibility unless I actually hold the same view about masturbation that Grisez does.[76]

Moore's argument shows that unless we grant the premise that 'self-integrity' is damaged by non-marital sexual acts, we need not accept the conclusion that we act with a bad will when we do these things. Only if the integrity of my acts were to require the 'procreative' element could I be guilty, in any moral sense, of harming my own integrity by failing to make all of my acts "open to" the good of "marriage". If my intrinsic sexual orientation makes this kind of "marital" (procreative) sexual attraction impossible for me, the possibility could not exist for me to be 'integrated' by heterosexual acts. Neither can my choice to perform non-"marital" (procreative) sex acts be an act of 'self-disintegration'.

John Finnis claims that non-marital sex acts cannot realize any intrinsic common good. Such acts, he says, cannot but be willed for instrumental reasons. Finnis claims that in such willing, "the partners treat their bodies as instruments to be used *in service of their consciously experiencing selves*; their choice to engage in such conduct thus dis-integrates each of them precisely as acting persons."[77] [my emphasis] But it is difficult to see how instrumental reasons for willing these non-marital sex acts (e.g. to express love or to give pleasure to one's partner, or to deepen the intimacy between oneself and another) dis-integrates them as agents. It is precisely because *consciousness directs* these instinctual drives towards interpersonal, consciously chosen ends, that we can see them as integral to our humanity. Absent this integration with consciousness and will, it is difficult to see how sex acts are anything more than a set of involuntary instinctual drives. Without the conscious subject willing to direct these drives in deliberate ways, it is difficult to see how we would make any moral judgments about them.

Implicit in the BGT proponents' use of the term "disintegration" is a particularly dubious definition of what its opposite means. "Integration" of the self, in their view, refers to the union of male and female reproductive organs as the essential and definitive thing that makes sexual partners experience their 'real common good'. Crucial to this view is the notion that the reproductive function of the human genitalia (even if not functional to that end due to infertility) is somehow definitive of, not merely a means to, unity with another human being. Neither subjectivity, nor the intended end goal of a person's behavior, is sufficient to define the personal reality of his or her marriage; rather, what makes the union a "marriage" is the biological union of opposite sexual organs, irrespective of any *actual* procreative capacity they may have. This seems hopelessly arbitrary. What, other than fixation on a tautology, makes the union of opposite sexual organs inherently more 'marital' or more integral to the couple's 'common good' than the union of their tongues or the union of their minds or their wills in a common activity or project?

Even if we were to accept the "one-flesh union" premise, Grisez and his followers would still need to show that such union is the only form of bodily communion of persons.[78] If he cannot then we may conclude that homosexuals can enjoy through their bodily union a form of bodily communion other than one-flesh union. As Moore says:

> The experience of intimacy they have in their intercourse may not be the experience of marital union, but it by no means follows that it is not the experience of any real unity between them. That could only be so if marital union were the only real unity between people, which is plainly not the case.[79]

Grisez and BGT theorists admit that development of moral doctrine (eg, in the case of slavery where the development of moral doctrine went from condoning to forbidding it [80]) occurs 'because of the unfolding understanding of the human good.'[81] But instead of explaining how this unfolding could take place, Grisez goes on the attack, and says that certain moral prohibitions are based on aspects of the human goods that are already understood. This raises the further question of how we can discern those aspects of the basic goods that are already understood as opposed to those that are not entirely understood and are, therefore, open to revision. Salzman asks, "Why is it that the aspect of the human good of justice that involves liberty in the case of slavery was open to refinement, with a corresponding revision of the norms deduced from the specifications of the **fpm**, while the human good of marriage and the prohibition of specific types of reproductive technologies, are not?"[82]

The strength of revisionism is that it can transform our conception of the basic goods and the norms founded on them in the light of human experience and progress. Experience challenges abstract generalisations about humanity/human nature. Salzman seems to grasp the most pressing issue for future debates about homosexual prohibitionism when he writes:

> "Finally, scientific experience, knowledge, and developments are posing new questions that require new answers. . . . For instance, the successful mapping of the human genome will have profound implications on our formulation of norms in light of the basic goods of life, knowledge and skilled performance. New norms will have to be formulated to determine what is and is not an ethical use of medical technology to restore or maintain health."[83]

We saw (above) how Bamforth and Richards argued that BGT deploys a peculiar form of 'cognitivism' since its self-evident views about sexual morality can only be understood as 'self-evident' from the perspective of faith in magisterial authority.[84] Such authority, say Bamforth and Richards, "immunizes these views from any kind of accountability to rational assessment of relevant matters of fact bearing on the issues."[85] I have suggested (above) that the BGT reading of the facts is too narrow and selective. The BGT's cognitivism, it seems, does not represent development beyond the kind of reasoning used by St. Paul. As noted in Chapter 1, whether or not "non-marital" (homogenital) forms of sexual expression constitute 'natural' variants of human sexuality is not 'self-evident' by virtue of a theological/moral set of definitions of 'nature' but is an empirical question, and as such is 'self-evident' only to the extent that it reflects good evidence. Today, vast human experience coupled with research into human genetics and early brain development promise the best means of resolving what is or is not a 'natural' (i.e. naturally occurring) variant of human sexuality.

The BGT does allow for the possible unfolding understanding of a basic good based on experience that would allow for the complete reversal of a specific moral norm, and it is very clear on the primary criterion for justifying such a development: the magisterium is the only authority that can judge in this area.[86] Revisionists and most citizens in liberal democracies reject the notion that the Catholic magisterium is the ultimate determinant of moral truth irrespective of evidence and argument. History justifies such caution. For revisionists, the basic goods are knowable through human experience and good evidence. The material norms that guide behavior are contextually dependent and "the anthropology on which 'human fulfillment' is dependent can evolve as well, with repercussions for understanding the basic goods."[87]

Timothy Chappell says that it is plausible to claim that there is no more explaining an action once one has claimed that it is aimed at achieving the good of, say, friendship or knowledge. But to say that marriage is an intrinsically intelligible end of action in the same way "seems quite hopeless".[88] It is perfectly intelligible to ask why marriage is a good thing in a way that it is arguably not intelligible to ask why friendship or knowledge are good things. It seems that whatever it is that makes marriage a good thing is explicable in terms of the other basic goods anyway. Grisez himself virtually admits that what makes marriage a good is that it instantiates other basic goods when he writes that "marriage is a special kind of open-ended community".[89] But, says Chappell, to admit this is surely just "to admit that marriage is *not* a basic good, but a case of the basic good of sociability."[90] This leaves unanswered whether all marriages always conform to the basic good of sociability. It would only be so if all marriages were good marriages. Divorce statistics suggest that many marriages are not conducive to the mutual wellbeing of both partners, and may sometimes be destructive or abusive.

The inclusion of marriage among the basic goods also overlooks the fact that there are many cultural conceptions of marriage. Which of these conceptions of marriage found in different societies is *the* "basic good of marriage"? Is a polygamist partaking of the basic good of marriage when he takes his seventeenth wife? Does a twelve year-old girl partake in the basic good of marriage when her family give her to a man more than twice her age?

Grisez argues that "the givenness and fundamental unalterability of natural inclinations account for the unalterability of the principles of natural law. . ."[91] This appears to make 'natural inclinations' or 'givens' of human nature - plus the will to conform to them -- sufficient to an understanding of human personhood. Revisionists do not dispute that unalterable natural facts and life circumstances form a significant part of our human experience. Jean Paul Sartre described these unalterable aspects of an individual's situation as 'facticity'.[92] This category includes those aspects of my being that are fixed, e.g. upbringing, parents, social or economic situation, one's personal past history, race, sex, and disability. It probably includes sexual orientation as well. But these do not, in themselves, constitute a normative account of what we must do. Rather they set the limits within which it is possible for us to make decisions and take responsibility. George himself admits that whatever does not depend on free choices is not the responsibility of the individual, and is ultimately God's responsibility.[93] (So, at least here, he accepts that 'ought implies can'.)

In his *Treatise of Human Nature*, David Hume famously (or notoriously) claimed reason is, and ought only to be, the slave of the passions. Hume's idea was that reason's fundamental purpose is to serve ends determined by the natural inclinations. By contrast, Kant felt that reason's purpose was not only as a means to get whatever we happen, naturally or instinctively, to want.[94] Rather, reason is what allows us to discern what we ought to want, or which ends we ought to seek, irrespective of our arbitrary, self-centered, and sub-voluntary desires. The BGT has a distinctly Humean flavor that makes Hittinger's "recoverist" label quite fitting. Chappell quotes *Hume's Enquiry Concerning the Principles of Morals* where the latter asserts that the ultimate ends of human action are never accounted for by reason, but recommend themselves entirely to the sentiments.[95] Chappell says it is doubtful whether, in Hume's view, there can be any serious moral theory at all. Hume's theory leaves no room for a distinction between selfishness and morality. Consequently, the only ethic he could take seriously was egoism – the notion that we should only ever act altruistically because it is in our own interests to do so, primarily because altruism gives us a kind of refined pleasure.

The Grisez school seems to follow Hume in giving ethical significance to our natural inclinations. They claim our natural inclinations are neither arbitrary nor contingent.[96] They are universal and binding upon all human beings in a universal way. It follows that natural inclinations can furnish us with some foundations for ethics – namely an account of the basic goods. These goods are recognized by all humans just as such. Even if this is so, BGT defenders offer no guidelines for choosing if conflicts should arise between fulfillment of my self-interested human well-being and the interests/well-being of others. Aristotelian, Kantian and modern liberal ethicists, by contrast, see the uniquely human capacity for reason as what separates us from other species, and from 'swine' (pace Mill[97]). Mill's understanding of 'pleasure' gives to human pleasure a much higher form than the satisfaction of, say, pigs. He follows Epicurus in adopting a definition of 'pleasure' that involves "absence of pain in the body and of trouble in the soul". In a letter to Menoeceus, Epicurus expressed his view that pleasure is not possible in the absence of prudence, honor and justice. He could not divorce the concept of pleasure from that of virtue. Mill too felt that, not only were the social and interpersonal virtues a 'higher' form of pleasure than those of satisfying basic physical needs, but that the self-determination and autonomy necessary to an ethical life were what made liberty so valuable.

Revisionists, proportionalists and liberals do not dispute that there are many pre-moral/material goods that appeal to any human being simply by virtue of our natural inclinations (instincts). They also agree that facts, including facts about human nature, ought to be relevant to moral evaluations of human acts. But they reject the idea that moral values are implicit in particular involuntary biological facts of nature.

The Grisez school have distinguished their ethics from rational egoism (or, in Robert George's words, from a "Humean theory of ethics") by excluding pleasure from the basic goods. The BGT school claim that pleasure is not an "intelligible good" and therefore not a basic good (although it is, apparently, a basic motive or instinctual drive common to the human species). The action done solely in pursuit of pleasure is fully explicable ('intelligible') --- but physical pleasure does not necessarily contribute to "integral human fulfilment". The Grisez school have found it necessary to add a distinction between 'sensible goods' and 'intelligible goods'. In *Christian Moral Principles*, Grisez writes:

> "If one confuses sensible and intelligible sources of motivation and takes pleasure and pain to be basic principles of human action, one's conception of action will be distorted. There is an intelligible aspect under which one can choose pleasure and seek to avoid pain, namely, the lessening of tension or increase in harmony among various parts of oneself. [But] emphasis on pleasure and pain tends to focus concern upon oneself and to distract attention from the larger possibility of finding one's fulfillment by participation in community, ultimately the heavenly fellowship."[98]

Timothy Chappell argues that this begs the question, since nobody can be confusing "sensible and intelligible sources of motivation" unless that distinction actually exists, which is precisely what Grisez has yet to prove.[99] The Grisez school distinguish their ethics from Hume's ethics by denying that pleasure is a basic good. Physical pleasure is not, for them, an 'intelligible' good, since it does not necessarily contribute to integral human fulfilment. But we might point out that nor does 'marriage' *necessarily* contribute to integral human fulfilment. Grisez says that pain does not have the character of a privation, and it is "no less beneficial to the organism than pleasure."[100] Even so, the relegation of pleasure to a mere 'sensible' good and not an 'intelligible' ("basic") one is difficult to comprehend in light of the BGT school's original definition of the basic goods as 'anything that is actually desired as an end-in-itself'. Since they think our natural inclinations are neither arbitrary nor contingent but universal and binding upon all human beings in a universal way, it is strange that pleasure is left out of the 'natural inclinations'. Why marriage is desired as an end in itself while pleasure is not is difficult to comprehend.

The new natural law theorists merely propose, and claim they need only propose, that there are good things that are intrinsically valuable for human beings as such. Revisionists are cautious in accepting this premise, for it makes no distinction between pre-moral/material values (food, shelter, survival, health, reproduction) and moral values (pursuing these things in responsible and appropriate ways). BGT seems to presuppose that pursuing the right set of (external, material) goods is always equivalent to having a good (internal, morally upright) motive.

Crucially, revisionists and proportionalists make a distinction between pre-moral (material) goods/evils and moral goods/evils. If six million Jews die because of an epidemic disease this is a pre-moral evil, and is correctly viewed as bad, because it is unpleasant and destructive of human flourishing. But if six million Jews die because of a humanly orchestrated holocaust, this is a *moral* evil, and we do well to ascribe blame to those responsible. We ascribe blame to agents, not to acts. Likewise, if a child is born into a privileged American family and can afford to eat three square meals a day, this is a pre-moral good. A full human belly is good in the sense that it is pleasant and contributes to good health. But we don't shower *moral* praise on people for feeding their appetites, as this is only natural and instinctive, just like the desires to procreate or to avoid pain. Often the human predicament demands that we are forced to choose between material goods and moral goods, such as when we might have to forego a material good in order to avoid a moral evil. Arguably, eating, gaining knowledge, marrying and reproducing are motivated by subconscious selfish instinct, not by voluntary *moral* choice. Most people intuitively distinguish between selfish, instinctive behavior that is to one's own benefit and moral behavior, which is other-regarding. There is nothing about natural human pre-moral goods, either singly or collectively, that automatically makes them inherently morally choiceworthy. Rather, the basis for judging an act right or wrong is the proportion of premoral goods to evils brought about within the total personal situation.

BGT advocates identify all non-marital sex acts as immoral on the assumption that, in willing such acts, "the partners treat their bodies as instruments to be used *in service of their consciously experiencing selves*; their choice to engage in such conduct thus dis-integrates each of them precisely as acting persons."[101] As noted above, Grisez expunges the notion of human agency from his "one flesh union" definition of marriage so that sub-voluntary functioning of glands and organs, not the intentions of the partners, are what 'make' the union exclusive and indissoluble. Grisez conflates the choosing of the exterior act (the material act) and the 'end' of the agent's will (self-disintegration). This implies that the agent knows or accepts the BGT premise that such acts do constitute self-disintegrity. This just begs the question, since the explanation of how 'marriage' constitutes a *moral* norm for choosing is only given with reference to its inclusion within a putatively infallible and exhaustive set of **pre-moral** goods that hold for *all* human beings, whether straight or gay.

BGT seems not only to presuppose, but also to recommend, a kind of universal psychological egoism. As George puts it, "the **fpm** directs us, in choosing partial fulfilments, to treat every possible human fulfilment as an essential aspect of integral human fulfilment."[102] This treats the sum of pre-moral goods (ie. heterosexually self-interested ends) as though they were necessary (but not sufficient) conditions of any moral choice, ignoring the fact that many people, both Christians and liberals, (a) are not heterosexual and (b) think moral choices often involve precisely the demand that we sacrifice some pre-moral goods for the well-being of *other people*.

An ethic that remains in the self-interested realm of goods cannot adequately explain why we are morally obligated to protect any good for *other* persons. Hittinger has argued that the Grisez/Finnis system has not adequately addressed this issue. Finnis seems to recognise the problem. He has questioned whether it is even possible to reconcile individual and communal participation in the human goods.[103] He is aware that the theory leaves unresolved the question whether *my* good and the well-being of *my communities* relates to any more *comprehensive* human participation in good.[104] In reference to certain unsettled questions regarding friendship, Finnis is compelled to inquire whether there is any further way to understand why it is reasonable to sacrifice oneself for a friend or a community. An ethic that lacks a notion of the common good, or which does not give a prominent account of how other-regarding behaviour ought to be guided, will find itself entangled in a certain "conflict of opportunities" between my own well-being and that of others. Finnis says, "in the absence of any answers to such questions, the basic human values will seem, to any thoughtful person, to be weakened, in their attractiveness to reasonableness, by a certain relativity or subjectivity[105] --- not so much the 'subjectivity' of arbitrary opining, but rather the 'subjectivity' of the '*merely* relative to us' (where 'us' has an uncertain but restricted reference)."[106] Finnis argues that a concept like friendship with God is necessary in order to dispel the anxiety that practical reasonableness is ultimately tantamount to a refined form of self-cultivation.[107]

Revisionists and proportionalists refuse to treat pre-moral goods as though they were normative goods without taking into account the inter-subjective, relational, social contexts within which they are pursued. There are many commonly recognised duties (eg. don't betray a friend, don't betray a spouse) that are not to my advantage in every case. Intuitively we tend to make a distinction between morality and selfishness. BGT cannot make that distinction in any consistent way.

Russell Hittinger credits Finnis with acknowledging the problems inherent in the BGT, but says that he never resolves them. Instead Finnis concludes that the "assumptions" concerning a personal God would, "if verified," entitle us to "remove the question mark with which I originally introduced the basic value of religion."[108] Finnis continues, "And this would not only explain, in principle, how self-sacrifice in friendship can make sense; it also would account for our obligation to favour the common good."[109] By his own admission, Finnis's problem is that the values of religion, friendship, and the common good are left under a "question mark" until he can find some way to verify this religious perspective. Hence, the obligation to "favour" the common good is left pending.[110] Grisez, by contrast, moves into revealed religion in order to remove the problem. Either way, the tension between the selfish and other-regarding sense of 'good' cannot be resolved in the absence of some over-arching (more valuable) good that could guide us in choosing between realising the goods for ourselves and realising them for others. It would seem that the Grisez/Finnis project fails to succeed by reason alone, since a 'God of the ethical gaps' would have to be proposed in order to make it into an other-regarding ethical theory.

The Thomistic anthropological model has been an ambiguous contribution to resolving the differences between divergent accounts of how best to preserve what is 'basic' to human nature. The neo-scholastic interpretation of Aquinas's moral philosophy has led to much dispute precisely on the question of the normativity of (human) nature.[111] Grisez interprets Aquinas as saying that ultimately any choice has its intelligibility by reference to the intelligible end(s) for which it is done. We need to be clear that the dispute is not over whether human nature is the standard for ethics, and so normative in a sense, but whether the physical (and involuntary) aspects of human well-being/fulfilment exhaust a proper understanding of what is most essential to that nature. Therefore, everything hinges on the operative model of human 'nature,' which is why the methodology employed in the anthropological inquiry is so important. Since Aquinas's methodology is so influential in the Catholic understanding of human nature, there is much dispute over how it aids the anthropological inquiry, and to which conclusions it leads.

"If there is one thing on which Grisez and Thomas are at one", says Ralph McInerny, "it is in their insistence on starting-points, or principles. Principles are important, of course, because they affect everything else that follows from them."[112] Thomas, like Aristotle, questions the treatment of man's ultimate end, that is, the human good. On his view, the search for moral principles involves human actions, and begins by asking what all of those actions commonly exhibit; what is true of all of them? Aristotle shows us that anything must be a compound of matter and form. Thomas begins by seeking truths common to all distinctively *human* acts as such.

Grisez interprets[113] Aquinas to mean that ultimately any choice has its intelligibility by reference to the intelligible end(s) for which it is done. But Grisez defines only one kind of 'ends' as intelligible -- material (pre-moral) goods. In Thomas, by contrast, what characterises a human act as such is that it is undertaken (*willed*) for some (*intended*) end. We are answerable for such acts precisely because they are in our power and proceed from cognitive power and will. The mind sets an end that is willingly pursued. Activities which can truly be ascribed to a human agent but which do not proceed from him in this way (e.g. digesting, balding, breathing, tripping, being sexually aroused, etc.) may be called 'acts of a man' but not 'human acts'. Human acts are voluntary.[114] "Moral acts are specified by the end, for moral acts and human acts are the same." (*ST*, IaIIae, q. 1, a.3) Thomas understands the human good as that for which all human acts are undertaken. This is what he means by the ultimate end.[115]

Grisez diverges from Thomas here. In *Practical Principles* Grisez introduces a distinction between intelligible goods that include the choices by which one acts for them ("reflexive" intelligible goods) and those for which this is not the case (the "substantive" goods). This is a distinction that Grisez refers to elsewhere throughout his work. As Chappell says, "The substantive goods correspond closely to humans' nature as a particular kind of mortal animal. The "reflexive" goods reflect a different aspect of being human: that it involves rational agency "through deliberation and choice".[116] In *Practical Principles*, Grisez identifies the substantive intelligible goods as life, knowledge and aesthetic experience, and excellence in work and play. It would seem, then, that Grisez **does** acknowledge some sort of distinction between **instinctive** and **intentional** goods/evils, although this 'distinction' is questionable, since he does not treat one as more distinctively human than the other (to do so would contradict the incommensurability thesis). Chappell concludes, correctly in my view, that "the [Grisez School] are like Hume (and unlike Aristotle, Aquinas or Mill) in positing a plurality of different basic objects of desire or goods."[117]

Thomas devotes the second section of the *Prima Pars* to ticking off eight candidates for the ultimate end, and finding all of them wanting. There can be a plurality of candidates for the role of ultimate end, but Thomas allows only one defensible winner of the role. This is what makes his ethics 'teleological'. This end is present in the agent's intention as the 'end of ends' for personal activity. It is variously described as "self fulfilment" (*impletio sui*), "the notion of ultimate end" (*ratio ultimi finis*), "perfection of the agent", the "satisfaction of all desires" or the whole or "total good" or "happiness" (*beatitudo*).

In his *Groundwork of the Metaphysics of Morals*, Section 1, Kant (like Aquinas) surveyed a wide variety of candidates that might count as unconditional, universal, absolute goods. He proffers abilities such as the 'talents of the mind' (e.g. intelligence and judgement), qualities of character (e.g. courage, prudence, tenacity, wit) and the 'gifts of fortune' (e.g. health, life itself, wealth, privilege) and even happiness. We might note that some of these pre-moral goods coincide with the Grisez/Finnis lists. But Kant concluded that none of these is an absolute moral good. He rejected each for the same reason. All of them could be used instrumentally to make the human situation morally worse. For example, if a person of bad will is intelligent, courageous, quick-witted, and wealthy these merely increase his capacity for evil. All of these pre-moral qualities, while they have their limited appeal, can on occasion be instrumental to creating thoroughly bad human outcomes. This means that none of them is intrinsically good ('good without qualification'). They can only be described as good or bad (in the *moral* sense) relative to the human intentions ('ends') for which they are used and the impact they have on others. Thus, it is the agent's intention within an interpersonal context that determines the moral worth of the object, not the object (i.e. material means) that is significant for the *moral* status of the agent's intention. It is having the right intention *vis-à-vis* the total personal situation and outcomes (not the right means/object) that makes the good will 'good'.[118]

For Kant, as for Aristotle, "good action is itself an end." Kant concluded in his *Groundwork* that "It is impossible to conceive anything at all in the world, or even out of it, which can be taken as good without qualification, except a good will."[119] This is entirely consistent with Thomas's understanding that material actions will be taken to be good only insofar as the *ratio boni* (i.e. the ultimate end, what the good will wills) is taken to be realized in them.

Thomas rejects the suggestion that the ultimate end consists of a plurality of things because he always employs a distinction between the meaning of the end and the material means. In other words, he is cautious not to treat material goods as though they had an intrinsic moral value apart from the meaning imputed to them by rational moral agents within interpersonal contexts. The *ratio boni* is not drawn from things called good, rather it is conceptually prior to, and distinct from, them. The ultimate end is never a means (a material, pre-moral good). Good is first and primarily to be understood as ultimate end (the end goal sought by the agent).

Human action is a special case in that pre-moral goods function as ends in the biological processes that Thomas referred to in article one (digesting, balding, experiencing sexual attraction/arousal towards various people, etc.). 'Acting according to reason' is often given as an account of the *human* good. Aquinas shares Aristotle's view that rational activity is *peculiar to man* and that to do it well is a sufficient basis for saying that the agent is good. Thomas follows Aristotle in observing that we have a word for the ultimate end, namely "happiness" (*eudaimonia*). Aristotle held that while *eudaimonia* may require the support of "external goods," their possession should not be mistaken for *eudaimonia* itself. *Eudaimonia* is active, it is a way of living; "good action is itself an end," he believed. This shifts 'basic goods' for humans from involuntary (passive) aspects of their nature to the creative, conscious faculties. As John Cooper has appreciated, for Aristotle, "*eudaimonia* is necessarily the result of a person's own efforts; success, of whatever kind, could only count as *eudaimonia* if due to one's own efforts".[120]

By contrast, Grisez contends that unless human persons "have possibilities which are not yet defined, there is no room for them to unfold themselves through intelligent creativity and freedom."[121] The BGT school includes amongst the goods that are properly 'basic' to human flourishing both involuntary goods (in the sense that they are 'given' not made) and goods that are products of human effort and will, and then stipulates (via the incommensurablility thesis) that it is impossible for an ethic to prioritize one over the other, since both are equally essential to "integral human fulfillment".

The kind of well-being that Aristotle and Thomas held was the proper end of *human* action was not defined in terms of holding some complement of material possessions, but in living one's life in a certain way. Individual well-being must be "self-authored". It is precisely because of this understanding of *eudaimonia* that revisionists prize agency and autonomy so highly, and especially the freedom to engage in putatively 'immoral' (i.e. unconventional) *victimless* acts.

The **fpm** directs us, in choosing partial fulfillments, to treat *every* possible human fulfillment as an *essential* aspect of integral human fulfillment.[122] This seems to be an incoherent sentence – it gives with one hand what it takes with the other. It allows that we have to make choices, but then says our choices must not treat some part of a set as ***more* essential** than others, which is exactly what 'choice' entails. The **fpm** either requires us or does not require us to treat every possible aspect of human fulfillment as essential to each one of our choices. It cannot do both. The example of the altruist who voluntarily subjects herself to medical experimentation for the good of the wider community brings the problem into focus. The choice of other citizens **not** to make such altruistic sacrifices cannot be a moral evil unless we all have an obligation to remedy all of the ontic/material evils that we could. We do not. This is because we have no moral obligation to act to positively promote some pre-determined set of pre-moral goods (this would be an unjustified encroachment on our liberty). Our moral obligation is, rather, **not to** deliberately inflict ontic evils that could be avoided. If we could be ***legally compelled to promote*** a particular (religious or moral) notion of 'the good life' then, even if we could succeed, our doing so would not be motivated by a good will, but by a prudent one. This kind of public morality is not consistent with the aim of making people virtuous, unless virtue is indistinguishable from self-interest. To many sincere Christians, this would also seem contrary to the inviolability of conscience.

Aristotle and Aquinas were aware that 'rational activity' means many things. Both Thomas and Grisez realise that practical reason can be instrumental to fulfilling ends that are not morally good. Grisez is clear that the 'intelligibility' of an end is not sufficient to make it morally good. There are intelligible reasons, for example, to kidnap a child and subject her to experiments for the good of medical knowledge. This is not unintelligible. But it is morally wrong ("unchoiceworthy"). However, the reason why it is wrong is very different in Grisez than in Aquinas.

Thomas envisions two kinds of rational activity: (1) intellectual virtues which give the *facultas* but not the appetitive disposition to use it. One cannot become good just by philosophizing. (2) moral virtues/virtues of appetite – in which intellectual virtues direct practical choices. In the *Summa*, IaIIae, q. 94, a.2, having established that the first principle of the practical order is "the good is to be done and pursued and evil avoided", Thomas indicates how it is that one passes from the first principle to others. The first principle is foundational with respect to all other principles in the practical order. "Because good has the note of end and evil has the contrary note, reason naturally grasps as good all those things to which man has a natural inclination and consequently as to be pursued in action, and the contrary of these are grasped as evils to be avoided." Grisez follows Thomas this far. It looks as though Thomas ultimately **does** allow for a plurality of ultimate (natural) ends after all: "those things to which man has a natural inclination". For Grisez, this is where the theory stops. One does moral evil when one fails to treat all of the natural ends as equally valuable, or when one fails to "remain open to" any of the basic ontic goods. George concedes that the basic goods are 'pre-moral' (or 'ontic') goods as opposed to moral goods. Only pointless activity is "un-choiceworthy". We need to have a way to distinguish morally upright decisions from those that are merely rational/intelligible. Yet this is exactly what the Grisez/Finnis school fails adequately to explain. As I showed above, their theory does not offer any means of getting beyond rational egoism. It cannot help us to decide when, or even whether, we ought to pursue basic goods for ourselves and when to sacrifice 'our' goods for the good of *others*.

Where Grisez sees 'good' as the pursuit of a multitude of incommensurable natural ends, Thomas sees a hierarchy amongst the natural ends, because *an ultimate end is presupposed*. This is what makes his theory 'teleological'. Man actively seeks his good. Man is a complex organism comprising many appetites, including natural inclinations. A nature as such is ordered to some end as its good or perfection. By 'nature' Thomas means the intrinsic principle in changeable things. Particularizations of the human good presuppose the human good as such, the desire for the ultimate end. The precepts that bear on the other natural inclinations (for survival, for reproduction, etc.) express their relation to the ultimate end: man's overall good.

BGT, says Salzman, is teleological because it grounds morality in human goods – the goods of real people living in the world of experience. But then the BGT shifts from a methodologically teleological explanation of its foundations to a *de facto* use of deontological absolute moral norms on certain ethical issues (primarily issues of sexual ethics). Therefore, Salzman says, [BGT] is clearly not a teleological theory because its proponents insist "that the basic goods are incommensurable". A necessary requirement for any teleological normative ethics is that pre-moral values or disvalues (i.e. basic goods or aspects of those goods) are commensurable.

But worse, the incommensurability of values is also built into the definitions of the values, eg. 'skillful work and play'. Anyone can recognize that work and play are opposites. In order to achieve the good of successful or 'skillful' work, one must neglect the good of play. In order to play and to develop one's skills in play, we need to be freed from the obligation to work. But this choice involves not being "open to" one of two basic goods. Hence the BGT characterizes both of these conflicting values under the single rubric of "skill" as "skillful work and play", thus pre-empting any conflict between them by conflating them into a single concept or 'basic good'. Other dilemmas arise between 'life and health'. One person might choose against the good of 'health' (his own) in order to donate a kidney to save another person's 'life', or one might undergo torture (foregoing good health) in order not to betray a friend whose life is endangered by the torturers. Similar problems can be seen in the conflation of "justice and friendship". Justice means being impartial, and friendship involves being partial to one's friends. This dilemma is evaded by defining the conflicting values as a single concept, thus *apparently* eliminating any actual conflict between them by theoretically obfuscating the fact that they are opposite values.

BGT posits certain absolute or 'exceptionless moral norms' forbidding specific acts that can never be chosen, regardless of consequences, because choosing such acts necessarily violates a basic good.[123] I would put this differently, by saying that BGT allows a select set of pre-moral goods to function as ultimate ends, whereas neo-Scholastic, revisionist and proportionalist theories always see the pre-moral, involuntary, goods as *relative* to the ultimate, distinctively *human,* good. Grisez and Finnis depart from previous natural law methodologies by maintaining that pre-moral facets of human nature constitute a natural law method for deriving moral norms.[124] Where BGT interprets 'ends' as material objects to be pursued, revisionists and proportionalists interpret 'end' primarily in terms of agency or motive within a social context. Revisionists disagree with the BGT's premise that pre-moral goods have intrinsic human value in any context.

Revisionist critics may agree with Finnis/Grisez that we should will the basic goods for ourselves and for others. They might also agree that it is humanly impossible in all of one's actions to achieve the good for both oneself and for others. That said, unless we abandon the commonsense axiom that 'ought implies can', human impossibilities cannot provide a moral guideline for choosing. This moral requirement seems, rather, to paralyze all choice. Seeking the human good involves voluntary aspects of character, and cannot be imputed to human nature, or its involuntary aspects, in an abstract sense. The respect and dignity that we accord uniquely to humans *as such* rests upon our belief that we alone possess the potential for this kind of voluntary moral self-development.

So far I have examined three naturalist arguments as they apply to homosexual behaviour: that of St. Paul in Romans 1, that of St. Thomas Aquinas as deployed in Catholic doctrine, and that of the Basic Goods Theorists (pioneered by Grisez and Finnis). Each of these ethical approaches in its own way implies a tension between the homosexual and his own created nature. In the next chapter I will turn my attention to more recent attempts by Christian ethicists to link moral language to involuntary aspects of biology. In recent decades Christian bioethicists have responded to a growing body of evidence that supports the homosexual essentialist hypothesis – that gay people are 'born that way'. A wider acceptance of the possibility of homosexual essentialism has increased the pressure on Christian prohibitionists to be consistent with their own demand to 'read the language of the body in truth'. In addition the 'new gay essentialism' appears to have produced a tension between doctrinal assertions that homosexuality is an 'objective disorder' and the ordinary conception of 'health' as 'functioning in accordance with one's given nature'. With more and more 'out' gay people flourishing and leading seemingly healthy, productive lives, Christian ethicists were faced with the daunting task of explaining the 'disease' of homosexuality in terms extrinsic to the individual homosexual subject. The question of whether they have succeeded in so doing will occupy the next chapter.

1   Hittinger, Russell, _A Critique of the New Natural Law Theory_, Notre Dame, Indiana, University of Notre Dame Press, 1987, p. 1.

2   Hoose, B. Proportionalism: The American Debate and Its European Roots, Washington, DC: Georgetown University Press, 1987.

3   Hittinger, Op. Cit., p. 5.

4   Grisez, Germain, Contraception and the Natural Law, Milwaukee, Wisconsin, Bruce, 1964, p. 60.

5   George, Robert P., In Defense of Natural Law, Oxford University Press, 1999, p. 17.

6   Ibid., p. 18.

7   Ibid., p. 10.

8   Ibid., p. 37. From this we can already glean how this approach is profoundly at odds with modern liberalism. The idea that all human beings have a preordained 'end' to which their lives must conform (pursue) conflicts with the liberal notion that individuals may be free to pursue their own vision of the good life and that the development of individual character that this fosters is an ultimate human good.

9   Ibid.

10  Ibid.

11  Ibid., pp. 40-41.

12  According to Grisez, Aquinas did not give us a systematic account of moral norms that could guide a decision between two courses of action. He did not, as Basic Goods Theory does, establish a connection between the intelligibility of the ends (arrived at by 'practical rationality') and specific moral rules.

13  George, Op. Cit., p. 45.

14  Finnis, John, Natural Law and Natural Rights (Clarendon Law Series), Oxford University Press, 1980, pp. 86-89.

15  Germain Grisez, Joseph Boyle, and John Finnis, "Practical Principles, Moral Truth, and Ultimate Ends in Natural Law" in Natural Law: Volume I. (ed.) John Finnis. 1991: Dartmouth (UK), p. 103-4.
    Grisez lists seven basic goods in Vol 1 of _The Way of the Lord Jesus_. In a list taken from Grisez and Russell Shaw (_Fulfillment in Christ: A Summary of Christian Moral Principles_. Notre Dame, IN: University of Notre Dame, 1991, p. 55) the two goods of self-integration and authenticity are included.

16  Grisez, Germain, The Way of the Lord Jesus, Vol. 2: Living a Christian Life, Quincy, Ill., Franciscan Press, 1993, pp. 555-69, esp. p. 568.

17  They seem to regard proportionalism as indistinguishable from Utilitarianism. In Chapter 3 I explained that proportionalists differ form Utilitarians in rejecting the use of morally bad means to the achievement of good ends. For proportionalists, the ends do not justify _morally_ bad means, and so individual rights would not be sacrificed to the wellbeing of the 'greatest number'. On the

other hand, if the means entails only an evil in the pre-moral sense (material harm) then the deliberate production of a good can justify the doing of an evil. If it could not, self-sacrifice would be ruled out as immoral. Proportionalists do not view pre-moral evils associated with the means as discrete actions, but see them as elements of a single action (determined by its object, or intended purpose).

[18] George, Robert P., In Defense of Natural Law, Oxford, England, Oxford University Press, 1999, p. 49.

[19] Grisez's eight modes of responsibility appear in The Way of the Lord Jesus: Christian Moral Principles, Chapter 26, and correspond to questions D, E, F, G, H, I, J and K in that order. The modes are intended to specify the first principle of morality by indicating the specific ways in which it is to be sought. The eight modes are as follows: 1. One should not be deterred by felt inertia from acting for basic intelligible human goods. 2. One should not be pressed by enthusiasm or impatience to act individualistically for basic human goods. 3. One should not choose to satisfy an emotional desire except as part of one's pursuit of a basic human good. 4. One should not choose to act out of an emotional aversion except as part of one's avoidance of some intelligible evil. 5. One should not, in response to different feelings towards different persons, willingly proceed with a preference for anyone unless the preference is required by the intelligible human goods themselves. 6. One should not choose on the basis of emotions which bear upon empirical aspects of intelligible goods in a way which interferes with a more perfect sharing in that good. 7. One should not be moved by hostility to freely accept or choose the destruction, damaging, or impeding of any intelligible human good. 8. One should not be moved by a stronger desire for one instance of an intelligible human good to act for it by choosing to destroy, damage, or impede some other instance of an intelligible human good.

[20] Grisez, Germain, The Way of the Lord Jesus, Christian Moral Principles, Chapter 7, Question G, Para. 2. Accessed online at http://www.twotlj.org/G-1-7-G.html on 20 January, 2012.

[21] George, Op. Cit., p. 51.

[22] John Finnis, Joseph M. Boyle, Jr. and Germain Grisez, *Nuclear Deterrence, Morality and Realism* (Oxford: Clarendon Press, 1987), 283.

[23] Grisez, Germain, Boyle Joseph M., and Finnis, John, 'Practical Principles, Moral Truth, and Ultimate Ends,' *American Journal of Jurisprudence*, 32, 1987, pp 99 & 123.

[24] This inverts the revisionists' understanding of human action. The 'reason' for action is not supplied by the willing agent and his intended purposes (motives), but by the static set of goods by which his will is passively 'directed'. This pictures the will being subordinate to the practical reasons intrinsic in a set of

static and enduring 'goods' that are always good, independent of the agent's motives for wanting them.

25 Grisez, Germain, <u>The Way of the Lord Jesus, Vol. 2: Living a Christian Life</u>, Quincy, Ill., Franciscan Press, 1993.
Chapter 9, p. 568.

26 Ibid., p. 570.

27 Ibid., p. 578.

28 Ibid., p. 633.

29 Ibid., p. 634.

30 George, Robert P. and Bradley, Gerard V., 'Marriage and the Liberal Imagination,' *Georgetown Law Journal*, 84 1995, pp. 301-20.

31 Ibid., pp. 301-2.

32 Finnis, John, 'Law, Morality and "Sexual Orientation"', *Notre Dame Law Review* 69/5 (1994), p. 1066.

33 Goldsworthy, Jeffrey, 'Fact and Value in the New Natural Law Theory,' *American Journal of Jurisprudence*, 41, 1996, 21, 38-45. See also: Bamforth, Nicholas and Richards, David A.J., <u>Patriarchal Religion, sexuality and gender: a critique of new natural law</u>, Cambridge University Press, 2008, pp 285-6. (In ethics, non-cognitivism is one of a number of views that deny that moral sentences are genuine statements. That is, they may be justified as ways of living or from within a particular form of life, but they do not ground distinct types of knowledge. Non-cognitivists maintain that moral judgments cannot be known since moral propositions do not express anything true or false about the world.)

34 George, George, Robert P., <u>In Defense of Natural Law</u>, Oxford University Press, 1999, p. 37.

35 See, for example, Bamforth, Nicholas and Richards, David A.J., <u>Patriarchal Religion, sexuality and gender: a critique of new natural law</u>, Cambridge University Press, 2008, pp 285-6.

36 Grisez, Germain, <u>The Way of the Lord Jesus: Vol. 1, Christian Moral Principles</u>, Chicago, Franciscan Herald Press, 1983, p. 100.

37 Bamforth, Nicholas and Richards, David A.J., <u>Patriarchal Religion, sexuality and gender: a critique of new natural law</u>, Cambridge University Press, 2008, pp 285-6.

38 Ibid., p. 186.

39 Divine Command Theory is the meta-ethical position that moral propositions derive their meaning from God's attitudes. For example, to say 'murder is wrong' means the same thing as 'God prohibits murder'.

40 Grisez, Op. Cit., p. 10.

41 This is particularly worrying from a liberal standpoint given what George says about punishment: "I argue . . . that the injustice which justifies criminal punishment on the retributive view need not inhere in the underlying

immoralities of the acts that are prohibited under the criminal law. . . the breach of a duty to obey a law that is not in itself unjust --- even a law prohibiting putatively victimless wrongdoing --- constitutes an injustice, and may justly be punished under the retributive law." (George, 1999, p. 11)

42    George, Op. Cit., p. 55.

43    For example, George (1999, p. 37) writes: "The crucial point is that under this [neo-scholastic interpretation of natural law] sound practical thinking depends upon a methodologically prior speculative (metaphysical, -- or 'ontological' – and theological) inquiry."

44    George, Op. Cit., p. 37.

45    Clack, Beverley, Sex & Death: a reappraisal of human mortality, Cambridge, Polity Press, 2002, p. 110.

46    Commentators could argue that there is tension between claims that the goods are not based on intuition and claims from members of the same school that they are self-evident. For example see Finnis, John, Natural Law and Natural Rights, Clarendon Law Series, Oxford University Press, 1980, p. 160. Under the sub-heading 'The Variety of Human Opinions and Practices' Finnis suggests what is at the core of natural law theorizing: "It amounts to no more than saying that any sane person is capable of seeing that life, knowledge, fellowship, offspring, and a few other such basic aspects of human existence are, as such, good, i.e. worth having, leaving to one side all particular predicaments and implications, all assessments of relative importance, all moral demands, and in short, all questions of whether and how one is to devote oneself to these goods."

47    McInerny, Ralph, 'Grisez and Thomism' in Biggar, Nigel and Black, Rufus, The Revival of Natural Law, Ashagate, 2000, p. 67.

48    If this were the case, then our sexual actions, unlike our other actions, would conveniently not be subject to the dictates of reason and consciousness, but instead would have an intrinsic 'reason' of their own, independent of the reflective intervention of the human ratio. Indeed, this approach to ethics harkens back to the 'preceptive' model favoured by traditional Catholic doctrine, according to which "spouses must read the language of the body in truth" and any act which frustrates the procreative purpose (telos) assigned to the sexual act (by God) is a "lie in the language of the body". As such, the exterior shape or structure of the act is prioritised over agency and intent in a moral evaluation of it. The agent's purposes, circumstances and relationships would be rendered morally irrelevant. This seems decidedly counterintuitive and certainly conflicts with what we now know about human sexuality, not to mention human agency.

49    George, Op. Cit., p. 52.

50    Grisez, Germain, Living a Christian Life, p. 473, in Salzman, Todd, A., 'The Basic Goods Theory and Revisionism: A Methodological Comparison on the

Use of Reason and Experience as Sources of Moral Knowledge', *Heythrop Journal* XLII, 2001, p. 427.

51 Salzman, Todd, A., 'The Basic Goods Theory and Revisionism: A Methodological Comparison on the Use of Reason and Experience as Sources of Moral Knowledge', *Heythrop Journal* XLII, 2001, p. 428.

52 See Salzman, Ibid., pp. 428-9.

53 Ibid., p. 429.

54 Ibid., p. 439.

55 Ibid., (his emphasis)

56 Ibid.

57 Grisez, Boyle and Finnis, 'Practical Principles, Moral Truth and Ultimate Ends', 1987, pp. 99, 123.

58 An equally serious problem is that this logic assumes that simply not to actively promote or participate in marital sex is tantamount to acting against it. This is a false dilemma. Even worse, if ought implies can, then impossibilities cannot provide the guiding ideal by which we measure our moral failures. George wants it both ways. He says that we *cannot* choose to bring about integral human fulfillment (George, 1999, p. 68). No set of humanly possible choices *can* bring about overall human fulfillment (George, 1999, p. 51). "No human . . . set of choices can realize anything more than aspects of complete human well-being." But, in spite of his clear understanding that integral human fulfillment is impossible to bring about through human choosing, he nevertheless claims ". . . but we can chose compatibly with a will to integral human fulfillment." (George, 1999, p. 68). The standard, then, "is not how close we come to bringing about integral human fulfillment in our choices . . . rather, it is whether our choices are compatible with a will to integral human fulfillment." (George, 1999, p. 68.) But why we should will to let our choices be guided by an impossible ideal, as opposed to a humanly possible one, is a mystery, and certainly does not seem rational.

59 George, Op. Cit., p. 52.

60 Chappell, Timothy, '*Natural Law Revived: Natural Law Theory and Contemporary Moral Philosophy*' in Nigel Biggar and Rufus Black, Eds., <u>The Revival of Natural Law: philosophical, theological and ethical responses to the Finnis-Grisez school</u>, Aldershot, England, Ashgate, 2000, p. 32.

61 George, Op. Cit., p. 48.

62 Ibid., p. 53.

63 Grisez, Germain, <u>The Way of the Lord Jesus, Vol. 2: Living a Christian Life</u>, Quincy, Ill., Franciscan Press, 1993, p. 568.

64 Ibid., p. 570.

65 Moore, Gareth, 'Natural Sex: Germain Grisez, Sex, and Natural Law' in <u>The Revival of Natural Law</u>, Biggar & Black, Eds., 2000, p. 225.

66   Grisez, Op. Cit., p. 578.

67   Moore, Op. Cit., p. 228.

68   Grisez, Op. Cit., p. 633.

69   Ibid., p. 634.

70   Ibid., p. 635.

71   Ibid., p. 635 n. 162.

72   Ibid., p. 653.

73   Ibid., p. 650.

74   Grisez, Germain, The Way of the Lord Jesus, Christian Moral Principles, Chapter 26, Question K. Accessed online at http://www.twotlj.org/G-1-7-G. html, accessed on 20 January, 2012.

75   Robert P. George and Gerard V. Bradley, 'Marriage and the Liberal Imagination,' Georgetown Law Journal, 84 (1995), pp. 301-2.

76   Moore, Op. Cit., p. 233.

77   Finnis, John, 'Law, Morality, and "Sexual Orientation," 69 Notre Dame Law Review, 1994, p. 1066.

78   Moore, Op. Cit., p. 237.

79   Ibid.

80   Only in 1890 did Pope Leo XIII denounce the institution of slavery.

81   Grisez, Germain, The Way of the Lord Jesus, Volume 1: Christian Moral Principles, Chicago, Franciscan Herald Press, 1983, p. 902.

82   Salzman, Todd, 'The Basic Goods Theory and Revisionism: A Methodological Comparison on the Use of Reason and Experience as Sources of Moral Knowledge' in Heythrop Journal, XLII, 2001, p. p. 442.

83   Ibid., p. 444.

84   Robert George says it seems to him "that appeals to self-evidence, when properly understood, do not fail to provide a solid foundation for moral reasoning. In any event, they provide no less solid a foundation than appeals to the facts of human nature." (George, 1999, p. 88) To me, this looks a lot like intuitionism, although Grisez denies this.

85   Bamforth, Nicholas and Richards, David A.J., Patriarchal Religion, Sexuality and Gender: a critique of new natural law, Cambridge University Press, 2008, p. 186.

86   Grisez, Germain, The Way of the Lord Jesus, Volume 1: Christian Moral Principles, Chicago, Franciscan Herald Press, 1983, pp. 10-11.

87   Salzman, Op. Cit., p. 445.

88   Chapell, Op. Cit., p. 38.

89   Grisez, Germain, The Way of the Lord Jesus, Vol. 2: Living a Christian Life, Quincy, Ill., Franciscan Press, 1993, p. 569.

90   Chapell, Op. Cit., p. 39.

91  Grisez, Germain, The Way of the Lord Jesus, Volume 1: Christian Moral Principles, Chicago, Franciscan Herald Press, 1983, p. 182.

92  Sartre, Jean Paul, *Being and Nothingness: An Essay on Phenomenological Ontology*, Chapter 4, (1958) transl. Hazel E. Barnes, intr. Mary Warnock, London: Methuen.

93  George, Op. Cit., p. 42.

94  This is arbitrary, as it varies from one person to the next and so cannot provide any principled reason for preferring one person's 'intelligible' desire over another's when the two conflict.

95  "It appears evident that the ultimate ends of human action can never, in any case, be accounted for by *reason*, but recommend themselves entirely to the sentiments and affections of mankind, without any dependence on the intellectual faculties. Ask a man *why he uses exercise*; he will answer *because he desires to keep his health*. If you then enquire, *why he desires health,* he will readily reply, *because sickness is painful.* If you push your enquiries farther, and desire a reason *why he hates pain*, it is impossible he can ever give you any. This is an ultimate end, and is never referred to any other object." [Hume] cited in Chappell, Timothy, 'Natural Law Revived: Natural Law Theory and Contemporary Moral Philosophy' in Nigel Biggar and Rufus Black, Eds., The Revival of Natural Law: philosophical, theological and ethical responses to the Finnis-Grisez school, Aldershot, England, Ashgate, 2000, p. 34.

96  Chappell, Op. Cit., p. 43.

97  In *Utilitarianism* (1863), Chapter 2, 'What Utilitarianism Is.', Mill wrote:

98  Now, such a theory of life excites in many minds, and among them in some of the most estimable in feeling and purpose, inveterate dislike. To suppose that life has (as they express it) no higher end than pleasure- no better and nobler object of desire and pursuit- they designate as utterly mean and grovelling; as a doctrine **worthy only of swine**, to whom the followers of Epicurus were, at a very early period, contemptuously likened; and modern holders of the doctrine are occasionally made the subject of equally polite comparisons by its German, French, and English assailants. [my bold]
Online edition published by eBooks@Adelaide, Last updated Sun Aug 29, 2010.
Grisez, Germain, The Way of the Lord Jesus, Volume 1: Christian Moral Principles, Chicago, Franciscan Herald Press, 1983, p. 121.

99  Timothy Chappell, 'Natural Law Revived: Natural Law Theory and Contemporary Moral Philosophy' in Nigel Biggar & Rufus Black, Eds., The Revival of Natural Law: Philosophical, theological and ethical responses to the Finnis-Grisez School, Ashgate (Aldreshot, England), 2000, p. 36.
I would add that basic goods theory does not explain how its list of basic goods fundamentally differs from natural instincts, like the drive to pursue pleasure and avoid pain. Kant too argued that pleasure and pain could not serve as basic

moral principles for human action, and would have agreed with the BGT's assertion that if one makes these into principles of action, one's conception of action will be "distorted". Yet BGT defenders fundamentally disagree with Kant's claim that an agent should actively employ *reason* in a particular situation to determine if or when a particular pre-moral good should be pursued.

[100] Grisez, Op. Cit., p. 120.

[101] Finnis, John, 'Law, Morality and "Sexual Orientation"', *Notre Dame Law Review* 69/5 (1994), p. 1066.

[102] George, Robert P., In Defense of Natural Law, Oxford University Press, 1999, p. 51.

[103] Finnis, John, Natural Law and Natural Rights, Clarendon Law Series, Oxford University Press, 1980, p. 372.

[104] Ibid.

[105] This was precisely Kant's concern: that ethics would become relativistic and subjective, rather than fair, reciprocal and universalizable. Kant rejected premoral goods as intrinsic to ethics because they are contingent, subjective and arbitrary.

[106] Finnis, Op. Cit.., p. 373.

[107] Finnis, John, Fundamentals of Ethics, Georgetown University Press and Oxford University Press 1983. p. 48.

[108] Finnis, Natural Law and Natural Rights, 1980, p. 410.

[109] Ibid, p. 406.

[110] Hittinger, Russell, *A Critique of the New Natural Law Theory*, Notre Dame, Indiana, University of Notre Dame Press, 1987, p. 153.

[111] George, Op. Cit., p. 37.

[112] McInerny, Ralph, 'Grisez and Thomism' in Biggar & Black, Eds., The Revival of Natural Law: philosophical, theological and ethical responses to the Finnis-Grisez school, Aldershot, England, Ashgate, 2000, p. 53.

[113] McInerny (p. 53) says it is not clear whether Grisez sees himself as interpreting Aquinas correctly, or as improving upon him, by making explicit what he supposes is implicit in Aquinas. He openly admits his dissatisfaction with what considers inadequacies in Thomas. On the matter of starting points it is not clear, however, whether Grisez is a critic of what Thomas taught, or whether he sees his own offering as a version of it.

[114] McInerny, Op. Cit., p. 56.

[115] Whether there **is** an ultimate end of human action, some single good for the sake of which they are all undertaken, is a separate question.

[116] Chappell, Op. Cit., pg. 38.

[117] Ibid, p. 37.

[118] Thomas explains why there could not be a plurality of ultimate ends: *"I answer that we can speak of ultimate end in two ways, in one way, with reference to its*

*meaning, in another way, with reference to that in which the meaning is taken to be realized."* (ST, IaIIae, q.1, a.7) It seems this is a source of some confusion. Apparently Grisez has chosen to describe the human good with reference to the material things *in which the meaning is taken to be realised* (i.e. in which it is "intelligible").

119    Kant, Immanuel, <u>Groundwork of the Metaphysics of Morals</u>, translated, with analysis and notes, by H J Paton in *The Moral Law*, London: Hutchinson & Co. 1972, p. 59.

120    Cooper, John M., <u>Reason and Human Good in Aristotle</u>, Indianapolis, Hackett, 1986, p. 124. Also see *Nichomachean Ethics* 1099a 31-b8; 1099b 18-30; 1140b 7.

121    Donagan, Alan, <u>The Theory of Morality</u>, Chicago, University of Chicago Press, 1977, p. 26. (cf. Hittinger, p. 11)

122    George, Robert P., <u>In Defense of Natural Law</u>, Oxford University Press, 1999. p. 51.

123    Salzman, Op. Cit., pg. 436.

124    See Hittinger, Russell, <u>*A Critique of the New Natural Law Theory*</u>, Notre Dame, Indiana, University of Notre Dame Press, 1987, pp. 10-13.

# CHAPTER 5

## *New Directions in Christian Discourse since the 90's: Towards a Homophobic Bioethic*

There is widespread agreement between religious and secular institutions in Western liberal democracies that ethics ought to be **related to** (not identical with) facts about human nature. However, there are serious lingering disagreements over which facts ought to be emphasized, and how new discoveries about human nature ought to impact on ethics.

This chapter explores the various ways in which conservative Christians, especially in America, have responded to the new hypothesis of homosexual essentialism by changing their verdict on homosexuality from a type of voluntary immoral behavior to a an innate *predisposition to* immoral behavior (a defect in the very nature of the person).

In 1991 neurobiologist Simon LeVay claimed to have found a difference in brain structure between gay and straight men. LeVay focused on a region of the hypothalmus, a small area located near the pituitary gland at the base of the brain. In both rats and humans the hypothalmus is smaller in females than in males. In a blind study, LeVay examined cross-sections of tissue taken from forty-one autopsies of gay men, straight men, and straight women. His research showed that a particular nucleus of the anterior hypothalmus known as INAH-3 was on average two or three times greater in volume in heterosexual males than in females and homosexual men.[1]

LeVay offered the modest conclusion that this finding suggests that sexual orientation has a biological substrate -- that is, homosexuality may be innate. LeVay went on to speculate that, if sexual orientation is somehow a function of the genetically controlled sexual differentiation that occurs in the early foetus, then it must somehow be influenced by genes.

LeVay is convinced that homosexuality is a 'third sex' or 'third gender', hard-wired into the individual's body and mind. In *Queer Science* LeVay upheld the theory that gays are born, not made.[2] He recounted the work of past researchers intent on finding gay genes, gay hormonal environments in the womb, and gay ways of thinking.

LeVay's social arguments hinge on his science. He supposes that, if we think of people in same-sex relationships as a 'distinct category' of human beings, social stigma and discrimination are less likely to occur. This 'distancing' of homosexuality from the category of heterosexuality will mitigate any 'instinctive aversion' straight people might experience when contemplating what gays do in bed. LeVay's rationale is that if people regard homosexuality as distinct from heterosexuality, people will be less likely to see gay people as defective or dysfunctional heterosexuals.

In a similar vein, Dean Hamer and his research team at the National Cancer Institute have produced some evidence that male homosexuality - in some instances - is genetic. Hamer wrote in a 1993 issue of *Science*, "We have now produced evidence that one form of male homosexuality is preferentially transmitted through the maternal side and is genetically linked to chromosome region Xq28."[3] His comments in the journal *Science*, authored by Hamer and four other scientists at the National Cancer Institute, reported "a linkage between DNA markers on the X chromosome and male sexual orientation."[4] The research team concluded that there is a 95.5 percent certainty that the predisposition for homosexuality exists in a gene, or several genes, near the end of the long arm of the X chromosome inherited from the mother.

In *The Science of Desire* (1994) Hamer nevertheless claimed, "the social constructionist theory is not likely to be disproved anytime soon, since its content is too amorphous ever to be tested."[5] Hamer agrees with constructionists that human sexual expression is a mysterious and complex phenomenon that cannot be reduced to biology, but makes a distinction between "human sexual expression" and sexual orientation, noting that the latter may indeed be heritable and genetic.

The advent of biotechnology and genetic research has apparently provoked a shift in the direction of Christian discourses around homosexuality that is inconsistent with the naturalist approaches of the past. Even before the biotech advances of the 1990's, it was becoming apparent that Western scientific and medical establishments were beginning to produce evidence that threatened to demythologize the polarization of 'normal' heterosexuals and 'unnatural' or 'disordered' homosexuals. Kinsey's reports of 1948 and 53 had suggested that homosexuality was the primary sexual orientation for around ten percent of the general population. The American Psychiatric Association dropped homosexuality from its list of mental disorders in 1973. The American Psychological Association Council of Representatives adopted the same measure in 1975.

It is perhaps not surprising that in the same year, the Catholic Church issued a document, *"Declaration on Certain Questions Concerning Sexual Ethics"* (*Persona Humana*), that represented a significant shift in its thinking on sexual matters. It acknowledged, for the first time, the existence of persons for whom homosexuality is "an innate instinct" which is "constitutive of their emotional and sexual identity". Catholic doctrine on the matter flowed from an interpretation of Aquinas, who apparently had managed to unite the normal and the normative on the assumption that all human beings were by nature heterosexual. Therefore, following the 1975 Declaration, if the church was to preserve her prohibition of homosexual acts she needed to show how something that seemed to occur naturally could nevertheless be interpreted as profoundly unnatural, or objectively 'disordered'. Natural law ethics rest first and foremost on observations of nature, and this creates a problem for those who would prohibit[6] homosexual acts, since homosexuality seems to be a constant throughout natural history and across many species of animals. If only a tiny proportion of humankind is naturally and unavoidably homosexual, then Aquinas's logic would appear to be deeply flawed on its own terms.

To resist this conclusion, the church had a difficult task. She needed to explain how homogenital sex, which is in accordance with the homosexual's given nature and harms no one (and arguably benefits many), nevertheless constitutes immoral behavior ('sin'). Perhaps aware of the difficulty of their position, the Congregation for the Doctrine of the Faith produced another document in 1986, *Letter to the Bishops of the Catholic Church on the Pastoral Care of Homosexual Persons*, in which then prefect Joseph Ratzinger cited St. Paul's use of homosexuality as an exemplary case of disharmony between creator and creatures. In point 5 of this document, he states:

> In Romans 1:18-32, still building on the moral traditions of his forebears, but in the new context of the confrontation between Christianity and the pagan society of his day, Paul uses homosexual behavior as an example of the blindness which has overcome humankind. Instead of the original harmony between Creator and creatures, the acute distortion of idolatry has led to all kinds of moral excess. Paul is at a loss to find a clearer example of this disharmony than homosexual relations. Finally, I Timothy 1, in full continuity with the Biblical position, singles out those who spread wrong doctrine and in verse 10 explicitly names as sinners those who engage in homosexual acts.[7]

This was an implicit denial of the (still inconclusive) evidence that homosexuality exists in nature as part of creation. As such it represents a tacit attempt to back-peddle on the admission in the 1975 document that homosexuality is "an innate instinct" which is "constitutive of their emotional and sexual identity".[8] Perhaps aware of the fragility of this denial (pending further evidence as to the origins of homosexuality), Ratzinger also put forward a simple natural law argument about marriage as the only appropriate context in which the use of the sexual faculty is morally acceptable. This entailed moral condemnation of any form of pre-marital or extra-marital sexual activity not appropriate to the procreative union of one male and one female.

The new empirical research that strengthened the case for homosexual essentialism in the 1990's might have provided a basis for the extension of full human rights to gay and lesbian persons. Or it could have destabilized the traditional Christian prohibitionist stance *vis-à-vis* homosexual activity.

Indeed, in his August 2010 decision overturning California's Proposition 8, which defined marriage in the state as being solely between a man and a woman, U.S. District Court Judge Vaughn Walker wrote:

> "Proposition 8 targets gays and lesbians in a manner specific to their sexual orientation and, because of their relationship to one another, Proposition 8 targets them specifically due to sex. Having considered the evidence, the relationship between sex and sexual orientation and the fact that Proposition 8 eliminates a right only a gay man or a lesbian would exercise, the court determines that plaintiffs' equal protection claim is based on sexual orientation, but this claim is equivalent to a claim of discrimination based on sex."[9]

The significance of this was that Walker made explicit the relationship between the behavior in question (gay sexual relationships) and the nature of those who would wish to enter into them. He linked sex and sexual orientation, showing that to discriminate against a particular kind of (consenting) sexual relationship was tantamount to discriminating against a particular kind of person, and made the appropriate analogy to sexual discrimination.

Fifteen years prior to Walker's decision, Andrew Sullivan had provoked an intellectual storm with the publication of his manifesto for social change, *Virtually Normal: an Argument About Homosexuality*. The 1995 book sent shock waves through the Vatican and America's conservative Christian 'think-tanks'. Appearing as it did in the wake of the public 'gay gene' revelations of LeVay and Hamer, Sullivan's argument laid down the gauntlet to moralists who still claimed, despite the evidence for homosexual essentialism, that homosexual behavior was inherently immoral.[10] Sullivan, an American practicing Catholic, spelled out the logical consequences of the Church's 1975 response to the growing sociological and psychological evidence that, for a small proportion of the human species, homosexuality is constitutive of their emotional and sexual nature. He demonstrated, in eloquent detail, why the Church had failed in its subsequent attempts to formulate a coherent argument to strengthen its condemnation of homosexual activity. He pointed out that the Church (following St. Thomas's reasoning) needed to explain how things that occur in accordance with a person's nature are somehow against human nature in general. Aquinas's answer had been to suggest psychological sickness, or what the modern church calls an "objective disorder".[11]

But this left unanswered the thorny question of what defines a "disorder" and what counts as "objective". To Sullivan, the Church seemed to be abandoning it's own *a posteriori* methodology. I've argued (above) that the Church's methodology is only nominally 'a posteriori'. It reads nature or 'the natural' through the lenses of a religious worldview in such a way that "God's invisible nature" can be discerned regardless of the visible aspects of nature discerned by means of scientific methodology. Sullivan argued that the church had gone *beyond* Thomas to explain how aspects of a person's given nature are somehow against human nature in general. Church documents located the homosexual disorder *within the constitution of the person* – as part of his or her intrinsic emotional identity. The implication was that 'creation' itself was flawed. The Vatican maintained that the homosexual disposition is morally neutral (like any other mental or physical illness) but that the homosexual is morally culpable in *acting upon* this disposition. In popular parlance the Church's reasoning was woven into a mantra that urged Christians to "love the sinner" but "hate the sin". Meanwhile, from a secular standpoint, the homosexual's status as inherently 'disordered' was beginning to resemble the debunked superstition that left-handed people are 'sinister' and should not use their left hands.[12]

In attempting to make sense of the Church's reasoning, Sullivan addressed the widespread analogy between a genetic predisposition to homosexuality and a genetic predisposition to alcoholism.[13] There is a clear pattern within both Catholic and Protestant theological discourses of linking the two – a pattern that emerged only *after* the Catholic Church's public acknowledgement that homosexuality may be an intrinsic condition.

In January 1991 theologian-bioethicist J. Robert Nelson, in a document titled *Christian Social Action*, attacked the reductionist application of evolutionary theory to social behavior.[14] Defending the older, and normative, concept of unity between soul and body, spirit and matter, in the whole person, he claimed that in Biblical anthropology, "an accepted model of the human person has prevailed" that is still normative for "a probable majority of people of [Christian] heritage."[15] In a strikingly modern turn, Nelson argued that, while the brain is the locus of the mind, mind nevertheless transcends the physico-chemical activity of the brain and the neurosensory system of the body. "This transcendence," he said, "is palpably demonstrated by the exercise of the will in making decisions and directing the actions of the body."[16] In a section subtitled 'susceptibilities' Nelson went on to discuss "predictable dispositions toward various kinds of abnormal behavior." He said, "these are not diseases in the strict sense, but pre-determined patterns of personal behavior." He made a division between those patterns of behavior, such as schizophrenia, that are "not morally reprehensible" and "other types of behavior morally decried by the arbiters of a good society, but toward which the person may be genetically determined. Alcoholism is one of these; sexual aberration is another."[17] Nelson concludes that the emerging knowledge of genetic causation of "morally deplorable behavior" is an "enlarging factor" in the search to understand personal and moral therapy of the whole, psychosomatic person.[18]

This response represents one of the earliest attempts (by a non-Catholic theologian) to simultaneously acknowledge that homosexuality is 'natural' and to stigmatize it as 'abnormal' or 'morally reprehensible' at the same time.

Several years later, in their 1994 response to what they described as a homosexual movement that presents itself as, *inter alia*, "an appeal for extension of civil rights to minorities", the members of the Ramsey Colloquium expressed concerns that many today doubt that we can speak of what is normatively human. Sponsored by the Institute on Religion and Public Life, the Ramsay Colloquium was a group of twenty-one Jewish and Christian conservative theologians, ethicists, philosophers, and scholars whose members include the 'New Natural Law' authors Robert P. George and Russell Hittinger. Their document misrepresented growing doubts over the normative status of heterosexuality as a wholesale rejection of *any* normatively human attributes. It was not. Rather, the doubts were about the way *they* (Christian prohibitionists) had defined what is 'normatively human'. Instead of revising their views on human sexuality to reflect the new empirical data, they decided to redefine the new data in ways that would incorporate it into their *existing* concept of what constitutes 'normative' human sexuality. In their 1994 paper '*The Homosexual Movement: a Response*' the Colloquium's authors stated:

> "When some scientific evidence suggests a genetic predisposition for homosexual orientation, **the case is not significantly different from evidence of predispositions toward other traits—for example, alcoholism or violence.** In each instance we must still ask whether such a predisposition should be acted upon or whether it should be resisted. Whether or not a homosexual orientation can be changed—and it is important to recognize that there are responsible authorities on both sides of this question—we affirm the obligation of pastors and therapists to assist those who recognize the value of chaste living to resist the impulse to act on their desire for homogenital gratification."[19] [my bold]

By claiming that homosexuality is not significantly different from predispositions towards alcoholism or violence, the colloquium's traditionalists implied that homosexuality is a 'defect' in need of fixing.[20] Whether alcoholism and violence really *are* innate tendencies (as opposed to voluntary patterns of behaviour) remains questionable.[21] Whether or how they might compare to homosexuality needs further analysis.

Like Nelson, The Ramsey Colloquium's members compared a genetic predisposition to homosexuality to predispositions towards alcoholism and violence. They affirmed the obligation of pastors and therapists to help individuals resist their desire to act on homosexual impulses. Suddenly, the homosexual was being constructed less as a sinner in rebellion against God (or creation) than a patient in need of compassionate treatment from other human beings. The Rev. Louis P. Sheldon, president of the Traditional Values Coalition in the United States, said that, if a biological cause of homosexuality were found, then, "we would have to come up with some reparative therapy to correct that genetic defect."[22]

In 'Lessons From the Cloning Debate: The Need for a Secular Approach', Wesley J. Smith[23] predicted that, since expectant parents are already pressured to terminate pregnancies when prenatal testing has disclosed Down Syndrome or other genetic anomalies, we should not be surprised if, as our knowledge about the interaction of genes increases, other non-health-related "undesirable" traits might also be rejected. On the list of potential targets for this kind of eugenic weeding, Smith includes "those diagnosed as having a propensity toward obesity, homely features, alcoholism or other addictive behaviours, homosexuality, undesirable stature, poor athletic ability, low intelligence, criminal or other anti-social behaviour, and so on…"[24]

And in a similar vein, Gary DeMar[25] explained why a genetic cause for homosexual desire should not prevent us from refusing to describe the condition as 'normal': "All of us have **sinful desires. Alcoholics still desire alcohol.** Former smokers who have quit still desire a cigarette. People who have lost weight crave the foods they love. … Adulterers mend broken marriages."[26] [my bold]

Andrew Sullivan's provocative argument in *Virtually Normal* (1995) showed why the analogy between alcoholism and homosexuality does not work. He pointed out that the act of having a drink is immoral only for alcoholics, while moderate drinking is perfectly acceptable for non-alcoholics.

Sullivan need not even have granted the premise that the act of having a drink is *immoral* for alcoholics. While having a drink may harm the alcoholic and deepen his condition of dependency, this is not yet a *moral* issue unless it can be shown that the act of drinking alcohol is 'other regarding' behavior that produces a victim, i.e. another person who is substantially harmed by the act. In the absence of a victim, the act ceases to be morally significant. In modern liberal democracies this insight about morally relevant behaviors is enshrined in John Stuart Mill's principle of harm, which specifies that the only justification for interference in the private lives of citizens is to prevent harm to *others*. Moreover, the definition of 'harm' must go beyond behaviors that merely offend others' tastes or sensibilities. Mill and classic liberals defined harm much more narrowly than contemporary politicians do; 'harm,' in its politically significant sense, meant causing substantial harm to the victim's "permanent interests" as a progressive being.[27] Mill distinguishes between harm and mere pain. Stubbing one's toe is painful but not harmful in the politically relevant sense, while brainwashing someone by closing off a vast number of possible actions is harmful although it may never have been attended by pain.[28]

Mill understood human well-being as self-authored; self-regarding actions are those pertaining to the very creation of our selves. For this reason Mill sees liberty as serving individuality, and the human well-being that flows from it.

Interestingly, Mill also makes reference to the alcoholic, as an exemplary case from which we can glean those aspects of behaviour that might justly be subject to interference by the state:

> "Drunkennesses, for example, in ordinary cases, is not a fit subject for legislative interference; but I should deem it perfectly legitimate that a person, who had once been convicted of any act of violence to others under the influence of drink, should be placed under a special legal restriction, personal to himself; that if he were afterwards found drunk, he should be liable to a penalty, and that if when in that state he committed another offence, the punishment to which he would be liable for that other offence should be increased in severity. The making himself drunk, in a person whom drunkenness excites to do harm to others, is a crime against others." [On Liberty, Chapter V] [29]

Evidently the restrictions do not apply to 'ordinary cases' of drunkenness, but only to those in which a tendency to drunken violence towards others has *already been established*. There is nothing about drinking that automatically causes anti-social behaviour, and much evidence points in the opposite direction, suggesting that alcohol more often leads to social behaviour.

Even if we follow Sullivan in granting the weak premise that alcoholism *per se* is immoral, Sullivan identifies another weakness in the alcoholism analogy. The analogy with alcoholism does not work because alcoholism does not reach to the core of the human condition in the way that homosexuality does. It is questionable whether alcoholism is constitutive of a person's inner nature, or refers to a pattern of choices. If alcoholism is overcome the alcoholic does not become less him or herself but more fully able to realise his or her potential. By contrast, if homosexuality is overcome by renunciation of homosexual acts, the person is "liberated" into pain, repression, isolation and grief. The repression of one's intrinsic homosexuality is the abandonment of intimacy and the evisceration of one's emotional core. To quote Sullivan, "It preserves the persona at the expense of the person."[30] The church's admission that homosexuality is "an innate instinct" which is "constitutive of [some persons'] emotional and sexual identity", when combined with their proscription of homosexual acts, begins to seem strange. It would seem the Catholic Church acknowledges that the entire human species is not intrinsically heterosexual, but nevertheless wants everyone to *act* as though it were.

Medical sociologists note that, in the absence of physiological causation, claimants often propose 'compulsivity' as the cause of deviant behaviour and as a justification for medical status.[31] There is much less evidence of genetic or biological causation in the case of criminal behavior and compulsive addictions than there is for homosexual orientation. But even if these other tendencies to act in destructive or harmful ways share with homosexuality a biological etiology, there is nevertheless a difference. Homosexuality is not in itself a tendency to act in destructive or harmful ways. No one disputes the biological causation of **hetero**sexuality. Nor does anyone seem to be interested in seeking to prove it. Yet alleged 'diseases' such as sex addiction or genetic compulsion to sex crimes like rape or pedophilia are treated as distinct from the involuntary **heterosexual** impulse that accompanies them. In the case of the heterosexual rapist, it is the 'criminal' gene, as distinct from the 'heterosexual' gene, that is singled out for 'defective' status. In the case of the homosexual, there is no explanation given for why simply *being* homosexual is sufficient to acquire the status of a 'defect'. Unlike the other behaviors it is compared to (pedophilia, 'polyamorous' relationships or incest), homosexuality is not treated as a separate deviation unrelated to the basic sexual orientation of the subject. Rather, homosexuality *per se* is deemed to lead to destructive or morally evil behavior. Yet there is no evidence for why this should be so. The inner logic for describing homosexual behavior as 'undesirable' or morally wrong must be theological or entail a belief that heterosexuality is a necessary component of any 'healthy' form of sexual expression. But if heterosexuality and homosexuality both have biological roots, there can be no basis for defining heterosexuality as humanly 'normal' or 'ideal' unless it can be shown that heterosexuality is intrinsically beneficial or that homosexuality is intrinsically harmful in some observable sense. Otherwise the identification of sexual 'health' with heterosexuality is tautologous. Definitions are notoriously difficult to argue with.

Having rejected the alcoholism analogy, Sullivan argues that a better comparison to homosexuals is the sterile couple, who are unable, by no fault of their own, to participate in the procreative goodness of heterosexual marital sexual union. The Church's stance is that the immorality of homosexual acts (as with masturbation, extramarital sex, premarital sex) lies in the fact that it is not open to the possibility of procreation in a divinely blessed marital bond. Catholic prohibitionists argue that the union of male and female speaks to the core nature of sexual congress and to its virtuous instantiation. But surprisingly Sullivan does not vigorously attack this claim, although it is perhaps the weakest reasoning marshalled to support the Roman Catholic Church's prohibitionist stance. (I have criticized this reasoning in chapter 4.)

Sullivan might have pointed out, for example, that heterosexual marital acts are not intrinsically good in any **moral** sense, and to uphold heterosexual procreative intercourse *per se* as a supreme moral standard for human sexual conduct, as Catholic teaching does, is to change the meaning of morality altogether. In the modern West, there is broad consensus that we are morally responsible only for the volitional aspects of our behaviour, and not for those aspects of our character and behaviour that stem from biology alone.[32] The Church's approach is mistaken because it appears to confuse pre-moral goods and moral goods. It selects biological aspects of human nature and renders them equally (if not more) essential as a basis for norms about sexual ethics than moral agency and volitional aspects of 'personhood'. While sterility may be a pre-moral evil (according to one reading of the Thomistic rationale that the 'final end' of the reproductive organs is procreation), this has no bearing whatever on a **moral** evaluation of sterile persons' sexual acts. If it did, we could conclude that procreative unitive sexual acts are morally virtuous simply because fertilization might result from them while non-procreative unitive acts (e.g. of sterile couples) are immoral simply because it cannot.

If we are consistent, we will immediately see that, if the moral rightness of a sexual act does not depend upon the potential fertility of the act, as it most certainly does not, then nor can the immorality of a sexual act depend upon a lack thereof. In a *moral* evaluation of any kind of human act, the intention of the agent in performing it matters. So too does the impact of the act on other human beings. The Church's sexual ethics seem to undermine this post-Enlightenment view of what constitutes moral responsibility. However, the Church does not seem to be interested in the basis for moral evaluation operative in a modern secular legal context. Perhaps this apparent indifference to the moral and legal framework of modern liberal democracies is what led Sullivan to conclude that, insofar as the prohibitionist politics is "effective, it is unreasoned; and insofar as it is reasoned, it is increasingly marginal. In a liberal society, which engages citizens with reasons rather than believers with doctrines, it has begun to fail to be a politics at all."[33]

One could think that the church is not interested in mixing religion and politics, but prominent spokespeople from the Catholic and Evangelical right joined forces in 2009 to issue their *Manhattan Declaration*, a manifesto calling upon their "fellow citizens, believers and non-believers alike" to embrace and defend what they claimed were "fundamental truths about justice and the common good".[34] Chuck Colson, one of the declaration's authors, called it "a wake-up call—a call to conscience—for the church" and a "crystal-clear message to civil authorities that we will not, under any circumstances, stand idly by as our religious freedom comes under assault."[35] The authors of this document (chiefly Colson and Robert George, a leading advocate for the 'new natural law') claimed that marriage is intrinsically about procreation, and that where this understanding of marriage erodes, "social pathologies of every sort quickly manifest themselves".[36] In addition the document acknowledges that there are those who are "disposed towards homosexuality" only to then qualify this with "just as there are those disposed towards other forms of immoral conduct." More than fifteen key American Catholic leaders had signed the Declaration upon its release. Others signed it later. Prominent figures like Timothy Dolan, Archbishop of New York and Donald Wuerl, Archbishop of Washington D.C. were amongst the signatories to this manifesto, which sent a powerful message that the Roman Catholic Church is prepared to engage in political battles over public policy alongside evangelicals in the United States. In the next chapter we will see how Christian involvement in the formation of bioethics public policy took shape, both in the United States and the United Kingdom.

1   See Simon LeVay, 'A Difference in Hypothalamic Structure Between Heterosexual and Homosexual Men,' *Science*, August 30, 1991, pp. 1034-1037.

2   LeVay, Simon, <u>Queer Science: The Use and Abuse of Research into Homosexuality</u>, Cambridge mass. The MIT Press, 1996.

3   Dean H. Hamer, Stella Hu, Victoria L. Magnuson, Nan Hu, Angela M. L. Pattatucci, 'A Linkage Between DNA Markers on the X Chromosome and Male Sexual Orientation' *Science*, New Series, Vol. 261, No. 5119 (Jul. 16, 1993), pp. 321-327. (The same year, Germain Grisez, whose new natural law approach was discussed in the previous chapter, added 'marriage' to his list of basic goods, the neglect of which would constitute a moral error.)

4   Ibid.

5   Dean Hamer & Peter Copeland, <u>*The Science of Desire: The Search for the Gay Gene and the Biology of Behavior*</u>, New York: Simon & Schuster, 1994, p. 177.

6   Here I have adopted Andrew Sullivan's term "prohibitionists" for those who argue that homosexual acts are morally wrong, not from bigotry but from a serious tradition of thought that posits heterosexual union as the normative form of human sexual expression. This view is associated with a politics that seeks to cure or punish people who practice homosexual acts, and to deter all the others who might be tempted to stray into the homosexual milieu. (see Sullivan, Andrew, <u>Virtually Normal: an argument about homosexuality</u>, New York, Vintage Books, 1995, pp. 21- 22)

7   See full text of the document online at: <u>http://www. vatican.va/roman_curia/congregations/cfaith/documents/ rc_con_cfaith_doc_19861001_homosexual-persons_en.html</u>

8   Apparently, at about the same time, Catholic bishops in the United States defied their own doctrines on the sanctity of life to defend eugenic research being carried out under the auspices of The March of Dimes. For the full story see: <u>http://www.catholictradition.org/Life/march-dimes.htm</u>

9   United States District Court for the Northern District of California, Kristin M. Perry, Sandra B Steir, Paul T. Katami and Jeffrey J. Zarrillo v. Arnold Schwarzenegger, No C 09-2292 VRW, pp. 120-121.

10  Sullivan, Andrew, <u>Virtually Normal: an argument about homosexuality</u>, New York, Vintage Books, 1995, p. 38.

11  Ibid., p. 41.

12  The left hand was used as a classification mechanism that symbolized natural evil, a metaphor from ancient Hebrew and Mesopotamian culture that was integrated into mainstream Christianity by early Catholic theologians such as Ambrose of Milan. See: ***Ambrose of Milan: political letters and speeches*** / translated with an introduction and notes by J.H.W.G. Liebeschuetz, (Liverpool, England: Liverpool University Press, 2005).

Robert Hertz, a student of Emile Durkheim, published an essay titled "*The pre-eminence of the right hand: A study in religious polarity*" in 1909. Hertz noted that a huge set of values and associations had been accorded to a small biological asymmetry. Left-handedness is everywhere less common than the dominance of the right. It is a convenient marker on which cultures have erected an edifice of symbolic associations that are nearly as universal as any symbol can be.

13    Sullivan, Andrew, <u>Virtually Normal: an Argument About Homosexuality</u>, New York, Vintage Books, 1995, pp. 43-45.

14    First coined by E.O. Wilson, a Pulitzer Prize winning Harvard biologist, the term 'sociobiology' refers to the application of evolutionary theory to social behaviour. Sociobiology expands standard Darwinian evolutionary theory to the domain of human behaviour, which sociobiologists see on a continuum with animal sociality. According to the *Stanford Encyclopedia of Philosophy*, critics of human sociobiology regard standard sociobiological models as "inadequate to account for human behaviour, because they ignore the contributions of the mind and culture. A second criticism concerns genetic determinism, the view that many social behaviours are genetically fixed. Critics of sociobiology often complain of its reliance on genetic determinism, especially of human behaviour, and claim that it provides tacit approval of the status quo. If male aggression is genetically fixed and reproductively advantageous, critics argue, then male aggression seems to be a biological reality (and, perhaps, a biological 'good') about which we have little control. This seems to be both politically dangerous and scientifically implausible."

15    Nelson, J. Robert, 'Genetic Research Broadens the Understanding of Humanness' in <u>What is Life?,</u> Christian Social Action, 1991, p. 268.

16    Ibid.

17    Ibid.

18    Ibid., p. 269.

19    Accessed online at <u>www.OrthodoxyToday.org</u>

20    For example, the Ramsey Colloquium explicitly stated that "When some scientific evidence suggests a genetic predisposition for homosexual orientation, the case is not significantly different from evidence of predispositions toward other traits, such as alcoholism or violence." The members of the colloquium urge therapists and pastors to assist people in resisting the impulse to act on their desire for homosexual gratification. This statement was re-printed in *The Month*, July 1994, pp. 260-265.

21    See Benn, Piers, 'Can Addicts Help It?' in *Philosophy Now* Magazine, Issue 80, Aug/Sept 2010, pp. 17-20. Benn, a lecturer at the Imperial College School of Medicine in London, has argued that 'disease' models are conceptually linked to the idea of powerlessness and that assumptions underlying the medicalization of

alcoholism (alcohol addiction) rest on the belief that the cause of the addiction is a disorder outside of the addict's will. AA folkore and literature, he says, contribute to a 'disease model' in which individuals accept that recovery is not possible on their own, but only with the aid of a Higher Power – God. Benn argues there is no justification for regarding alcoholism as a disease. Even a partly genetic explanation (where there is conclusive evidence to implicate genetic factors in some cases of alcoholism) does not imply that people with 'alcoholic' genes are *compelled* to drink. At most, it explains why some people are more inclined than others to become alcoholics. Even if genetic factors caused alcohol to abnormally boost the brain's production of pleasure-enhancing hormones dopamine and seratonin, this would not be compulsion.

[22]   Quoted in Larry Thompson, "Search for a Gay Gene", TIME (12 June, 1995).

[23]   Smith is a lawyer, author and Senior Fellow at the *Discovery Institute*'s Center on Human Exceptionalism. The *Discovery Institute* is a public policy think tank best known for its advocacy of intelligent design creationism. Smith is also a special consultant for the U.S. based *Center for Bioethics and Culture*.

[24]   Smith, Wesley, J., J.D., 'Lessons from the Cloning Debate' in <u>Human Dignity in the Biotech Century: a Christian Vision for Public Policy</u>, Charles W. Colson and Nigel M. de S. Cameron, Eds., Downers Grove, Il., InterVarsity Press, 2004, p. 198.

[25]   DeMar has authored over twenty books and is head of *American Vision*, a non-profit Christian ministry in the United States, founded in 1978.

[26]   'My Genes Made Me Do It', The AmericanVision.Org, Aug. 26, 2009.

[27]   In 'On Liberty' in Chapter 1, introductory, Mill states: "It is proper to state that I forego any advantage which could be derived to my argument from the idea of abstract right as a thing independent of utility. I regard utility as the ultimate appeal on all ethical questions; but it must be utility in the largest sense, grounded on the **permanent interests** of man as a **progressive** being. Those **interests**, I contend, authorize the subjection of individual spontaneity to external control, only in respect to those actions of each, which concern the interest of other people. If any one does an act hurtful to others, there is a prima facie case for punishing him, by law, or, where legal penalties are not safely applicable, by general disapprobation." In Chapter V Mill elaborates the conditions under which one might suffer emotional pain as a result of disappointment in a competitive institution, and says that "society admits no right, either legal or moral, in the disappointed competitors, to immunity from this kind of suffering; and feels called on to interfere, only when means of success have been employed which it is contrary to the general interest to permit — namely, fraud or treachery, and force." (see Collini, Stefan, Ed., <u>On Liberty and Other Writings</u>, Cambridge University Press, 1989, p. 14.)

[28] McCabe, Helen, 'On Liberty: an introduction', in *Philosophy Now* Magazine, Issue 67, November/December 2009, pp. 7-8.

[29] Collini, Stefean, Ed., <u>On Liberty and Other Writings</u>, Cambridge University Press, 1989, p. 98.

[30] Sullivan, Op. Cit. p. 189.

[31] Conrad, Peter and Schneider, Joseph W., <u>Deviance and Medicalization: From Badness to Sickness,</u> Philadelphia, Temple University Press, 1992, p. 47.

[32] In English common law, *mens rea* is considered to be an ingredient of all criminal offences, although some minor statutory offences are punishable irrespective of it. While common law defines an act as a voluntary or involuntary bodily movement, the Model Penal Code which has been incorporated into US criminal law stipulates that the act must be voluntary. Under the principles of English common law, an act alone does not make a person guilty of committing a crime. Illegal intent is also required. The legal concepts of 'diminished responsibility' and the McNaughten rules also reflect in principle the inseparable relationship between voluntary intent and moral guilt.

[33] Sullivan, Op. Cit., p. 55.

[34] 'Manhattan Declaration: a summary', pg. 1, 2009 (drafting committee: Robert P. George, McCormick Professor of Jurisprudence, Princeton University, Timothy George, Professor, Beeson Divinity School, Samford University, Chuck Colson Founder, the Chuck Colson Center for Christian Worldview, Lansdowne, VA).

[35] Colson, Chuck, 'The Manhattan Declaration; Defending Life, Marriage and Freedom', Nov. 20, 2009, at http://www.breakpoint.org/commentaries/13534-the-manhattan-declaration

[36] "The Manhattan Declaration: a call of Christian conscience", at http://www.manhattandeclaration.org/the-declaration/read.aspx, 'marriage' section, paragraph 2.

# CHAPTER 6

# *Heterosexist Christian bioethics:*
# *a cartography & critical evaluation*

In the Anglo-American Christian literature on sexual ethics in the 1990's, one sees homosexual behavior being treated less as a rebellious deviation from 'created' nature (as in Paul's epistles) and more as an innate disease or disorder. This suggests a tension between the traditional Christian imperative to conform to one's 'created' biological nature and the growing evidence for a 'gay gene' that was being widely circulated at the time. For the sake of accuracy, it is probably more accurate to speak of a 'biological substrate' for homosexuality (or indeed for sexual orientation, of whichever type). Regardless, the traditional concept of 'health' is the organism's functioning in accordance with its given nature (unless there is a good reason not to). Applying the 'disease' label to the (still theoretical) homosexual biology was therefore becoming more difficult to reconcile with new evidence suggesting that the homosexual orientation is in many cases a naturally occurring variant of human sexuality.

One way of explaining how the disease metaphor could be applied to homosexuality in these circumstances was to suggest that acting according to one's given homosexual nature endangers or harms *others* in some significant way. The pedophile provides a model example of such a 'diseased' individual (where the harm is extrinsic to the subject). In March 2013, pediatric neurosurgeon Dr. Benjamin Carson compared same-sex relationships to pedophilia and bestiality on Fox News.[1]

But again, there are problems with this comparison. First, whether pedophilia ought to be considered a 'disease' or a 'crime' hinges on whether the pedophile is capable of self-restraint. If his nature *compels* his behavior (and not merely his attraction), then his behavior is determined, so he cannot be held personally responsible for it. In these circumstances it would seem to make sense to label his condition a 'disease'. But if he *is* capable of controlling his unconventional (and in this case *harmful)* urges, then his decision to act on his attraction to children is a moral vice, not a 'disease'. Current social attitudes and penal policies tend to treat the pedophile's behavior as a moral outrage and a crime, which implies a rejection of determinism. Presumably, moral outrage is directed at the pedophile because of both the belief that he could have acted otherwise and the harm done to non-consenting victims of his behavior.

Attempts to explain the homosexual 'disease' in terms extrinsic to the homosexual person are more problematic, especially in light of evidence that 'out' gay people are flourishing and making valuable contributions to society. The discourse had to shift to explain the 'disease' in new terms that could re-define it as an innate tendency to 'sinful' *behavior.* This meant that all homosexual acts *as such* had to be harmful to others or morally evil in some sense. The homosexual was "sick" because of his innate tendency to do morally evil things (namely, to have sex with consenting adults of the same sex).

But there was a price to be paid for viewing homosexual orientation as an innate tendency to 'sinful' behavior. The explanation for why a homosexual orientation was 'disordered' or 'defective' had to be given in terms of the behavior to which it led, and this implied that, for homosexuals (and maybe for a minority of other 'disordered' types) bad behavior is causally determined by one's 'disordered' predisposition, rather than by one's free choices. This implies **both** that homosexuals do not have free will **and** that something about homosexual actions *per se* is intrinsically morally evil. The argument required two contradictory premises: (1) that the 'sinful' behavior was rooted in a naturally occurring trait, and (2) that the voluntary will of the agent (which apparently does not exist) caused the 'sin', which explains why the agent could be held blameworthy for choosing to *act upon* the evil tendency.

This reasoning created two problems. First it suggested that a small subset of harmful or destructive behaviors is biologically determined. This would mean that for some 'sins' or crimes we ought to treat the offender medically, as a patient who is sick, while for other sins/crimes we ought to treat the offender as a responsible moral agent, and punish him for his bad choices. With respect to the homosexual, the Christian Right's prohibitionist language seemed to waver between the two. While labeling homosexual orientation an 'objective disorder' and suggesting that it needed a cure, the Christian right's prohibitionist literature also asserted that the homosexual agent's innate predisposition was morally neutral and only his voluntary behavior to be sexually active made him a "sinner", i.e. bad. The latter view was accompanied, almost invariably, by the popular platitude: "Love the sinner, hate the sin." Second, and more importantly, Christian prohibitionists' proclamations failed to explain why *all* homosexual acts are intrinsically evil or sinful, since there seems to be no victim and no harm in most homosexual acts, while other 'sins' clearly produce victims and indisputable harm. For homosexual behavior, the reverse was true -- many people seemed to be much healthier and happier because they had chosen to express, and not to repress, their disposition to homosexual behavior.

Despite its fundamental disagreements with the foundations of secular ethics in liberal democracies, the Catholic Church has made attempts to modernize its doctrines and to reduce the tensions between post-Enlightenment ways of thinking and its own. The post-medieval focus on intention and agency guided the church, in its 1968 encyclical *Humanae Vitae,* to incorporate new proclamations on the importance of the "unitive" aspect of heterosexual congress into its documents on the subject. The relevant remarks appear in Section II., 'Doctrinal Principles'. Question 11, *'Observing the Natural Law'* begins by stating that sexual activity between husband and wife does not cease to be legitimate even when, for reasons independent of their will, it is foreseen to be infertile. After all, even within God's plan it can be observed that each and every act of sexual congress does not lead to new life. This is followed by the more problematic assertion that men are nevertheless urged to the observance of the precepts of natural law according to which "every marital act must of necessity retain its intrinsic relationship to the **procreation** of human life." [my bold] It would seem that the intrinsic relationship to the procreation of human life is precisely what is lacking in the union of an infertile couple, as in the many unions in which fertilization does not take place. However, the next question, '*Union and Procreation*', Question 12, goes on to explain that this doctrine is "based on the inseparable connection, established by God, which man on his own initiative may not break, between the **unitive** significance and the procreative significance which are both inherent to the marriage act." Importantly, the "intrinsic relationship to the procreation of human life" that belongs to the infertile couple is not to be understood literally, as a biological potential to conceive new life. Rather, it is "because of laws written into the actual natures of man and of woman", and according to which, "if each of the essential qualities (unitive and procreative) are preserved", then "the marriage act fully retains its sense of true mutual love and its ordination to the supreme responsibility of parenthood to which man is called."

The church teaches that heterosexual couples, even when infertile, preserve the procreative potential because of "laws written into the natures of men and of women." But this overlooks research which suggests that homosexuality is "written into the natures" of approximately ten percent of men and women. Furthermore, it is difficult to understand these "laws" in biological terms if the "procreative potential" they represent does not actually depend upon the ability to procreate. In the case of infertile couples, the heterosexual union can only preserve the procreative potential in a symbolic sense. The "laws written into the actual natures of men and women" are indeed just that - they are not inherent in, but *inscribed* (through human, cultural constructs) onto the natures of men and of women. They function as symbolic markers on which the church has erected an edifice of associations and ethical norms. Just as left-handedness, because of its relative rarity, had been used as a classification mechanism that symbolized natural evil, so homosexuality is transformed into an illegitimate form of sexual expression. The position expressed in *Humanae Vitae* (1968) is explicitly reiterated in the 2009 *Manhattan Declaration*:

"That is why in Christian tradition, and historically in Western law, consummated marriages are not dissoluble or annullable on the ground of infertility, even though the nature of the marital relationship is shaped and structured by its intrinsic orientation to the great good of procreation."[2]

Partly to alleviate the tensions that arose from excluding individual agency from sexual morality altogether, *Humanae Vitae* gave equal weight to the unitive aspect of the marital bond. The significance of "unitive" is that it ensures that the sexual acts in question, in addition to being symbolically procreative, are **consenting**. This seems intuitively correct, for there is nothing about the biological fact of procreative sex that makes it sufficient as a *moral* standard. Procreative sexual behavior is not *inherently* virtuous, as we know from countless stories of abuse, pedophilia, exploitation and rape (including marital rape). In order to preserve her stance against homosexual activity, the church only needed to show that acts **lacking** the procreative potential are immoral. She didn't need to argue that potentially procreative sexual activity is a sufficient condition for morally virtuous sexual behavior. Had she argued that procreative potential is sufficient, she would have had to admit as morally acceptable various non-consenting forms of sexual behavior (rape, pedophilia, etc). The church needed only to maintain that procreative potential is a *necessary* condition for virtuous sexual conduct, without which sexual acts are rendered 'sinful'.

But many, including faithful Catholics, did not find this convincing. We need only ask whether there could be unitive and mutually beneficial sexual acts that are *not* potentially procreative, and here again we find that the answer is a resounding 'yes'. Even from the most heterosexist standpoint, there are many non-procreative sexual intimacies (including sexual intercourse between sterile couples and post-menopausal couples, including oral and anal sexual acts, involving pre-marital and post-marital couples, or contracepting heterosexual couples) that do not implicate the participants in any kind of moral vice. The symbolic importance attached to the 'one man and one woman' form of marriage and sexual intimacy has significance for some believers within the Christian community. For others, it does not.

From the standpoint of modern ethics, in which agency and harm to others are crucial standards by which an act takes on moral contours, the burden of proof is on the Church to show that there is something inherently harmful about non-procreative consenting sex acts *per se*. But 'victims' of consenting homosexual acts have been conspicuously absent. In liberal democracies, the presence of a 'victim' is an important test for whether the state can justifiably interfere in an individual's liberty. Therefore, it is particularly alarming that the authors of *The Manhattan Declaration* call upon **civil authorities** to proscribe homosexual unions that they say harm Christian conservatives' definitions of marriage and the common good. Instead of producing human victims, Christian prohibitionists resort to the claim that it is their *definition* of 'marriage' (a religious definition of marriage) that is threatened by legalizing homosexual marital unions. In an address to half a million Catholics at the shrine of Fatima on May 13, 2010, Pope Benedict XVI condemned same-sex marriage as an "insidious and dangerous" challenge to society and the common good.[3] And Cardinal Jorge Bergoglio, now Pope Francis, supported these sentiments in describing [marriage equality] as a destructive pretension against the plan of God. He asserted that the legalization of gay marriage is much more than a mere political issue and claimed that it should instead be viewed as "a machination of the Father of Lies that seeks to confuse and deceive the children of God."[4]

In similar fashion, *The Manhattan Declaration* of November 20, 2009 stated that marriage is an objective reality "that it is the duty of the law to recognize and support for the sake of justice and the common good." The authors claimed that the common good of civil (not Christian) society "is damaged when the law itself . . . becomes a tool for eroding a sound understanding of marriage..."[5] Presumably, a 'sound' understanding of marriage is a conservative Christian understanding of marriage. But this begs the question as to whose rights are really being violated by a law that continues to uphold the Christian definition of marriage within a Western liberal democracy whose Constitution stipulates that the state must remain neutral between different visions of the good life and is explicitly prohibited from endorsing a particular religious worldview.

Sullivan was correct to conclude that civil marriage is a social and public recognition of a private commitment and denying it to homosexuals is the most public affront possible to their public equality.[6] Moreover, the heterosexuality of marriage is intrinsic only if marriage is understood to be intrinsically procreative.[7] However, no civil marriage license is granted on the condition that the couple bears children; and no marriage is less legal if it remains childless.[8] The denial of civil marriage to homosexuals constitutes a quintessential case of proactive discrimination by the state against homosexual persons as such. The *Manhattan Declaration*'s authors invert the reality of the situation in claiming that justice and the common good are undermined when the law becomes a tool for eroding a 'sound' (i.e. Christian) understanding of marriage. When the law does uphold a single religious standard for marriage, it is in breach of the establishment clause of the First Amendment[9] and represents a classic case of state discrimination against non-Christian understandings of marriage.[10]

The *Manhattan Declaration*'s claim about the immoral status of all homosexual acts[11] also begs important questions. Whether any moral value attaches to heterosexual intercourse within marriage depends upon the same criteria that any moral evaluation does: a moral agent, a moral 'patient'/victim, harm/benefit, and intentional behavior. Once we take these into account, we realize that marriage has no intrinsic moral value independent of that erected by Christian doctrine. At best, it has pre-moral value for heterosexuals. *Actual* marriages are as good or as bad as the parties to them choose to make them. Sex acts are potentially beautiful, ugly, abusive, sublime, crude, ecstatic, loving, cruel, selfish, unselfish, nurturing, exploitative or humiliating. Which of these a sexual act becomes is not determined by whether the participants are married. Vast human experience tells us that marriage is not a necessary condition for morally acceptable sex acts; nor is a non-marital context sufficient to characterize them as 'immoral'.

Christian prohibitionists speak to a circle of initiates who understand their symbolic definitions and assent to them from within a context of prior commitment and faith. Belief in the symbolic importance of marriage and procreative potential for all sex acts is similar to belief in the transformation of bread and wine into the body and blood of Christ. I do not say this derisively but rather to point out that the ritualized eating of bread with its internal meaning ("as body of Christ") for members of the faith is not empirically falsifiable because it is not intended to contain a proposition that could be rendered true or false by the production of objective evidence. Rather it is "true" for those who already accept the definitions on faith. 'Truth' in this context is not a test of whether proposition 'p' corresponds to some independent state of affairs that can be empirically tested, but refers to the meaningfulness of the proposition for insiders who already believe in a set of propositions because of their faith or their "worldview". In this sense, to establish marriage as the exclusive domain in which sexual conduct can rightfully occur depends entirely upon the success with which institutional values and 'sacramental meaning' can be inscribed onto 'nature' by a religious subculture (or in America, by a religious majority).

For the most part, Christian prohibitionists have not hidden the fact that they wish to protect not human victims of harm, but a public definition of 'marriage' with roots in Christian tradition. Chief among the alleged social goods that marriage is supposed to protect is the family as a basic social unit. But here again, there is little evidence that homosexual marriage would do any actual harm to *real* families. Since prohibitionists concede the existence of people for whom homosexuality is "an innate instinct" constitutive of their identity, they must also acknowledge that these people are also members of heterosexual families. The distinction between "families" and "homosexuals" is empirically false. The stability of existing families *is* threatened partly by how homosexuals are treated within them. As many as 50 percent of LGBT teens experience a negative reaction from their parents when they come out; 30 percent experience physical abuse and 26 percent are kicked out of their homes. LGBT children comprise 40 percent of all homeless youth and family rejection is the primary cause. Additionally, LGBT adults who report family rejection are six times more likely to be depressed, three times more likely to use illegal drugs and eight times more likely to have attempted suicide than non-rejected young adults.[12] Christian prohibitionists don't want gay sons and daughters in their families at all, even though they produce gay sons and daughters. Gay fathers and mothers who are passing as heterosexual find the charade unbearable; spouses are betrayed, children are abandoned and families are broken.[13] While Christian conservatives sometimes imply that homosexuals are promiscuous and lead depraved, shallow lives, they have also opposed social incentives like gay marriage that would help gay and lesbian people **not** to live promiscuous lives. Homosexuals who have no choice to be homosexual are unwanted by their conservative Christian families anyway, so they do not pose a threat to the family, except by staying within the familial unit to which they were born. Knowing they are unwanted, many choose to leave. Since homosexuality is constitutive of their intrinsic nature, they are not choosing homosexuality over heterosexual marriage; and so they are not sending any social message that heterosexual family life should be diminished.[14] There is no reason to believe that we cannot celebrate the traditional heterosexual family and also celebrate stable homosexual relationships. Many families already do.

The way that (predominantly Protestant) prohibitionist theologians have dealt with the apparent healthiness of homosexuals who express their sexuality by engaging in sexual acts is twofold. First, they use appeals to vividness[15] in producing few but widely publicized testimonials by "ex-gay" persons who now claim to lead happy, healthy heterosexual lives after undergoing secular "reparative therapy" or Christian counseling within "ex-gay ministries" such as *Exodus International* or *CORE Issues*, a Northern Ireland-based group which claims to support gay and lesbian men and women who wish to change sexual preference and expression. In her analysis of the ex-gay movement, Surina Khan, an associate analyst at Political Research Associates, says that it "offers a vehicle for publicly questioning the very sexual and social identity of homosexuals and, by extension, undermining their claim to civil rights legal protections. After all, the argument goes, if lesbian and gay people need not be homosexuals, because with God's help or through reparative therapy they can "heal" themselves, then civil rights for gay/lesbian/bisexual/transgender people are not needed.[16] Sara Diamond identifies this as a repackaging of the Right's "no special rights" theme, an idea that casts civil rights as limited to ethnic minority groups. The "special rights" theme relies on the argument that sexual orientation is not a basis for discrimination and that gay/lesbian/bisexual/transgender people simply want to win legitimacy for their "deviant" behavior by putting it on a par with immutable characteristics such as skin color.[17]

Rev. Mario Brugner is one of many ex-gay lecturers. His book *Setting Love in Order* explains how to confront "the personal confusion associated with sexual and relational brokenness in all its forms."[18]

In the early part of this century, with much publicity for ex-gay counseling circulating in the United States, the American Psychiatric Association found it necessary to reaffirm its 1973 stance. They adopted a resolution that says there's no scientific evidence showing that therapy can make gay people straight. On August 4, 2009 they issued their statement, '*Appropriate Therapeutic Responses to Sexual Orientation*', which advises treatments that "increase family and school support and reduce rejection of sexual minority youth." The report also states: "Some difficulties arise because the professional psychological community considers same-sex sexual attractions and behaviors to be a positive variant of human sexuality, while some traditional faiths continue to consider it a sin, moral failing, or disorder that needs to be changed."[19] The Christian right's pundits responded with claims that the APA's reports and statements are "pseudoscientific"[20] whereas reparative therapies are based on valid and reasonable information.[21]

Meanwhile, in the UK, the British Medical Association found it necessary to ban 'conversion therapies' targeted at altering a person's sexual orientation. More than two-thirds of the BMA's doctors voted to end such therapies in their codes of practice. This motion was adopted following the results of a 2009 survey conducted by London's University College revealing that one in six British psychiatrists and counsellors would still offer conversion therapies to GLBT people. Dr. Tom Dolphin of the BMA's Junior Doctors Committee told journalists, "Treating same-sex attraction as a disease that can be cured has an insidious effect to pathologise what is part of the normal spectrum of human sexuality."[22]

The fifth edition of the American Psychiatric Association's *Diagnostic and Statistical Manual of Mental Disorders* (DSM-5) went under review by a new panel. An updated edition was published in May 2013. The manual standardizes and defines the diagnostic criteria for a host of psychiatric conditions, including sexual aberration. At stake is the potential medicalization or pathologizing of certain unconventional sexual behaviors under the auspices of empirical science. Currently catalogued disorders include sadism, voyeurism, erectile disorders, transvestism, and pedophilia. The panel's *Sexual and Gender Identity Disorders Work Group* distinguished 'paraphilic disorders' from atypical human sexual behavior by defining the former as those sexual desires and behaviors that cause mental distress to a person or make the person a serious threat to the psychological and physical well-being of other individuals. At first glance, this looks reasonable. It requires the threat of harm to both the **physical** and psychological well-being of others. However, the document goes on to explain that a minimum requirement for diagnosis is that people with atypical sexual interests have a sexual desire or behavior that merely involves another person's psychological distress.[23] This makes virtually any atypical sexually behavior fair game for diagnosis.

Homosexuality was removed from the DSM in 1973 but this move was hotly contested by religious conservatives and could still be reversed. Dr. Charles Moser, an affiliate of the Institute for Advanced Study of Human Sexuality in San Francisco, has recommended the removal of all *paraphilias* (unusual sexual interests) from the DSM, claiming that such a move would force transgressors to accept responsibility for criminal sexual behaviors and deny them the use of pathology as a mitigating factor.[24]

A second strategy deployed by religious prohibitionists[25] has been to adopt the terms "lifestyle" and "lifestyle choices" to refer to homosexuals and homosexual behavior. The Christian right's leading organizations made this discourse all pervasive in the 1990's.[26] This rhetoric represented an implicit denial that homosexuality *is,* like heterosexuality, constitutive of a person's fundamental nature or identity or that, while it is constitutive of some people's fundamental identity, it is nevertheless bad when acted upon.

Ted Peters is exemplary of this stance.[27] In his 1997 book *Playing God: Genetic Determinism and Human Freedom*, he began to speculate on what it would mean for social toleration of homosexuality if indeed there is a 'gay gene'. Peters was not convinced that the discovery of genetic homosexuality would lead to increased social acceptability and protection against discrimination for gay and lesbian persons. Although homosexual essentialism may aid in the defense of homosexuals against anti-gay constructivists who presume that homosexuality is voluntary, it will not protect them against those who believe that homosexual orientation leads to immoral behavior, and so should be treated as one of many other genetic *defects*, on a par with breast cancer. Peters asked whether we ought to praise genetic science for helping us to find a medical way to cure our society of homosexuality.

Despite these comments, Peters took a skeptical stance towards the scientific evidence for genetic homosexual orientation, and concluded that such science is in doubt. Nevertheless, he hesitantly accepted that our biological substrate, which is "heavily influenced by our genes" is likely to predispose some individuals to what we know as a homosexual orientation. Peters set out hypothetical arguments about how Christians should respond to homosexual essentialism.

On the one hand, he said, if we can establish that the basis for sexual orientation lies in the genes we inherit, then this puts sexual orientation into a category comparable to eye color, height, skin pigmentation, or other bodily features that, in themselves, are morally neutral. But Peters claimed that genetic essentialism does not in itself prevent homosexuality from being lumped in a category with other undesirable genes.

In this respect, his Protestant perspective is consonant with *The Pastoral Care of Homosexual Persons* (1986), in which Joseph Ratzinger claimed that an "overly benign interpretation had been given to the homosexual condition itself" in the church's 1975 document. Hence, the 1986 document expressly **rejected** the notion that homosexual orientation *per se* is neutral, or even good, while also expressing the view that "the particular **inclination** of the homosexual person is **not a sin**". Instead, the 1986 letter explains that homosexuality "is a more or less strong tendency ordered toward an intrinsic moral evil; and thus the inclination itself must be seen as an objective disorder." To give this claim some content, point 6. in the 1986 pastoral letter references a Biblical passage:

> Providing a basic plan for understanding this entire discussion of homosexuality is the theology of creation we find in Genesis. God, in his infinite wisdom and love, brings into existence all of reality as a reflection of his goodness. He fashions mankind, male and female, in his own image and likeness. Human beings, therefore, are nothing less than the work of God himself; and in the complementarity of the sexes, they are called to reflect the inner unity of the Creator. They do this in a striking way in their cooperation with him in the transmission of life by a mutual donation of the self to the other.

This seemed to suggest that, while homosexuals may be created that way after all, they are not created 'in the image of God'. The 'fallen creation' motif took root in The Ramsay Colloquium's 1994 'Response to the Homosexual Movement'. Its authors stated:

> "What is in accord with human nature is behavior appropriate to what we are meant to be—appropriate to what God created and calls us to be.

> In a fallen creation, many quite common attitudes and behaviors must be straightforwardly designated as sin. Although we are equal before God, we are not born equal in terms of our strengths and weaknesses, our tendencies and dispositions, our nature and nurture." (section IV - 'The Claims of the Movement')

Two approaches have dominated the various Catholic and evangelical responses to homosexuality in the 1990's. The first was to suggest that, pending further evidence, homosexuality is a lifestyle choice rather than what Sullivan calls "an essentially involuntary condition that can neither be denied nor permanently repressed".[28] But the second, and more predominant, approach was to acknowledge that homosexuality occurs in nature as an involuntary condition but to fuse this observation with theological pseudo-science to pathologize the condition as a 'disorder' in need of therapeutic or medical treatment. The 'therapeutic' trend in theological discourses around homosexuality became more pronounced in the late 1990's and continued into the twenty-first century, in which pathologization of the homosexual predisposition is now the dominant approach.

The presuppositions about sexual ethics that underpin the Christian prohibitionist stance also inform Christian bioethics. In his essay on human cloning, 'Christian Vision for the Biotech Century: Towards a Strategy' Nigel M. de S. Cameron[29] recommends that Christians and their communities be 'educated' by what Leon Kass[30] has called the 'wisdom of repugnance'. Kass's concerns centre on human dignity and the subtle ways in which our attempts to assert technological mastery over human nature could end up dehumanizing us by undermining various traditional meanings such as the meaning of the life cycle, the meaning of sex, the meaning of eating, and the meaning of work.[31] In brief, Kass has argued that the repugnance we feel towards incest, bestiality, and other practices (he does not directly mention homosexuality) is an indication of natural emotional expression of deep wisdom, beyond reason's power fully to articulate. While Kass does not explicitly address homosexuality, his views on it may be inferred from what he says about sex:

> "Thanks to the sexual revolution, we are able to deny in practice, and increasingly in thought, the inherent procreative teleology of sexuality itself. But, if sex has no intrinsic connection to generating babies, babies need have no necessary connection to sex. Thanks to feminism and the gay rights movement, we are increasingly encouraged to treat the natural heterosexual difference and its pre-eminence as a matter of "cultural construction." But if male and female are not normatively complementary and generatively significant, babies need not come from male and female complementarity."[32]

And:

> "Sexual reproduction — by which I mean the generation of new life from (exactly) two complementary elements, one female, one male, (usually) through coitus — is established (if that is the right term) not by human decision, culture or tradition, but by nature; it is the natural way of all mammalian reproduction."[33]

While Kass is right to say that male-female union is the natural way of all mammalian *reproduction*, it would be mistaken to say the same of all mammalian *sexuality*. Scientists have observed homosexual behavior occurring naturally in as many as 450 species of non-human animals. Like the conservative Catholic thinkers with whom Kass associates,[34] he holds the view that "whether or not we know it, the severing of procreation from sex, love and intimacy is inherently dehumanizing". This begs the question. Kass assumes what he needs to prove – namely that homosexuality is not within the spectrum of healthy human sexuality. He seems to harbor a bias against natural biodiversity, which could have a role to play in species (not just individual) survival. Kass slides from a sound premise about mammalian reproductive nature to a conclusion about human sexual nature more generally.

Kass's approach to genetic manipulation is carefully merged with his invalid conclusions about human sexuality. His arguments against cloning human beings leave open the possibility of genetic therapy for 'curing' homosexuality. What he finds 'profoundly dehumanizing' about cloning is that it is instrumental making – the animals cloned are designed "as means to serve rational human purposes":

> "How does begetting differ from making? In natural procreation, human beings come together, complementarily male and female, to give existence to another being who is formed, exactly as we were, by what we are: living, hence perishable, hence aspiringly erotic, human beings. In clonal reproduction, by contrast, and in the more advanced forms of manufacture to which it leads, we give existence to a being not by what we are but by what we intend and design."[35]

The allusion to "perishable, hence erotic" in the list of things that make us what we are, ties in with Kass's understanding that human sexuality is inherently the expression of the will to reproduction and hence immortality (i.e. genetic survival). Homosexuality need only be described as lacking the potential for natural procreation in order to designate it a 'disorder'. Kass's manner of distinguishing begetting from making allows genetic therapy for homosexuality to fall under "begetting" or to be seen as a variant of "natural procreation" since the parents would be forming a child exactly as they are (i.e. inherently reproductive). He says:

> "These biological truths about our origins foretell deep truths about our identity and about our human condition altogether. Every one of us is at once equally human, equally enmeshed in a particular familial nexus of origin, and equally individuated in our trajectory from birth to death — and, if all goes well, equally capable (despite our mortality) of participating, with a complementary other, in the very same renewal of such human possibility through procreation. Though less momentous than our common humanity, our genetic individuality is not humanly trivial."[36]

Kass's privileging of abstract notions of what constitutes our "common humanity" over genetic individuality is accomplished by moving away from *a posteriori* descriptions of the natures of particular humans to abstract, *a priori* definitions of human nature. This move allows Kass to interpret the capacity for procreation as more "momentous" to our humanity than our genetic individuality. But for homosexuals, the generically 'human' capacity for sexual reproduction is presumably ruled out by sexual attraction to the same sex. On this view, the genetic individuality of the homosexual includes an incapacity for reproduction, and this doesn't "go well". But Kass's *a priori* premise - that our common humanity *is* generically heterosexual -- is exactly what he needs to prove. Most evidence points to the contrary – namely, that heterosexuality is no more essential to our 'common humanity' than maleness, right-handedness or brown hair. This interpretation furnishes "deep truths about our identity" only by ignoring empirical evidence about our identity. It also ignores the fact that homosexuals are not incapable of reproduction, but only of sexual attraction to the opposite sex, which does not necessarily prevent homosexuals from reproducing.

When he says, "In natural procreation, human beings come together, complementarily male and female, to give existence to another being who is formed, exactly as we were, by what we are...", Kass's thinking borrows from the new molecular biology in giving historical and ontological primacy to the hereditary molecule, such that the organism is merely DNA's way of making another DNA molecule. The sociobiologists' central dogma is that the gene is ontologically prior to the individual and the individual to society. Theologian J. Robert Nelson, too, alludes to the sociobiologists' claim that "the only purpose of genes is to reproduce more of the same, whatever the organism may be".[37] The exclusion of homosexual orientation from this "whatever" is assured by the reproductive purpose intrinsic to all genes. So, Kass says parents would be forming a child who, like themselves, is "aspiringly erotic" (in the exclusively heterosexual, procreative sense in which Kass understands 'eroticism').

But, as Rose, Lewontin and Kamin point out, if taboos against homosexuality are genetically or pre-socially inscribed in our nature (as the "wisdom of repugnance" would suggest), then social legislation and rhetoric to enforce them would be obsolete: "A *natural* repugnance should require no *legal* shoring up in this way."[38] [my emphasis] Moreover, it is not true that there are universal homosexuality or incest taboos. In the case of incest, Rose et. al. also point out that it is not possible to map social definitions of kin directly onto genetic ones.[39] Claims about what is "naturally" repugnant draw on the biological determinist assumption that the social organization of contemporary Christian Western society reflects social structures that are universal and inevitable. According to this kind of determinism, a disordered brain (or today, a disordered gene) is,

> "seen as the cause of an unacceptable interaction of individuals and social organizations. The political consequence is that, since the social institution is never questioned, no alteration in it is therefore contemplated; individuals are to be altered to fit the institutions or else sequestered to suffer in isolation the consequences of their defective biology."[40]

In his 1993 book, _The New Genesis: Theology and the Genetic Revolution_, Ronald Cole-Turner[41] described humans as participants, through genetic engineering, in redemption. This outlook was taken up by Michael J. Reiss[42] and Roger Straughan[43] in their 1996 book _Improving Nature?: The Science and Ethics of Genetic Engineering_. Reiss and Straughan use the language of "redemption" in the sense of 'restoration.' Their idea is that genetic engineering can help to overcome 'genetic defects' caused by harmful mutations.[44] In this way, genetic engineering can help to restore creation to a fuller, richer existence and can play an important role without encroaching on the scope of divine activity.

In this vein, Reiss and Straughan argue that humans may have a theological responsibility, even a duty, to use genetic engineering to root out imperfections in the natural world, including those found in humans. Viewed in this light, genetic engineering can be seen as a tool with the potential to "eliminate harmful genetic mutations, reduce suffering and restore creation to its full glory."[45] Comments like this seem to gloss an important distinction, to wit, the difference between medical interventions that reduce the suffering of a patient and those that presuppose a Christian (non-medical) understanding of what constitutes creation's "full glory". Presumably the latter could furnish a basis for 'enhancement' of patients who do not suffer from any known medical disease. As recently as March 2015, Irish bishop Kevin Doran tacitly equated homosexuality to Down's syndrome on Ireland's News Talk Breakfast radio. In response to the question whether he believed being born gay was as God intended, he responded: "That would be to suggests that if some people are born with Down's syndrome or Spina Bifida, that that was what God intended either."

In their chapter devoted to 'theological concerns' Reiss and Straughan note that all of the world's religions have teachings concerned with creation and human nature.[46] Both authors write from a Protestant perspective and are of the view that religions have distinctive claims to knowing what is right and wrong, based on sacred scriptures, teachings and traditions, and 'our conscience.' They then note that natural law has been invoked to support both religious and non-religious writers in support of their arguments, albeit in different ways. The authors go on to list a number of problems with natural law arguments, including (1) the difficulty of defining exactly what is 'natural' and (2) natural law arguments commit the naturalistic fallacy.

Reiss and Straughan then shift their theological musings to the question, 'What is to be *our* role in creation?' That we *do* have a role is presupposed, so the authors merely want to define what this role ought to be theologically, given that we are in fact creating new types of organisms through genetic engineering.

They go on to outline some religious objections to genetic engineering, including one that looks similar to Francis Fukuyama's or Jeremy Rifkin's objections that there are extrinsic considerations such as assurances of safety or promises about the ultimate benefits to us all.[47] In *Our Post Human Future* (2002), Fukuyama notes that genes have been compared to an ecosystem, where each part influences every other part. He cites Edward O. Wilson's admonition that, "in heredity as in the environment, you cannot do just one thing. When a gene is changed by mutation or replaced by another gene, unexpected and possibly unpleasant side effects are likely to follow."[48] Fukuyama says that the 'Law of Unintended Consequences' would apply to germline engineering[49] in spades: "A gene affecting one particular disease susceptibility might have secondary or tertiary consequences that are unrecognized at the time that the gene is reengineered, only to show up years or even a generation later."[50] As an example, Fukuyama discusses how repairing the gene for sickle-cell anemia might therefore increase susceptibility to malaria, something that may not matter much for people in North America but would harm carriers of the new gene in Africa. In a similar vein, Rifkin's *The Biotech Century: Harnessing the Gene and Remaking the World* (1998) cautioned against embracing "what is likely to be the most radical experiment humankind has ever carried out on the natural world" without first examining the complex risks, pitfalls, and dangers that accompany the biotech revolution.[51] Among these he notes the "potentially catastrophic consequences of an accidental or deliberate release of deadly genetically engineered biological warfare agents", a narrowing of the gene pool and loss of genetic diversity, and the eugenic implications of a new era of genetic engineering tools. Both Fukuyama and Rifkin have called for more public debate and discussion around the impact and consequences of genetic engineering, particularly its social and political ramifications and its impact on our common understanding of human nature. Reiss and Straughan dismiss this type of cautionary advice as a wholesale rejection of "modern medicine" and describe it as though it were nothing more than over-cautious nagging paternalism, to which the authors compare "similar objections ... raised in the nineteenth century when the first anesthetics were developed..."[52]

This analogy needs to be examined much more meticulously than Reiss and Straughan permit. Objections to "modern medicine" or to genetic therapies tout court are not the same as objections to using them for the purpose of irreversibly altering the nature of human beings, especially for cosmetic or eugenic purposes. "Modern medicine," or more accurately "advances in genetic science", are simply means for achieving human ends. Fukuyama rightly points out that what the political community decides are appropriate ends are not ultimately scientific questions but political or moral ones.[53] The situation may in fact be the inverse of what Reiss and Straughan represent: instead of a small, over-cautious group of naysayers holding back "progress" the situation may be that the public are being subjected to an unending flow of glowing and uncritical reports of the marvelous breakthroughs on the genetic frontier, with little effort to examine the accompanying dangers.[54] As Rifkin points out, genuine debate has been marginalized and stifled "by an establishment that views every question, query, and reservation as a direct and immediate assault on free inquiry and science itself. Critics have been repeatedly represented as 'luddites, vitalists, fearmongers, and fundamentalists' for broaching concerns over where the new science is headed."[55] The critics' reservations are far from anti-progressive or anti-scientific. The concerns they've expressed are not with science itself, but with the socio-political ends to which it could be directed. The chilling flippancy with which critics' questions have been met led the German philosopher Jürgen Habermas to preface his essays on the future of human nature by denying that he is, in raising questions about the implementation of welcome advances in scientific knowledge, categorically opposing them.[56] Critics seem to find themselves on the defensive before they've even begun to express their worries.

Objections to the unregulated use of embryo screening and genetic manipulation for non-medical enhancement also arise from different concerns and highlight different kinds of risks than the objections raised in the nineteenth century when the first anesthetics were developed. Reiss and Straughan even compare Christian Scientists, who reject all modern medicine, to those who, like myself, Rifkin, Fukuyama, and Habermas have serious concerns about the long-term consequences and unforeseen effects of genetic engineering, and in particular manipulations intended only for enhancement, rather than to relieve the patient of physical suffering. Harvard university professor Michael Sandel compares genetic enhancements to cosmetic surgery, because it employs medical means for non-medical ends -- ends unrelated to curing or preventing disease, repairing injury, or restoring health.[57] However, unlike elective cosmetic surgeries, parental interventions in the genetic inheritance of their children leave no room for consent. Placing serious concerns over the manipulation of human life in the same category with fears of medical progress misrepresents and trivializes the former. Even Leon Kass, chairman of the President's Council on Bioethics from 2001 to 2005, recognizes that the new biotechnology touches and threatens the deepest matters of our humanity: bodily integrity, identity and individuality, lineage and kinship, freedom and self-command, eros and aspiration, and the relations and strivings of body and soul.[58]

What Fukuyama wants to protect from future biotech advances is "the unity or the continuity of human nature, and thereby the human rights that are based on it."[59] Fukuyama and other critics are far from dismissing the new biotechnology wholesale. According to Fukuyama, we can distinguish between good and bad uses of biotechnology.[60] Fukuyama's critique focuses on the potential to re-open possibilities for social engineering. Nevertheless, he acknowledges that germ-line manipulation, in which changes are passed down to the individual's offspring, has "obvious attractions for the treatment of inherited diseases such, as diabetes."[61] Among his main concerns is how the new technologies increase our ability to manipulate the source of all human behavior, the brain. Both Fukuyama and Rifkin express reservations about embryo selection and the degree to which all medical technologies can be used for enhancement rather than therapeutic purposes.[62] While somatic gene therapy changes the DNA of somatic cells, and therefore affects only the individual who receives the treatment, germ-line manipulation threatens to embed one generation's social preferences in the next by making changes to the genotype that are subsequently passed down to the individual's offspring.[63] The worry is that social engineering will merely use biotechnology as a new and more efficient means of achieving ends that, in the past, would have been dismissed as encroachments on individual liberty and privacy. Is Rifkin so wrong for asking what it will mean to be a human being in a world where babies are "genetically designed and customized in the womb and where people are identified, stereotyped, and discriminated against on the basis of their genotype?"[64] "What is ultimately at stake with biotech," says Fukuyama, "is not just some utilitarian cost-benefit calculus concerning future medical technologies, but the very grounding of the human moral sense."[65] When Rifkin says "our very sense of self and society will likely change, as it did when the early Renaissance spirit swept over medieval Europe more than seven hundred years ago"[66] he is referring to a shift away from a meritocracy to what he calls a 'genetocracy'. Reflecting on the unbounded prospects for man to design and mould human life extrinsically, Robert L. Sinsheimer, a molecular biologist at the California Institute of Technology, described this new kind of human agency as an opportunity to transition to a whole new pitch of evolution. He described this as nothing less than "a cosmic event".[67] Medicine moves from the era of self-discovery to one of self-mastery.

Reiss and Straughan describe objections to the exploitative nature of scientific progress and innovation as variations on the "playing God" objection, noting that Christianity has been criticized for its anthropocentrism and its failure to responsibly exercise stewardship over the natural world. This has sometimes resulted in a rapacious, exploitative attitude towards nature.[68] Reiss and Straughan survey a number of theological approaches (Hindu, Jewish and Buddhist) to 'stewardship' in order to demonstrate that there is agreement amongst the world religions that humans have a responsibility as to how they use the creation. They use the word 'mutuality' to describe a relationship between man and nature that does not carry overtones of hierarchy and superiority. In addition, they use the interpretative language of "co-creation" to suggest that we are "co-workers or co-explorers with God."[69] The reasoning, in their own words, is that since creation is an ongoing process, humans have begun consciously to influence the course of that continued creation, in a way that includes altering the future of the world year by year, as we "cause some species to become extinct and alter the genetic constitution of others."[70] One problem with this interpretative discourse is that the language disguises the fact that this is not merely describing what we humans do, but evaluating it as a positive, even Godly, form of creation (as opposed to "destruction" – even though it involves "causing some species to become extinct").

Reiss and Straughan go on to present a number of theological responses to genetic engineering, but for my purposes the most interesting are those that accept it partially or wholly. One of the theological responses they seem to think exemplary is that of Ronald Cole-Turner.[71] Reiss and Straughan highlight the way that Cole-Turner interprets genetic manipulation as 'restoration' and they almost seem to be recommending that the discourse should be altered accordingly:

> "Here redemption is being used in the sense of 'restoration'. The idea is that genetic engineering can help to overcome genetic defects caused by harmful mutations. In this way, genetic engineering can help to restore creation to a fuller, richer existence and can, Cole-Turner maintains, play an important role without encroaching on the scope of divine activity.
>
> It can perhaps be argued, in this vein, that humans may have a theological responsibility, even a duty, to use genetic engineering to root out imperfections in the natural world, including those found in humans. Viewed in this light, genetic engineering can be seen as a tool with the potential to eliminate harmful genetic mutations, reduce suffering and restore creation to its full glory." [72]

The crucial 'idea', however, is not "that genetic engineering can help to overcome genetic defects caused by harmful mutations". Rather, the politically and morally significant idea is that mutations that cause differences *are* 'harmful' or constitute 'defects'.

According to Jeremy Rifkin, the discovery of the DNA double helix in the 1950's brought with it a new set of metaphors and a new language for describing biological processes that changed the way molecular biologists perceive genetic mutations. Molecular biologists diverged from the standard perspective of evolutionary biologists when they began describing mutations not as different readings or versions of a relatively stable archetype, but as "errors" in the code. This shift from the notion of genetic mutations to "errors", says Rifkin, "represents a sea change in the way biologists approach their discipline."[73] This raises the question of what constitutes the 'harm' when we speak of 'harmful mutations' in this manner. This whole outlook contains un-stated premises. The very language of 'defect', 'abnormality', 'disease' and 'risk' presupposes an image of the perfect human being, a kind of proto-type of perfection.[74]

Since the passage above suggests that the genetic mutations which prevent this 'fullness' are 'harmful' or 'defective' we must ask to whom this harm is being done, and in what the harm or defectiveness consists. If the harm/ defectiveness of the homosexual gene is to the reproductive functions of our genitals, then there are two problems. First, homosexuals are not infertile, and even if they were, reproductive technologies could help to restore homosexual fertility to "its full glory". Second, any argument that treats empirical premises as automatically disclosing moral norms, without further explanation, runs into the naturalistic fallacy. Reiss and Straughan agree that some versions of natural law reasoning run into problems for this very reason.

More complex issues are raised in respect of germ-line therapy. Germ-line cells are found in the ovaries and testes and give rise to eggs and sperm, respectively. Changes to germ-line cells can be passed on to children and succeeding generations. Changes to these cells may have wider implications than changes to somatic cells (i.e. all the other cells in our body). By 1995, over 200 trials for somatic gene therapy had been approved.[75] Some human diseases caused by genes can already be treated by conventional means. Some genetic conditions are already preventable by restrictive diets, showing that both genes and environment play essential parts in human development and health. It seems that both genes and environment are involved in manifestation of traits, such that changes to the environment can prevent some genetic diseases from manifesting.

A condition affected by many genes is called a 'polygenic' condition or trait. Human skin color is one example of such a trait. Eye color is also determined by several genes. The vast majority of human traits are determined polygenically. The scope for gene therapy is likely to be more limited than many at first predicted, due to the environmental components of many diseases as well as the polygenic nature of various conditions. Prohibitionists are aware of the difficulty in ascribing homosexual behavior to genes, since homosexual behavior has not as yet been correlated exclusively or directly to a single gene. Some sociobiologists speculate that the difficulty in specifying the genetic marker for the trait may be explicable by epigenetics – the study of how environmental factors give cues that 'switch on' the genetically coded potential for a behavioral trait. The gene is pictured as intrinsically coded to provide a fixed and stereotyped response to the appropriate stimulus.

But, if homosexuality is manifest or expressed only in some environments, then in what sense is it innate? We could argue that the homosexuality gene is 'triggered' by the relatively tolerant attitudes found in London, England while it does not express itself in environments of religious intimidation. It grows difficult to distinguish between a genetic predisposition being 'triggered' into existence and one that is pre-existing but repressed by external taboos, which, when removed or circumvented, allow the tendency to 'express' itself. When the Iranian President Mahmoud Ahmadineja said that homosexuality does not exist in Iran[76] he was understood as meaning that, in a country where homosexuality is punished by death, homosexuals do not express their orientation. This does not mean that the biological predisposition to homosexuality does not exist in Iran. In Iran the only legal option for homosexuals who wish to 'live out' their homosexuality is gender reassignment surgery, which is commonplace there.[77]

Reiss and Straughan begin their discussion of 'somatic gene therapy for other traits' by reminding the reader that "part of the very essence of our being human is that we, above all the other organisms with which we share this planet, have the potential to transcend much of our biological heritage. We are far more than our genes."[78] The authors look to a hypothetical future scenario in which it would be possible for somatic gene therapy to reduce the likelihood of someone being violently aggressive or homosexual. As with the alcoholism analogy, homosexual orientation is being treated as one of many **undesirable** tendencies. But what is lacking is an explanation of what homosexuality and violent aggression have in common *qua* 'undesirable'. In the case of alcoholism, the harm done is to oneself and one's own potential fulfillment. Tendencies to violent aggression, if acted upon, are harmful to others. In the case of homosexuality, there is no harm at all, and most homosexuals are far happier expressing their homosexuality than repressing it. This does not mean that they should express it in any context or manner. The voluntary aspect of self-restraint is always important in guiding *any* of our involuntary tendencies. A tendency to violent aggression is not itself immoral; what *is* immoral is acting upon it in the wrong way, at the wrong time and in the wrong context. The same predisposition to violent aggression that is potentially harmful to others can, when exercised in the proper context, be beneficial to oneself or others. A boxer or an American football player who had no tendencies to violent aggression would be a very bad sportsman indeed. Violent aggressive tendencies are not behaviors or acts. So long as these tendencies exist in human agents, people can choose to express them in constructive or destructive acts. The argument that a tendency *causes* an act reifies behaviors, re-describing them as material properties located in the brain or genes. In ordinary persons, predispositions must be combined with the agent's will in order to become 'harmful' or undesirable forms of behaviour. There is nothing in the 'predisposition' itself that dictates how the agent will express it. The homosexual predisposition, like the heterosexual predisposition, can be suppressed, expressed in violent or aggressive ways, or expressed in healthy, appropriate ways.

Reiss and Straughan note that legal bans on somatic gene therapy for violent aggressive tendencies or homosexuality run into problems. First, most countries already spend much energy and effort trying to outlaw and prevent these behaviors. Some homosexuals are still working with psychotherapists who are supposed to help them to change their sexual orientation. The implication is that somatic gene therapy could be a much more efficient way of dealing with 'problems' that are already consuming a lot of energy. Somatic gene therapy becomes simply a more efficient and economical means to ends which society (or an intolerant segment of society) already regards as desirable. In its evaluation of the merits of mapping and sequencing the human genome, the United States government's now defunct Office of Technology Assessment expressed a popular sentiment when it concluded that "one of the strongest arguments for supporting human genome projects is that they will provide knowledge about the determinants of the human condition" including those diseases "that are at the root of many current societal problems."[79]

First, Reiss and Straughan gloss over the fact that what most countries already spend energy and resources trying to outlaw and prevent is violent aggressive **behavior**, not a violent and aggressive 'orientation' or genes. It is violent *behavior* that consumes public resources, not violent genes. The implication, though indirect, is that social conditions or circumstances external to the individual are never causes of violent interactions between individuals and 'society'. The social interactions that provoke violent responses are ruled out as a target for reform, since they do not constitute the problem. The problem must be internal to the individual who is not content with the social situation. This kind of causal explanation of social problems undermines the legitimacy of claims that social relationships or institutions may be systemically unjust. The growth of biological determinist discourses in the early 1970's was precisely a response to increasing demands for social justice that could not (or would not) be met. From Malcolm X to labor unions, to the women's movement and welfare rights organizations, these were demands that challenged, threateningly, fundamental assumptions about the inherent good – or primacy – of the existing order. The rise of a new paradigm of biological determinism deflated the pressure of these demands by undermining their legitimacy.[80]

Jonathan Beckwith, a professor of microbiology and genetics at Harvard University, has expressed his concern that the new genetic science is becoming a facilitator for a eugenics-based politics. To ignore the interactive causes of disease and to focus exclusively on the gene as

> "explanatory of disease and social problems tends to direct society's attention away from the other means of dealing with such problems. . . Genetic explanations for intelligence, sex role differences, or aggression lead to an absolving of society of any

responsibility for its inequities, thus providing support for those who have an interest in maintaining these inequities."[81]

Furthermore, if one of the prospective uses of somatic gene therapy is to prevent violent crime, the presumption is that somehow a 'tendency' or an *intended* act is a 'crime' despite the absence of both a harmful act and a victim. Reiss and Straughan make oblique references to crime (they use "violent aggression") in its current forensic sense, but in the therapeutic scenario they describe, they are not merely referencing but *re-defining* forensic terminology and its presuppositions quite radically. In its ordinary legal context, a 'crime' can only be defined as such retrospectively, because something has already been done to a 'victim'. The background presupposition in our current legal system is that bad acts don't *have to* be done, but they are anyway, because a free moral agent *chooses to act* upon bad intentions. The will of a free human agent, not his bad predisposition, is causally responsible for the act. If we are prepared to punish people for a tendency to act in a particular way, how can this tendency be established except retrospectively, by pointing backwards at a pattern of past acts? If we are prepared to punish people for what they merely 'intend' to do, we must also be prepared to reward people for good intentions before a virtuous deed is done. 'Crime,' as it is presently defined, depends upon the concepts of (1) moral agency, i.e. a free, adult, rational human being, capable of understanding right from wrong and (2) a 'victim', i.e. a morally significant being(s) who is unjustly harmed by the intentional acts of a moral agent, and (3) volitional, as opposed to accidental, action. The definition of a criminal is always retrospective, not prospective, because the freedom that allows a criminal to choose to act on his intentions is what makes him blameworthy when he decides to commit an immoral act. Until he acts, it is assumed that he continues to have the freedom to choose differently. To think otherwise would be tantamount to thinking that he was a kind of automaton, unable to guide or direct his involuntary instincts. Again the idea would be that bad behavior is hard-wired in the subject. If we were to accept this thesis as a more general explanation of human action, we would not be able to hold people morally responsible for their actions, whether good or bad.

The best we could hope for would be to steer people's desires (and so their behavior) in the same way that we might train a pet.

Today we are seeing a worrying revival of the type of thoroughgoing biological determinism that characterized the work of criminologists Cesare Lombroso (1835-1909) and Pierre Paul Broca (1824 – 1880). Both claimed that inherited physical characteristics were determinative of mental and moral traits. Both popularized the view that "biology is destiny". Lombroso's criminal anthropology depended upon this deterministic presupposition. While no one a decade ago would have given serious consideration to Lombroso's idea that one can tell a murderer by the shape of his or her head, it is now said that one can do so by the shape of his or her chromosomes.[82] But, as Jeremy Rifkin has warned, government efforts to redefine violent crime as a "health" issue shift the public debate from environmental and political factors that affect crime (like lack of educational opportunity, poverty and unemployment) to genetic 'errors' within subjects that can be controlled or weeded out.[83]

The presupposition of modern liberal efforts to reduce aggressive or violent behavior is **not** that some subset of individuals has an innate and uncontrollable tendency towards violence. Rather it is that we all share, to varying degrees, violent tendencies, but that we also have free will, and thus a responsibility to exercise control over whatever our given dispositions may be, especially where they cause unjustifiable harm to others. This is the background against which "our current efforts" to reduce crime take place. The Straughan/Reiss proposed use of somatic gene therapy does not make modern liberal methods of fighting crime more reliable; it undermines the modern liberal view of what constitutes 'crime' altogether.

Moreover, it is certainly debatable whether violently aggressive behavior and homosexuality belong in the same category. The association of these two phenomena is specious. The two behaviors are analogous in virtually no sense other than the repugnance felt towards them by the authors. Luckily, Reiss and Straughan seem entirely aware of this when they state that their choice of examples (violent behavior and homosexuality) highlights the social construction of disease. But instead of attempting to criticize this as a bogus form of 'medicine' the authors are content to say that a disease "is, in a sense, a relationship between a person and society"[84] and that "many diseases or disabilities are as much a reflection of the society in which the person lives as they are the product of the genes and internal environment of that person."[85] This incorporates a social aspect into the definition of disease, rather than limiting it to "the internal environment of the person." Indeed, it suggests that disease just is a given society's dis-ease (i.e. discomfort) with certain biological facts or with certain unconventional, or inconvenient, behaviors. Perhaps it is not surprising that some liberals harbor a creeping suspicion that biotech is going to be the new front on which social conservatives plan to fight their so-called 'culture war'.

Reiss and Straughan do express some concern over the issue of **consent** in somatic gene therapy for socially undesirable traits, but they make no important distinction between violent aggression and homosexuality. They argue that it might be acceptable for a person convicted of a violent crime to consent to rehabilitative therapy, psychological or somatic, aimed at behavior modification. But it is quite another issue to allow a parent to decide on behalf of a fetus or an infant that its genes should be modified to make it less aggressive or less gay. Reiss and Straughan cite the Clothier Committee's conclusion: "In the present state of knowledge any attempt by gene modification to change human traits not associated with disease would not be acceptable."[86] But this offers little comfort, given what they've already said about disease (i.e. that it "is, in a sense, a relationship between a person and society"). In this context, some worry that 'disease' will come to merely reflect a society's desire to change humans who do not conform to prevailing assumptions about the inherent good of the existing order. In the early 70's, the Soviet state responded to political dissidence among members of the Soviet intelligentsia by subjecting protestors to psychiatric investigations, which then led to pseudo-scientific diagnoses. The role of this plainly political use of psychiatry was to medicalize a political question. As Rose et. al. point out,

> "It is important to see that it was not so much that the Soviet protestors were being punished for their protest, . . . Rather, the state seemed concerned to invalidate a social and political protest by declaring the protestors to be invalids, sick, in need of care

and protection to cure them of their delusions that there were any blemishes on the features of the Soviet state."[87]

Germ-line therapy is especially contentious because alterations to the human germ-line impact succeeding generations and so affect more than just the individual concerned. This practice has been widely rejected by religious and secular opponents, despite the fact that germ-line alterations are already well established for micro-organisms, plants and animals. Reiss and Straughan argue that if germ-line therapy may currently be too risky, it is difficult to imagine that it will continue to be so indefinitely. It seems likely that new technological and scientific advances will allow the risks to be minimized, and the authors predict that in time it will be viewed as acceptable. As for the irrevocable effects of germ-line therapy, Reiss and Straughan also predict that techniques will be developed so that it too will one day become reversible.

To the question of its necessity, they argue that germ-line therapy might be able to produce certain benefits that could otherwise not be realized. But this is too vague. It does not allow us to distinguish between truly medical 'benefits' to the individual, and benefits to the society (or some segment of it). Given that Reiss and Straughan see 'disease' as largely a "socially constructed" concept, and raise no serious ethical concerns about a prospective scenario in which somatic gene therapy provides a more efficient way of reducing the likelihood of someone being homosexual (since so much energy is *already* being spent in "trying to outlaw and prevent these behaviors") we can infer what kinds of "benefits" they mean. The benefits are discernible only with reference to the Christian majority's view of what constitutes a 'good life'. This kind of paternalism is deeply at odds with modern liberalism's emphasis on the individual's right to pursue his own vision of the good life.

Reiss and Straughan consider possible moral objections to germ-line therapy on the grounds that it harms biodiversity. Evolution depends upon genetic variation. Reiss and Straughan begin by denying that germ-line therapy is going to significantly decrease human variation. Secondly, they argue that germ-line therapy may indeed lead to a future in which there is more genetic variation -- as some parents opt for certain genes for their children and other parents opt for others. However, since the premises of their argument are conservative, it is highly doubtful that they think the gene therapy they are recommending will lead to value pluralism, since that seems to be precisely the kind of 'problem' that these therapies are designed to root out, more efficiently than the current means of promoting 'shared' social values and social definitions of 'perfection'. Third, they say the obligation to eliminate suffering resulting from genetic disease might outweigh the evolutionary benefits of genetic variation. This seems to miss the possible dependency of human health on genetic variation. It also sets up an opposition between biodiversity (and its evolutionary benefits) and the presumed parental duty to eliminate their offspring's suffering. As applied to homosexuality, this is a false dilemma. Homosexuality does not cause suffering for gay offspring anyway; stigma does. Even if it did cause 'social' or parental suffering, the assumption is that displeasure with another's harmless diversity (precisely *because of* his otherness) is adequate grounds for overriding the benefits associated with biodiversity. This displeasure is also supposed to outweigh all the reasons for forbidding altering an individual's genetic make-up without his consent. This is certainly ethically questionable.

In response to concerns that germ-line therapy could be used for eugenic purposes, the authors ignore the prospect of free-market parental screening and selection for eugenic enhancement or negative eugenics, and mention only the rather fantastical idea that 'dictators' could produce a certain kind of person. This is a straw man. Opponents of germ-line therapy are far more concerned about permitting unregulated parental selection of traits than about a 'dictator' producing Aryan blue-eyed babies. Their concern seems justified in light of the stance taken by leading evangelicals like Ted Peters and Albert Mohler (below). Ted Peters says we could reject the anti-gay position and argue, "if it's natural, it's normal." But, says Peters, if homosexuality is as morally 'normal' as eye color, hair color, or height, then no moral code could justify preferring one sexual orientation to the other. But this just begs the question why anyone would ever choose to select for sex or sexual orientation at all. If there were no sense that one sexual orientation is inferior to the other, people wouldn't feel the need to interfere with the natural genetic make-up of their offspring. Peters supposes that homosexual and heterosexual parents would have equal rights to express their sexual preferences regarding their progeny such as they presently have in many cultures vis-à-vis sex selection. This approach apparently leaves any moral responsibility associated with eugenics in the hands of private individuals.

Having misrepresented their opponents' concerns as the unrealistic fear of a state-imposed eugenics, Reiss and Straughan then attack *these*, weaker, concerns by claiming, "dictators have had, have now, and will have far more effective ways of controlling people." This completely contradicts what they have already said (above) in defense of somatic gene therapy -- the latter being a much more efficient way of dealing with 'problems' that are already consuming a lot of energy, such as violent aggression or homosexuality. We have seen that, in their view, somatic gene therapy is simply a more efficient and economical means to ends that 'society' already deems desirable. The same would be true of germ-line therapy. Instead of appealing to the public's fear of tyrannical 'dictators' we could point to the longstanding liberal fear of a 'tyranny of the majority'.

Reiss and Straughan also note in passing a few conditions that ought to be met to ensure that the use of germ-line therapy is not so unpopular as to be objectionable. But this assumes popularity is the test of whether a practice is, in principle, acceptable. The question of whether germ-line therapy is objectionable is a separate issue to whether it is popular. Theologian Ian Barbour has argued that widespread public approval must first be secured, since the therapy will affect unborn generations who cannot themselves give informed consent to treatment.[88]

Reiss and Straughan seem to think the importance of our genetic make-up is overstated. If they mean that genetic facts do not automatically reveal moral values, this is uncontroversial. We have already noted that aspects of genetic make-up, if treated as behaviors rooted inside a person, overstate the extent to which biological urges direct our will and our choices. But if our genetic make-up were not a factor *at all* in influencing the kinds of free choices we are likely to make (such as the choice to pursue homosexual relationships) then there would be little impetus to alter it for socially desirable 'therapeutic' purposes, and even less need to persuade the majority that eugenic 'therapies' for sexual orientation are unproblematic. The question is less whether pre-natal manipulation of biology will be effective than whether it ought to be permitted.

Another approach to the 'gay gene' theory comes from Ted Peters. Reverend Peters asks whether the discovery of a genetic cause for heterosexuality or gay bashing should influence the way we regard these phenomena. Homophobia is so widespread in the human race that it is reasonable to think it could be genetic.[89] In the future, could gay bashers cite genetic evidence to claim that their behavior is morally neutral? They need not wait until the future. Let us suppose, for argument sake, that heterosexism is genetic (for heterosexuals). First, I would not grant that this genetic condition, as described by Peters, is analogous to homosexuality. Peters slides too easily between 'heterosexuality'/'homophobia' and 'gay bashing'. Heterosexuality (or homophobia) *per se* says nothing about the actions of the person with a heterosexual/homophobic disposition. Like acts of gay sex, gay bashing is a free action, not a biological trait. Steven Rose et. al. point to the practice of reifying behaviors – describing them as properties or objects located in the brain.[90] Reification is too often *presupposed* in reductionist forms of biological determinism. The biological property is not an outcome of disinterested scientific research but is part of the ideological framework informing it. If there were a genetic desire to behave violently towards homosexuals, this intrinsic desire would not, in itself, make acting on that desire a moral good. Humans are free to choose whether to act on their innate desires. Homosexuals have never denied this. Indeed, an individual's moral character is formed by these choices. Gays could argue that we can love the sinner but hate the sin of gay bashing. (And here the 'sin' would really be a moral evil, unlike gay sex, which has no victim.) How or whether one responds to one's natural inclinations and desires is a moral issue only when, and only *because*, that choice benefits or harms other morally significant beings. Peters himself says that the *expression* of the undesirable or anti-social predisposition is morally wrong, rather than the predisposition itself. Liberals agree.

Peters takes another tack, suggesting that individuals who inherit genes that predispose them towards behaviors that are presumed to be socially disruptive, undesirable, and immoral ought to exercise self-discipline as free moral agents. Notice that Peters does not use the word 'harmful'. If he had, we would instantly see that genetically predisposed gay bashers ought to exercise self-discipline while homosexuals need not. But even if we accept his carefully crafted terminology to describe the kinds of behaviors that require self-discipline, "undesirable" would equally apply to gay bashing, as it is violent, unjust and certainly not desirable to the victims. Heterosexuals might describe homosexual behavior as "undesirable" if they were required to participate in it. But then, no one is requiring that heterosexuals be gay anyway. Peters's example of the genetic gay-basher reasonably elicits the "love the sinner, hate the sin" formula. It is only the *expression* of the undesirable or anti-social predisposition that is morally wrong. To put it another way, it is not a gene that is violent or bigoted. It is a *person* who is violent or bigoted. It is not a gene that gay bashes. It is a *person* who gay bashes. The 'hate the sin' formula is correctly applied to gay-bashing but misleadingly applied to homosexuality because for the latter there is no harm in the behavior that could make it a sin (or "undesirable"). Not only is homosexual behavior not harmful, but the expression of a homosexual's disposition can be seen as a beneficial moral choice when it is an expression of love and self-giving that enriches other people, while harming no one. It is a moral good in the same way that any free act of love that benefits others is good. Peters might protest that homosexuality offends other people or causes them psychological distress, or insults their religious sensibilities. But liberal democracies would be burdened with endless legal disputes if every insult or instance of disgust were legislated. Liberal democracies do not, and should not, regard as serious harm the kinds of ordinary discomfort with other peoples' lifestyles or self-regarding behaviors that all of us experience with regularity. The traditional liberal definition of harm is thicker. It is defined as harm to our permanent interests as progressive beings. This kind of harm interferes with our agency, self-determination or bodily sovereignty. It is a kind of harm that strikes at the core of our human integrity and dignity, and prevents our development as individuals. Cocooning adults in cotton wool does not prevent actual harm, it prevents intellectual and moral growth and limits tolerance towards others.

Homosexual behavior is not transformed into a moral virtue by a genetic predisposition to homosexuality. And no one has ever claimed that it is. Peters seems to attack a straw man that he himself has erected. Homosexuals do not claim that their innate homosexuality determines their actions any more than heterosexuals claim that they lose their free will by virtue of being heterosexual. In either case, the agent still decides whether and how to act upon her biological predisposition. What distinguishes homophobic actions as morally bad is that there is a free moral agent, an intentional action, and a victim who is unjustly harmed by the act(s). By contrast, in consenting homosexual acts, there is no victim and no harm. This fact has prompted some Christian conservatives to disseminate misleading propaganda about the kinds of harm homosexuality causes. For example, American evangelicals like Rick Warren and Scott Lively who do missionary work in Uganda have promoted a book by Richard A. Cohen, a Christian "conversion therapist", in which the author claims that up to forty per-cent of homosexuals are directly linked to child molestation. Again, this is an attempt to link homosexuality to some kind of extrinsic harm, like violence or aggression. This kind of misinformation campaigning in the guise of missionary work has influenced anti-gay public policy in Uganda.[91] American anti-gay activist Scott Lively has campaigned vigorously to convince people in Uganda and other countries that gay people are out to recruit their children and destroy their societies.[92] Political Research Associates have produced a more comprehensive report about the influence of American evangelical involvement in anti-gay politics abroad in a report titled, *Colonizing African Values: How the U.S. Christian right is transforming sexual politics in Africa.*

There can only be two types of arguments to give substance to the claim that a homosexual trait is either (1) morally 'undesirable' or (2) 'defective' in a material, pre-moral sense. Either it is harmful to others or it is self-destructive. The kind of injury caused by alcoholism or violence can be demonstrated by ordinary empirical means. In the case of homosexuality, on the other hand, the only discernible damage is that done to a *definition* of nature or to an ideal that has become socially entrenched. There are no real victims of homosexuality while there are real victims of homophobia. We have seen the sense in which homosexuality poses a threat to cultic/

cultural definitions of nature and, hence to the social organization of sexuality. In this sense homosexuality does 'cause' social problems, in much the same way that the Copernican revolution or the sexual revolution of the sixties upset the cosmological and patriarchal paradigms of their epochs. Desegregation in the American South and ending apartheid in South Africa caused social 'problems' and disruption too, but that alone did not make them humanly unworthy activities. To date, there is very little evidence to show that homosexual behavior is destructive or harmful to others or to society. With respect to the alleged harm to the social institution of marriage, there is even evidence to the contrary. When the *Associated Press* compiled divorce statistics from data supplied by the *U.S. Census Bureau* and the *National Center for Health,* the data showed that the highest divorce rates were found in the Bible Belt. "*Tennessee, Arkansas, Alabama and Oklahoma round out the Top Five in frequency of divorce... the divorce rates in these conservative states are roughly 50 percent above the national average*" of 4.2/1000 people. The Barna Group conducted a similar survey with similar results, while atheists and agnostics had the lowest divorce rates.

Nevertheless some authors have attempted to produce medical evidence to show that homosexual acts are inherently self-destructive. Thomas Schmidt provides a wealth of information on this topic. In his book *Straight and Narrow?* there is a chapter titled 'The Price of Love' in which Schmidt attempts to show that homogenital sex between males is self-destructive, and he provides graphic medical evidence in support of this claim.[93] Although Schmidt deals with three categories of harm associated with homosexual practice: psychopathology, physical afflictions, and AIDS, I will here only treat the issue of physical afflictions.[94] Literature on the other two categories is abundant and, in the case of psychopathology, highly controversial. The balance of evidence shows that depression and other psychological problems related to homosexuality stem from social stigma and repression, rather than from homosexual orientation itself.[95] Whatever psychopathological 'harm' can be attributed to homosexuality is slanted unless treated partially as an issue of socialization and social maladjustment, which may say more about the harmful effects of stigmatization and prejudice than it does about homosexuality.[96] As Denies Overbye has remarked, "We know too little about the biochemical cocktail that is the brain, and all too much about how stigmatized children live down to our expectations."[97] There is, it seems, no neutral social context for such a discussion and Schmidt's claims profit by omitting this fact. Furthermore, on many of the issues discussed, such as promiscuity, Schmidt limits his statistics to gay *males*, which may reveal more about *males* than homosexuals.

In discussing the physical afflictions associated with homosexuality, Schmidt comments at length on those associated with male homosexual anal intercourse. His point is to show that homosexual acts are inherently self-destructive. In similar fashion the Colorado-based *Family Research Institute*, a Christian think tank, have produced and distributed a prolific body of informative pamphlets aimed at showing why homosexuality is self-destructive, including one entitled *Medical Consequences of What Homosexuals Do*. This pamphlet draws the bulk of its data from studies of patients in treatment settings, rather than from a large, random survey of members of the general population. Its focus is on high-risk groups already suffering from the effects of sexually transmitted disease and is not representative of the behavior of homosexuals as a whole. A more comprehensive and balanced view is provided by the Wellcome survey conducted by Wellings et al. (1994).[98]

In his attempt to prove that homosexual behavior is physically harmful to gay males who practice it, Schmidt gives his readers a graphic account of "the anus's internal susceptibility to damage."[99] This ignores the fact that a large percentage of gay males do not engage in anal penetrative sex at all (the majority do not according to the National Survey of Sexual Attitudes and Lifestyles II, 2000-2001), while many heterosexuals do.[100] Anal sex is not even a defining characteristic of homosexuality, much less a destructive one.

This aside, even if the medical data were absolutely accurate, this treatment of the 'harm' of homogenital sex acts is astonishingly crude in its understanding of human sexuality. Heterosexual intercourse is not always good for the health of the participants (take rape or pedophilia for example). But more importantly, this reduction of sexual acts to their biological aspect would seem equally grotesque and 'harmful' were it to turn its gaze to heterosexual reproduction, the only difference being that females suffer most of the 'harm' associated with it. Instead of looking at the ripping and tearing of membranes inside the anus we might instead turn our attention to the bleeding and tearing that accompany the loss of female virginity or childbirth, or to the frequency of cystitis or sexually transmitted diseases associated with penetrative heterosexual intercourse. But to focus on the physical aspect of sexual acts without regard for their unitive and affective aspects is to place them in a material realm that ignores the complexity and integrity of human persons. Schmidt neglects to mention the *un*pleasant minutiae of heterosexual intercourse and female anatomy and, consequently, the physical harm associated with homosexual and heterosexual acts is not given a balanced presentation. With regard to heterosexual acts, Schmidt takes for granted a distinction between pre-moral evil (e.g. pain, physical damage, tearing of membranes, etc.) and moral evil (evil which is related to the intentional aspect of an agent's behavior). For example, he does not think it morally wrong that females suffer terrible pain and are sometimes torn apart in childbirth. He clearly assumes that the good of heterosexual intercourse for the couple is proportionate to the suffering and injury the female may (eventually, if pregnant) endure as a result. Yet in his treatment of homosexual acts, Schmidt never sees the good of the love shared between the couple as proportionate to the minor physical injuries they may suffer as a result, thereby giving disproportionate weight to the damage done to the anus in comparison to the love expressed between two persons.

Other theologians have taken a more subtle approach in describing the harm of homosexuality. Recognizing that anal intercourse is not exclusive to homosexuals and that homosexual activity does not produce any special category of observable harm, they have used medical language to embed homosexuality within a disease discourse. In March 2007 the Rev, Albert Mohler Jr, a leading voice in the 16 million-strong Southern Baptist Convention began to use the discourse of "fallen creation" and "natural imperfections" in connection with homosexuality. Mohler's language echoed *Persona Humana* (1975) in both acknowledging that involuntary homosexuality exists and simultaneously describing it as a pathological condition in need of a cure.[101] This language pre-empts any association between essentialist theories of homosexuality and social tolerance for homosexual behavior. Mohler was using this language in response to an article in the now defunct US-based *RADAR* magazine. The *RADAR* article explored a hypothetical future medical scenario in which a mother-to-be grapples with the question whether to have a homosexual baby. Tyler Gray, the article's author, suggested that screening for behavioral traits like homosexuality in the womb is an immanent possibility. Gray cited London's *Sunday Times*, in which experts predicted that within a decade hormonal patches would be offered to parents that would allow them to change the sexual orientation of their fetus. Gray went on to state "there's little doubt that expectant parents will soon be able to screen their embryos and choose one with the 'correct' sexual preference." [102] Gray astutely pointed out that the procedure known as Preimplantation Genetic Diagnosis (PGD) already allows doctors to screen for more than 1,300 chromosomal disorders. The same techniques can also allow medics to screen for traits such as eye color, hair color and height before implanting the embryo in the uterus. Gray predicted that "as geneticists map the location of the genes responsible for more complex behaviors and pinpoint, once and for all, those that help determine homosexual orientation, such traits, too, will factor into would-be parents' decisions to implant an embryo and carry it to term – or to toss it and all of its undesirable qualities in the trash."[103]

Albert Mohler, Jr. described homosexual activists' reactions to the possibilities outlined in the *RADAR* article as a form of the naturalistic fallacy: "… the discovery of a biological cause for homosexuality would lead to the normalization of homosexuality simply because it would then be seen to be natural, and thus moral."[104] This description of homosexuals' reactions to the 'gay gene' thesis, like that of Peters (above), attacks a straw man rather than the actual arguments of homosexual rights activists. The homosexual activists' position is erroneously depicted as a version of the Christian right's own past arguments – namely that because something is 'natural' it is automatically morally good (because it reflects 'creation'). Homosexual activists argue the opposite. They understand, along with many thoughtful Christians, that observations about what occurs with regularity in nature are descriptive, not prescriptive, and therefore morally neutral.

In his list of ten points on how "to think in genuinely Christian terms" about the future possibilities outlined in the *RADAR* article, Mohler claimed that "the human genetic structure ... shows the pernicious effects of the Fall and of God's judgment."[105] This reasoning appears to be consonant with the Ramsey Colloquium's 1994 statement, in which intrinsic homosexual orientation was viewed in light of 'fallen creation':

> "In a fallen creation, many quite common attitudes and behaviors must be straightforwardly designated as sin. Although we are equal before God, we are not born equal in terms of our strengths and weaknesses, our tendencies and dispositions, our nature and nurture. We cannot utterly change the hand we have been dealt by inheritance and family circumstances, but we are responsible for how we play that hand. Inclination and temptation are not sinful, although they surely result from humanity's fallen condition. Sin occurs in the joining of the will, freely and knowingly, to an act or way of life that is contrary to God's purpose."

This reasoning contains several problematic assumptions. First, it offers no method of discerning exactly which parts of the human genetic structure manifest 'pernicious' effects of original sin, nor which types of inclination and temptation (aspects of humanity's condition) are 'fallen'. Second, it implies that *some* aspects of the human genetic structure reflect God's punishment or 'judgment' against Adam and Eve for the Fall. The pernicious effects of ***human*** moral failure are written into the homosexual's very nature, put there by God as punishment for their heterosexual progenitors' disobedience. Should we assume some sort of a Calvinistic doctrine of predestination whereby only some of Adam and Eve's offspring are singled out for heterosexual salvation, while others are doomed to lives of homosexual repression and misery, or homosexual activity and subsequent punishment in hell? If so, it is difficult to see how this innate divine punishment for the Fall could be just, since it arbitrarily targets only a small portion of Adam and Eve's offspring for divine retribution. Third, this seems to require a particularly sadistic picture of a God who both creates homosexuality and plants it in human nature to punish *some* humans for Adam and Eve's abuse of freedom, and then rewards those unfortunate individuals for not acting in accordance with the nature He implanted in them. Moreover, it would seem that St. Paul's moral exhortations against those who rebel against their God-given nature (and hence all creation) cannot be used to condemn homosexuals after all, but instead would make a virtue of rebellion against 'creation'. Yet Mohler specifically alluded to Paul's reasoning to explain why homosexuality is a 'sin' in the first place. The argument is circular.

Mohler seems to agree with liberals that moral responsibility hinges on freedom of choice: we may not choose our temptations, or the situations we find ourselves in, but we are nevertheless absolutely responsible for our decisions and actions.[106] His reasoning is almost existentialist. If this is the case then it makes no sense to say that we are 'sinners' by virtue of 'the fall' or 'fallen creation'. We can only be called 'fallen' for *our own* sins, since it is our will, not our fallen nature, which ultimately makes us act on evil temptations. If the Fall is God's way of holding Adam and Eve accountable for *their* bad choices, rather than unjustly blaming them for His own design flaw, then He should be consistent and hold all human individuals responsible for their own sins in the same manner, rather than punishing otherwise innocent individuals for the sins of their progenitors.

As to the scientific evidence pointing to biological causation for sexual orientation in some individuals, Mohler says, "The biblical condemnation of all homosexual behaviors would not be compromised or mitigated in the least by such a discovery. The discovery of a biological factor would not change the Bible's moral verdict on homosexual behavior."[107] Mohler's view, like that of the Catholic Church, is neutral on the homosexual 'condition' but morally condemns the homosexual *behaviour*. His reasoning follows the same reasoning as the "love the sinner, hate the sin" creed. But it also runs into the same contradictions.

Reverend Ted Peters reaches almost identical conclusions. Starting from the premise that the gay gene constitutes a "predisposition to engage in socially unacceptable behavior, or what some might call sin,"[108] Peters says we can identify homosexuality as one of many other innate predispositions, "such as lust or greed or similar forms of concupiscence which are shared with the human race generally."[109] All of these undesirable background conditions constitute the state of original sin into which we are born. Again, the allusion is to an ethic that is pre-modern, and obsolete in modern liberal democracies. Knowing what constitutes a 'sin' presupposes a Christian worldview that many citizens in liberal democracies do not share. Christian definitions of 'sin' often depend not upon any actual harm to others, but upon offense to beliefs and attitudes based on faith, scripture or doctrine.

Mohler says that we sin against homosexuals by insisting that they choose their temptations. But he goes on to say that we all (whatever our sexual orientation) are absolutely responsible for "what we do with sinful temptations".[110] Homosexual activists agree with Mohler that we are all equally morally responsible agents, whatever our sexual orientation and whatever our sexual temptations. Homosexual activists have never argued that a biologically fixed sexual orientation prevents one from being a free, responsible moral agent, although heterosexual rapists and their defense attorneys *have* sometimes argued thus. Patriarchal societies, too, have circulated the myth that men have an innate instinct for promiscuity that makes them exempt from criticism for sexual infidelities or promiscuity, while deploying the double standard that women who behave promiscuously are 'sluts'. The widespread double standard that treats sexual promiscuity as natural for men and 'dirty' for women has prevailed in Catholic cultures.

Mohler's view that we all have sinful temptations is not in dispute. What *is* in dispute is the notion that homosexual acts are 'sins'. Mohler and his Christian conservative allies assume without argument that homosexual acts *per se* are amongst the sins by which people are tempted, even though there is no victim of this 'sin' as there is for most others. The rationale for defining homosexual acts as 'sins' can no longer be furnished by simply claiming that the 'sin' consists in the homosexual's rejection of his own nature (the nature intended by God). So Mohler must insist, as he does, that "no scientific finding can change the basic sinfulness of all homosexual *behavior*."[111] Mohler identifies homosexuality as a particular "pattern of temptation"[112] and says that those who commit same-sex acts are responsible for the choice to commit the sinful act. The temptation is to behavior that has *already* been pre-defined as a **moral** evil. When we probe into *why* a homosexual act is 'sinful' or a moral evil, Mohler's recourse is to the Bible, and specifically to Paul's reasoning in Romans: ".. the Bible … places this condemnation in the larger context of the Creator's rightful expectation of our stewardship of the sexual **gift.** All manifestations of homosexuality are thus representations of human sinfulness and rebellion against God's express will."[113] In his follow-up blog of 16 March, Mohler tries to make this more explicit by quoting 1 Corinthians 6:9-11 where Paul includes homosexuality or its cognates in a list of behaviors that are to be condemned. It is through sanctification or "justification in the name of the Lord Jesus Christ" that those who were once homosexual sinners have been saved. However, the argument is circular; it assumes what it needs to prove - namely that homosexual acts per se *are* morally evil. Given the recent sociological and genetic data about natural variants of human sexuality, the burden of proof is on Mohler to show that homosexual behavior is anything but responsible stewardship of one's own sexual gift.

Mohler went on to say that the homosexual tendency to sin (the pattern of temptation to homosexual acts) is encompassed within a more general human tendency to sin, as "we are all sinners from the start" having been "born with a huge moral defect".[114] For this more general moral defect, Mohler says there is only one cure: the cross of Christ. The doctrine of original sin is seldom given such a literal interpretation, since it flies in the face of modern ethics. Even Mohler himself appears uncomfortable with the notion that individuals can be born sinners prior to making any free choices. In his blog of 16 March, Mohler says moral responsibility does not require absolute moral choice. But it does require *some* choice, and Mohler clearly sees this as what is morally significant. Citing what seems to be an example taken from Sartre, he says "a soldier in battle may not have chosen to be in a situation of moral anguish, but he is still absolutely responsible for his decisions and actions. Those who commit homosexual acts, whoever they are and whatever their biological profile, are absolutely responsible for their sin."[115] But again, the argument fails to show how a soldier in battle (who has to take responsibility for his decision to kill other people) is analogous to a homosexual (whose acts will harm no one unless for reasons having nothing to do with homosexuality *per se*). Homosexuals and their defenders would fully agree that homosexuals are absolutely responsible for their sins. They merely disagree that homosexual acts *per se* are 'sins'.

When Christians talk about restoring creation to 'it's full glory' or of 'imperfections' we must assume that we have some working definition of what 'perfection' or 'fullness' consists in. No doubt heterosexuality will be a part of that definition. But, since Christian authors also suggest that the genetic mutations which prevent this 'fullness' are 'harmful' or 'defective' we must ask to whom this harm is being done, and in what the harm or defectiveness consists.

Christian prohibitionists know that the discovery of a gay genotype or some similar underlying biological marker would make it illogical to blame homosexuals for their natural tendency to 'deviate' from the norm. Indeed it would place their sexuality within the spectrum of natural human sexuality. Knowing this, some Christian prohibitionists have begun using a narrative of pathology to preserve the stigma accorded to homosexuality perhaps to provide the impetus for parents to look to new biotechnology for a 'therapeutic' response to it. Biotechnology would seem to offer parents future opportunities to eradicate the biological cause(s) of homosexual orientation from their offspring. By no means am I suggesting that a gay gene accounts for all homosexual behavior. Homosexual behavior cannot be entirely eliminated by eradicating 'gay genes'. Nor am I suggesting that everyone who participates in homogenital acts is born with a genetic predisposition to homosexuality. However, the fact remains that, for those who are apparently genetically or biologically predisposed to homosexuality, there is cause to worry that it will become a target for eugenic 'therapy'.

Since the nineties, advances in biomedical technology have brought us to the brink of realizing what Francis Fukuyama predicted in 2002: that within twenty years we would have at our disposal the means for parents to drastically reduce the likelihood of having a gay child. As I mentioned at the beginning of this chapter, as recently as August 2010 the American broadsheets announced that a prenatal pill used to treat congenital adrenal hyperplasia could have the side effect of reducing the likelihood of homosexuality in females treated with the drug. The news prompted wide discussion of the future trajectory of chemical and biotech engineering for eugenic purposes, and homosexuality was singled out as a key target for prenatal manipulation.

In his response of 18 August, 2010 Joe Carter, web editor of *First Things*, a leading American Catholic publication[116], said that, although conservative Christians will abhor the prospect of aborting gay children, many of them will be amenable to changing sexual orientation in the womb.[117] The prenatal treatment, he said, offers a humane solution for a moral problem. Carter then attempted to forge a rapprochement between gay activists and conservative Christians, suggesting that if gay activists could agree that homosexual behavior requires free choice then conservative Christians might be willing to join them in protesting against eugenic therapies aimed at changing someone's future behavior while still in the womb. This was a straw man. Gay people have never denied that their sexual behavior, like all of their conscious behavior, is the result of free choice. Rather, they disagree with the Catholic claim that the behavior in question (consenting homosexual behavior between adults) constitutes a moral problem.

Carter said gay activists could be "harming their cause even more if they continue to argue that homosexual behavior is normal and acceptable simply because it has a basis in our biological nature."[118] This is just another straw man. First, if homosexuality does have a basis in some people's biological nature, this tells us only that homosexuality is a natural variant of human sexuality. It does not entail that all homosexual behavior is "acceptable" since that would be a moral question that has to do with the voluntary ways in which agents choose to express their predispositions. The situation is exactly the same for the heterosexual.

Second, liberals and gay activists completely agree with Carter when he says that the kind of biological reductionism that treats human behavior as explainable by chemical and physical laws undermines both moral autonomy and the dignity of the individual. The problem with such reductionism is that it re-describes behaviors as properties or objects within the individual's brain or gene. Many reject this deterministic model because they see human action as directed by free will. We may have all kinds of dispositions, but we nevertheless have responsibility for our behavior because we make decisions about how, when and whether to express them.

Carter's readers need to be reminded that he is protesting against a Christian argument, not the gay activists' one, when he refers to the notion that a sexual "orientation is normal and acceptable simply because it has a basis in our biological nature." First, this conflates "normal" and "acceptable", treating them as though they were equivalent terms. "Normal" is a descriptive term about what constitutes average behavior. Homosexuals could reasonably argue that homosexuality is "normal" for those who possess a biological predisposition for homosexuality. This would not be to make any value judgment about the various ways in which homosexual individuals then express their same-sex attraction. It would merely be to say that homosexuality is a natural, though less common, variant of human sexuality. "Acceptable" is an evaluative term. It implies that something ought to be accepted because it is morally permissible or at least not harmful. Homosexuals can, and should, argue that homosexual orientation *per se* is both normal and acceptable prior to any evaluation of particular homosexual acts.

Homophobic Christians, not gay activists, have attempted to wed the mere biological fact of procreative 'complementarity' or the presumed 'naturalness' of heterosexuality to some kind of judgment about its superior moral status - despite the fact that a heterosexual orientation can be expressed in many morally bad ways (e.g. rape, pedophilia, exploitation, abuse, etc). None of these behaviors are made more acceptable because of their underlying heterosexuality. Heterosexual attraction, because it is involuntary, is irrelevant to a moral assessment of the behaviors to which it leads. An assessment of the ethics of any sexual behavior requires consideration of the *voluntary* aspects of that behavior - i.e. whether it is consenting and whether it is injurious to others. Whether or not a sexual action is "acceptable" or "desirable" has everything to do with these considerations and nothing to do with the sex or sexual orientation of the agents involved. The voluntary aspects of behavior and its consequences are what matter to the moral assessment of all human action, whether sexual or not.

Homosexuality *per se* could not be a predisposition to immoral behavior unless it could be shown that something about one's sexual orientation causes one to harm or injure others or to coerce non-consenting sex. There is no evidence to show that this is the case. The mere attraction one feels for the opposite or the same sex does not override free will and so cannot be an excuse for bad (immoral) behavior. Heterosexuals, more than homosexuals, have attempted to use their sexual orientation to excuse all kinds of bad choices - rape and infidelity being key examples. But this does not cut any ice among those of us who reject biological determinism. Thankfully, both liberals and Catholics can agree on that much.

The existence of a 'gay gene' or some other biological substrate for homosexual orientation is germane to the defense of gay and lesbian civil rights precisely because of our shared liberal belief in human free will and moral responsibility. Conservatives agree with liberals in rejecting biological determinism because it undermines the traditional moral belief that the root cause of an agent's behavior is his free will. Our common belief in free will is what allows us to hold individuals responsible for their choices and actions (whether sexual or not). As Carter so lucidly explained:

> "This acceptance of the "medicalization" of sexual orientation is misguided. Treating orientation as a malady promotes a reductionist view in which human behaviour is explainable by chemical and physical laws. As we've seen in other areas of bioethics, reductionism inevitably undermines both moral autonomy and the dignity of the individual."[119]

While liberals see personal responsibility and harm as central to the social regulation of behavior (sexual or otherwise), some conservatives have begun to look to the invention of new sexual diseases to justify interventions into sexual orientation because it justifies using biotechnology to regulate sexual behavior. Instead of treating homosexuality as a medical problem, Carter wants Christians to treat it as a moral problem, preventable in utero by medical or pseudo-medical means. But moral problems presuppose the autonomy of the individual. Treating involuntary biological sexual orientation in utero is in tension with the presupposition that homosexuality *is* a *moral* problem.

However, attempts to assign a 'disease' status to the homosexual predisposition will be unnecessary anyway if the liberal eugenics movement succeeds (see Chapter 7). In this sense, the Christian 'disease' discourse only performs an auxiliary function, providing parents with a medical meta-narrative that guides or justifies their reprogenetic decisions. (Reminder: the term 'reprogenetics' was coined by molecular biologist Lee Silver of Princeton University and refers to the merging of reproductive and genetic technologies. Silver distinguishes reprogenetics from eugenics in that the former would be voluntarily pursued by individual parents with an aim to improve their children - a policy of which Silver approves - whereas eugenics are compulsory and imposed upon citizens by governments for particular ultimate goals.) Parents' right to make such decisions is defended by liberal eugenicists who claim intervening parents enjoy a 'presumption of liberty'. Christian conservatives collude with the allegedly 'liberal' eugenics movement primarily in assuming that parents *do not have to justify* interventions into the genetic make-up of their offspring. According to liberal eugenicists, the burden of proof is on liberals to show what harm is done by parents in selecting the (aesthetic *or behavioral*) traits of their offspring.

For Christian figureheads like Mohler and George, who regard human embryos ontologically and morally as having full moral standing, selective abortion is not an option. This would presumably rule out Preimplantation Genetic Diagnosis (PGD). Assuming that antenatal genetic screening for homosexuality will not be used to override the Christian ban on abortion, it seems there are two viable options left for the Christian 'liberal' eugenicist whose aim is to prevent the birth of a homosexual child. Both would aim at modification rather than destruction of an embryo with the unwanted trait. The first would involve screening for homosexuality and then using somatic gene therapy to eliminate the undesired trait. Somatic gene therapy typically involves giving a person 'healthy' DNA to override the effects of their own 'malfunctioning' DNA. Changes to somatic cells alter a trait in an individual, but cannot be passed on to future generations.

The second hypothetical option would be to screen for homosexuality and then use germ-line therapy to eliminate the unwanted trait. Germ line cells (the cells found in the ovaries or testes that give rise to eggs and to sperm) can indeed be passed on to succeeding generations. Germ-line therapy would not only eradicate the trait from the individual but also from his or her offspring. Germ-line manipulation is presently regarded as too risky and is widely rejected. However, germ-line therapy has obvious attractions for inherited diseases. A number of somatic therapy trials have been conducted in recent years, with relatively little success. The problem with this approach is that the body is made up of trillions of cells; for the therapy to be effective, the genetic material of what amounts to millions of cells has to be altered. The somatic cells in question die with the individual being treated, if not before; the therapy has no lingering generational effects. Germ-line engineering, by contrast, is what is done routinely in agricultural biotech and has been successfully carried out in a wide variety of animals. Modification of the germ line requires, at least in theory, changing only one set of DNA molecules, those in the fertilized egg, which will eventually undergo division and ramify into a complete human being.[120]

Moreover, somatic therapy may never prove effective in addressing diseases involving functions dependent on structure such as the brain.[121] Zimmerman and other proponents of germ-line therapy argue for an extension of the interests of the patient to include the "interests of the entire genetic legacy that may result from intervention in the germ line."[122] Zimmerman argues for the right of parents to make choices on how best to protect their unborn children during pregnancy. To deny them the opportunity to take corrective action in the sex cells or the embryonic cells, he argues, would be a serious breach of medical responsibility. It falls to critics of liberal eugenics to explain why "countless individuals should be subjected to possibly painful, intrusive, and potentially risky somatic therapy when the gene or genes responsible for their diseases could be more easily eliminated from the germ line, at less expense, and with less discomfort."[123] The presupposition of this argument is quite revolutionary. Zimmerman is assuming that we have a positive obligation ***to intervene to prevent*** ontic evils that cause others to suffer. Liberals only argue that we have a negative obligation ***not to cause*** ontic evils that can easily be avoided.[124]

In a personal statement attached to '*Reproduction and Responsibility: The Regulation of New Biotechnologies*', a report by the President's Council on Bioethics (March 2004), Robert P. George includes himself among the members of the Council who favor protecting human life from the very beginning by banning the use of living human embryos at any stage of development as disposable research material. [125] This would likely include a ban on IVF. But, since he is in the minority on this view, George recommends limiting the number of days beyond which the law tolerates deliberate embryo killing. "It is important to understand," he says, "that the Council's recommendation here is *not* to authorize embryo-destructive research up to a certain limit. It is only to prohibit such research beyond a certain limit. Because in the absence of legislation this research remains unrestricted, a prohibition of embryo-destructive research beyond a certain limit does not amount to authorizing research up to that limit." This is emphasized by his addition of a further "pledge" to establish a yet more complete protection for human life in *all* stages of development. However, George sees no need for Catholics to prove their consistency on pro-life issues anyway[126]. The distinction George wants to preserve between authorizing and prohibiting is academic, and most readers will see that placing a limit on prohibitions amounts to the same thing as a limited authorization of the same activity. Moreover, George has been a vociferous opponent of homosexual civil rights, such as the right to marriage, but is less vociferous in opposing PGD and IVF. Whether there will be any substance to the pledge to press for more complete protection for human life in *all* stages of development remains to be seen.

Leon Kass, who chaired the President's Council on Bioethics from 2001 to 2005 and is a fellow of the American Enterprise Institute,[127] asks how we will proceed ethically if our traditional notions of human fulfillment and flourishing cannot be culturally sustained.[128] He asks how we will judge whether an alterable genetic predisposition toward homosexuality, should it be diagnosable *in utero*, ought to be regarded as a treatable condition.[129] But Kass already has answers to these questions, which he has provided elsewhere.[130] Kass has stated that the Bible provided him with "an account of human life that can more than hold its own with the anthropological and ethical teachings offered by the great poets and philosophers," with "teachings of righteousness, humaneness, and human dignity . . . that were undreamt of in my prior philosophizing."[131] Kass believes that the Book of Genesis provides philosophical teachings, accessible to all, about the human condition and how it may be improved. In this sense his outlook echoes that of *The Pastoral Care of Homosexual Persons* (1986), in which Joseph Ratzinger rested his claim that homosexuality "is a more or less strong tendency ordered toward an intrinsic moral evil; and thus ... an objective disorder" on this reference to Genesis:

> Providing a basic plan for understanding this entire discussion of homosexuality is the theology of creation we find in Genesis. God, in his infinite wisdom and love, brings into existence all of reality as a reflection of his goodness. He fashions mankind, male and female, in his own image and likeness.

Like Pope Benedict XVI, Robert P. George and Rev. Ted Peters, Leon Kass objects to the decoupling of sex from procreation. He identifies the cultural upheavals of the sexual revolution as the beginning of a pernicious denial of the inherent procreative teleology of sexuality itself. Kass was an early critic of reproductive technologies like in vitro fertilization because he was concerned that their use obscures truths about the essence of human life and society that are embedded in the natural reproductive process. But he later endorsed the *marital* use of IVF.

The expectation that Christians would overlook their past reservations about IVF or other 'artificial' reproductive technologies in the interests of eliminating human diseases or dysfunctions (as defined by their doctrine) is not completely without basis. On 2 March, 2007 Albert Mohler clearly articulated his position on parental use of genetic interventions to 'cure' homosexuality: "If a biological basis is found, and if a prenatal test is then developed, and if a successful treatment to reverse the sexual orientation to heterosexual is ever developed, we would support its use as we should unapologetically support the use of any appropriate means to avoid sexual temptation and the inevitable effects of sin."[132] Soon afterward Mohler backtracked and qualified this by saying he would not support gene therapy but might support other treatments, such as a hormonal patch.[133]

Bob Edgar, executive secretary of the National Council of Churches, noted that Mohler's statement set off reverberations that cut both ways – to Christian conservatives on the radical right it had the unfortunate effect of validating the claim that homosexuality is God's creation (natural), but other hardliners[134] commended Mohler for giving publicity to the view that homosexuality is a "disorder" in need of a cure.

Homosexuals are understandably wary about the discovery of a 'gay gene' not necessarily because they think such a discovery is inconsistent with the demands of truth, but because they fear the political motives driving it. If a 'gay gene' or similar biological marker(s) were to be discovered, the way could then be paved for gay fetuses to be aborted or gay embryos to be 'engineered' back to heterosexual 'health' -- a proposition that enjoys currency among religious and non-religious liberal eugenics proponents. Even if religious leaders do not openly endorse PGD or liberal eugenics, they will have the option of simply allowing free market liberal eugenics to become ever more standardized, and can always claim that their weak protests were "powerless" against the secular liberal forces driving it.

Astute homophobic religious leaders tend not to allude to the possibility of a pre-natal gay genocide because the very existence of a 'gay gene' would completely undermine every existing moral argument marshaled to justify their homophobia. As noted in Chapter 1 of this book, Christian homophobia is based almost invariably on a naturalist ethical theory that assumes healthy human sexuality is heterosexual to the exclusion of other variants.[135] If the existence of a 'gay gene' or similar biological marker(s) destroys the 'naturalist' model that for centuries has been the sole basis for homophobia, it destroys the grounds for a discriminatory eugenic engineering policy *a forteriori*. This is the catch-22 for Christian prohibitionists. Therefore advocates of reprogenetic modification of sexual orientation, whether motivated by religious belief or financial incentives, have a vested interest in forestalling public debate about eugenic interventions to 'cure' homosexuality until the genetic marker(s) for the trait is/are isolated and the technological procedures for intervening to 'cure' it are ready to go to market.

This analysis of the prohibitionists' strategy will sound less alarmist if we take into account the inconspicuous standardization of practices like male circumcision, selective abortion for sex-selection (legal in the US) and the widespread use of PGD, all of which are already being retroactively exploited by liberal eugenics supporters to shrug off moral misgivings as "too late".[136] As Barbara Katz Rothman has argued, there is reason to consider these possibilities now:

> "The scientists quickly speak up: that isn't possible, they reassure us, you don't understand the genetics involved. Five years later, of course, that is possible, and then it is too late to decide whether or not to do it: we wake up to find it done."[137]

In the middle of the last century, Max Weber predicted that Western capitalist societies would gradually evolve into an "iron cage" -- a technically ordered, rigid, dehumanized society.[138] Instead of a technological utopia that could set us free, Weber saw the coming of a bureaucratic "polar night of icy darkness" that would limit individual human freedom and potential.[139] In a similar vein, Rose et. al. see bureaucratic efficiency as the preferred means by which possessors of social power achieve their ends, since the resort to violence is a distinct disadvantage to those who use it. It is clearly better if the power struggle can be moved to the institutional level – since these institutions themselves are in the hands of the possessors of social power, the outcome is better assured.[140]

The Nuffield Council on Bioethics[141] is effectively the most influential bioethics policy advisory body in the UK. In their Genetic Screening Supplement, its authors are clear that measures enacted by the Council of Europe to prevent the use of the results of genetic tests for non-health reasons would apply only in countries that have ratified the *Convention for the Protection of Human Rights and Dignity of the Human Being with regard to the Application of Biology and Medicine* (later referred to as the *"Convention on Human Rights and Biomedicine"*). This does not include the UK.[142] John Harris, one of the UK's most vocal proponents of liberal eugenics sits on both the UK Human Genetics Commission and the Ethics Committee of the British Medical Association. The documents of these advisory bodies in some instances appear slanted in favor of liberal eugenics. The language they adopt reflects this, for instance, by assuming presumptive liberty for parents and opposing this to the more controversial population screening programs:

> "Genetic testing is carried out for patients who are at risk and who are actively seeking advice, whereas screening could be viewed as an imposition (by the state) with a presumption of benefit. From this perspective, the ethical responsibilities of those introducing screening programmes are greater. Strong scientific evidence of effectiveness on clinical outcomes and the minimisation of harm should be fundamental requirements. This evidence base should also include explicit assessment of the ethical, social and legal issues which may be involved."[143]

This seems to reassure readers that the genetic testing mechanisms will be actively sought by patients (consistent with "liberal eugenics") as opposed to a state-imposed screening program with some presumption of benefit (paternalism). But the point of this section is to argue that ethical responsibilities are greater when screening is introduced by the state, as opposed to when it is positively sought out by patients. This sidesteps the moral objections to liberal eugenics.[144]

The European Union's *Charter of Basic Rights*, Article 3, guarantees the right to bodily and mental integrity, and contains "the prohibition of eugenic practices, especially those that have as their goal the selection of persons." Article 21, 'Non-discrimination' contains the provision that

> "1. Any discrimination based on any ground such as sex, race, colour, ethnic or social origin, genetic features, language, religion or belief, political or any other opinion, membership of a national minority, property, birth, disability, age or sexual orientation shall be prohibited."[145]

The Charter "**does not extend** the ability of the Court of Justice of the European Union, or any court or tribunal of Poland or **of the United Kingdom**, to find that the laws, regulations or administrative provisions, practices or action of Poland or of the United Kingdom are inconsistent with the fundamental rights, freedoms and principles that it reaffirms." This amendment to the EU's Charter of Basic Rights (which appears in the 2009 Treaty of Lisbon) effectively prevents the Charter from being applicable to the United Kingdom and Poland.

Even less will fears of a stealth strategy for introducing these eugenic liberties seem overblown if we take into account the conspicuous reluctance of the Nuffield Council to address the issue in advance. In section 7.12 of the Nuffield Council's 'Genetic Screening Supplement' ('Future Considerations') the members acknowledge the existence of a "danger that commercial pressures could result in premature application of screening programs before they are clinically useful or where the benefits are weak." However, they recommend that care "is taken not to exaggerate the potential of screening (or testing) for susceptibility genes to improve health, since to do so could lead to false assumptions and unnecessary anxiety", especially amongst "lobbying groups" exerting pressures and "whose perspectives on screening for particular diseases may not reflect the overall body of evidence." And in an appendix they "recognize that there is a whole area of serious concern about genetic screening for human traits that are in no sense diseases. These issues have been brought to the fore by recent controversies about gender choice, and about the so-called 'homosexuality gene'. We do not dismiss these issues. They call for discussion by professionals with skills other than those represented in our Working Party."[146]

Leading Catholic figureheads have also exhorted their allies to maintain a deliberate silence on pressing bioethical issues. Robert P. George and William L. Saunders[147] have asked how anyone can blame politicians and others for perceiving the Church as another interest group when the United States Catholic Conference (USCC)[148] itself reports that it has over fifty Congressional "legislative priorities" for 1991-92.[149] George and Saunders do not suggest that leading Catholics should not influence public policy. To the contrary, their remarks about the USCC "talking too much" appear in the context of an appeal to Catholics to influence public policy much more effectively than they presently do. George and Saunders accuse Catholics like Associate Justice William Brennan, president John F. Kennedy and Fr. Robert Drinan (a law professor at Georgetown University) of betraying Catholic authorities by influencing public policy in ways that do not reflect Church teaching. The authors "name and shame" ten members of the United States Senate because they did not vote to ban partial-birth abortion; the authors literally use the word 'shame' and later recommend bringing back the practice of 'shunning' Catholic leaders who betray church teaching.[150] But George and Saunders also counsel the USCC to "desist from pronouncing specific prescriptions on matters that are subject to honestly disputed questions of fact and prudential judgments", including questions of strategy on pro-life political action.[151] George and Saunders claim that the USCC's excessive talking is partly to blame for the failure of Catholic efforts to influence public policy regarding bioethical issues in the United States.[152]

It would be naïve to overlook the vested interests of a research field already relying on the capital market for funding. A global life-science industry is already beginning to exert unprecedented control over the vast biological resources of the planet.[153] The concentration of power is impressive, with the top ten agrochemical companies controlling 81 percent of the $29 billion global agrochemical market. According to Jeremy Rifkin, ten life science companies control 37 percent of the $15 billion per year global seed market. The world's ten major pharmaceutical companies control 47 percent of the $197 billion pharmaceutical market. The life sciences companies are anxious to exploit the enormous potential of the new biotechnologies and are devoting considerable funds to research and development and licensing agreements. An estimated $7.5 billion annually is invested in-house on biotechnology programs.[154] Global pharmaceutical companies also spent more than 3.5 billion dollars in 1995 buying up biotech firms. These same life science conglomerates spent approximately 1.6 billion dollars in 1995 in licensing arrangements with biotech firms.[155] Novartis, the world's largest agrochemical company, the second largest seed company, the second largest pharmaceutical company, and the fourth largest veterinary medicine company, also has a huge stake in the new field of genetic medicine. In 1995, Sandoz -- now Novartis --- purchased Genetic Therapy Inc. for $295 million. The Maryland-based firm held a license on a broad patent covering the technique for removing cells from a patient, modifying their genetic makeup, and returning them to the patient's body.[156]

Biotech research is bound up with investors' interests, creating a "dynamic which threatens to steamroll the inherently slow-paced process of ethicopolitical opinion formation in the public sphere."[157] This "steamrolling" is implicit in The Nuffield Council's '*Genetic Screening: A supplement to the 1993 Report*' (2006) Section **7.6,** which states:

> "Ensuring that appropriate attention is given to issues of consent and counseling is both time and resource-intensive and there are concerns that, if genetic screening became more widespread, these demands should not become so burdensome as to slow the introduction of new programmes or to restrict existing programmes."

The Nuffield Council expressly derives its legal principles for policy regulation from, *inter alia, The Convention For the Protection of Human Rights and Dignity Of The Human Being with Regard To The Application of Biology and Medicine* (Council of Europe, Oviedo, 4 April, 1997), (heretofore 'the Convention'). Although the Convention provides that tests to detect a genetic predisposition or susceptibility to a disease may be performed **only for health purposes**, the Nuffield Council notes that the Convention does, however, provide (in Article 26) that the restriction of predictive genetic tests to *health purposes only* may be overridden where prescribed by law and necessary in a democratic society in the interest of public safety, for the prevention of crime, for the protection of public health or for the protection of the rights and *freedoms of others.*

This loophole in the Convention's legal principles appears to be designed precisely to allow for negative eugenics, while also permitting the eugenic interventions to be framed as "protection of the rights and freedoms of others". This caveat is included (or hidden?) in a footnote, as though it were hardly important. Yet its effect is to protect parental liberty for genetic screening for positive and negative eugenic purposes. I am here using Habermas's distinction between positive (enhancing) eugenics and negative (healing) eugenics. Negative eugenics is based on a moral point of view that commits us to the "logic of healing", which obliges us, in our dealings with second persons, from instrumentalizing them. It burdens us with the responsibility of justifying an anticipated consent that at present cannot be sought. Assumed consensus should, he argues, only be invoked to prevent evils that are unquestionably extreme and likely to be rejected by all. The moral demand not to instrumentalize second persons saddles us with the responsibility of drawing a line between negative eugenics and enhancing (positive) eugenics.

Parental liberty is valuable, but whether it should override the liberty of their offspring to express their own biological sexual natures in ways that harm no other person is a question that needs to be debated now, before the new therapies go to market. Some liberals believe that parental liberty over-steps when it is used as a euphemism for illegitimate political paternalism. The kind of 'harm' such parental interventions aim to prevent is not harm to the child or to any particular human individual, but to the dominant, fallible and increasingly fragile cultural value of heterosexism. The question whether Western liberal democracies ought to allow parental reprogenetic interventions aimed at these ends will occupy the next chapter.

1   See Katherine Stewart, 'Whither America's Religious Right?', *Guardian* online edition, 7 April 2013, accessed online at: http://www.guardian.co.uk/commentisfree/2013/apr/07/whither-america-religious-right.

2   George, Robert, George, Timothy and Colson, Chuck (the draft committee of the 2009 *Manhattan Declaration*), see 'marriage', p. 7.

3   "The Pope Condemns 'insidious' same-sex marriages", *The Daily Telegraph*, London, Friday May 14, 2010, p. 20.

4   Matthew Cullinan Hoffman, 'Homosexual 'Marriage' is a Machination of the Devil, Argentinean Cardinal Warns', LIFESITENEWS.COM, July 9, 2010, accessed online at http://www.lifesitenews.com/news/archive//ldn/2010/jul/10070902

5   *Manhattan Declaration*, 'marriage', p. 7.

6   Sullivan, Op. Cit., p. 179.

7   Ibid.

8   Ibid.

9   Bill of Rights, Amendment I: "Congress shall make no law respecting an establishment of religion, or prohibiting the free exercise thereof; or abridging the freedom of speech, or of the press; or the right of the people peaceably to assemble, and to petition the government for a redress of grievances."

10  For Judge Vaughan Walker's decision overturning California's Proposition 8, see: http://www.scribd.com/doc/35374462/California-Prop-8-Ruling-August-2010

11  The *Declaration* states: "We also acknowledge that there are those who are disposed towards homosexual and polyamorous conduct and relationships, just as there are those who are disposed towards other forms of immoral conduct." After brief remarks about how these people deserve compassion and that 'we', no less than 'they', are sinners, the Declaration continues: "We call on the entire Christian community to resist sexual immorality." It further states, "… the rights of parents are abused as family life and sex education in schools are used to teach children that an enlightened understanding recognizes as 'marriages' sexual partnerships that many parents believe are non-marital and immoral."

12  'The Psychological Impact of LGBT Discrimination', *Psychology Today* online edition, accessed 24 June, 2015, post published by Michael Friedman, Ph.D. on Feb. 11, 2014 in Brick by Brick.

13  Sullivan, Op. Cit., p. 104.

14  Ibid., p. 111.

15  Misleading Vividness is a fallacy in which a very small number of particularly dramatic events are taken to outweigh a significant amount of statistical evidence. This sort of "reasoning" has the following form:
    1. Dramatic or vivid event X occurs (and is not in accord with the majority of the statistical evidence) .
    2. Therefore events of type X are likely to occur.

16   See 'What Is the Ex-Gay Movement?', www.publiceye.org, 2008.

17   Sara Diamond, Not by Politics Alone: The Enduring Influence of the Christian Right, New York, NY, Guilford Press, 1998.

18   Quoted in *The Belfast Telegraph*, "Protests Planned at Gay 'Cure' Church Forum", 20 Feb, 2010.

19   Cited in Father Benedict Groeschel, "Appalled by 'The' Psychological Association" in *National Catholic Register*, September 6-12, 2009 Issue.

20   Father Benedict Groeschel, a Catholic, claims that the APA's August 2009 statement is an "abuse of research" and suggests that his readers protest and demand that the APA distance itself from "this pseudoscientific presentation." (see *"Appalled by 'The' Psychological Association'* in National Catholic Register, September 6-12, 2009 Issue).

21   Dr. Joseph Nicolosi is a leading proponent of reparative therapy. He has long been the inspiration behind the National Association for Research and Therapy for Homosexuality. More information can be found at http://www.NARTH.com and http://www.JosephNicolosi.com.

22   Sydney *Star Observer*, "BMA: You Can't Cure Homosexuality", Friday 2 July, 2010. http://www.starobserver.com.au/news/australia-news/new-south-wales-news/2010/07/02/bma-you-cant-cure-homosexuality/27530

23   www.dsm5.org/Documents/Paraphilic%20Disorders%20Fact%20Sheet.pdf

24   Moser, Charles and Peggy J. Kleinplatz, 'DSM-IV-TR and the Paraphilias: An Argument for Removal', paper presented at the American Psychiatric Association annual conference, San Francisco, California, May 19, 2003.

25   Here I include:
**Political/Advocacy groups:** American Family Association, American Life League, Campaign for Working Families, Center for Reclaiming America, Christian Coalition of America, Concerned Women for America, Constitution Party, Eagle Forum, Faith and Action, Family Federation for World Peace and Unification, Family Research Council, Focus on the Family, State Family Policy Councils, Moral Majority Coalition, National Right to Life Committee, Priests for Life, Traditional Values Coalition, Vision America
Media: Christian Broadcasting Network, Christian Examiner, Coral Ridge Ministries, Covenant News.com, Insight Magazine, Liberty Channel, Presbyterian Layman, Salem Communications, Ten Commandments News, Washington Times, World magazine, World Net Daily
**Think Tanks & Publishers:** Acton Institute, American Vision, Chalcedon Foundation, Discovery Institute, Free Congress Foundation, Institute for Creation Research, Institute on Religion and Democracy, Summit Ministries, Wallbuilders
*In the UK the *Centre for Social Justice* plays a similar role. It is a thinktank set up by the former Tory leader Iain Duncan Smith, and has heavily influenced

David Cameron's beliefs on subjects such as the family. It is presently headed by Philippa Stroud, a high-flying prospective Conservative MP for Sutton and Cheam who founded a church that tried to "cure" homosexuals by driving out their demons through prayer. The CSJ reportedly claims to have formulated as many as 70 of the Tory party's policies. (See Jamie Doward, Cal Flyn and Richard Rogers in *The Observer*, Sunday 2 May 2010.)

**Educational Institutions**: Ave Maria Law School, Christ College, Liberty University, New Saint Andrews College, Patrick Henry College, Regent University, University of Bridgeport

**Legal Organizations**: Alliance Defence Fund, American Center for Law and Justice, Americans United for Life, Foundation for Moral Law, Home School Legal Defense Association, Liberty Counsel, Rutherford Institute, Thomas Moore Law Center

26   The official position of the Southern Baptist Convention, the largest evangelical organization in the United States with over 16 million members, states that homosexuality is not a "valid alternative lifestyle." In a similar vein, the US-based *Family Research Council* claims it "does not consider homosexuality, bi-sexuality, and transgenderism as acceptable alternative lifestyles or sexual 'preferences'; they are unhealthy and destructive to individual persons, families, and society." Likewise, Liberty Counsel, a far-right legal organization affiliated with the late Jerry Falwell's Liberty university, promotes a website called 'Hope for Homosexuals' that publishes testimonials of ex-gays showing that many have walked away from the "homosexual lifestyle".

27   The Rev. Dr. Ted Peters is an ordained pastor in the Evangelical Lutheran Church in America and Professor of Systematic Theology at Pacific Lutheran Theological Seminary and the Graduate Theological Union, Berkeley, California. As a research scholar he is affiliated with the Center for Theology and the Natural Sciences (CTNS). He is editor of the journal *Dialog,* and author of numerous works in theology, including *God-the World's Future* (1992), *Playing God? Genetic Determinism and Human Freedom* (1996), *Science, Theology, and Ethics* (2002), and *Evolution from Creation to New Creation* (2003).

28   Sullivan, Op. Cit., p. 170.

29   Nigel M. de S. Cameron, an Evangelical Christian, is President of the Center for Policy on Emerging Technologies in Washington, DC, and a Research Professor at the Illinois Institute of Technology. Cameron is Dean of The Wilberforce Forum, is former Provost and Distinguished Professor of Theology and Culture at Trinity International University/ Trinity Evangelical Divinity School in Deerfield, Illinois. Known internationally for his work on bioethics, Dr Cameron founded the journal Ethics and Medicine and the Centre for Bioethics and Public Policy (bioethics.ac.uk) in London, England; he also chairs the board of the Center for Bioethics in the Church (thecbc.org).

[30] Kass headed President Bush's Council on Bioethics from 2002 to 2005.

[31] Bostrom, Nick, 'A History of Transhumanist Thought', in *Journal of Evolution and Technology*, Vol. 14, Issue 1, April 2005.

[32] Leon R. Kass, *The Wisdom of Repugnance*, Catholic Education Resource Center, www. Catholiceducation.org/articles/medical_ethics/me0006.html

[33] Ibid.

[34] In Tallying the New Bioethics Council: Has Leon Kass Stacked the Decks? (*Reason* Online Edition, January 23, 2002), Ronald Bailey describes President Bush's 18-member Council on Bioethics thus:

"Most of the members of the council are communitarians. They generally believe that modern American society focuses far too much on individual autonomy at the expense of social responsibility. They want to reshape American society around a set of core values and often express hope for a larger role for religion in public policy and public discourse. A surprising number of the council members, including Kass, are closely associated with the neoconservative religious magazine *First Things*."

Among the members of Kass's Council were Robert P. George and Gilbert Meilaender, both signatories to the Ramsey Colloquium's 1994 response to homosexuality and both members of the American Enterprise Institute, a Washington-based neoconservative think-tank dedicated to free-market capitalist economics and social conservatism whose members read like a who's who in American right-wing politics.

[35] Ibid.

[36] Kass, Leon, 'The Wisdom of Repugnance', http://www.catholiceducation.org/articles/medical_ethics/me0006.html

[37] J. Robert Nelson, 'Genetic Research Broadens the Understanding of Humanness' in *What is Life?*, Christian Social Action, Jan. 1991, p. 269.

[38] Rose et. al., *Not In Our Genes: biology, ideology and human nature*, New York, Penguin, 1990, p. 137.

[39] Ibid.

[40] Ibid., p. 21.

[41] Cole-Turner is a founding member of the International Society for Science and Religion and currently serves as its Vice-President.

[42] Reiss is Chief Executive of Science Learning Centre London, Vice President of the British Science Association, Honorary Visiting Professor at the University of York, Docent at the University of Helsinki, Director of the Salters-Nuffield Advanced Biology Project, a member of the Farm Animal Welfare Council and editor of the journal Sex Education. He is Assistant Director of Research, Consultancy and Knowledge Transfer at the institute of Education, University of London. He is also an Anglican priest.

[43] Dr Roger Straughan is Reader in Education at the University of Reading, specialising in moral education and ethics. He has written extensively on ethical issues arising from genetic technologies, particularly concerning animals and plants.

[44] A key issue here will be what constitutes 'harm' or 'harmful' in this context. Is this a medical term or a pseudo-medical category? We might ask what criteria are used to define 'harm'. Is the harm to the patient's well-being, or to public or parental values (religious or otherwise) that the patient somehow fails to instantiate? We have already seen how homosexual relationships 'harm' a religious definition of marriage, but this is a very specific kind of harm that requires prior faith in a set of religious definitions.

[45] Reiss M.J. and Straughan R., Improving Nature?: The Science and Ethics of Genetic Engineering, New York: Cambridge University Press, 1996., p. 89.

[46] Ibid., p. 69.

[47] Ibid., p. 79.

[48] E. O. Wilson, 'Reply to Fukuyama,' in The National Interest, no. 56 (Spring 1999), pp. 35-37.

[49] While somatic gene therapy changes on the DNA of somatic cells, and therefore affects only the individual who receives the treatment, germ-line changes are passed down to the individual's offspring.

[50] Fukuyama, Francis, Our Post Human Future: Consequences of the Biotechnology Revolution, New York: Farrar, Starus & Giraux, 2002, p. 78.

[51] Rifkin, Jeremy, The Biotech Century: Harnessing the Gene and Remaking the World, New York: Tarcher/Putnam, 1998, p. X.

[52] Ibid.

[53] Fukuyama, Francis, Our Post-Human Future: Consequences of the Biotechnology Revolution, New York: Farrar, Straus & Giraux, 2002, p. 186.

[54] Rifkin, Jeremy, The Biotech Century: Harnessing the Gene and Remaking the World, New York: Tarcher/Putnam, 1998, p. x.

[55] Ibid., p. xii.

[56] Habermas, Jürgen, The Future of Human Nature, Cambridge, Polity Press, 2003, p. 12.

[57] Sandel, Michael J. The Case Against Perfection: Ethics in the Age of Genetic Engineering (Cambridge Mass. & London, England: Belknap Press of Harvard University Press, 2007), p. 9.

[58] Kass, Leon R., The Wisdom of Repugnance, Catholic Education Resource Center, www.catholiceducation.org/articles/medical_ethics/me0006.html

[59] Fukuyama, Op. Cit., p. 172.

[60] Ibid., p. 10.

[61] Ibid., pp. 76-77.

[62] Fukuyama p. 19, Rifkin, p. xiii.

63 Fukuyama, Op. Cit., p. 94.
64 Rifkin, Op. Cit., p. xiii.
65 Fukuyama, Op. Cit., p. 102.
66 Rifkin, Op.Cit., p. 1.
67 Sinsheimer, Robert L., 'The Prospect of Designed Genetic Change', *Engineering and Science Magazine*, April 1969 (California Institute of Technology), reprinted in Ruth F. Chadwick, Ed. Ethics, Reproduction and Genetic Control, London, Routledge, 1994, pp. 145 -146.
68 Critics of Christianity have suggested that this is due partly to the establishment of a dualism of man and nature absent in Asian and pagan religious belief systems. Beverley Clack (*Sex & Death, 2002*) suggests something similar to this in her analysis of Platonic idealism and the Augustinian concept of 'sin'.
69 Reiss and Straughan, Op. Cit., p. 84.
70 Ibid.
71 Cole-Turner, Ronald, The New Genesis: Theology and the Genetic Revolution, Louisville Kentucky, Westminster/John Knox Press, 1993.
72 Reiss and Straughan, Op. Cit. p. 89.
73 Rifkin, Op. Cit., p. 145.
74 Ibid.
75 Ibid, p. 207.
76 On 24 September 2007, while speaking at Columbia University.
77 Beginning in the mid-1980s, transsexual individuals have been officially recognized by the government and allowed to undergo sex reassignment surgery. As of 2008, Iran carries out more sex change operations than any other nation in the world except for Thailand. The government even provides up to half the cost for those needing financial assistance and a sex change is recognised on the birth certificate.
78 Reiss and Straughan, Op. Cit., p. 212.
79 U. S. Congress, Office of Technology Assessment, *Mapping Our Genes*, July 1988, p. 84.
80 Rose et. al, Op. Cit., p. 22.
81 Beckwith, Jon, 'A Historical View of Social Responsibility in Genetics', American Institute of Biological Sciences, 1993, p. 332.
82 Rose, et. al., Op. Cit., p. 26.
83 Rifkin, Op. Cit., p. 159.
84 Reiss and Straughan, Op. Cit., p. 215.
85 Ibid.
86 Clothier Committee (1992). *Report of the Committee on the Ethics of Gene Therapy.* London: HMSO.
87 Rose, et. al., Op. Cit., p. 166.

[88] See Reiss, Michael, 'Genetic Engineering: Should We Make People in Our Own Image?' http://www.google.co.uk/search?hl=en&source=hp&q=Ian+Barbour+and+consent+and+treatment&aq=f&aqi=&aql=&oq=, accessed on 20 Sept., 2010 and 'What Sort of People Do We Want?', Notre Dame Journal of Law, Ethics and Public Policy, 1999.

[89] Peters, Rev. Ted, Playing God: Genetic Determinism and Human Freedom, New York, Routledge, 1997.

[90] Rose et.al., Op. Cit., p. 7.

[91] Gettleman, Jeffrey, 'Americans' Role Seen in Uganda Anti-Gay Push' in The New York Times online edition, January 3, 2010, http://www.nytimes.com/2010/01/04/world/africa/04uganda.html accessed on January 5, 2010.

[92] Montgomery, Peter, 'Loving Uganda to Death: the Global Reach of Far-Right Christian Hatred, Religious Dispatches online, March 24, 2013, religiondispatches.org/archives/sexandgender/6926/loving_uganda_to_death_the_global_reach_of_far_right_christian_hatred/

[93] See Schmidt, Thomas E., Straight and Narrow?: Compassion & Clarity in the Homosexuality Debate (Leicester, England: Inter-Varsity Press, 1995), chapter 6, esp. pp. 100-137.

[94] As for his discussion of AIDS, Schmidt overlooks the fact that in Africa an AIDS pandemic has taken 22 million lives in less than 20 years. The Catholic Church and its bishops have everywhere extolled abstinence and fidelity and denounced the use of condoms, with the head of the Catholic Church in Mozambique even proclaiming his belief that some European-made condoms are infected with HIV deliberately. The international community continues to be distressed at the effects of the Catholic Church's policy on condoms, because the reality is that *married* women living in Southern Africa are at higher risk of becoming infected with HIV than unmarried women. Extolling abstinence and marital fidelity do not protect her, because in all likelihood she is already monogamous and faithful. It is her husband who is likely to have contracted HIV out of wedlock. Yet refusing a husband's sexual advances risks ostracism and indigence in African cultures. Biologically females are twice as likely to become infected with HIV through unprotected heterosexual intercourse than males. In many countries women (including wives) are rarely able to negotiate condom use and are more likely to be subjected to non-consensual sex. Suggesting that abstinence is a "solution" to AIDS in these circumstances is anything but "compassionate" towards women and effectively condemns them to death and makes orphans of countless children - hardly a way to end gender discrimination or to promote healthy marriage and family life. The Joint United Nations Program on HIV/AIDS (UNAIDS) specifically noted the need for countries to **expand** access

to condoms within five years, a move that most conservative Christians would certainly oppose.

[95] Indeed, given the stresses created by sexual stigma and prejudice, it would be surprising if some of them did not manifest psychological problems (Meyer, 2003). The data from some studies suggest that, although most sexual minority individuals are well adjusted, non-heterosexuals may be at somewhat heightened risk for depression, anxiety, and related problems, compared to exclusive heterosexuals (Cochran & Mays, 2006).

[96] see, e.g. Goffman, Erving *Stigma* and Kardiner, A. and Ovesey, L., *The Mark of Oppression*.

[97] Denies Overbye, 'Born To Raise Hell?', *Time*, Feb. 21, 1994, v.143, no. 8, p. 76.

[98] Wellings, K., Johnson, A.M., Wadsworth, J. and Field, J. (1994) the National Survey of Sexual Attitudes and Lifestyles, Blackwell Scientific Press, London.

[99] Schmidt, Thomas E., Straight and Narrow? : Compassion and Clarity in the Homosexuality Debate, Leicester, England: Inter-Varsity Press, 1995, p. 117.

[100] The 2002 National Survey of Family Growth (NSFG), surveyed over 12,000 men and women aged 15 to 44. Results show that 34 percent of men and 30 percent of women reported engaging in anal sex at least once.

[101] See the 1975 *Declaration on Certain Questions Regarding Sexual Ethics* (*Persona Humana*) VII, para. 2.

[102] Tyler Gray, 'Is Your Baby Gay?: Pretty Soon, a DNA Test Could Tell You', *RADAR* Online, March 2007, p. 2. http://www.radaronline.com/from-the-magazine/2007/03/is_your_baby_gay_1.php

[103] Ibid.

[104] Mohler, Rev. Albert, Jr., 'Is Your Baby Gay? What If You Could Know? What If You Could Do Something About It?' at www.AlbertMohler.com posted Friday, March 2, 2007, p. 2.

[105] Ibid., p. 3.

[106] Ibid., pp. 3- 4., point 9.

[107] Ibid., p. 3., point 4.

[108] Peters, Ted, *Playing God: Genetic Determinism and Human Freedom*, New York, Routledge, 1997, p. 96.

[109] Ibid.

[110] Mohler, Op. Cit., p. 4, point 9.

[111] Ibid., pp. 3 & 4.

[112] Ibid., p. 4, point 10.

[113] Mohler, Rev. Albert, "*Was it something I said? Continuing to think about Homosexuality*", http://www.albertmohler.com/blog,16 March, 2007, p. 2.

[114] Ibid., p 3., point 8.

[115] Ibid., p. 2, point 3.

116 Many of the Bush Presidency's Council on Bioethics were affiliated with this magazine.

117 Carter, Joe, 'Gay Gene Eugenics' in *First Things* online edition, August 18, 2010, p. 2. www.firstthings.com/onthesquare/2010/08/gay-gene-eugenics

118 Ibid.

119 Ibid., p. 2.

120 Fukuyama, pp. 76-7.

121 Zimmerman, Burke E., 'Human Germ-Line Therapy: The Case for Its Development and Use', *Journal of Medicine and Philosophy*, December 1991, p. 594.

122 Ibid., p. 596.

123 Ibid., pp. 597-98.

124 Gregory Stock of UCLA's School of Public Health has argued along similar lines in *Prospect*, as discussed in Chapter 6.

125 His statement was co-authored by Alfonso Gómez-Lobo.

126 In 'Bioethics and Public Policy: Catholic Participation in the American Debate', *Issues for a Catholic Bioethic*, Luke Gormally, Ed., London, The Linacre Centre, 1999, p. 292, Robert George and William L. Saunders say there has been too much effort by Catholic leaders to link the Church's pro-life witness to the whole range of sanctity and quality of life issues (capital punishment, welfare, housing, taxation, defense spending, international human rights policy, etc.). These efforts at consistency are wasted, they claim, since "no matter how careful they are to avoid sounding as though stopping abortion is the only thing they care about, American cultural elites" will "viciously attack them".

127 The *American Enterprise Institute for Public Policy Research* (AEI) is a Washington-based conservative think tank founded in 1943. Among its members are Michael Novak, who was a member of the Ramsay Colloquium, and other socially conservative economic libertarians.

128 Kass, Leon, The Hungry Soul: eating and the perfecting of our nature, Chicago and London, University of Chicago Press, 1999, p. 5.

129 Ibid., pp. 5-6.

130 See Leon R. Kass, "Making Babies: The New Biology and the 'Old' Morality", *The Public Interest*, Winter 1972; Leon R. Kass, "The Wisdom of Repugnance," *The New Republic*, June 2, 1997; Leon R. Kass and James Q. Wilson, *The Ethics of Human Cloning*, Washington: AEI Press, 1998.

131 Kass, Leon, 'Looking for an Honest Man: Reflections of an Unlicensed Humanist', text of 2009 Jefferson lecture at NEH website (retrieved May 22, 2009).

132 Mohler, Rev. Albert, Jr., 'Is Your Baby Gay? What If You Could Know? What If You Could Do Something About It?' at www.AlbertMohler.com posted Friday, March 2, 2007, p. 3.

[133] Duke, Lynne, 'A Pre-Birth Determination', *Washington Post* online, March 18, 2007, p. 1.

[134] For example, Rev. Bob Schenck, a pastor of the Evangelical Church Alliance.

[135] Where it is not based on natural law reasoning, Christian homophobia is based on the authority of the Bible irrespective of any argument. The Euthryphro dilemma sufficiently deals with such claims, as Biblical authority could justify *any* abhorrent behavior. Few Christian fundamentalists would agree that it would be right to, say, rape or murder innocent children just if the Bible contained a command to do so.

[136] Habermas, Jürgen, *The Future of Human Nature*, Cambridge, Mass., Polity, 2003, p. 19.

[137] Katz Rothman, B., Genetic Maps and Human Imaginations, New York: WW Norton, 1998, p. 37.

[138] Benhabib, Seyla, and Fred R. Dallmayr. The Communicative Ethics Controversy: Studies in Contemporary German Social Thought, MIT Press, 1990, pp. 29-32.

[139] Weber, Max, Weber: Political Writings (Cambridge Texts in the History of Political Thought), Peter Lassman. Ed., Trans. Ronald Speirs, Cambridge University Press, 1994. xvi.

[140] Rose et. al., Op. Cit., p. 64.

[141] The Nuffield Council on Bioethics does most of the work of a national bioethics advisory body in the UK. This is despite the fact that the government in 1999 decided **not** to create an official national bioethics advisory board. This decision was taken on the basis that the Nuffield Council, together with other scientific advisory committees, such as the British Medical Association, already fulfilled the role. Instead, the Human Genetics Commission (HGC) and the Agriculture and Environment Biotechnology Commission (AEBC) were established to advise the government on developments in biotechnology in those respective areas. The AEBC was disbanded in 2005, but the HGC continues to be an active and influential organization. The Nuffield Council meets with members of the HGC regularly to exchange information about current and future work. The HGC is the UK Government's advisory body on new developments in human genetics and their applications. The HGC advise the government on human genetics with a particular focus on the social, ethical and legal issues.

[142] See **6.9** of the Nuffield Council's 'Genetic Screening Supplement', July 2006. For a full list of signatories see: http://conventions.coe.int/Treaty/Commun/ChercheSig.asp?NT=164&CM=8&DF=21/05/2011&CL=ENG

[143] See **7.5** of the Nuffield Council's 'Genetic Screening Supplement', July 2006.

[144] Objections raised by those such as Jürgen Habemas, Francis Fukuyama, Jeremy Rifkin, Michael Sandel and myself, among others.

[145] Protocol 30 on the application of the Charter of Fundamental Rights to Poland and the United Kingdom (2007).

[146] Appendix A: Conclusions and Recommendations from Genetic Screening: Ethical issues1993 (Chapter 10: Conclusions), What is Not Covered in This Report 3.

[147] Both George and Saunders were members of the *Ramsay Colloquium* of The Institute of Religion and Public Life in New York. I remind my readers of the Colloquium's stance on homosexuality: "Our statement is directed chiefly to debates over public policy and what should be socially normative. We share the uneasiness of most Americans with the proposals advanced by the gay and lesbian movement, and we seek to articulate reasons for the largely intuitive and pre-articulate anxiety of most Americans regarding homosexuality and its increasing impact on our public life." Saunders now works for the ultra-right Family Research Council in Washington D.C. where he is Senior Fellow and Director of their Center for Human Life and Bioethics.

[148] This organization began in 1966, following Vatican II. It issued approximately seven pastoral letters per year between 1966 and 1967 on a wide range of social issues, including "peace and Vietnam", "race relations and poverty", "the government and birth control", "abortion", Panama-U.S. relations", "the introduction of the family viewing time during prime time", and 'farming" to name just a few.

[149] George, Robert and Saunders, William L., 'Bioethics and Public Policy: Catholic Participation in the American Debate', *Issues for a Catholic Bioethic*, Luke Gormally, Ed., London, The Linacre Centre, 1999, p. 292.

[150] Ibid., p. 298.

[151] Ibid., p. 292.

[152] Ibid. Other reasons they cite for this failure are defensiveness in engaging the opposition, when they should be on the offensive on the abortion issue. Additionally, they say there has been too much effort by Catholic leaders to link the Church's pro-life witness to the whole range of sanctity and quality of life issues (capital punishment, welfare, housing, taxation, defense spending, international human rights policy, etc.). These efforts at consistency are wasted, they claim, since "no matter how careful they are to avoid sounding as though stopping abortion is the only thing they care about, American cultural elites" will "viciously attack them.

[153] Rifkin, Op. Cit., p. 9.

[154] Ibid., p. 68.

[155] Rural Advancement Foundation International, "The Life Industry," RAFI Communique, September 1996, p. 1 http:www.rafi.ca/rafi/communiqué/fltxt/19964/html cited in Rifkin, p. 68.

[156] Rifkin, p. 69.

[157] Habermas, Op. Cit., p. 18.

CHAPTER 7

# The Limits of Parental Liberty

In July and August 2010, the US media buzzed around the story of a New York doctor who had used a prenatal pill to treat congenital adrenal hyperplasia, a condition that 'masculinizes' female babies and causes them to be born with ambiguous genitalia.[1] The controversy centered on the fact that the pill also had the effect of reducing the chance that females treated with the drug would be lesbian. Critics called it the first step towards engineering in the womb for sexual orientation.[2] Prenatal treatment for congenital adrenal hyperplasia offers (whether intentionally or not) the first possibility to test the potential for chemically steering a child's sexual orientation in the womb. Kenneth J. Zucker[3] added, "[The hormonal treatment] theoretically can influence postnatal behavior, not just genital differentiation."[4] The controversy surrounding the potential to chemically prevent homosexuality prompted a consortium of medical groups led by The Endocrine Society[5] to produce updated guidelines on treatment of congenital adrenal hyperplasia in September 2010. The authors recommended that prenatal therapy continue to be regarded as experimental. Thus they did not recommend specific treatment protocols. Instead they suggested that prenatal therapy be pursued through protocols approved by Institutional Review Boards at centers capable of collecting outcomes data on a sufficiently large number of patients so that risks and benefits of treatment could be defined more precisely.[6]

Only when the projected hopes for genetically modifying future childrens' sexual orientation come to light can we fully discern the impetus behind the recent publicity push for therapeutic language of seeking a 'cure' for homosexuality and the resurgent popularity of 'reparative' therapies and 'lifestyle transformation' testimonials like that which appeared in a *London Times* article of January 2010, in which a 41 year-old ex-gay man, Patrick Muirhead, claimed "Loving your own sex occurs in nature, without artificial triggers. But it is still not average behavior. Homosexuality is an aberration; a natural aberration."[7]

As noted in the previous chapter, advocates of free market genetic modification for homosexuality, whether motivated by religious belief, financial incentives or both, have a vested interest in forestalling public debate about eugenic interventions to 'cure' homosexuality until the biomedical technology for doing so is ready to go to market. It is urgent, therefore, that those who have serious concerns about interventions of this type make their case against legalizing these procedures now. Since what is at stake is the future of human nature, it is important that the public be well informed about ethical objections to liberal eugenics. It is also desirable that those who insist on having this debate not be dismissed as 'Luddites' or fear-mongers who wish to slow the progress of science and modern medicine. Like Habermas, I see no need to categorically oppose all uses of pre-natal screening and genetic therapy. Our aim is simply to ask whether, and if so how, the implementation of these achievements might impact our self-understanding as responsible agents. "Do we want to treat the new possibility of intervening in the human genome as an increase in freedom that requires normative regulation – or rather as a self-empowerment for transformations that depend simply on our preferences and do not require any *self-limitation*?"[8] Normative restrictions on the treatment of embryonic life need not be directed against genetic interventions as such. The problem is not genetic engineering but the manner and scope of its use.[9]

Some of the promises and benefits of unregulated reprogenetics[10] presuppose both determinism and paternalism deeply at odds with the liberal emphasis on individual rights and responsibilities. Eugenic approaches to improving the behavior of other individuals threaten to destabilize the underlying liberal consensus that individuals are responsible for their own moral character, and that others' wishes are insufficient to override the individual's authority to govern his own life in socially responsible ways. "What is ultimately at stake with biotech," says Francis Fukuyama, "is not just some utilitarian cost-benefit calculus concerning future medical technologies, but the very grounding of the human moral sense."[11] The "human moral sense" to which he refers is the notion that human individuals are distinct from other species of animals in their ability to direct and control their involuntary instincts. Because of this distinctively human capacity for free choice, humans alone are given the rights, dignity, and responsibilities accorded to moral agents. The gains in human rights and liberties of the nineteenth and twentieth centuries have been underpinned by a broad belief that what is common to *all* human beings, regardless of ethnicity, sex, sexual orientation, religion or disability, is our capacity for making free choices and forging an individual identity through our efforts. As I said in chapter 4, we experience our achievements as the products of our efforts and we measure our failures (and those of others) only against potentials we (or they) actually possess. Our experience of ourselves as responsible agents is essential to the *moral* evaluation of human action in a way that involuntary natural endowments are not.

Whether under the auspices of religion or science, historical attempts to assign moral value to involuntary, biological aspects of human nature have been fraught with confusion. St. Paul's anthropological presuppositions about the domination of *sarx* over will, along with his concept of 'original sin' as intrinsic in the nature of all persons, are the theological precursors to contemporary forms of biological reductionism and determinism. By problematizing human nature and human agency, Paul paved the way for external authorities to impose order on the perceived dangers they represented. Today's attempts by liberal eugenicists and transhumanists to problematize human nature *as such* hark back to Paul's pre-modern anthropological archetype by diminishing the importance of free will both for the moral evaluation of human behavior and the aspiration to improve it.

A typical example of this confusion comes from a prominent advocate of liberal eugenics, Professor Julian Savulescu of the Uheiro Centre for Practical Ethics at Oxford University[12]. Savulescu begins from the premise that human nature is 'problematic'. He argues that humans can, and should, be "liberated" from their biological "constraints".[13] Savulescu says this is partly because we are simply ill-suited to the environment we have created for ourselves. Social justice also dictates that we should enhance human nature in various ways, and Savulescu claims it would be "moral neglect" *not to* do so. He makes an analogy between malnourishing your child and failing to intervene to improve your child's diet. His reasoning is that not enhancing the child has the same *effect* as failing to nourish them, since we have a prima facie duty *to improve others' well-being*. Savulescu accuses some of *morally* neglecting the needs of others, and yet his proposed cure for this is to remove their inability to do otherwise. First, it is doubtful that we are unable to do otherwise, as many parents *do* provide for their children's needs and many adults are charitable to others. Second, he wants to remove moral responsibility from the perpetrators of this "moral" neglect on the grounds that they are not capable of moral responsibility anyway. The reasoning is circular.

Savulescu admits that the very people who will develop and select these cures are equally in need of them and that the bioenhancement technologies are open to abuse and misuse. His only reply to this criticism is to remind us that our present situation is so desperate that it must override the risks associated with this kind of bioenhancement. Savulescu dismisses critics of yet more unreflective technological advancement of obstructing the proposed remedy to the dire situation that was allegedly caused by too much technological advancement.

In addition, Professor Savulescu puts forward an 'existential' argument to the effect that the world is "different" in an unprecedented way: we no longer live in a safe world. The availability of enriched uranium and biological weapons poses an ever-present threat to peace and stability. Since human beings have 'moral limitations' (such as psychopathology) which can be 'cured' by biological intervention, the world will be made safer from danger by doing so. As Savulescu says, "psychological states place us at great risk." Professor Savulescu refers to his own (questionable) concept of "the biology of moral dispositions" and says it leads us to ponder how, *not whether*, we should enhance human nature. But it is doubtful whether 'dispositions' that are determined biologically *are* correctly described as 'moral dispositions' at all. Modern philosophers acknowledge that morality applies only to an agent's decision to **act** upon a biological disposition in particular circumstances where doing so will cause bad consequences for morally significant others. Much of Savulescu's argument trades on reification of behavior patterns – a tendency *to act* in a particular way is re-defined as a condition or entity within the biology or brain chemistry of the person. If the seemingly value-neutral medical term 'psychopathology' can stretch to voluntary behavior patterns, then I agree that there is a lot of 'sick' behavior in this world. But I would demure from transferring the use of medical language to patterns of so-called "sick" acts. It seems doubtful that all perpetrators of bad acts were '*born* that way' and had no choice to behave differently. Is every white-collar criminal who is "getting away with it" (often in a corporate culture that encourages ruthlessness) incapable of behaving differently? It is more likely a certain culture (not a "disease") allows these people to feel impunity when acting selfishly and being rewarded with huge profits for doing so.

Savulescu points out how most of the damage we do nowadays is not only through deliberate acts (for which we feel morally responsible) but omissions (for which we do not feel responsible). His point is that, for the victims of this civic neglect, it would seem that increasing their well-being and preventing them harm are equivalent values. This may be so, but using biotech to enhance the 'morality' of those whose omissions cause harm is not the only available solution.

Savulescu says proponents of moral bioenhancement claim only that we are "not biologically or genetically doomed to cause our own destruction," so we ought to embrace the newfangled means available to enhance human morality. Hence his ostensible appeal to our moral sense of responsibility. However, Savulescu also makes the contradictory claim that "our natural moral psychology does not provide us with the means to prevent [our downfall]," which is another way of saying that we *are* biologically doomed to cause our own destruction.

Abandoning the modern, autonomous model of human behavior and moral responsibility has serious implications. As Francis Fukuyama and Jeremy Rifkin have appreciated, we are in the throes of one of the great transformations in human history.[14] If we are to adopt a Nietzschean perspective on human nature that takes us beyond 'good and evil' then "we need to accept the consequences of abandoning our best natural standards for right and wrong and to do so with our eyes open."[15] Modern concepts of jurisprudence, justice, forensics, and even political democracy presuppose that moral agency and its attendant responsibilities are grounded in the autonomy of the individual.

By contrast, transhumanists[16] follow Nietzsche in urging us towards a future stage of 'post-moral' development in which subconscious drives and instincts will be regarded as paramount for assessing, directing and improving human behaviour.[17] The transhumanist agenda includes making reprogenetics safely available to all persons. Nick Bostrom of Oxford University claims these "will become increasingly relevant and practical in the coming years as these and other anticipated technologies come online."[18] In the early 90's, proponents of unregulated reprogenetics combined liberal cultural politics and laissez-faire economic policies with a liberal eugenic biopolitics. In *Citizen Cyborg* (2004), James Hughes set forward what he termed "democratic transhumanism," which joined transhumanist biopolitics with social democratic economic politics and liberalism.[19] He argued for safe and universally accessible biotechnology that will aid us in the achievement of a post-human future while respecting the sovereignty of individuals over their own bodies.

Social Darwinism is the backdrop against which unregulated use of reprogenetic enhancements make sense. Social Darwinism provides the rationale that, if social or economic inequalities are biologically determined, attempts to remedy them by social means, as proposed by liberals, reformists, and revolutionaries, "go against nature".[20] Typical of this outlook is Professor Savulescu's claim that social or economic circumstances do not account for differences in character and behaviour (presumably it is the other way round). The social Darwinist paradigm allows us to view the social and economic status quo as 'the natural order of things' rather than seeing it as the outcome of political and institutional forces driven by human decisions and individuals' choices and values.[21] It reduces all reasons (human goals, choices) to mere causes (value-neutral backward-looking explanations). This naturalistic paradigm lends a sense of inevitability to the social order. In this sense, it provides the modern scientific equivalent to St. Paul's ancient perspective, expressed in Romans 13: "there is no authority except from God, and those that exist have been instituted by God. Therefore he who resists the authorities resists what God has appointed, and those who resist will incur judgment." (vv. 1-2) Nowadays, few would claim that social realities and relationships of power are the result of God's appointment or providence. But many would argue in a similar vein that the political realities are 'inevitable' and 'natural' – the outcome of 'natural superiority' or 'survival of the fittest' - rather than owing to social and economic privilege, choices, political policies and economic arrangements made by powerful individuals.

By locating the ultimate causes of human behavior and social institutions in the subconscious, involuntary substrate of human biology, proponents of social Darwinism create a demand for new forms of paternalistic, authoritarian social control. According to this paradigm, 'evil' 'sinful' or 'criminal tendencies' reside within the natures (or biological 'predispositions') of persons, undermining their potential to lead morally good lives. This paternalistic way of thinking provides the justification for 'experts' (or medical professionals) to intervene in order to re-direct the individual's behavior according to his own, or society's, "best interests". This presupposes that some moral guardians are infallible or at least know better than the individual what kinds of behavioral dispositions will be 'best' (either for his own good or for the good of society). Interventions of this nature *presuppose* the absence of the necessary conditions for moral responsibility in the individual, and then actively remove moral responsibility from the individual on that basis, relocating it in external authority figures or paternalistic social institutions.[22]

To appreciate the significance of ethical disagreements that are developing alongside the biotech advances of recent decades, it is necessary to understand the political backdrop against which they are being fought.

Since the late eighteenth century, Western political systems have been so shaped by liberal values that they are generically classified as "liberal democracies". This wide consensus on liberal values prompted Francis Fukuyama to argue in his 1992 book *The End of History and the Last Man* that the advent of Western liberal democracy may signal the end point of humanity's socio-cultural evolution and the final form of human government.

Historically, liberals were critics of the injustice of a feudal system in which social position was determined by the 'accident of birth'. If the revolutions of the eighteenth century and the liberal reforms of the nineteenth meant anything it was the rejection of the principle that merit was hereditary.[23] Liberals also challenged the authority of the established church and supported the movement towards freedom of conscience in religion. Influenced by the Enlightenment belief in universal reason, liberal thinkers of the 18th and 19th centuries demanded reasoned justifications for political powers. No longer would superstition or tradition suffice as explanations for political authority.

Liberals also championed a vision of human flourishing linked to autonomy. For John Stuart Mill, autonomy was not valuable for its own sake but for its conduciveness to the development of individuality, which he thought indispensable to human wellbeing. In the third chapter of '*On Liberty*', John Stuart Mill (1806–1873) outlined why individuality was essential to human well-being. He urged that free scope should be given to varieties of character (so long as this did not cause injury to others) and thought it desirable that "individuality should assert itself" in things that do not concern others.[24] Mill claimed that where a person's "rule of conduct" came not from within but from slavish obedience to "the traditions or customs of other people", a principal ingredient of human happiness would be lacking.[25] He identified individuality as "quite the chief ingredient of individual and social progress".[26] As a utilitarian, Mill saw rights, defined in terms of negative liberty, not in abstract terms but as serving the permanent interests of man as a progressive being. Mill's understanding of what constitutes human well-being draws strikingly on virtue theory. The ancients had claimed that virtue was essential to happiness, if not entirely constitutive of it[27]. The ancient ethical conception of happiness as a whole life well lived is distinct from the modern psychological conception of happiness as a feeling of contentment produced by the satisfaction of being able to fulfill whatever desires we happen to have. Both Mill and his predecessor Wilhelm Von Humboldt worried that the notion of virtue as a good in itself would be supplanted by a notion of virtue as instrumental to procuring fleeting physical and material pleasures.[28] The morally vicious individual, no less than the morally virtuous individual can enjoy the contentment of having his desires satisfied, whether the objects desired are rightly or wrongly desired. On the psychological conception of happiness as contentment, individuals achieve happiness when they get what they want, regardless of whether what they want is something they also need and regardless of whether what they want is innocuous or harmful. The psychological conception of happiness is competitive (rather than reciprocal) since its attainment by one individual may depend upon the deprivation of it for another. When happiness is so conceived, the right to pursue it cannot be secured *for all*.

Mill's rejection of this psychological notion of happiness in favor of the notion of happiness as virtue (in the sense of a whole life well lived) separates his utilitarianism from the more crude understanding of utility as "the greatest good for the greatest number." When happiness is conceived as a whole life enriched by the cumulative possession of all the goods that human beings rightly desire because they are naturally needed, then the pursuit of happiness becomes *cooperative* rather than *competitive*. One agent's pursuit of this kind of happiness does not conflict with another's efforts to achieve it. No institution or government can confer moral virtue upon a human being or make her a person of good moral character. Happiness conceived as a well-lived life cannot be secured for all by governments or laws. However, it is within the power of governments and social institutions to provide human beings with the external conditions (e.g. negative liberty) indispensable to the pursuit of this kind of happiness. This will not ensure its attainment. It will only ensure that **all** have the liberty necessary to its attainment. The interior perfection of character that is moral virtue is the only one within our power and subject to free choice on our part.[29] Our possession of all other goods depends to some degree upon external circumstances beyond our control.

Mill argued that individual decision-making and originality are what make liberty worth having. He saw liberty as an indispensable condition for the pursuit of happiness. Mill and Humboldt followed the ancients in interpreting 'happiness' not as holding some compliment of material (or biological) possessions, but in living one's life in a certain way. As John Cooper has appreciated, for Aristotle, "*eudaimonia* is necessarily the result of a person's own efforts; success, of whatever kind, could only count as *eudaimonia* if due to one's own efforts."[30] The value liberals place on negative liberty and the private sphere comes from an understanding of individual well-being not as a commodity that can be handed from one person to another, but as an active, self-authored quality of life. Whether asserted to resist an oppressive government or domination and violence from other individuals, rights function as means of placing control over action in a person's own hands.[31]

By the early 90's political liberalism had lost its influence in America (except in the economic sphere where libertarian policies continue to dominate). The media strategies of social conservatives like Irving Kristol, Richard Mellon Scaife, John Olin and Roger Ailes allowed them to slant coverage of the news.[32] Today it seems science, backed by humanists on the left and neo-conservatives on the right, is retaining its influence in shaping American discourse and policy. However, science is increasingly presented as 'objective' and therefore supremely good. It is regarded as the 'best' means of determining social policy, and the demand that public policies should be 'in keeping with the scientific evidence' or the notion that progress is hampered by viewpoints devoid of scientific grounds, threatens to misrepresent science as more value-neutral than it really is.

In the contemporary Anglo-American West, science is accorded the authority that once went to the Church. Science replaces the Church as the ultimate legitimator of bourgeois ideology.[33] To oppose 'science' is not merely to transgress human conventions but eternal and unchanging laws of nature. As Rose et. al. say, "The social order was still seen to be fixed by forces outside humanity, but now these forces were natural rather than deistic. If anything, this new legitimator of the social order was more formidable than the one it replaced."[34] Some argued that science was the ultimate in epistemic domination; it provided the discursive framework for a new mode of oppression that forced its results on everyone in a post-religious age. Philosopher of science Hilary Putnam claimed that scientists play a crucial role in determining the meanings of words and Steven Rose[35] could declare in 1984 that science had become the new source of legitimacy for ideology.

In a 1998 article, David Fernbach leveled a series of sophisticated criticisms against the claims of the 'New Gay Science'. He argued that even if empirical evidence suggests that the cause of homosexual orientation is biological, it is nevertheless an oversimplification to assume that there is "a one-to-one fit between any of these supposed biological indicators and a homosexual orientation."[36] Fernbach suggests that the *biological* definition of gay identity is associated with the reactionary aim of defending homosexual behavior against "the zealots of religion who especially perceive homosexuality as willful misconduct."[37] But Fernbach also claimed, in the same article, that the dangerous 'eugenic aspect' of the biological gay identity has enjoyed favor amongst homophobic religious zealots and also amongst the very biologists associated with the genetic discoveries, many of whom are gay men. The fact that the gay scientist and author Simon LeVay, for example, would not oppose a woman's right to abort a lesbian or gay fetus, is interpreted by Fernbach as indicative of:

> "a radical breakdown of the traditional ideological nexus between biological gay identity and social tolerance. The whole enterprise of giving the spontaneous sense of 'being born that way' an up-to-date scientific backing is undermined by the very advance of biology; the forces of patriarchy and oppression simply prepare to do battle on the new ground of genetic technology. Indeed, because the entire research program that the gay biologists adhere to is premised on the assumption that homosexuality is a social problem, Hamer and LeVay are drawn from their original purpose of justifying the gay minority into scenarios remarkably similar to those of their homophobic colleagues."[38]

The anxieties expressed by Fernbach are certainly not to be dismissed lightly. If the previous chapter shows anything it is that the traditional nexus between biological gay identity and social tolerance has indeed broken down and continues to be eroded. Fernbach's perspective suggests that the odds against social justice for homosexuals grow worse in direct proportion to the objectivity of the search for scientific truth about the etiology of homosexuality. Fernbach observes that we are living in an increasingly 'eugenic age' which he perceives as a direct threat to homosexuality.

In 2004, Charles W. Colson, co-author of the 2009 *Manhattan Declaration*, edited a compilation of essays containing many viewpoints on how a distinctively Christian bioethics ought to approach issues like human cloning, inheritable genetic modification and the commercial use of genes, cells and tissues[39]. An analysis of these essays is indicative of the ways in which the prohibitionist stance towards homosexual acts is being woven into a bioethics that rationalizes eugenic or 'therapeutic' treatment of the homosexual tendency or 'condition'. The authors collectively reject inheritable genetic modification (IGM) by means of which real or perceived 'enhancements' would accrue to offspring in an irreversible way.[40] However, they do not rule out work in biotechnology that will lead to cures for diseases and disabilities which leaves open the question of how a Christian bioethics will look upon homosexuality. As liberal eugenicist author Nicholas Agar explains:

"The problem is that it is difficult to make the therapy–enhancement distinction principled. It is hard to find definitions of disease suitable to serve as a moral guideline for genetic technologies. **Social constructivists consider diseases to be states to which society takes a negative attitude. Cancer seems to satisfy the requirements of this definition, but so might homosexuality and practicing a religion different from the norm in your society.** Objectivist accounts avoid these difficulties by making the definition of disease independent of our attitudes. According to the most widely advocated version of this view, I suffer from disease when some part of me fails to perform its biological function. For example, cholesterol deposits on the arteries constitute or conduce to disease because they impede the heart in the performance of its function, which is to pump blood. The problem with this way of defining disease is that it may sometimes set goals irrelevant to human flourishing. Suppose we were to discover that homosexuality was a consequence of malfunction in the part of the brain responsible for sexual attraction. Should this rather obscure fact about biological functioning count more than the fact that many homosexual people seem to be living excellent lives?"[41] [my bold]

As for the problems presented by finding a principled way to make the therapy-enhancement distinction, Agar is not convinced Christians living in liberal democracies need find one at all. Similarly, Professor Julian Savulescu claims that 'disease' is an arbitrary and indefinable standard. Agar and Savulescu are prominent defenders of 'liberal eugenics'. Liberal eugenicists begin from the premise that attempts to draw a 'principled' line between therapy and enhancement are impossibly fraught. Therefore, given the liberal presumption of liberty that places legal restraints on state interventions into the private sphere, the burden of proof rests with liberals to show how or why enhancements based on parental preference are harmful. In the absence of any proof of harm, parents ought to be permitted to exercise their liberty by modifying the genetic make-up of their children as they see fit. This seems to allow for state neutrality with respect to genetic interventions while protecting parental liberty to select traits in ways that do not restrict the autonomy of the child.[42] Consequently, this type of eugenics is regarded as non-coercive. Liberal eugenics offers parents the liberty to define disease as 'states to which society takes a negative attitude'. As Agar puts it: "Access to information about the full range of genetic therapies will allow prospective parents to look *to their own values* in selecting improvements for future children. By contrast, authoritarian eugenics would do away with ordinary procreative freedoms. Liberal eugenicists instead propose a radical extension of them."[43]

Despite internal tensions in Western culture between its Judeo-Christian roots and their Enlightenment critique, Christian conservatives today have at their disposal an ostensible means of avoiding the apparent dilemma between the desire to promote their own version of public morality and the dominant liberal injunction to protect the sovereignty and liberty of the individual to pursue his own vision of 'the good life'. 'Liberal eugenics' leaves eugenic decisions to the market, driven by the demands of consumers. Defenders of liberal eugenics are content to transfer the socio-political responsibility for eugenic decisions to the discretion of parents. This seems to qualify as a 'liberal' form of eugenics because the state does not impose any single vision of the 'good life' on future generations of individuals subject to it. Rather, it leaves individual parents the 'moral space' within which to make such value judgments for themselves (and for their offspring). Consequently, it could be argued that the future direction of human nature will be determined not by an institutional dictator with utopian plans for social engineering, but by parents and what they perceive to be best for the wellbeing of their offspring.

Liberal eugenicists claim that, in this respect, liberal eugenics is not significantly different from traditional child rearing. They argue that there is no substantial difference between helping our children to achieve happiness and success by providing training and education and providing it by means of bioengineering. Not to use the best means available to improve our children's prospects for happiness and success could even be construed as a culpable omission, or a form of neglect.

If there are legitimate ethical objections to unlimited parental liberty in the use of reprogenetics, they must be widely disseminated independently and on their own terms. Otherwise, they risk being misrepresented from within the context of liberal eugenicists' discourses. In this chapter I wish to propose some tentative ethical objections to liberal eugenics and in particular to genetic interventions aimed at altering the subject's sexual orientation.

### i. A tyranny of the majority is as dangerous to individual liberty as a tyrannous government.

Nicholas Agar and other liberal eugenicists begin by acknowledging the difficulty of making a clear distinction between medical therapeutic uses of genetic manipulation and eugenic ones. Any intervention to remove a negative trait could just as easily be construed as the creation of a positive, or 'enhanced' state of well-being. Since many diseases are socially constructed, Agar says it is hard to find definitions of disease that could serve as a moral guideline for regulating use of eugenic technologies.[44] Disease definitions vary between socially constructed definitions ('states to which society takes a negative attitude') and objectivist definitions (those independent of social attitudes). Allowing a patient's 'diseased' status to be defined (*and treated* without her consent) as any state "to which society takes a negative attitude" not only fails to protect the individual from the tyranny of the majority, it legitimizes subjecting individuals to such a tyranny by new, more powerful, biotechnological means. Medicine will be enlisted to do the work that punishment and moral exhortation did in the past, by providing new, more efficient and irrevocable ways of expressing the majority's intolerance for perceived 'social ills'.

In the case of homosexuality, this is particularly troubling, given the social stigmatization of those who act according to their biological homosexual predispositions. Interventions undertaken for eugenic purposes (e.g. to make the sexual orientation of offspring more closely resemble the narcissistic goals of their parents) would have the effect of homogenizing the human species. This would be true whether the means is preimplantation genetic diagnosis (PGD),[45] somatic or germline genetic modification. Where homosexuals are already a minority, parental liberty to eradicate homosexuality from their offspring would have the effect of making them more so.

As Agnes Fletcher has noted, everyone experiences limitations, whether they be physical, intellectual, or sensory. The determining factor in terms of quality of life is society's response to these limitations in terms of attitudes or barriers to participation.[46] Fletcher claims, correctly in my view, that searching for medical solutions to perceived social ills is wrong. It is akin to lightening the skin of a black child in order to protect him from racist discrimination or abuse, instead of addressing the social ills of racism. This diverts attention from the work needed to remedy social intolerance. Worse, it is a form of 'blaming the victim' for social ills that derive from prejudice and fear of difference. As such, we might see pseudo-medical solutions to social ills becoming more prevalent as consciousness of victimization and pressure to remedy social injustices increase.[47]

In the previous chapter I examined how theologian bioethicists Reiss and Straughan see nothing problematic in the notion that somatic or even germ-line therapy might provide more efficient and less politically contentious forms of social repression. After all, disease is, "in a sense, a relationship between a person and society."[48] Instead of treating the issue of consent as an important one, without which it would be unethical to use germ-line therapy to treat persons for socially defined "ills", Reiss, Straughan and Ian Barbour all assume that where consent is lacking, a majority can simply remove the individual's right to informed consent in matters of 'therapy' for a disease which is here defined as largely a "socially constructed" concept. The implication is that treatment intended to alter the genetic makeup of a person to make him or her conform, without consent, to a socially popular or religious idea of 'health' is morally acceptable so long as a sufficient majority say so. This subverts, without argument, the most basic assumptions upon which the rights of individuals in modern liberal democracies rest. It would seem this is precisely why Barbour, Reiss and Straughan share a concern that it will be unpopular. Even if only half of all parents in the United States were to use bioengineering to 'straighten' their children, this would be likely to lower tolerance for the now smaller minority of homosexuals who remain, and this (increased) social stigma could be avoided by altering the child's sexual orientation according to the preferred social norm. As Michael Sandel has observed, "the Promethean instinct is infectious."[49] The practical effect of legalizing such a practice would be to gradually create a situation where there is an ever-stronger impetus to use it.

John Stuart Mill expressed worry about this kind of social pressure to conform to a uniform type. In *On Liberty* (1859) he was adamant that "if resistance waits till life is reduced nearly to one uniform type, all deviations from that type will come to be considered impious, immoral, even monstrous and contrary to nature."[50] Mill thought that when people become unaccustomed to diversity, they also become less tolerant of it.

The unpopularity of a policy permitting such arbitrary (pseudo)medical interventions into the biological make-up of other persons comes to light in view of our basic individual rights. For Mill, we lack freedom if we are coerced by other human beings.[51] He defined freedom as the absence of interference by others, which is minimally necessary for "pursuing our own good in our own way."[52] Mill and other Utilitarians defended rights as instrumental to human interests (interests which maximize human wellbeing). Chief amongst these interests is protection from harm. The importance of being an individual and taking an active role in shaping our own lives is what justifies placing constraints on others. Mill understood that a popular and powerful majority was as much a threat to individual liberty as a tyrannous government. In the first Chapter of *On Liberty* he was at pains to expand the protection of the individual beyond just protection from the state to a full protection from oppression by "the will of the most numerous or most active part of the people; the majority, or those who succeed in making themselves accepted as the majority."[53] Mill argued that the abuse of power by a tyrannous majority is as dangerous as any other abuse of power. The tyranny of the majority, while it may at first operate through the mechanisms of state, can become an even more formidable social oppressor because it is more insidious and "leaves fewer means of escape, penetrating much more deeply into the details of life."[54] For these reasons Mill urged that protection must extend beyond protection from the magistrate to protection also against

> "*the tendency of society to impose, by other means than civil penalties, its own ideas and practices as rules of conduct on those who dissent from them; to fetter the development,* **and, if possible, prevent the formation,** *of any individuality not in harmony with its ways, and compel all characters to fashion themselves upon the model of its own.*"[55] [my emphasis]

Whether to resist an oppressive government or domination and violence from other individuals, rights function as means of protecting the 'moral space' minimally necessary for "pursuing our own good in our own way." Reprogenetic approaches to improving individual moral well-being threaten to destabilize the underlying liberal conviction that others' wishes are insufficient to override a person's authority to govern her own life. The form of popular bioengineering proposed by Anglo-American advocates of "liberal eugenics"[56] and theologians like Reiss, Straughan and Barbour is deeply at odds with the liberal concept of rights and the sovereignty of the individual.

This is a key problem, and one that cannot be overcome by popular consensus alone, although this too should be sought. The current consensus that Reiss, Straughan and Barbour suggest we should strive to overcome by 'popular consent' is the liberal notion that the rights of individuals (especially the rights to consent and autonomy) trump other utilitarian considerations about what produces the most happiness for the majority.

To desire and pursue non-harmful things that may be socially 'disruptive' (i.e. unconventional or distasteful to others) is precisely the definition of freedom. To choose my own desires, or to choose between competing desires, is essential to moral agency and to personhood. This liberty is not absolute. Liberals accept the limits imposed by the harm principle. Exposure to 'socially disruptive' ideas and lifestyles that sometimes cut against the grain of social convention is essential in order that real alternatives are possible. Liberal societies protect this freedom up to the point where it causes harm to others – not just harm to their tastes or attitudes but to their permanent interests as progressive beings.[57] Offending people is permissible (even intellectually healthy) because it allows us to test our ideas against the strength of others, even if we happen to find others' views or lifestyles distasteful or objectionable. If we are confident in our own views we ought to be willing to defend them, rather than treating them as dead dogmas or sacred shibboleths that must never be questioned. Defensiveness and hostility to difference most often stems from the fragility of one's own position, or an inability to defend it through reasoned argument. No one is infallible, so we can all learn from exposure to the ways or opinions of others. Even mistaken views sometimes contain partial truths from which we can learn. Censoring unpopular beliefs, by the exposure to which we might otherwise be educated, stunts human progress. For these reasons, J. S. Mill defended the widest possible liberty consistent with like liberty for all. He interpreted harm in a fairly narrow way, and explicitly did not include self-regarding behaviors (such as consenting sexual activity between adults) as 'harmful'. Nor did he include mere offence as truly harmful to man as a progressive being.

Classic liberalism's rejection of paternalistic interference into the private sphere except to prevent harm *to others* places the burden of proof squarely on those who wish to interfere in the behavioral predispositions of future children to prevent them from desiring sexually unconventional choices. To justify such interference into the genetic makeup of individuals, 'liberal' eugenicists or concerned parents must show why homosexual behavior is harmful. In the absence of such proof, future human beings must be left alone and permitted to opt for homosexuality.

It may be that the liberal eugenicist will claim that *anyone* in a liberal society can opt for homosexuality, regardless of his *biological* predispositions. It would seem to follow that defending the biological sanctity of the individual will do nothing to protect his or her future liberty. The freedom to engage in harmless unconventional sexual behaviors is protected precisely because the harm principle cannot justify placing limits on consenting adult sexual behavior of any kind. Few liberals would dispute this point. After all, most liberals agree that human beings have free will, so a biological predisposition for homosexuality does not *determine* (i.e. compel) gay behaviours anyway. But this is to obscure the point. A biological substrate, while it does not *compel* the homosexual individual's particular choices, does seem to *direct* the individual's sexual attraction in predictable ways. If it did not, there would be no market for the bioengineering technique in the first place and we wouldn't be having this argument about legalizing it. Reducing the biological substrate for homosexual attraction (if one exists) will almost certainly reduce homosexual behavior. The purpose of the reprogenetic interventions will be to eliminate individuals' voluntary homosexual behavior by eliminating their involuntary biological predisposition for it. The practical effect sought by those who use such reprogenetic interventions will be to reduce homosexual behavior. This will happen not by taking away the individual's free will, but by biologically steering the direction in which it is most likely to be expressed.

Voluntary sexual acts are related to sexual attraction, which is involuntary. This relationship points to an important distinction that can help us to discern why interventions aimed at *behavioral* modification are particularly troubling to liberals in a way that cosmetic modifications would not be.

The argument against bioengineering sexual orientation is not that making people heterosexual will deprive them of all liberty to engage in homosexual acts. In a liberal society they could still opt for homosexuality. But in fact they wouldn't. This is the most salient reason why heterosexist parents would wish to use reprogenetic intervention. Their purpose for using it on their offspring would be to prevent homosexual behavior by preventing the kind of underlying sexual attraction that makes it appealing. The objection, therefore, is that 'straightening' future generations denies to others the right to live *their* own lives uninhibited by the social values of others.

Those who uphold the liberal values of toleration and diversity accept that no individual has an absolute right to be sheltered from the fallible beliefs and practices of others, and much of our upbringing has the practical effect of subjecting us to ideas that we may not willingly share with our parents or older generations. However, reprogenetics differs from ordinary social conditioning and indoctrination in that its coercive force completely removes the individual's ability to respond. In this sense it is not reciprocal and not equal. Its aim is to permanently alter the very *will* of the individual to make it conform to that of others. As Mill says, the individual needs protection from the tendency of a powerful majority **"to fetter the development, and, if possible, prevent the formation, of any individuality not in harmony with its ways, and compel all characters to fashion themselves upon the model of its own."** [my emphasis]

Parental liberty is valuable, but it does not override the liberty of their offspring to express their own biological natures in ways that harm no one. So called 'parental liberty' over-steps when it is used as a euphemism for illegitimate political paternalism and eugenics.[58] The kind of 'harm' such parental interventions aim to prevent is not harm to the child or to any other individual, but to the dominant, fallible and increasingly fragile cultural values of heterosexism or homogeneity. These socially conventional values, if they must be biologically introjected into others in order to make them conform, are deeply paternalistic and authoritarian. Insofar as they aim at fashioning others in our own image, they are also deeply narcissistic.

Whether or not parental interventions aimed at such ends should be legally permitted in Western liberal democracies is doubtful.

Liberal eugenics (if intended to determine the patient's future desires and harmless behaviors) would violate existing legal protections for the sovereignty of the individual (and negative liberty). It would furnish new means of irrevocably inscribing the fallible social values of some into the very nature of others without their consent, and its ultimate consequences would be a socially and biologically engineered tyranny of the majority. As such, the 'liberal' eugenics movement threatens to dismantle core tenets of modern liberalism. Francis Fukuyama expressed concern that a new biotechnology powerful enough to reshape what we are will open up once again possibilities for social engineering that the past century's "utopian planners" had given up on.[59] It seems to me he was correct.

**ii. Eugenic interventions aimed at behavior modification remove responsibility from individuals and make them dependent upon others in a way that undermines our sense of personhood. The transference of responsibility for an individual's moral wellbeing from himself to others will lead to an explosion of parental responsibility and a concomitant decrease in 'parental liberty'.**

As Michael Sandel explains, the real problem with unlimited parental liberty to enhance their children by means of biotechnology is the explosion of responsibility.[60] Responsibility for individual fulfillment would go beyond that individual. For liberals, the interior perfection of character that is moral virtue is the only one within our power and subject to free choice on our part. The notion that interior perfection of character is **not** wholly within our own power, but depends upon the interventions of others, is not only a *consequence* of bioengineering enhancements, but a *presupposition* of them. This presupposition needs considerable argument, since the default position of modern liberalism is non-interference with individual liberty in the absence of harm to others. Michael Sandel argues that, if liberal eugenics continues unfettered, parents could become responsible for choosing, or failing to choose, the right traits for their children.[61]

Let's put this into context: once pre-natal screening and selection for sexual orientation become standardized techniques, parents who once saw giving birth to a homosexual child as a matter of chance will feel judged or blamed. This creates a burden of decision for parents that did not exist before. Although prospective parents remain free to choose whether to use prenatal testing and whether to act on the results, the choice is now to act or to omit to act, and parents will be responsible for either choice they make. Such a presumption of responsibility (for the moral well-being of others) would not necessarily grant people the 'moral space' in which to decide for themselves whether to turn away from others' (perceived) needs. This expansion of responsibility would be especially likely given what we've said (above) about the proportionate increase in stigmatization that would accompany a decrease in homosexuality. If one believed that well-being could be bestowed upon one person by others, then people could be *obligated* to provide well-being for one another. By contrast, liberals merely require that people not inflict harm on others when it can easily be avoided.

But it could be argued that there is little difference between an increase in well-being and a decrease in harm. It would seem that increasing someone's well-being and preventing them harm are equivalent values (pace Savulescu). But this places the burden of one person's happiness on another's shoulders. Moreover, it ignores the key issue: liberals and virtue ethicists reject the notion that the individual's *eudaimonia* could be *provided by others*. Consequently, the absence of harm/interference is **not** sufficient for well-being, but is the necessary condition for its achievement. As such, the absence of harm is more valuable to an individual's *eudaimonia* than well-being bestowed *by others* could ever be. Citizens in a liberal state do not have a claim right to assistance in good living, but they do have a claim right to those minimal mechanisms necessary to provide the conditions within which it is possible to pursue it for themselves. Chiefly, this involves protection from interference by others.

Mill argued that self-determination is essential to human happiness because the wisdom of others is fallible and sometimes too narrow. Individuals know and care more about their own situation than anyone else who might claim to be acting in their "best interests". Moreover, people start with different circumstances and life experiences and have different needs; they are more like trees (organic and individual, with deep roots and growing in different directions) than trains (manufactured for one purpose and destined to one pre-ordained 'end').[62]

In *A Theory of Justice* (1971), John Rawls offered a brief endorsement of liberal eugenics based on justice.[63] Even in a society that agrees to share the benefits and burdens of the genetic lottery, he wrote, "It is in the interests of each to have greater natural assets. This **enables** him to pursue a preferred plan of life."[64] The parties to the social contract "want to ensure for their descendants the best genetic endowment (assuming their own to be fixed)."[65] Eugenic policies are therefore required as a matter of justice. "Thus over time a society is able to take steps at least to preserve the general level of natural abilities and to prevent the diffusion of serious defects."[66] Rawls sees the equal distribution of biological goods as tantamount to the equal distribution of other, political and material goods. Without the minimum necessities (education, health care, housing) people do not have equal liberty, since they do not have equal opportunities to take advantage of the negative liberty afforded to them. This justifies state interventions to redistribute wealth. A state sponsored redistribution of biological 'wealth' (or 'natural assets') would be intended to meet the minimal condition necessary to allow us "to pursue a preferred plan of life".

This leaves unanswered the question of what constitutes "greater natural assets" or "the best genetic endowment" or "serious defects". For Rawls, the "just society" guarantees to individuals the freedom to choose how they want to spend the time they have for living and to realize a personal conception of the "good life" according to their own abilities and choices.[67] Habermas notes that, "in a constitutional democracy the majority may not prescribe for minorities aspects of its own cultural form of life by claiming for its culture an authoritative guiding function."[68] The program of today's Anglo-American 'liberal eugenicists' is comparable with liberalism, says Habermas, "only if enhancing genetic interventions neither limit the patient's opportunities to lead an autonomous life nor constrain the conditions for her to interact with other persons on an egalitarian basis."[69]

When genetic disease prevention becomes safe and widely accessible, failing to use it for those who have severe heritable diseases would be construed as causing them harm. It would seem that increasing someone's well-being and preventing them harm are to be treated as equivalent values after all. In what sense, then, can liberals argue that the absence of harm is more valuable to an individual's *eudaimonia* than well-being bestowed *by others* could ever be? Addressing this question pinpoints the kind of harm liberals are chiefly concerned to prevent. While physical harm limits our liberty in obvious ways, so too do forms of paternalistic interference that diminish the agent's autonomy. Truly 'serious' diseases are harmful to human fulfillment for the same reason that paternalistic interference is harmful: both leave the individual dependent on others for basic life functions or plans that ought rightly to belong to the individual. Self-determination is limited or impaired.

It seems Rawls's argument could justify state-sponsored eugenic policies for the prevention of serious biological defects that would otherwise leave persons in a permanent state of dependency. The principled distinction between therapy and enhancement (as discussed in vii., below) could help us to reach a consensus in defining which kinds of biological defects are sufficiently 'serious' to warrant intervention.

Liberal eugenics implies more state compulsion than first appears. Many liberal eugenicists argue that liberal reprogenetics are not only unobjectionable, but may even be morally required.[70] Buchanan et. al. defend liberal eugenics on the grounds that it does not harm the child's right to "an open future".[71] I have expressed my reservations about the claim that interventions aimed at behavioral modification *do* harm the child's right to an open future, and are expressly intended to foreclose future options that intervening parents dislike. Genetic interventions are morally permissible provided the enhanced capacity is an "all-purpose" means, and so does not point the child toward any particular career or life plan. By Rawls's own account the obligatory interventions, if there are any, could not include those that preclude the "pursuit of a preferred plan of life" and would have to leave individuals the freedom to choose how they want to spend the time they have for living and to realize a personal conception of the "good life" according to their own abilities and choices. The genetic assets required and equally distributed would have to be "all-purpose means" (functions) not directed at any preferred set of ends.[72] There could be no valid reason for defining heterosexuality as "an all-purpose means".

First, intervening to change sexual orientation is patently motivated by the wish to point the child *away from* a particular kind of life and (by elimination) *towards* its opposite. But more importantly, what starts out looking like a free choice can easily be transformed into an obligation, says Sandel.[73] If we interpret the enhancements as general "all-purpose" means, useful in carrying out virtually any life plan, then withholding this from the child could be seen, pace Rawls, as unjust deprivation tantamount to denying the child an education. The closer such capacities are to being truly generic, all-purpose goods, the less objection there would be from the state to ensure that they are equally distributed. So, says Sandel, "liberal eugenics does not reject state-imposed genetic engineering after all; it simply requires that the engineering respect the autonomy of the child being designed."[74] It is doubtful whether it even meets that minimal requirement.

### iii. Bad ends cannot be made better by 'good' means.

James Watson, the biologist who, along with Francis Crick, discovered the double-helix structure of DNA, sees nothing wrong with genetic engineering and enhancement, so long as they are freely chosen rather than state imposed.[75] While critics argue that non-therapeutic reprogenetic interventions are nothing but a form of "free-market" or "privatized" eugenics, defenders of unregulated reprogenetics reply that to remove the coercion is to remove the very thing that makes eugenic policies morally repugnant. But adopting alternative means does not render the ends more acceptable.

Francis Fukuyama has cautioned that social engineers will merely use biotechnology as a new and more efficient means of achieving ends that, in the past, would have been dismissed as encroachments on individual liberty and privacy. While liberal eugenics do not expressly impose any single vision of the 'good life' on all redesigned individuals, they represent a different means of imposing many people's identical visions of the 'good life' on others without their consent, and this is part of what was wrong with authoritarian, state-imposed eugenics. If we currently accept that there is something morally objectionable about allowing a powerful majority to impose its will and its values on a relatively powerless minority, even to the point of exterminating their genotype, then achieving these ends by new means will not make them less objectionable. A form of non-authoritarian eugenics in which the moral culpability for the homogenizing eugenic goal is shared amongst many individuals, is nevertheless a form of utopian social engineering; it is simply a more popular one.

The hopes for genetic enhancement today fall to the marketplace, and regulating this "genetic supermarket" will only be a matter of public debate if there is a perceived need for legal regulation. Some fear that the ultimate consequences of parental liberty to alter, or screen for and select, sexual orientation will be a pre-natal gay genocide.[76] To many, it seems that genetic 'therapy' aims at the nefarious end of eradicating homosexuals but merely accomplishes it by less flagrant means. But if we agree that the goal of eugenics (or prenatal genocide) is morally objectionable, then achieving it by parental liberty is no better than achieving it by state-sponsored social engineering or state planned extermination.

Liberal eugenics defenders argue that a gay 'genocide' is not the goal of genetic 'therapy' anyway. Therapy aims at curing (or changing) the subject rather than exterminating him or her altogether.[77] Only in light of these anticipated counter-arguments can we now see why defenders of liberal eugenics must ensure that genetic interventions to modify sexual orientation must be made to appear analogous to *reparative therapies*, or innocuous choices, and must not be perceived as equivalent to 'purging' an unpopular 'other' from the gene pool. Making the ends of 'parental liberty' appear innocuous, even 'healthy', as opposed to sinister or 'purging', makes it much easier to transfer delivery of these goals to new means. Only if the public becomes suspicious of the ends will it become equally wary of the means.

## iv. Unilateral interventions undermine the moral recognition of autonomy proper to a community of legal equals.

Even if all could agree that genetic interventions aimed at altering sexual orientation are the moral equivalent of 'purging' homosexuals from the gene pool, the illiberal aim of dictating a preferred scope of sexual behaviors would not be the only problem with 'liberal' eugenics. Liberals, and many Christians, tend to assume that by 'moral responsibility' we mean that each of us carries the sole responsibility for giving ethical shape to our own lives. Eugenic interventions aiming at behavioral modification reduce the modified patient's ethical freedom by irreversibly steering his choices away from a particular field of options according to the will of a third party. Genetic manipulation dismantles the underlying assumption that each of us equally enjoys reciprocity of rights and duties. The dangers of constraining the ethical freedom of a genetically modified person can never be ruled out *a priori* since the person concerned can never give their prospective consent. Attributing or assuming the patient's consent can never be easily justified except in cases where there is a prognosis of extreme suffering or limitation for the individual concerned. Arguably, assumed consent is only justified to prevent extreme evils rejected by everybody.

The irreversible choice a person makes in redesigning another person's genome for behavior modification jeopardizes the necessary condition for the autonomous agent's self-determination. Such interventions undermine egalitarian interpersonal relations by initiating a new kind of paternalistic relationship that is asymmetrical in several respects. While parenthood is inherently asymmetrical insofar as parents beget their children and children do not beget their parents, this dependence only engages the child's existence, not his essence.[78] Eugenic interventions aimed at behavioral modification revoke the usual reciprocity between persons of equal birth. Where a paternalistic intervention has re-directed the course of the dependent person's life history, or confined it to within preferred boundaries, the latter may interpret but not revise or reverse this intervention. Nor is the relationship reciprocal. The product cannot draw up a design for its designer.[79] This would preclude a symmetrical relationship between programmer and product. The programmer would have the liberty to act as the co-author of the 'product's' life. This is a liberty that the product would not have vis-à-vis the 'programmer' (reprogenetic engineer). The unilateral ability of producers/reprogenetic engineers to dispose over the direction of another person's life history undermines the mutual recognition of autonomy proper to a moral and legal community of free and equal persons.

### v. The presumption of liberty cuts both ways.

Liberal eugenicists argue that biotechnologies furnish a more legitimate means of social engineering, since the impetus for it will not be state planning, but consumer choice. This overlooks the fact that the consumer's liberty of choice is in direct conflict with the negative liberty of the 'patient' and his presumptive right to non-interference. It is surprising, therefore, to find so many intelligent defenders of liberal eugenics arguing as though parents were entitled to a presumptive liberty that their progeny are not. Molecular biologist Lee Silver of Princeton University represents the predominant view when he claims that "a liberal society that values freedom above all else" will be hard pressed to find "any legitimate basis for restricting the use of reprogenetics."[80]

For liberal homophiles, the urgency of so doing comes into sharp focus in light of the routine discussion of homosexual orientation as a key candidate for 'therapeutic' interventions. Biologist James Watson created a stir when he controversially expressed the view that, if a gene for homosexuality were discovered, he would support the decision of a pregnant woman to abort a foetus that carried it.[81] When accused of homophobia, he claimed he was merely expressing support for a much broader principle – that prospective parents should be free to abort foetuses for any reason of genetic preference.[82]

On this (allegedly) liberal view, the state would seemingly not be justified in preventing parents from inscribing their own heterosexist values into the genetic make-up of their unborn children. But, as Jürgen Habermas has observed, this program is compatible with political liberalism only if enhancing genetic interventions do not limit the opportunities to lead an autonomous life for the person genetically treated. It would seem that in the case of interventions to change sexual orientation, where the very point of the eugenic intervention is to eliminate the child's potential for types of behavior the parents dislike, the parents' eugenic freedom collides with the negative liberty of their children. The presumption of liberty cuts both ways.

In the case of altering someone else's sexual orientation, the purpose of the intervention into the other's genetic make-up (without her consent) is to eliminate a behavioral disposition to act in a particular way that is harmless but 'distasteful' to others. Having a particular biological sexual orientation does not eliminate the agent's autonomy, but it does ensure that the freedom he has will be directed towards particular kinds of ends. To deny this is to pretend that (involuntary) sexual attraction does not influence the kinds of voluntary choices an individual will make. The burden of proof shifts back to the "liberal" eugenicist to show why the patient's liberty to engage in private, consenting sexual behavior with a partner of his own sex is harmful to others. The presumption of liberty must favour the bodily sovereignty and sexual liberty of the patient. Unless parents can show how or why their preferred 'enhancements' prevent harm to others, they should not be permitted to interfere in the prospective liberty of their future offspring.

Habermas is correct to argue that intervention into "the prenatal distributions of genetic resources means a redefinition of those naturally fixed ... scopes for possible decision within which the future person will one day use her freedom to give her own life its ethical shape."[83] In this case, her ethical freedom has been intentionally changed by a prenatal design, such that she is made to share the authorship of her life with someone else. In the case of genetic manipulations intended to alter other people's sexual orientation, the very motive for the intervention is to make someone else behave the way we want them to by curtailing their ability to desire certain types of harmless sexual choices.

When Gregory Stock says that "efforts to block new technologies that might change our natures would require policies so harsh and intrusive that their harm would be far greater than that feared from the technologies themselves"[84] the implication is that our current failure to bioengineer our children is harsh, intrusive and harmful. Indeed more harmful even than the consequences of allowing us to dispose over future generations by inscribing our values into their genotypes. However, the burden of proof is on those who want to intervene to alter the genotypes of other, otherwise healthy human beings to show what harm is prevented to others by so doing. Stock thinks "policies in Britain to block innocuous choices like the sex of a child are a good example of undesirable state intrusion."[85] Stock's outlook is worrying partly because there are valid reasons to be concerned about the effects of sex selection. In China for example, by the second decade of the twenty-first century, up to one fifth of its marriage-age male population will not be able to find brides.[86] In India, census statistics have revealed a widening gap between girls and boys over the past three decades. A report published in *The Lancet* noted the remarkable growth in selective abortion of female fetuses in India, where the laws against selective abortion of girls are routinely flouted. The 2011 census revealed that the ratio of girls to boys aged under seven is now 915 girls per 1,000 boys, the lowest since records began in 1961.[87] Furthermore, sex selection is based on sexism. As such, sex selection perpetuates the harmful effects of sexism on girls and women. If legalized, it not only makes them into a minority, reducing what little social power they have, it also legitimates their inferior status by legalizing measures to prevent their existence. Yet Stock sees the fact that one generation are writing sexist ideas into future generations as harmless. Why not just argue that sexism is harmless? Stock says that sex selection does not harm children but benefits them because they are the 'right' sex for their parents.[88] A child of the 'wrong' sex is harmed because he or she is a disappointment to his or her parents. Thus, concludes Stock, no serious externality arises from sex selection.[89] The notion of "externality" presupposes that the harm to others or to society is the sole measure of whether limitations ought to be imposed on sex selection. As a liberal I have to agree. However, I disagree with Stock's claim that there are no serious externalities arising from sex selection. It is estimated that by 2020 there could be more than 35 million young "surplus males" in China and 25 million in India. The evidence shows that serious externalities *do* develop as a result of sex selection, as well as from the sexism from which it springs. Stock must think that the increase in sexism and its effects on girls and women are not harmful and so do not constitute a 'serious externality'. Many would disagree.

A liberal society that values freedom above all else, therefore, is not too hard pressed to find a legitimate basis for restricting the use of reprogenetics. We can muster substantial evidence to show that selectivity of this non-therapeutic kind leads to serious externalities. It harms others. This gives us the justification needed to impose legal restrictions on parental liberty. Liberal eugenicists, then, need to get busy finding a legitimate justification for restricting the scope of harmless behaviors open to their progeny.

**vi. Liberals are not inconsistent in opposing eugenic manipulation while defending the right to abortion.**

Many liberals[90] who object to parental interventions to change the sexual orientation of their offspring will not object, in principle, to abortion. This would appear to involve them in a dilemma. Pro-life Christians and others might demand to know why anyone would object to altering a fetus that they wouldn't object to killing. Since genetic manipulation would take place in the embryonic stage of development, it is difficult to see why liberals' fears about the instrumentalization of persons would not apply in spades to the practice of abortion.[91]

But this assumes that pro-choice liberals share with conservative Christians the premise that embryos have an ontological and ethical status equivalent to that of persons. Liberals need not give embryos the moral and ontological status of persons in order to object to manipulations aimed at changing a future person's behaviour. Pro-choice liberals do not think that a foetus has an absolute right to life because this would entail the belief that individuals in liberal democracies have a moral obligation to create actual persons from potential ones. Again, this involves an explosion of our existing responsibilities vis-à-vis other persons. It would mean that somehow non-existent persons 'need' or are even 'entitled' to exist and that existing individuals have a moral responsibility to make it so.

Liberal objections to reprogenetics aimed at behavioral modification are not directed at the protection of a potential human being but at the protection of an actual human being's potential for self-determination. Potential human beings do not have rights. Actual human beings do. Liberals' objections are directed at the ends sought by means of these interventions. The ends are expressly intended to curtail the liberty of future *existing* persons according to the will of others. The interventions only take place **because** (and only **if**) a particular potential human being **is** going to exist as an **actual** human being. The express purpose of the intervention is to change the nature and desires of an *actual* (not a potential) future person.

If our treatment of embryos intended for birth is subject to moral regulation in a way that embryo destruction is not, some might ask why PGD to select for heterosexuality should not be morally permissible. Even if liberals are not persuaded by the rather complex notion of respecting a special category of 'embryos intended for birth', there are negative externalities (see v, above) associated with PGD that ought to be sufficient to ban it, except where using PGD prevents serious harm to others. If used for screening out innocuous traits like homosexuality, the procedure would cause negative externalities similar to those associated with sex selection. We have good reasons for banning sex selection. Where it is used widely (with or without full legal permission) the harmful consequences in terms of sex imbalances and sexism ought to provide grounds for legally restricting these practices: they harm others. They harm the group targeted, because, with their numbers reduced, they suffer increasing discrimination. They also harm other groups, such as the 'surplus males' who cannot find wives. Allowing the selection legitimates and perpetuates discrimination against the targeted groups.

Since genetic interventions aimed at sexual behavior modification are undertaken to realize a qualitative determination of a particular kind of future life, their very purpose is to override the negative liberty of the future individual to prevent him from pursuing a set of life choices of which his 'designer' disapproves. The purpose of the intervention is to reduce the negative liberty of the individual to live *his own* vision of the 'good life' (in accordance with his nature) in a way that harms no one.

Bioengineering for eugenic purposes instrumentalizes *other persons*. It does not merely prevent potential persons from existing, but decides which types of persons ought to exist and how existing persons ought to behave.

The continued existence of a potential child is a separate issue to the continued existence of an actual child's potential(s). The presupposition of genetic behavior modification is that the treated embryo **will be born**. Therefore the object of the genetic manipulation is a future person in a way that the object of abortion is not. Genetic manipulation is directed at a future person's potentials while abortion is directed at a potential future person. The debate over the status of the embryo continues because there is no clear answer as to whether a fetus *is* entitled to the same legal status as a person. This is separate to the question of which choices, or kinds of options, ought to be open to a future human being. Whether potential human beings have an entitlement/claim right to life is an entirely different question to whether future living children ought to have their options/ dispositions foreclosed in advance by social guardians and/or engineers. Whether we have an obligation to make human beings is a separate question to which kinds of human beings we ought to make.

Whereas in the past, Christian conservatives saw biology and science as weakening Biblical authority and threatening a creationist account of human origins, this situation began to change after the 60's. Evangelical populism transformed into a culture war against modern liberalism. The voices leading the anti-communist scare were able to mobilize and redirect religious resentment away from conservative corporate giants trying to consolidate wealth to those who aimed to redistribute it.[92] The result was a tenuous alliance between corporate libertarians and religious social conservatives.

There are, however, serious divisions between the ethical-religious goals of pro-life Christians and the financial incentives of their neo-con libertarian allies. Stem cell research has brought these divisions into focus. Since extracted embryonic stem cells potentially can be made to grow into any cell in the human body, they are an extraordinary resource in the fight against Alzheimer's, Parkinson's, diabetes and other diseases. There is a perceived moral imperative, and huge financial incentives, to allow this research to continue. On the other hand, religious conservatives object to using those stem cells because they are extracted from embryos created for fertility treatments but not used to produce children. This involves deriving benefit from the destruction of human embryos --- which makes it morally equivalent to abortion.

Liberals would be well advised to exploit (or at least expose) the existing tensions between pro-business libertarians and some pro-life Christians. For example, in 2001 President Bush adopted a policy on stem cell research (which involves the destruction of embryos). His policy was intended to appease these two factions. He restricted federal funding to research carried out on *already existing* stem cell lines, so that no taxpayer funding would support any *further* destruction of embryos. In 2006 he vetoed a bill that would have funded new embryonic stem cell research saying he did not want the government "to support" the taking of innocent life. At the same time, he made no effort to ban it. Michael Sandel criticized this policy as inconsistent with pro-life policy and argument: "If harvesting stem cells from a blastocyst were truly on a par with harvesting organs from a baby, the morally responsible thing to do would be to ban it, not merely deny it federal funding."[93] If pro-life social conservatives were honestly persuaded that embryonic stem cell research is tantamount to infanticide, they would not only ban it. They would treat it as a grisly form of murder and subject scientists who performed it to criminal punishment. But while religious pro-life advocates do treat abortion as murder, and want it banned, they fail to demand the same of stem cell research. Sandel points out that if some doctors made a practice of killing children to get organs for transplantation, no one would take the position that infanticide should be ineligible for federal funding but allowed to continue in the private sector. Bush did not say that allowing embryonic stem cell research to continue is like allowing murder to continue, but this would be required for consistency if Bush really followed his own pro-life logic that embryos are inviolable human beings.[94] This shows that many religious people who invoke the 'equal-moral-status' position hesitate to embrace its full implications.

Robert P. George, while a member of the President's Council on Bioethics, did not actively demand a full ban on stem-cell research, but instead recommended limiting the number of days beyond which the law tolerates deliberate embryo destruction. He then argued that authorizing embryo destructive research up to a certain limit is tantamount to prohibiting it beyond a certain limit. By placing the emphasis on the prohibition, rather than on the authorization, George was able to maintain an apparent posture of opposition to it. But Sandel's example would make George's posture appear equally as odd as that of Bush. If some doctors made a practice of killing children to conduct research for the collective human good, no one would take the position that this type of infanticide should be permissible up to a certain age but prohibited beyond that age. George didn't say that allowing embryonic stem cell research to continue is like allowing murder of infants below a certain age to continue, but this would be required for consistency if he followed his own reasoning (in insisting that all embryos at any stage of development are inviolable human beings).

If pro-life Christians demand to know why anyone would object to altering a fetus that they wouldn't object to killing, liberals need not go on the defensive. Instead they might demand to know why anyone would object to aborting a fetus that they wouldn't object to destroying for research purposes.[95]

## vii. We can, and should, make a principled distinction between therapy and enhancement.

Both Fukuyama and Rifkin have expressed reservations about embryo selection and the degree to which all medical technologies can be used for enhancement rather than therapeutic purposes.[96] Jürgen Habermas shares their concern. He has attempted to make a principled distinction between (healing) negative eugenics and (more controversial) positive eugenics by arguing that the latter involves instrumental action in order to "collaboratively" induce, in the realm of objects, a state that is desirable according to one's own goals. In order to fully appreciate why this division between negative and positive eugenics is so controversial, we need to consider the problems with making a clear division between the two.

Nicholas Agar and other liberal eugenicists begin from the assumption that there is no principled way to make a distinction between therapy and enhancement.[97] Any intervention to remove a negative trait could just as easily be construed as the creation of a positive, or 'enhanced' state of well-being. Since many diseases are socially constructed, Agar says it is hard to find definitions of disease that could serve as a moral guideline for regulating use of eugenic technologies. Disease definitions vary between socially constructed definitions ('states to which society takes a negative attitude') and objectivist definitions (those independent of social attitudes). But when we consider the negative attitude society takes towards diseases like AIDS or cancer, it becomes difficult to know whether its status as 'disease' is socially constructed or objectivist. Objectivist accounts adhere to the view that 'disease' is defined by the failure of a biological function. But such failures do not, says Agar, always impede human flourishing. Many deaf people, for example, do not consider deafness to be a disability and some have supported a genetic test for deafness in order to ensure that their child will also be deaf.[98] There is, I think, an argument to be made that deafness is only perceived as a 'loss' or a malfunction *to hearing people*. There is something presumptuous and narcissistic about insisting that all people must be endowed with the same biological characteristics that have made *oneself* feel 'well' in order for *them* to feel fulfilled. Agnes Fletcher[99], writing from a 'disability equality perspective', has argued that our diversity as a species has innate value. She sees illness and impairment on a spectrum of human limitations that everyone experiences at some point in their lives, whether from illness or intellectual, sensory, or physical limitations. The key barrier to 'quality of life' is not the limitations themselves but society's responses and attitudes to them. Fletcher and other disabled people have expressed concern that the development of new biotechnologies and the 'choices' extended to parents are situated within a context of fears, myths and stereotypes about disability.[100] Disability rights advocates assert that there is an important distinction between the decision to have a child and the decision to have, or not to have, a particular child based on a single characteristic. Since such decisions are affected by the social context in which they are made, they have a wider impact than the individual.[101] Canadian academic and disability rights advocate Adrienne Asch identified a common tendency in prenatal diagnosis and discrimination more generally: a single trait is selected and identified with the whole person.[102] According to Asch, the characteristic is perceived as so important and so negative that it takes precedence over any positive qualities there might be in being alive.

In spite of these observations, we can attempt to make a tentative therapy/enhancement distinction principled. Therapeutic interventions are those alone that aim at *biological dysfunction that impedes human flourishing.* In cases where the prognosis is extreme suffering or limitation (especially where independence is impossible) we can be relatively certain that the concerned individual's consent can be assumed.[103] This anticipated consent on the part of the 'patient' is what justifies clinical interventions and allows us to designate these interventions as 'therapeutic' in a context of healing. Irrevocable decisions over the genetic design of an unborn person are always presumptuous (they assume our discernment in determining which genetic endowments will be 'best' for the lives of our children). As such, all such decisions ought, in principle, to depend upon consent. In cases where consent cannot be obtained, it can only be anticipated or assumed in circumstances where the intervention is to prevent *biological dysfunction that impedes human flourishing.* Habermas says we can only anticipate a wide consensus among otherwise highly divergent value orientations in situations where the intervention aims at the prevention of "extreme evils rejected by everybody".[104]

Chief amongst the 'evils' that we can assume there would be a general consensus to prevent is the removal of autonomy. Impairment of an individual's capacity for independent development and self-determination strikes at the core of what makes (adult) human life fulfilling. This impairment is more serious to the extent that the dependency it necessitates is permanent. This criterion could take us some way towards making more explicit what Habermas means by "extreme evils rejected by everybody" and may form a tentative basis for distinguishing between disabilities that do not impair fulfillment and more serious diseases or disabilities that do. All of us are dependent on others in various ways at various times in our lives. All of us are completely dependent as infants. But it seems uncontroversial that one of the necessary conditions for human fulfillment is independent self-determination and freedom of choice in how we spend the time we have for living.

If therapeutic interventions are those that alone aim at forms of biological dysfunction that impede human flourishing, homosexuality does not easily fit into this category. Homosexuality would only impede human flourishing for those individuals who are naturally heterosexually orientated. Agar acknowledges that many homosexual people seem to be living excellent lives. But he also suggests that homosexuality could be construed as constituting dysfunctional sexual attraction.[105] But equally, the homosexual genotype could be construed as a natural and healthy variant of human sexual attraction. Its benefits for the survival and health of the species (perhaps for keeping the population under control where resources are scarce) may not yet be fully understood. In 2014, broadcaster and naturalist David Attenborough said that the world's booming population – predicted to hit 11 billion by 2100 – will lead to our extinction unless something is done to tackle the problem.[106] At any rate, homosexuality has no obvious harmful effects.

It could be argued that permitting only genetic interventions that remove 'extreme evils rejected by everybody' will not rule out homosexuality as a target for therapy, since many *do* reject homosexuality as an extreme evil. When Christian figureheads talk about restoring creation to 'its full glory' or of 'imperfections' we must assume some working definition of what constitutes 'perfection' or 'fullness'. For some Protestant theologians (Cameron, Colson, Cole-Turner, Peters, Mohler, DeMar, Kass, et. al.), heterosexuality will be a part of that definition. But this is a tautology, not an argument. Despite the possible existence of a homosexual genotype, this view treats homosexuality as defective heterosexuality rather than as a separate but equally healthy variant of human sexuality. It assumes without argument or evidence that biodiversity cannot include non-reproductive types of sexual attraction, and that somehow diversity of this kind cannot have any use to the species. However, homosexuality is neither a pre-moral nor a moral evil. I hope my arguments in Chapter 6 for why homosexuality is no evil have gone some way to challenge that position.

My arguments, if they have any impact at all, ought to at least give us pause when considering whether to eliminate socially constructed 'diseases' from the gene pool. Among the most prevalent of these flawed social conceptions of 'disease' is the Vatican's notion that homosexuality is a biological tendency towards immoral forms of behavior. This places it on a par with pedophilia, which is currently looked upon as a biological compulsion for harmful, non-consenting, sexual behavior.

First, the notion that pedophilia *is* indeed so compulsive that it overrides the agent's free will is questionable, and so its status as a medical condition is in doubt. If pedophilia were a biological compulsion over which the affected agent had no freedom of choice, this would fail to explain the extremely emotional public indignation felt towards those who have the condition. Moreover, if homosexuality were a compulsion to bad behavior then it would be impossible for homosexuals to refrain from it. Yet this is precisely what the Vatican demand of homosexual persons. Upon reflection, the only kind of harm it causes for others is the difficulty they must endure in tolerating diversity. This is not harm to their permanent interests as progressive beings. Nor does their homophobic intolerance respect the reciprocity due to others.

Genetic behavioral modification ought to be ruled out as an especially dangerous category of bioengineering. This is because behaviors are not biological properties located in the gene or the brain. Human agents have free will and choose whether, how and when to express their biological predispositions. These free choices are the only thing that could conceivably make the resulting behavior morally bad. Genetic interventions directed at behavioral modification are intended to eradicate immoral behaviors. As such they deny the very autonomy that would justify a stance of moral disapproval towards other people's behavior. They aim at the wrong target in trying to manipulate behavior by changing involuntary aspects of character. The premise needed in order to remove a 'bad behavior' by redesigning someone's brain is that the brain is the cause of the bad behavior. But bad behavior *is* 'bad' (in the moral sense) because of the agent's freedom, not because of his biological predispositions.[107]

Much social disapproval is directed at behaviors that are (incorrectly) assumed to be immoral. For example, if homosexual behavior is immoral it cannot be so just because of the same sex aspect of the behavior, since there is nothing immoral about consenting homosexual sex acts *per se*. Only from an antiquated theological perspective could one see homosexual acts *per se* as immoral. If a liberal state were to permit the reprogenetic elimination of homosexuality because of its perceived immorality they would be granting a religious majority the right to inscribe its understanding of sexual ethics into the very nature of future human beings, and the species. This would be legally equivalent to state-sponsored religious genocide. Liberals defend the rights of homophobes to hold (and to express) any variety of irrational, homophobic or intolerant viewpoints. They may also live according to these beliefs, so long as their doing so does not encroach upon the liberty of others. However, a liberal state should never permit a religious majority to impose these beliefs on others in irrevocable ways that not only interfere in their autonomy, but also might lead to increased stigma and maybe eventually to the elimination of virtually all homosexuals.[108]

Habermas has suggested that we can draw a line between negative and positive eugenics by noting that the latter moves beyond the logic of healing - where healing is defined as the prevention of evils which one may assume to be subject to general consent. Religiously construed ideas of 'evils' where there is no ostensible harm to others are not subject to general consent. To legislate as though they were would be unconstitutional, at least in the United States.[109]

While Habermas understands the difficulty of distinguishing between negative (healing) goals and positive (enhancing) goals with respect to certain preventive interventions, such as strengthening the immunosystem or prolonging the lifespan, we can nevertheless use a simple regulative idea to govern such interventions based on a distinction between preventing evils and enhancing interventions. This principle is **assumed consent.** The intervening agent can anticipate or assume the consent of the patient preventatively treated when his action is guided by the clinical goal of healing.[110] This is in contrast to the perspective of a person who intervenes for manipulation of traits to induce in the patient a state that is desirable to her own goals. The definition of 'healing' hinges on the prevention of evils that one may assume to be subject to general consent. To make 'evils' more explicit and neutral vis-à-vis religious bias, I would recommend averting to the more specific and less morally fraught definition: <u>biological dysfunction that impedes human flourishing</u>.

While this definition will be controversial from the perspective of disability rights activists, this need not prevent us from ruling out homosexuality as a target for 'therapeutic' intervention, since homosexuality is not an 'evil' and does not impede human flourishing except in people who are heterosexual. Arguments to this effect could perhaps be marshaled to show that deafness is not an 'evil' that we can assume would be subject to general consent. It might be difficult to show that deafness impedes human flourishing, *except in people who were born with hearing*.

A distinction could still be made between homosexuality and deafness, however, on the grounds that homosexuals are not infertile, while deaf people do have impairment of a sensory function. Whether this sensory impairment impedes human flourishing is a question beyond the scope of this book, but to the extent that people born deaf do not experience it as such, it seems reasonable to doubt whether deafness from birth is the kind of 'evil' the prevention of which we could assume would be subject to <u>general</u> consent.[111] Assumed consensus can only be invoked, says Habermas, "for the goal of avoiding evils which are unquestionably extreme and likely to be rejected by all." If we view 'evils' in this more clinical light, we can distinguish negative eugenics by their aim: to prevent conditions that cause extreme suffering or limitation and therefore impair the quality of life of the patient. There are many heritable diseases that most of us can agree meet these criteria. Most of them limit the patient's autonomy in some permanent way.

In the case of homosexuality, some *heterosexual* parents could narcissistically assume that homosexuality is an evil the prevention of which one may assume to be subject to general consent. In his online article 'Gay Gene Eugenics' of August 18, 2010, Joe Carter at *First Things* magazine wrote:

*In 2002 Francis Fukuyama speculated that within twenty years we would be able to devise a way for parents to sharply reduce the likelihood that they will give birth to a gay child. Even in a society in which "social norms have become totally accepting of homosexuality," he argues, most parents would choose the treatment. Fukuyama is right. Even if homosexuality were considered a benign trait such as baldness or left-handedness, the majority of parents would opt to have a heterosexual child ("What if we want grandchildren?").*

But this would be likely to happen only because most people *are* heterosexual and would therefore experience *themselves* being gay as unfortunate. Heterosexual people might narcissistically assume that gay people cannot really be happy because *they* themselves would see the loss of *their own heterosexuality* as an 'evil'. Those born homosexual, however, see their homosexuality neither as a loss nor as an evil. Very few would consent to having it altered by others. The few that would alter it would most likely be motivated by reluctance to be subjected to social stigma. Most homosexuals look upon existing 'reparative therapies' aimed at making them heterosexual as a form of racist discrimination (or pseudo-medical abuse) rather than as a legitimate form of healing. It is only from a narcissistic, instrumentalizing perspective that one would want to prevent homosexuality *in a homosexual* person. One is not enhancing this person by making her adopt another (more prevalent) nature unless one can show that there is something inherently evil in difference or diversity. Yet most homosexual people would argue the opposite. They would say that their diversity, and being exposed to diverse others, has enriched their lives. Many with disabilities say the same.

If anything is necessary for the development of 'the perfect human being' it is self-determination. To remove from the individual the autonomy that makes him responsible for 'perfecting' himself [112] eliminates the moral dimension from the very concept of human 'perfection'. A 'good life' will no longer be conceived as a whole life well-lived, the product of individual effort and choice, but as a product of manufacture. This has prompted commentators to worry that new reproductive technologies encourage a consumerist attitude towards children.[113] In time, if viewed in this way, the 'good life' will be defined as some compliment of biological goods to which the individual will feel entitled in order to live (or to have?) a good life. Others will be held responsible for the quality of the individual's life, since this quality will be essentially dependent upon others. This presupposes that ethics is not about the scope of freedom the individual ought to have to act, but about whether the 'self' is a meaningful concept at all, except as defined from the outside, by others. By contrast, liberal moral philosophy pictures others *as* "other selves" – subjects with their own life goals and plans. This recognition of the other *as* an 'end in himself' is crucial to the liberal understanding of the self and explains the importance of equal protections reciprocally afforded to the 'other' under law.

I hope the above objections to unregulated reprogenetic liberty together make a case for treating these new human possibilities and opportunities with caution. I also hope they make more explicit what Francis Fukuyama and other critics mean in claiming that biotech poses a threat to the very grounding of the human moral sense.

[1]  The problematic notion that 'masculinity' is a biological condition rather than a socially constructed set of expectations about gender and appearance, etc. was not even addressed in the articles.

[2]  One such critic is Professor Alice Dreger, a bioethicist at Northwestern University. See 'Medical treatment carries possible side effect of limiting homosexuality' in *LA Times* online edition, August 15, 2010, by Shari Roan.

[3]  Zucker is a psychologist, sexologist and the head of the child and adolescent gender identity clinic at Toronto's Centre for Addiction and Mental Health. Zucker is known for his work in treating gender-variant children with reparative therapy to help them to conform to conventional behavioural expectations for male and female sexes. He is co-author, with Susan J. Bradley, of 'Gender Identity Disorder and Psychosexual Problems in Children and Adolescents'. In 2007, Zucker was chosen to be a member of the American Psychological Association Task Force on Gender Identity, Gender Variance, and Intersex Conditions, and in 2008 was named chair of the American Psychiatric Association workgroup on "Sexual and Gender Identity Disorders" for the 2012 edition of the DSM-5.

[4]  'Medical treatment carries possible side effect of limiting homosexuality' by Rachel Zammit Cutajar, in *MaltaToday* Online Edition, 16 August, 2010, http://www.maltatoday.com.mt/news/world/ medical-treatment-carries-possible-side-effect-of-limiting-homosexuality

[5]  According to their website, The Endocrine Society is an international body with 14,000 members from over 100 countries. The Society's diverse membership represents medicine, molecular and cellular biology, biochemistry, physiology, genetics, immunology, education, industry and allied health fields. Members of The Endocrine Society represent the full range of disciplines associated with endocrinologists: clinicians, researchers, educators, fellows and students, industry professionals and health professionals who are involved in the field of endocrinology. These professionals are dedicated to the research and treatment of the full range of endocrine disorders.

[6]  *Journal of Clinical Endocrinology and Metabolism*, September 2010, 95(9): 4133–4160, see sections 2.0 through 2.2 of the guidelines.

[7]  "The day I decided to stop being gay: Twenty years after he came out, Patrick Muirhead, 41, explains why he is suddenly feeling the appeal of the opposite sex", *The Times* of London, 18 Jan, 2010. http://www.timesonline.co.uk/tol/ life_and_style/men/article6990013.ece

[8]  Habermas, Jürgen, *The Future of Human Nature*, Cambridge, Mass., Polity, 2003, p. 12.

[9]  Ibid., p. 43.

[10]  The term 'reprogenetics' was coined by molecular biologist Lee Silver of Princeton University. The term refers to the merging of reproductive and genetic technologies. Silver distinguishes reprogenetics from eugenics in that the former

would be voluntarily pursued by individual parents with an aim to improve their children (a policy of which Silver approves) whereas the latter were compulsory and imposed upon citizens by governments for particular ultimate goals.

11    Fukuyama, Francis, <u>Our Post-Human Future: Consequences of the Biotechnology Revolution</u>, New York: Farrar, Straus & Giraux, 2002, p. 102.

12    Professor Savulescu is Director of the Oxford Centre for Neuroethics, which is one of three strategic centres in biomedical ethics in the UK funded by the Wellcome Trust. He is also Director of the Program on the Ethics of the New Biosciences, which is one of the 10 founding Institutes within the Oxford Martin School at the University of Oxford.

13    Savulescu, Julian, 'The BioRevolution and It's Ethical Implications', South Place Ethical Society, Sunday, 5 December, 2010.

14    Rifkin, Jeremy, <u>The Biotech Century: Harnessing the Gene and Remaking the World</u>, New York, Tarcher/Putnam, 1998, p. 4.

15    Fukuyama, Op. Cit.

16    The transhumanist agenda is to make enhancement options of various kinds -- preimplantation genetic diagnosis; genetic engineering; pharmaceuticals that improve memory, concentration, wakefulness, and mood; performance-enhancing drugs; anti-aging medicine; closer human-computer interfaces --- safely available to all persons. Notable transhumanists include: F. M. Esfandiary, Nick Bostrom of the faculty of philosophy at Oxford University, Julian Savulescu of The Uehiro Centre for Practical Ethics at Oxford University, David Pearce (author of *The Hedonistic Imperative*, is co-founder, with Nick Bostrom, of the World Transhumanist Association and sits on the board of the journal *Medical Hypotheses*), James Hughes (a sociologist at Trinity College in Hartford Connecticut), Mark Walker (a philosopher at the University of Toronto, then the editor of the *Journal of Transhumanism*), Allen Buchanan, a bioethicist and James B. Duke Professor of philosophy at Duke University. Greg Stock, John Harris, Gregory Pence, and Eric Juengst, among others, have also discussed the ethics of genetic engineering from a broadly transhumanist perspective. Julian Savulescu is a self-proclaimed 'moral transhumanist', arguing that biomedical research and therapy should make *homo sapiens* more human in the moral sense, even if they cease to be human in the biological sense.

17    In <u>*Beyond Good and Evil*</u>, Nietzsche called for the extra-moral period, when the value of an action will be judged by the non-intentional or instinctive motivation. We should, he argues, overcome morality and embark upon a post-moral world. For humans, says Nietzsche, the only given reality is instinct. Nietzsche apparently believed that instinct equals universal human nature. Moral judgments, he said, were at bottom irrational. Conscience is just 'instinct' by another name. Nietzsche maintained that most conscious thinking is guided by the instincts.

18 Bostrom, Nick, *Journal of Evolution and Technology*, Vol. 14, Issue 1, April 2005. Online version at http://www.nickbostrom.com/papers/historty.pdf, p. 12.

19 Hughes, J., *Citizen Cyborg: why democratic societies must respond to the redesigned human of the future*. Cambridge, MA: Westview Press, 2004.

20 Rose, Steven, Lewontin, R.C. and Kamin, Leon J., <u>Not in Our Genes: Biology, Ideology and Human Nature</u>, New York, Penguin Books, 1990, p. 7

21 Social Darwinism led to the notion of 'self-help' and promoted a blameless view of capitalism in which 'victims' made their own fate, and so any suffering that resulted was a consequence of their own failures. Nobody should rely on others, charities or the state (especially welfare) to help them. We succeed or fail according to our own efforts. In the 1990's this view was closely associated with economic libertarianism, according to which individual freedom means freedom to accumulate wealth and it is only natural that huge inequalities will result from this where there is free competition. Redistribution of wealth by means of taxation is illegitimate and constitutes an injustice to those more fit for survival, since the wealthy merit all of their advantages.

22 For example, a disordered brain (or today, a disordered gene) is "seen as the cause of an unacceptable interaction of individuals and social organizations. The political consequence is that, since the social institution is never questioned, no alteration in it is therefore contemplated; individuals are to be altered to fit the institutions or else sequestered to suffer in isolation the consequences of their defective biology." (Rose, et. al. p. 21) J. Robert Nelson's discussion of "predictable dispositions towards various kinds of abnormal behavior" fits this model neatly, since it presupposes that *behaviors* are located within the individual's biological make-up. Christian prohibitionists take this further by assuming, without compelling argument, that all homosexual *behavior* is **immoral**, not merely unusual or rare. This presupposes homosexual orientation is an innate tendency to act immorally. This belief provides the rationale that eliminating homosexuality in the womb will 'restore' human nature to its 'full glory'. At this stage, since no definite pre-natal eugenic solution has been safely found to 'cure' homosexuality, The Ramsay Colloquium, the Vatican and The Manhattan Declaration's signatories have recommended pastoral care and therapy to help homosexual individuals resist the impulse to act on their desire for 'sin' (homosexual gratification). As I pointed out, some others, including prominent Baptist Albert Mohler Jr. and Catholic Joe Carter, web editor of *First Things* magazine, have stated that Christians would broadly favor the use of reprogenetics to prevent homosexuality were such a genetic therapy to become safely available.

23 Rose et. al, Op. Cit., p. 25.

24 Collini, Stefan, Ed., <u>On Liberty and Other Writings</u>, Oxford University Press, 1989, p. 57.

25   In *On Liberty*, Chapter 3, Mill wrote that the free development of individuality "is one of the leading essentials of well-being." He identified the lack of recognition of this fact "by the common modes of thinking" as presenting the danger "that liberty should be undervalued". He thought it an "evil" that "the common modes of thinking" did not recognize "individual spontaneity" as having any intrinsic worth. (See Stefan Collini, Ed., On Liberty and Other Writings, Cambridge University Press, 1989. p. 57.)

26   Ibid.

27   One of the central claims of Plato's *Republic* is that justice is not only desirable for its own sake, but that it maximizes the happiness of those who practice it. Plato also espoused the view that the virtuous person cannot be harmed, as the only real harm is the loss of virtue. In the *Apology* (30b) Plato writes: "Wealth does not bring about excellence, but excellence makes wealth and everything else good for men, both individually and collectively." In Chapter 4 of the *Nicomachean Ethics* Aristotle identifies happiness (*eudaimonia*) as the good for which all humans strive. By '*eudaimonia*' he is not referring to a state of euphoria but to the activity of the soul in accordance with reason. Aristotle maintained that animate things (trees, animals, people, etc) have a *psyche*; this is what he means by 'soul'. Aristotle divides the soul into a rational and an irrational element. Human beings are uniquely capable of living according to the rational element. For Aristotle, human fulfillment means living according to our particular nature. In Chapter 8 of the *Nicomachean Ethics,* he identifies the good of the soul as higher than worldly goods and goods of the body. While all three are needed for complete happiness, Aristotle reaffirms that neither worldly good nor goods of the body can alone bring happiness. Happiness is an activity of the soul and the happy person leads a good life. In Chapter 9 Aristotle acknowledges that while virtue is a necessary condition for happiness, it is not a sufficient condition, since a virtuous person may nevertheless encounter adversity and misfortune. In Chapter 10 Aristotle concludes by reminding his reader that happiness is not a quality that can be attained instantly but must be measured over a whole life, and can best be determined only after one has died. He notes that it is better to lead a happy life than just a virtuous one, but claims that one cannot be happy and not virtuous. For Aristotle virtue is the best course of action, although the greatest happiness will come from being virtuous without adverse conditions.

28   Erica Stonestreet, 'On Individuality' in *Philosophy Now* Magazine, Issue 76, November/December 2009., pp. 17-18.

29   Adler, Mortimer, We Hold These Truths:Understanding the Ideas and Ideals of the Constitution, New York, Simon and Schuster, 1987, p. 58.

30   Cooper, John M., Reason and Human Good in Aristotle, Indianapolis, Hackett, 1986, p. 124. See also Nichomachean Ethics 1099a 31-b8; 1099b 18-30; 1140b 7.

[31]  Smith, Tara, 'Rights, Wrongs, and Aristotelian Egoism: Illuminating the Rights/ Care Dichotomy' in *The Journal of Social Philosophy*, Vol. 29 No. 2, Fall 1998, p. 9.

[32]  Kristol's obituary of 20 September, 2009 in London's **Guardian** claimed, "As editor, essayist, columnist and impresario, he exerted an extraordinary influence on the network of magazines, think tanks and grant-giving bodies, promoting the ideas he approved and those who could expound them, and ridiculing or excluding those who disagreed with him." His influence in "the two worlds of New York publishing and intellectual journalism and of Washington politics" was compared to that of "one of the great 'popes' of the Paris intellectuals." Kristol worked in London in the 1950s as editor of the literary magazine **Encounter**, which was later revealed to be essentially controlled by the Central Intelligence Agency. Kristol was entirely unashamed about what he saw as a virtuous struggle to counter the undue influence of anti-American ideas in Europe. Scaife spent tens of millions of dollars to turn The Tribune-Review of Greensburg, Pa., a small suburban daily he has owned since 1970, into a conservative challenger to the dominant and more moderate *Pittsburgh Post-Gazette*.

Scaife bankrolled the scandal-mongering *American Spectator* and many other right-wing enterprises. "It was effective," says New York Times columnist Paul Krugman, "because the typical news consumer didn't realize what was going on." Scaife's efforts famously managed to make Whitewater -- a $200,000 money-losing investment – synonymous with scandal, even though an eight-year, $73 million investigation never did find any evidence of wrongdoing by the Clintons.

The John M. Olin Foundation disbursed over $370 million in funding, primarily to conservative think tanks, media outlets, and law programs at influential universities.

Roger Ailes is president of Fox News and former media consultant to Republican presidents Richard Nixon, Ronald Reagan, and George H. W. Bush. He was also a consultant for Rudolph Giuliani's 1989 New York City mayoral campaign.

[33]  Rose et. al., Op. Cit., p. 31.

[34]  Ibid., p. 51.

[35]  Rose, along with co-authors R.C. Lewontin, and Leon J. Kamin, Op. Cit., p. 29.

[36]  Fernbach, David, 'Biology and Gay Identity', *New Left Review*, no. 228, March/ April 1998, p. 56.

[37]  Ibid., p. 49.

[38]  Ibid., p. 65.

[39]  Colson, Charles W. and Cameron, Nigel M. de S. eds., <u>Human Dignity in the Biotech Century: a Christian Vision for Public Policy</u>, Intervarstity Press, Downers Grove, Illinois, 2004.

40  This procedure is also known as 'germ-line' therapy or enhancement.

41  Kass, L.eon, Life, Liberty, and the Defense of Dignity: The Challenge for Bioethics, San Francisco: Encounter Books, 2002, cited in Agar, Nicholas, 'Designer babies: Ethical Considerations', April 2006 (ActionBioscience.org) http://www.actionbioscience.org/biotech/agar.html

42  Agar, Nicholas, 'Liberal Eugenics', *Public Affairs Quarterly* 12, no. 2, April, 1998, p. 137. Reprinted in Helga Kuhse and Peter Singer, Eds., Bioethics: An Anthology, Blackwell, 1999. (See also: Agar, Nicholas, Liberal Eugenics: In Defence of Human Enhancement, Oxford, England, Blackwell, 2004.)

43  Ibid., p. 171.

44  Agar, Nicholas, *Liberal Eugenics: In Defence of Human Enhancement*, Oxford: Blackwell, 2004, p. 79.

45  As Francis Fukuyama observed, "the first step towards giving parents greater control over the genetic makeup of their children will come not from genetic engineering but with preimplantation genetic diagnosis and screening." (Fukuyama, Op. Cit., p. 75)

46  Fletcher, Agnes, 'Disability as a Social Construct' in *Designer Babies: Where Should We Draw the Line?*, Institute of Ideas, London, Hodder & Stoughton, 2002, p. 17.

47  Rose et. al., Op. Cit., p. 23.

48  Reiss M.J. and Straughan R., Improving Nature?: The Science and Ethics of Genetic Engineering, New York: Cambridge University Press, 1996., p. 215.

49  Sandel, Michael, The Case Against Perfection: Ethics in the Age of Genetic Engineering, Cambridge Mass. & London, England, The Belknap Press of Harvard University Press, 2007, p. 89.

50  Mill, 'On Liberty', Chapter 3, in Collini, Stefan, Ed., On Liberty and Other Writings, Cambridge University Press, 1989, p. 74.

51  In On Liberty, Mill says: "Let us suppose . . . that the government is entirely at one with the people, and never thinks of exerting any power of coercion unless in agreement with what it conceives to be their voice. But I deny the right of the people to exercise such coercion, either by themselves or by their government." (See Collini, Stafan, Ed., On Liberty and Other Writings, Cambridge University Press, 1989, p. 20.)

52  "The only freedom which deserves the name is that of pursuing our own good in our own way, so long as we do not attempt to deprive others of theirs, or impede their efforts to obtain it. Each is the proper guardian of his own health, whether bodily, or mental or spiritual. Mankind are greater gainers by suffering each other to live as seems good to themselves, than by compelling each to live as seems good to the rest." (John Stuart MIll, 'On Liberty', in Warnock, Mary, Ed., Utilitarianism and On Liberty, Oxford: Blackwell, 2003, p. 97.)

53  John Stuart Mill, 'On Liberty', Chapter 1 in Collini, Stefan, Ed., <u>On Liberty and Other Writings</u>, Cambridge University Press, 1989, p. 8.

54  Ibid.

55  Ibid.

56  Among these are Nicholas Agar, Allen Buchanan, Dan W. Brock, Norman Daniels, Daniel Wikler, Gregory Stock and Ronald Dworkin. Robert Nozick and John Rawls also defend versions of liberal eugenics. *Independent* columnist Johann Hari has also expressed his support.

57  In *On Liberty*, Mill argued that we should all have freedom "to pursue our own good in our own way, so long as we do not deprive others of theirs, or impede their efforts to obtain it." Mill defended the maximum negative liberty to pursue our own interests by appeal to utility in its largest sense, "grounded on the permanent interests of man as a progressive being." (*On Liberty*, Chapter 1, introductory, 1859) Freedom, he argued, was necessary for 'mental well-being' and thus conducive to happiness. Mill supported liberty of thought and discussion of "any doctrine, however immoral it may be considered" by pointing out that "history teems with instances of truth put down by persecution, if not suppressed for ever, it may be thrown back for centuries." He says that we may offend, but not harm. Timidity with respect to minority views and unpopular opinions, argued Mill, may deprive others ("the world") of previously unknown truths, and such self-censorship would certainly not improve our mutual understanding of moral issues.

Mill did accept that in rare instances speech would constitute incitement to violence, but nevertheless did not reject such speech because of the *opinion* expressed, but only the context of volatility in which it was voiced. Mill is clear that acts such as cruelty and malice are properly the concern of society, and in extreme cases, the law. Whilst we may avoid, pity or dislike the person whose self-regarding actions we deprecate, we reserve punishment for those whose other-regarding actions have negative consequences. In Ch. 5 I have developed a long discussion of Mill's position on this in my discussion of his view of drunkenness.

Since the 1960's, adultery, homosexual activity, suicide and abortion have ceased to be illegal. Legal divorce is now widely available, and licensing laws have been hugely relaxed, with alcohol legally on sale for longer hours. These changes reflect society's view that we undertake certain endeavors and relationships at our own risk, and that part of our adult responsibility is accepting the consequences of our own decisions and improving ourselves over time on the basis of experience. Some local authorities are today moving away from Mill's liberal distinction between self-regarding behaviors and other-regarding behaviors, by making illegal a whole range of activities that liberals could argue ***do not*** cause harm to the permanent progressive interests of others. The smoking ban is a prime example of how recent governments have made activities that arguably are not harmful to others the proper concern of the law. Whether passive smoking does, in fact, kill is contested. Even if it does, the figure quoted by anti-smoking campaigners is usually around 46 untimely deaths per year. Most, if not all, of these could be avoided only if smoking was banned in the home, since this is where non-smokers are most exposed to the fumes of smokers. There is no question at all that the banning of private cars would save innumerable people from death and injury every day, as well as being a major factor in decreasing damaging air pollution. But Mill's harm principle does not require legal prohibition of all dangerous things, but all *intentionally* harmful other-regarding activity. Liberal societies *do* make murder, assault, rape and theft illegal because of the fact that they cause direct, deliberate and measurable injury to others in a way that mere offence does not. There will always be debate over what causes significant harm to others, but liberals tend to emphasize the need for negative liberty, except for activity that is incontrovertibly harmful to others. Western societies have defined intentionally harmful (unjustified) acts as crimes for many decades now, with wide consensus and a good deal of success.

58   I am here using Habermas's distinction between positive (enhancing) eugenics and negative (healing) eugenics. Negative eugenics is based on a moral point of view that commits us to the "logic of healing", which forbids us, in our dealings with second persons, from instrumentalizing them and burdens us with the responsibility of justifying an anticipated consent that at present cannot be sought. Assumed consensus should, he argues, only be invoked to prevent evils that are unquestionably extreme and likely to be rejected by all. The moral demand not to instrumentalize second persons is what saddles us with the responsibility of drawing a line between negative eugenics and enhancing eugenics.

59   Fukuyama, Francis, <u>Our Post-Human Future: Consequences of the Biotechnology Revolution</u>, New York: Farrar, Straus & Giraux, 2002, p. 15.

60   Sandel, Michael J, <u>The Case Against Perfection: Ethics in the Age of Genetic Engineering</u>, Cambridge Mass. & London, England: Belknap Press of Harvard University Press, 2007, p. 88.

61   Ibid., p. 87.

62   Mill, John Stuart, <u>On Liberty and Other Writings</u>, Collini, Stefan, Ed., Cambridge University Press, 1989, p. 60.

63   Sandel, Michael J., The Case Against Perfection: Ethics in the Age of Genetic Engineering, Cambridge, Mass & London, England, The Belknap Press of Harvard University Press, 2007, p. 77.

64   Ibid.

65   Ibid.

66    Rawls, John, *A Theory of Justice*, Cambridge, MA., Harvard University Press, 1971, pp. 107-108.

67    Habermas, Jürgen, *The Future of Human Nature,* Cambridge, Mass., Polity, 2003, p. 2.

68    Ibid., p. 3.

69    Ibid., p. 49.

70    See, for example, Allen Buchanan, Dan W. Brock, Norman Daniels, and Daniel Wickler, From Chance to Choice: Genetics and Justice (Cambridge: Cambridge University Press, 2000), pp. 27-60, 156-191, 304-345. Gregory Stock makes similar claims in Redesigning Humans: Our Inevitable Genetic Future. Nicholas Agar, in Liberal Eugenics: In Defence of Human Enhancement, p. 84, asks: "Isn't it just a fact that as people get healthier they tend to expect more of health services both for themselves and others? ... Within its range, THERAPY tends to support obligations rather than permissions. Expanding this range will bring a raft of new obligations, dramatically curtailing reproductive liberty. In the future, it will not be the case that parents will not be given the option to enhance their children, they will be required to do so." On p. 85 he continues: "... in the future full participation in political, social and economic life will sometimes require superior functioning." Agar is concerned that expanding the range of therapy beyond the treatment or prevention of disease will almost certainly force parents to enhance their children in various ways.

71    Buchanan, Allen, Brock, Dan W, Daniels, Norman and Wikler, Daniel, From Chance to Choice: Genetics and Justice, Cambridge: Cambridge University Press, 2000, pp. 27-60, 156-191, 304-345.

72    Even this may be too strong. Modern liberals don't think they're obligated to enable everyone to have the means to fulfil *all* the purposes anyone could wish to achieve. Rather, their interventions are to prevent disabling conditions so severe as to preclude a wide range of independent options. In a biological context, deafness may not allow a person to fulfil all possible purposes, but it still leaves open a wide range of autonomous life goals. Many deaf people would argue that deafness is 'disabling' only for those born with hearing. For those born deaf, it is no barrier to an independent, fulfilling life.

73    Sandel, Op. Cit., pp. 78-9.

74    Ibid., p. 79.

75    Ibid., p. 71.

76    I have outlined ample reasons to worry that this may be on the Christian right's agenda in Chapter 5, especially in light of comments by Joe Carter from *First Things*. See also, Rod Dreher, *"A Looming Gay Genocide?"* Tuesday, Jan. 9, 2007 on BeliefNet.com

77    In the case of Preimplantation Genetic Diagnosis, the procedure merely aims at selecting for birth an 'ideal' embryo from amongst other, less desirable embryos.

PGD would involve screening IVF generated embryos for the unwanted genetic trait, and then implanting unaffected embryos in the uterus. The procedure provides the option of commencing a pregnancy knowing that the baby is unaffected by the unwanted genetic trait. Catholics and some evangelical Christians object to IVF in principle, since it involves the creation and destruction of embryos. In their 2009 document *Life Giving Love in an Age of Technology*, the United States Conference of Catholic Bishops suggest that "Broader abuse is in the realm of science fiction at this point, although many scientists say it is possible and even should be welcomed: a "brave new world" in which human beings are tailored for genetic perfection, developed outside their mothers' bodies, and pre-selected for given roles in society. This would be the ultimate step toward a very efficient society in which the idea of human dignity may seem obsolete." (pp. 8-9)

Jürgen Habermas says secular objections to Preimplantation Genetic Diagnosis (PGD) are grounded in an opposition to (1) the conditional creation of embryos and (2) the nature of these conditions. The selectivity involved in PGD is instrumentalizing rather than therapeutic.

[78] Habermas, Op. Cit., p. 64.

[79] Ibid, p. 65.

[80] Silver, Lee, Remaking Eden: Cloning and Beyond in a Brave New World, New York, Avon Books, 1997, p. 4-7. Cited in Rifkin, p. 169.

[81] Watson made this remark in 1997, see 'Disgrace: How a giant of science was brought low' by Robin McKie in London and Paul Harris in New York, *The Observer*, Sunday 21 October 2007. See also: Victoria McDonald, 'Laureate advocates abortion of "gay babies" ', *Sydney Morning Herald*, 17 February 1997, p. 10. The article describes reactions to Dr James Watson's statement that '[i]f you could find the gene which determines sexuality and a woman decides she does not want a homosexual child, well, let her.'

[82] Bogan, Steve, "Nobel Winner Backs Abortion; For Any Reason,'" *Independent* (London), February 23, 2003, p. 13.

[83] Habermas, Op. Cit., p. 79.

[84] Stock, Gregory, 'Biotechnology: Our Slippery Slope?' in **Prospect** Magazine, June 2002, p. 16.

[85] Ibid.

[86] Fukuyama, Francis, Our Post Human Future: Consequences of the Biotechnology Revolution, New York, Picador, 2002, p. 81.

[87] See Prof. Prabhat Jha et. al, 'Trends in selective abortions of girls in India: analysis of nationally representative birth histories from 1990 to 2005 and census data from 1991 to 2011', *The Lancet* Early Online Publication, 24 May 2011. http://www.thelancet.com/journals/lancet/article/PIIS0140-6736(11)60649-1/

fulltext See also: Jeremy Laurance, *The Full Extent of India's 'Gendercide'*, The Independent, 25 May, 2011.

88    Stock, Gergory, Op. Cit., p. 18.

89    Stock says that while "a few interventions will arise that virtually everyone would find troubling" we can wait until actual problems occur before moving to control them. Stock claims we have the luxury of "feeling our way forward, seeing what problems develop, and carefully responding to them". But his argument is that unwarranted government incursions will delay medical advances. It is difficult to imagine that concerns over serious externalities that primarily affect powerless minorities will override financial incentives once the profit incentive kicks in.

90    While acknowledging that 'liberalism' as a political ideology is fractured between classic liberalism (or libertarianism) and modern liberalism, I am assuming that liberals, while they may differ over the extent to which the market ought to be regulated and over the degree to which capitalists may pursue wealth unfettered by social responsibilities, agree on making a distinction between public and private spheres and maintain that everyone should have maximal personal freedom consistent with like freedom of others.

91    As Dr. Marcy Darnovsky of The Center for Genetics and Society (CGS), a nonprofit information and public affairs organization, based in Berkeley, California remarked: "In their effort to make the idea of designer babies and human clones publicly acceptable, many advocates have adopted the language of reproductive choice. They have begun to argue explicitly that support for human genetic manipulation -- or at least, refusing to condemn those who may want to practice it -- is the "pro-choice" position. A recently published pro-germline engineering book, for example, is titled "From Chance to Choice." This reference is to Allen Buchanan, Dan W. Brock, Norman Daniels, and Daniel Wikler, *From Chance to Choice* (New York: Cambridge University Press, 2000).
Darnovsky says "This use of pro-choice language is likely to foster confusion between the unprecedented and unjustifiable practice of "enhancing" the genetic makeup of a future child, and the fundamental right to end an unwanted pregnancy. In some circles, it will take focused effort to make it clear that altering the genes of one's children and the genetic legacy of humanity is not among the reproductive rights for which so many women and women's organizations have struggled." (see 'Human Germline Manipulation and Cloning as Women's Issues', Nov. 20, 2000 at http://www.ourbodiesourselves.org/book/companion. asp?id=25&compID=67&page=8)

92    Gimbel, Steven, 'Global Warming, Intelligent Design and the Re-Ascendancey of the Pro-Scientific Political Left', www.butterfliesandwheels.com, 31 Jan, 2007, p. 2.

93   Sandel, Michael J., *The Case Against Perfection: Ethics in the Age of Genetic Engineering*, Cambridge Mass & London, England, The Belknap Press of Harvard University Press, 2007. p. 120.

94   Ibid., p. 121.

95   For a full analysis of the pro-life campaign's inconsistencies see Murray, Terri, 'Myth-Busting the Christian Right', myth 2., at The Center for Progressive Christianity, http://www.tcpc.org/library/article.cfm?library_id=519

96   See Fukuyama Op. Cit, p. 19 and Rifkin, Op. Cit., p xiii.

97   Agar, Nicholas, Liberal Eugenics: In Defence of Human Enhancement, Malden, MA and Oxford, England, Blackwell, 2004, p. 67, 79-84.

98   Middleton, *American Journal of Human Genetics*, 63(4), 1998, p. 1175-80 and Agar, pp. 12-13.

99   Fletcher works for The Disability Rights Commission and has surveyed disabled peoples' attitudes to developments in genetics. See 'Genes Are Us?', a RADAR survey, published by The Royal Association for Disability and Rehabilitation, London, 1999.

100   Fletcher, Agnes, 'Disability as a Social Construct' in Designer Babies: Where Should We Draw the Line?, Institute of Ideas, London, Hodder & Stoughton, 2002, p. 18.

101   Ibid.

102   see her collection of essays, 'Prenatal Testing and Disability Rights'.

103   Even if it cannot, it would be strange in a liberal context to presume that anyone has a legal obligation to assist another adult person in living where harmless means of avoiding it exist. If adult persons could assert a claim right to other's assistance for living, this would create an explosion of responsibility for all that would seriously impede negative liberty. In addition, it would render obsolete our current notion of moral virtue, since providing assistance to others would no longer be a charitable personal choice but a legal requirement.

104   Habermas, Op. Cit, p. 91.

105   Agar, Op. Cit., pp. 80-81.

106   Osborne, Hannah, 'David Attenborough: Women must be given control of their bodies, or mankind will perish', *International Business Times* online edition, Dec. 31, 2014.

107   Of course, it could be argued from a determinist standpoint that the agent cannot help but behave according to urges and drives that result in undesirable **outcomes**. Here, the human being is pictured as no different from other species in being unable to exert self-control over his innate urges. Then the purpose of the intervention would simply be to prevent/deter the undesirable behavior. To embrace this kind of determinism would require a sea change in our legal framework. The fact that adult citizens are responsible moral agents entitles them to basic rights on the one hand, and obligates them to accept moral

responsibility for their actions on the other. If we surrender our autonomy we must be prepared also to relinquish the rights that depend upon it. Our legal system *punishes* people for wrongdoing because of our assumption that the agent could have behaved otherwise. If we didn't believe in human responsibility, we would simply try to 'cure' people of their bad natures, rather than punishing them for their bad choices.

Recent studies, such as research into "brain-reading technology" carried out by John-Dylan Haynes at the Max Planck Institute for Human Cognitive and Brain Sciences, tends to presuppose a genetic basis for an ever-widening scope of undesirable human behaviors. Central to this outlook is a transition away from an agent-centered concept of crime to a behaviorist model of the 'criminal type'. This represents an ideological shift in forensic science that is politically conservative not only in its objectives but also in its assumptions.

[108] Some argue that homosexuality is primarily voluntary and not biological. Therefore, they argue, interventions to alter homosexual orientation will have little impact, since they aim at the wrong target. The preponderance of evidence is against this conclusion. The Royal College of Psychiatrists stated in 2007 (*Submission to the Church of England's Listening Exercise on Human Sexuality*): "It would appear that sexual orientation is biological in nature, determined by a complex interplay of genetic factors and the early uterine environment. Sexual orientation is therefore not a choice." Even if homosexual acts are a choice for a minority of self-identified homosexuals, the vast majority of homosexuals do not experience their sexual attraction to members of the same sex as a choice. This suggests that homosexual orientation has a biological cause that could, in principle, be subject to medical manipulation by social engineers or heterosexist parents. The specifics of *how* this would be done are irrelevant to the ethical question of whether it *ought to be permitted*.

[109] The First Amendment to the United States Constitution stipulates, "Congress shall make no law respecting an establishment of religion, or prohibiting the free exercise thereof". These two clauses together make up what are commonly said as the "religion clauses" of the First Amendment. The fact that homophobia is primarily a religious phenomenon makes protection from it's reach even more crucial. Already gays and lesbians are denied the same marital rights as heterosexuals based on the religious definition of marriage, which excludes any marital relationship that is not 'between one man and one woman'. This denies state-granted civil rights to a sexual minority based on a religious exclusion, and as such it has been challenged, correctly in my view, by Judge Vaughan Walker's decision (see Chapter 5, p. 1).

[110] In the case of PGD, moral weighing involves the degree of suffering the future person can be expected to face. Laws to limit PGD to a few severe genetic diseases could be justified on the grounds that preventing an unbearably

restricted future life is in the best interests of the future person concerned. But even so, says Habermas, making the distinction between life worth living and life not worth living *for others* remains disconcerting. (p. 69) It is extremely difficult to discern whether parents select the embryo based on *their own first person wish* for the child or on the assumption that *the second person himself* would refuse an existence subject to specific restrictions. Any such value judgment on behalf of others risks instrumentalizing them rather than adopting a clinical attitude oriented towards the goal of healing. Habermas says that only when we will be able to use gene-modifying interventions that make embryo selection unnecessary can we be sure that we have crossed the threshold from positive (enhancing) to negative (therapeutic) eugenics. (p. 69) Only then will we not have to weigh our responsibility to protect the "unwanted" embryo's life against the responsibility to prevent the future person from living with an unbearable handicap.

[111] Moreover, although there may be a case for parental ***choice*** to intervene to prevent deafness in a prospective child, parents could not be <u>obligated</u> to provide well-being for children unless the state removed negative liberty from individuals to ignore the needs of others. This would drastically expand the power of the state into the private sphere and seriously curtail the negative liberty afforded to individuals. It would be quite alien to liberal legal principles that merely require that people <u>not inflict harm</u> on others when it can easily be avoided.

[112] 'Bettering' himself is more realistic, and allows that he may have his own idea of what constitutes self-improvement.

[113] Fletcher, Op. Cit., p. 19.

# CONCLUSION

This book has traced the way in which a 'natural law' ethical methodology has been used and developed in conservative Christian (primarily Roman Catholic) teaching about homosexuality. I have attempted to demonstrate that Christian discourses about homosexuality in the 1990's shifted away from the 'preceptive' naturalist methodology deployed in Pauline and Scholastic Christian sexual ethics. This form of naturalism involved 'reading' from observations of natural phenomena moral goals or purposes, as though such purposes were written into nature (or parts of nature) itself. Following the emergence of evidence that suggested homosexual orientation had a biological component(s), the Christian methodology changed. Instead of resting ethical norms on descriptive accounts of nature, anti-gay Christian discourses after the 90's ceased to rest ethical norms on descriptive accounts of nature and began to do the reverse: they used Christian prescriptions to re-define the seemingly naturally occurring phenomenon of homosexuality as a "disorder" or "defect". Where once the anti-gay Christian literature had interpreted homosexual behavior as a form of rebellion against what has been inscribed in creation by 'God's invisible nature', it later pathologized homosexuality as an intrinsic disorder because of the extrinsic 'sinful' behavior to which it would lead. The Christian prohibitionist position seems to have transformed from the view that 'nature is good' (so our will should conform to it) to 'nature is flawed' (so it should conform to 'our' will to transform it or 'restore' it to its 'full glory').

In the wake of this methodological shift a new Christian bioethic emerged. It designates the homosexual as a key candidate for reprogenetic intervention. The envisioned interventions aim at sexual behavior modification to 'restore' a fallen creation to its full glory. This Christian conceptualization of homosexuality as an intrinsic 'disorder' comes from a theological worldview that cannot legally be imposed on unwilling citizens in secular states. However, Christian conservatives may soon be able to appeal to "liberal" eugenics to impose their theological sexual ethics on future generations in irrevocable ways. Arguments for liberal eugenics are not explicitly religious and appear to meet the liberal demand for state neutrality between diverse visions of 'the good life'. Liberal eugenics would protect parental liberty to intervene into the genetic make-up of offspring in order to re-define the naturally fixed scopes for possible decision within which the future person will one day use her freedom.

However, I have argued that reprogenetic interventions aimed at behavior modification do not meet the liberal demand for state neutrality between diverse visions of the good life. Placing the very nature of other people at the disposal of a Christian majority's will violates the individual's sovereignty to decide what constitutes 'the good life'. The liberty that allows us to determine for ourselves the shape of our lives is also what allows us to hold individuals morally responsible for immoral acts. This points to a weakness in the homophobic reasoning. Immoral behavior cannot be causally related to biology in the way that homophobic Christians assume it is. The new conservative Christian bioethic presupposes, along with socio-biology, that immoral *behaviors* are rooted not in the will of the agent, but in her biology. This view renders any coherent notion of individual moral responsibility obsolete. Liberals believe that freedom is a necessary condition for any coherent sense of moral responsibility at all. Therefore, the negative liberty necessary for moral autonomy should be equally distributed amongst all mentally competent adult citizens in a liberal state.

Pauline theology (along with it's anthropological assumptions, eg. about the domination of the *sarx* over the will, and its conceptualization of 'original sin' as inherent in the nature of the person) is a precursor to contemporary forms of biological reductionism. In his letter to the Romans, Paul repeatedly expresses his conviction that human beings (as a species; not individual humans) are incapable of responsibly exercising free will. "Let not sin," he wrote, "dwell in your mortal bodies to make you obey their passions" [Rom. 6:12] He even renounces consciousness of his actions, making nonsense of moral agency: "I am carnal, sold under sin. I do not understand my own actions . . ." [Romans 7: 14, 15] "Nothing good dwells in me, that is, in my flesh. I can will what is right but I cannot do it." [Rom. 7: 18] "I see in my members another law at war with the law of my mind and making me captive to the law of sin which dwells in my members. Wretched man that I am!" [Rom. 7: 21-24] With these statements Paul asserts his biological determinism in unequivocal terms. For almost two thousand years, St. Paul's pessimistic anthropology and his deterministic understanding of human nature rendered all human 'progress' or 'fulfillment' dependent upon external salvation. Like the Pauline salvation doctrine, modern liberal eugenicists aim at correcting human behavior *from the outside*. They begin by problematizing human nature (or aspects of it), and end by offering "biological liberation" from without.[1]

Contemporary sociobiology and the kind of reductionist, deterministic assumptions it makes about the nature of criminal or immoral behaviors, harkens back to a pre-modern anthropological archetype that underestimated and devalued the role of human agency. Under a modern and methodologically accepted rubric of science, it is resurrecting the old ideology that internalized the source of social evils in the individual's biological nature while externalizing the source of virtue and liberation in paternalistic social institutions or public authority figures. Serious implications flow from an abandonment of the modern, autonomous model of human nature – namely, the rejection of modern concepts of agency, democracy, crime and punishment, guilt and innocence, and our understanding that biological aspects of our persons are not relevant to moral appraisals of character. By locating the source (or cause) of immoral behavior in the **biological** nature of individuals, proponents of this view create an impetus for the development and implementation of new forms of paternalistic, authoritarian social control.

In rejecting the assumption that immorality (or some deterministic cause of immoral behavior) is intrinsic in the biological natures of some individuals, liberals find a broad basis for agreement with Christian conservatives and prohibitionists. As one of my opponents in the natural law debate, Robert George, has acknowledged,

> "In the absence of some free choice in human affairs, there could be no moral norms because such norms govern only free choices. Anyone who proposes a moral norm presupposes some free choice. But this presupposition does not establish that free choices are possible. It might be the case, after all, that no human actions are self-determined and, therefore, that there are no moral norms. If it is more reasonable to believe in complete determinism than in some free choice, then it is more reasonable to disbelieve than to believe in any moral norms."[2]

Insofar as genetic intervention to prevent homosexual behavior in a 'patient' might be intended to prevent *immoral* behavior, the argument for it is incoherent.

If we revive the ancient anthropological model under the auspices of "scientific progress" (making biotechnology fallen humanity's new 'saving grace') we lay the groundwork for transference of moral agency from the individual to medical experts, public health authorities, or parents. As responsibilities are removed from individual human agents, so too will be the rights that are their natural corollaries. We risk not only placing the very future of the human species in the hands of a subset of fallible human beings, but demolishing the modern concept of human agency. Human beings are creatures possessing both biological urges *and* the uniquely human ability to learn, develop, choose, and take responsibility for their actions. Humans are worthy of liberty, responsibility and self-determination. We will lose these values if we fail to protect the 'moral space' within which individual autonomy is exercised. If we open the door to a future where an individual's negative liberty may be colonized by the will of others acting 'in his best interests' or their own, we will remove from individuals both the liberty and the responsibility essential to living a 'good life'.

Cartesian dualism has received due ridicule within the academy because it posits a non-corporeal realm of freedom and will. But the ancient cosmic dualism is equally, if not more, fraught with inexplicable abstractions. It sets up a dualism between 'bad' human nature and 'good' super-human nature. In the past, the 'good' super-human nature was divine; today it is a vaunted 'super *man*' – a future human being, the product of genetic enhancement, who will represent an evolutionary leap beyond our current moral limitations.[3] It is urgent that the premises of this ancient form of dualism be challenged before we allow it to be fully resurrected today by sociobiologists, liberal eugenicists and pharmaceutical industry lobby groups. This 'new' (i.e. revived) anthropological model lays the groundwork for a removal of moral responsibility from the individual to extrinsic authorities, individuals or groups. Instead of the value of human life being intrinsically related to the individual's autonomous pursuit of goals of his own choosing, the value of his life will be defined from the outside.

Liberals remain ambivalent between viewing science and technology as objective instruments of progress and seeing science as providing ideologues with massively effective tools of destruction. Having witnessed the uses of the atomic bomb and chemical munitions, Edmund Husserl argued that science, divorced from its social context, had been transformed into a terrible evil.[4] Despite these philosophical insights, the pro-scientific left, especially in Europe, has tended to view science as *beyond politics* or immune from its pitfalls. I hope this book has revealed the urgency of rejecting this view. It is crucial that the challenge of addressing the political uses of science be met before these ends are divorced from their social context and left to the whims of corporations and consumers. A failure to do so may have irreversible effects on our shared sense of human agency.

Homophiles familiar with the traditional moral arguments against homosexual behavior know that they would be rendered implausible by the discovery of a 'gay gene' but are nevertheless painfully aware of the risks associated with such a discovery. Rather than placing future generations of homosexuals at the mercy of a potentially heterosexist eugenic policy, they choose instead to protect future generations of homosexuals by denying homosexual essentialism. The strategy is to annihilate their genetic 'kind' in theory so that others will not annihilate it in practice. This may seem like the lesser of two evils, given the potential danger of a prenatal gay 'gene-ocide'. But in reality it only delays the task of proving, once and for all, that homophobia is grounded on a serious mistake about natural human sexual variation.

The mere existence of a trait in 'nature' does not automatically assign it any particular positive *moral* value. But to think the existence of a 'gay gene' or similar biological marker(s) is irrelevant to the 'new gay eugenics' or the defense of gay and lesbian civil rights is myopic. The general public is not well acquainted with the 'naturalistic' basis for the stigmatization of homosexuals. If they were, they would be more likely to see that the automatic idealization or 'normative' status attached to heterosexuality flows from the (presumably now) baseless assumption that it is the only variety of human sexuality that nature (or "God") intended. In ancient Christianity, the 'given' aspects of the physical world were seen as categorically 'good' in the sense that they expressed divine intent. Traditionally, this was supposed to make them 'good,' as opposed to deviant behavioral tendencies that did not come directly from nature (or from God as the 'creator'). Religious perceptions of morality have long been colored by various attempts to derive 'ought' from 'is'. Today, biotechnology might soon offer religious homophobes the opportunity to change what human nature 'is' according to what they believe it 'ought' to be.

In the past, liberals and homosexuals worried about the intrusion of the state into the private lives of individuals. Today they have to worry about the opposite: that the personal decisions taken in the privacy of a doctor's consultation room will have an irreversible impact on public life and on the very nature of other people. Very soon, social conservatives could have at their disposal a new and powerful means of promoting their own vision of public morality within a liberal state. Without state imposition of any single vision of "the good life", social conservatives will nevertheless have a seemingly legitimate means of eliminating from human nature the biological basis for homosexual behavior. As I explained in Chapter 7, 'liberal eugenics' already provides the legitimating discourse for so doing.

Although it will be done by means of the free market, re-designing human nature presupposes a human ideal – one that will inform how or in which direction human nature should be improved. Even when not enforced by the state, there are always and in every culture prevailing ideas about what constitutes 'beauty' or 'success' or the 'ideal' human type. These ideas are human constructs. Regardless of how popular they may be, they are fallible. Often, they are the narcissistic projections of a popular majority's (or a powerful minority's) self-image. They do not tell us what human nature is; they tell us what some people wish it were.

One such idea of what constitutes a "good" human life is provided by the basic goods theory of ethics (see Chapter 4). This theory offers a particular set of 'goods' as universally definitive of "the good life" for all human beings, such that failing to promote any one of the goods that it claims is constitutive of "integral human fulfillment" is a moral evil. But choosing to ignore a basic good could be a moral evil only if everyone were obliged to promote a particular definition of the good life. Any ideology that proposes such an obligation is deeply at odds with the modern liberal state. Basic Goods Theory proposes just that, and defines immoral choosing as any choice in which any one of its basic goods is neglected. The Basic Goods Theory's conception of human fulfillment selectively excludes significant facts about human nature, such as the natural diversity that exists in human sexuality, and instead constructs its own abstract human sexual ideal that pictures human beings as universally heterosexual. It then makes its ideal a moral obligation, such that a failure to participate in it is deemed 'immoral'.

J.S. Mill and John Locke both cautioned against the socio-political promotion of any fallible vision of the good life as the benchmark for 'human fulfillment' or human 'integrity'.[5] For Locke, the natural light of reason reveals to all men, regardless of religious persuasion, certain moral truths, such as respect for others and reciprocity in one's dealings with others.[6] These truths cannot be trumped by religious values based ultimately on faith. Religious beliefs are neither objective truths nor certainties, and so it is appropriate that we recognize that they might be wrong. This should make us more tolerant of other views.

Locke and Mill thought that toleration of religious and other differences was 'agreeable' and that neither force nor authority should be used to create uniformity.[7] God has not entrusted any man to save the souls of others. Hence Locke thought that civil magistrates and powerful majorities are no less imperfect than anyone else. They do not represent some kind of special religious authority. In Locke's *Letter Concerning Toleration* (1689), he claimed that the toleration of those who hold different opinions on religious matters "is so agreeable to the Gospel and to reason, that it seems monstrous for men to be blind in so clear a light."[8]

Re-making human nature according to our wishes, instead of passively accepting all of its various manifestations is not, of itself, problematic. Indeed, each of us strives to make **ourselves** better (according to our potentials). Mill felt that this was an integral part of our humanity. He believed that happiness involves the knowledge that we're living as much as possible in accordance with our own conception of a good life, where 'good' means morally admirable as well as fulfilling and enjoyable. We could never achieve this sort of moral admiration from fearfully obeying the will of others, nor by blindly or slavishly adopting their fallible conception of the 'good life'.

Mill's conception of happiness involved a much more active idea of the self than that envisioned by political conservatism. He saw human individuals not primarily as passive bundles of connected ideas formed by heredity and biology, but as self-conscious, self-developing and self-creating.[9] Mill gradually relinquished his earlier belief that people are entirely moulded by their environment, and embraced the idea that they also form their own characters in keeping with their own ideas about what is good, right, beautiful, sympathetic and noble.[10] Liberals follow Mill in recognizing that not every way in which we might wish to express ourselves is consistent with the equal rights of others to do the same. Striving towards our own goals must be limited by the injunction not to harm the permanent interests of others in the process. Liberals accept limits to individual striving within a social context, in which each person has equal liberty to pursue his individual potentials and must not prevent others from doing the same.

This creative development of character from within, by decision and reflection, as well as by education from outside, is what Mill understood by 'individuality'. Active, self-authored individuality (along with the moral responsibility which flows from it) is arguably the basis of our human specificity, the 'factor X' that Francis Fukuyama claims is most threatened by the inflexible advance of unrestricted reprogenetics.[11] The liberal arguments about the importance of individuality to human happiness or wellbeing can, I hope, go some way to giving content to Fukuyama's 'Factor X'. He describes this mysterious source of human dignity by saying:

> "the demand for equality of recognition implies ... that when we strip all of a person's contingent and accidental characteristics away, there remains some essential human quality underneath that is worthy of a certain minimal level of respect – call it Factor X."[12]

For liberals, a "minimum level of respect" requires the 'moral space' afforded by negative liberty within which individual persons can pursue values that are genuinely their own – the only kind of 'values' worthy of the name. The ability to *create* value is arguably a minimal requirement of our humanity. Unless we continue to prevent the state, or any individual or group from invading the 'moral sphere' of free choice around individuals, we collude in hindering the development of their individuality, and also their full humanity.

If liberal homophiles want to prevent the eugenic use of biotechnology to 'weed' homosexuality out of the gene pool they need to respond to the arguments for liberal eugenics *now*, not when it is too late and the product has already gone to market. I hope this book will provide a starting point for taking up that challenge.

1    I've taken the phrase "biological liberation" from a presentation by Professor Julian Savulescu of the Uehiro Centre for Practical Ethics, Oxford University. He used this phrase in his address to the South Place Ethical Society ('The Biorevolution and It's Ethical Implications', 5 Dec., 2010).

2    George, Robert P., In Defense of Natural Law, Oxford University Press, 1999, p. 55.

3    This assumes that a biologically enhanced human being will be a morally perfect human being, as though our current moral failures were fully explicable by biology and not by the choices we make. It also fails to address the possibility that biological enhancements will merely augment the human power to do moral evil.

4    Gimbel, Steven, 'Global Warming, Intelligent Design and the Re-Ascendancy of the Pro-Scientific Political Left', butterfliesandwheels.com, 31 Jan, 2007, p. 2.

5    For Example, in 'On Liberty', Mill says "the opinion which it is attempted to suppress by authority may possibly be true. Those who desire to suppress it, of course, deny its truth; but they are not infallible. They have no authority to decide it for all mankind, and exclude every other person from the means of judging." (see Collini, Stefan, Ed., On Liberty and Other Writings, Cambridge University Press, 1989, pp. 20-21.)

6    Butler, Martin, Ed., AQA Philosophy AS: Student's Book, Nelson Thornes, 2008, p. 190.

7    (see Klibansky, Raymond, Ed., A Letter on Toleration, Translated from the Latin by J. W. Gough, Oxford: Clarendon Press, 1968, p. 65.)

8    Locke writes: "...the care of souls is not committed to the civil magistrate, any more than to other men. ... It does not appear that God ever gave any such authority to one man over another as to compel other men to embrace his religion." (see Klibansky, Raymond, Ed., A Letter on Toleration, Translated from the Latin by J. W. Gough, Oxford: Clarendon Press, 1968, p. 67.)

9    McCabe, Helen, 'On Liberty: an Introduction' in Philosophy Now magazine, Issue 76, Nov/Dec 2009, p. 6.

10    Ibid.

11    In Our Post Human Future, Consequences of the Biotechnology Revolution (2002) Fukuyama says "..... the deepest fear that people express about biotechnology is not a utilitarian one at all. It is rather a fear that, in the end, biotech will cause us in some way to lose our humanity....." (p. 101).

12    Fukuyama, Francis, Our Post-Human Future: Consequences of the Biotechnology Revolution, New York, Farrar, Straus & Giraux, 2002, p. 149.

# BIBLIOGRAPHY

Adler, Mortimer, We Hold These Truths: Understanding the Ideas and Ideals of the Constitution, New York, Simon and Schuster, 1987.

Agar, Nicholas, Liberal Eugenics: In Defence of Human Enhancement, Oxford, England, Blackwell, 2004.

Agar, Nicholas, 'Liberal Eugenics', *Public Affairs Quarterly* 12, no. 2, April, 1998, p. 137. Reprinted in Helga Kuhse and Peter Singer, Eds., Bioethics: An Anthology, Blackwell, 1999.

Alper, Joseph S. and Beckwith, Jonathan, 'Genetic Fatalism and Social Policy: The Implications of Behavior Genetics Research', *Yale Journal of Biology and Medicine* 66, 1993, pp. 511-524.

Bamforth, Nicholas and Richards, David A.J., Patriarchal Religion, Sexuality and Gender: a critique of new natural law, Cambridge University Press, 2008.

Benn, Piers, 'Can Addicts Help It?' in *Philosophy Now* Magazine, Issue 80, Aug/Sept 2010, pp. 17-20.

Berger P. and Luckmann T., The Social Construction of Reality: a treatise on the sociology of knowledge, New York: Anchor Books/ Doubleday, 1966.

Bostrom, Nick, 'A History of Transhumanist Thought', in *Journal of Evolution and Technology*, Vol. 14, Issue 1, April 2005.

Boswell, John, <u>Christianity, Social Tolerance and Homosexuality</u>, New Haven, Conn., Yale University Press, 1980, esp. pp. 112-13.

Buchanan, Allen, Brock, Dan W., Daniels, Norman, and Wikler, Daniel, <u>From Chance to Choice: Genetics and Justice</u>, Cambridge: Cambridge University Press, 2000.

Cahill, Lisa, 'Moral Methodology: a Case Study' in R. Nugent Ed., <u>A Challenge to Love: Gay and Lesbian Catholics in the Church</u>, New York, Crossroad, 1983.

Cahill, Lisa, <u>Between the Sexes: Foundations for a Christian Ethics of Sexuality</u>, New York, Paulist Press, 1985.

Cahill, Lisa Sowle, <u>Sex, Gender and Christian Ethics</u>, Cambridge University Press, 1996.

Carter, Joe, 'Gay Gene Eugenics' in *First Things* online edition, August 18, 2010, at <u>www.firstthings.com/onthesquare/2010/08/gay-gene-eugenics</u>, p. 2.

Catholic Council for Church and Society, 'Homosexual People in Society', Mt. Rainer, MD: New Ways Ministry, 1980.

Chappell, Timothy, '*Natural Law Revived: Natural Law Theory and Contemporary Moral Philosophy*' in Nigel Biggar and Rufus Black, Eds., <u>The Revival of Natural Law: philosophical, theological and ethical responses to the Finnis-Grisez school</u>, Aldershot, England, Ashgate, 2000.

Chiavacci, E., '*The Natural Law Yesterday and Today*', F. Festorazzi et al., <u>Nuove prospettive di morale coniugale</u>, Brecia, 1969, pp. 61-91.

Clack, Beverley, <u>Sex and Death: a reappraisal of human mortality</u>, Polity Press in association with Blackwell Publishers, Ltd., 2002, p. 111.

Cochrane, Donald B., 'Christian Opposition to Homosexuality', in James McNinch and Mary Cronin, (Eds.), I Could Not Speak My Heart: Education and Social Justice for LGBT Youth, Regina, Saskatchewan Canadian Plains Research Centre, 2004.

Cole-Turner, Ronald, The New Genesis. Theology and the Genetic Revolution, Louisville, Kentucky, Westminster/John Knox Press, 1993.

Colson, Chuck, 'The Manhattan Declaration; Defending Life, Marriage and Freedom' Nov. 20, 2009, at http://www.breakpoint.org/commentaries/13534-the-manhattan-declaration

Colson, Charles W. and Cameron, Nigel M. de S., Eds., Human Dignity in the Biotech Century: a Christian Vision for Public Policy, Downers Grove, Il.: InterVarsity Press, 2004.

Conrad, Peter and Schneider, Joseph W., Deviance and Medicalization: From Badness to Sickness, Philadelphia, Temple University Press, 1992.

Cooper, John M., Reason and Human Good in Aristotle, Indianapolis, Hackett, 1986, p. 124.

Collini, Stefan, Ed., On Liberty and Other Writings, Cambridge University Press, 1989.

Countryman, L. William, Dirt, Greed & Sex : Sexual Ethics in the New Testament and Their Implications for Today, London: SCM Press, 1988, pp. 45-65.

Curran, Charles E., 'Absolute Norms in Moral Theology,' in Norm and Context in Christian Ethics, edited by Gene Outka and Paul Ramsay, New York: Charles Scribner's Sons, 1968, pp. 139 – 173.

Curran, Charles E., 'Sexual Ethics: A Critique' in Issues in Sexual and Medical Ethics, University of Notre Dame Press, Notre Dame/London, 1978, pp. 30-49.

Curran, Charles E. and Richard A. McCormick, S.J., Eds., <u>Readings in Moral Theology No. 1</u>. <u>Moral Norms and Catholic Tradition</u>, New York, Paulist Press 1975.

Crysdale, Cynthia S. W., 'Gilligan's Epistemological Challenge: Implications for Method in Ethics.' *The Irish Theological Quarterly* 56 (1990b), pp. 31-48.

Fernbach, David, 'Biology and Gay Identity', *New Left Review*, no. 228, March/April 1998.

Finnis, John, <u>Natural Law and Natural Rights</u>, Clarendon Law Series, Oxford University Press, 1980.

Finnis, John, 'Law, Morality, and "Sexual Orientation,"' Notre Dame Law Review, no.69, 1994.

Finnis, John, Boyle, Joseph M. Jr. and Grisez, Germain, <u>Nuclear Deterrence, Morality and Realism,</u> Oxford, Clarendon Press, 1987.

Flannery, Kevin S.J., 'Practical Reason and Concrete Acts' in <u>Natural Law & Moral Inquiry: Ethics, Metaphysics, and Politics in the Work of Germain Grisez</u>, Ed. Robert P. George, Georgetown University Press, 1998, pp. 107-134.

Fletcher, Agnes, 'Disability as a Social Construct' in <u>Designer Babies: Where Should We Draw the Line?</u>, Institute of Ideas, London, Hodder & Stoughton, 2002.

Foucault, Michel, <u>The History of Sexuality, Vol. 1: An Introduction</u>, Vintage Books Edition, 1990, pp. 5, 53, 56, 119, 150,151.

Fromm, Erich, <u>The Fear of Freedom</u>, Edited by Karl Mannheim, London, Keegan Paul, 1942, p. 8.

Fuchs, Josef, 'The Absoluteness of Moral Terms,' *Gregorianum* 52,1971.

Fuchs, Josef, 'The Absoluteness of Behavioural Moral Norms' in An Introduction to Christian Ethics, A Reader, Ronald P. Hamel and Kenneth R. Himes, Eds., New York, Paulist Press, 1989.

Fukuyama, Francis, Our Post-Human Future: Consequences of the Biotechnology Revolution, New York: Farrar, Straus & Giraux, 2002.

Fukuyama, Francis and Stock, Gregory, 'Prospect Debate - Biotechnology: Our Slippery Slope?' in *Prospect* Magazine, June 2002.

George, Robert P., In Defense of Natural Law, Oxford University Press, 1999.

George, Robert P. and Saunders, William L., 'Bioethics and Public Policy: Catholic Participation in the American Debate', *Issues for a Catholic Bioethic*, Luke Gormally, Ed., London, The Linacre Centre, 1999, pp. 274-300.

George, Robert P. and Bradley, Gerard V., 'Marriage and the Liberal Imagination,' *Georgetown Law Journal*, 84 (1995), pp. 301-20.

Gilligan, Carol, In a Different Voice: psychological theory and women's development, Cambridge, Mass, Harvard University Press, 1982.

Gimbel, Steven, 'Global Warming, Intelligent Design and the Re-Ascendancey of the Pro-Scientific Political Left', www.butterfliesandwheels.com, 31 Jan, 2007.

Goldsworthy, Jeffrey, 'Fact and Value in the New Natural Law Theory,' *American Journal of Jurisprudence*, 41, 1996, 21, pp. 38-45.

Gray, John, Men are From Mars Women are From Venus, New York: HarperCollins, 1992.

Grisez, Germain, Contraception and the Natural Law, Milwaukee, Wisconsin, Bruce, 1964.

Grisez, Germain, The Way of the Lord Jesus, Volume 1: Christian Moral Principles, Chicago, Franciscan Herald Press, 1983.

Grisez, Germain, The Way of the Lord Jesus, Vol. 2: Living a Christian Life, Quincy, Ill., Franciscan Press, 1993.

Grisez, Germain, 'The First Principle of Practical Reason: A Commentary on the Summa Theologiae, Question 94, Article 2.', Natural Law Forum 10, 1965, pp.168 – 201.

Grisez, Germain, Boyle, Jospeh and Finnis, John, 'Practical Principles, Moral Truth, and Ultimate Ends,' American Journal of Jurisprudence, 32,1987.

Grisez, Germain and Shaw, Russell, Fulfilment in Christ: A Summary of Christian Moral Principles, Notre Dame, Indiana, University of Notre Dame Press, 1991.

Groeschel, Father Benedict "Appalled by 'The' Psychological Association" in National Catholic Register, September 6-12, 2009 Issue.

Gula, Richard M., Reason Informed By Faith: Foundations of Catholic Morality, New York, Paulist Press, 1989.

Gula, Richard M., 'The Meaning and Limits of Moral Norms' in An Introduction to Christian Ethics, A Reader, Ronald P. Hamel and Kenneth R. Himes, eds., New York, Paulist Press, 1989, p. 470 ff.

Habermas, Jürgen, The Future of Human Nature, Cambridge, Mass., Polity Press, 2003.

Hays, Richard B. 'Relations Natural and Unnatural: A Response to John Boswell's Exegesis of Romans 1', Journal of Religious Ethics 14, no. 1, 1986, pp 184-215.

Hittinger, Russell, *A Critique of the New Natural Law Theory*, Notre Dame, Indiana, University of Notre Dame Press, 1987.

Hoose, Bernard, <u>Proportionalism: The American Debate and Its European Roots</u>, Washington, DC, Georgetown University Press, 1987.

Hoose, Bernard, 'Proportionalism: a Right Relationship Among Values', *Louvain Studies* 24,1991.

Houston, Rev. Walter, 'Homosexuality and the Bible' in <u>Homosexuality: A Christian View</u>, The Homosexuality Working Party of the United Reformed Church, Ed., 1991.

Hughes, Gerard, 'Natural Law Ethics and Moral Theology' in *The Month*, March 1987.

Hughes, James, <u>Citizen Cyborg: Why Democratic Societies Must Respond to the Redesigned Human of the Future</u>, Cambridge, MA, Westview Press, 2004.

Hume, David, <u>An Enquiry Concerning Human Understanding</u>, Harvard Classics Volume 37, Copyright 1910 P.F. Collier & Son, public domain released August 1993.

Irvine, Janice, 'Reinventing Perversion: Sex Addiction and Cultural Anxieties' *Journal of the History of Sexuality*, University of Chicago Press, vol. 5, no. 3, Jan. 1995.

Jaggar, Alison M. & Struhl, Karsten J., 'Human Nature' in Warren T. Reich, Ed., <u>Encyclopedia of Bioethics</u>, Vol. 2., New York: Simon & Schuster, 1995.

Janssens, Louis, '*Ontic Evil and Moral Evil*,' in <u>Readings in Moral Theology, No. 1</u>, Curran & McCormick, Eds., New York: Paulist Press, 1975, pp. 40-93.

Janssens, Louis, 'Norms and Priorities in a Love Ethics,' in *Louvain Studies* 4, Spring 1977.

Kant, Immanuel, <u>Groundwork of the Metaphysics of Morals</u>, translated, with analysis and notes by H J Paton in *The Moral Law*, London, Hutchinson & Co., 1972.

Kass, Leon R., 'The Wisdom of Repugnance', Catholic Education Resource Center, <u>www. Catholiceducation.org/articles/medical ethics/me0006. html</u>

Kelly, Kevin T., <u>New Directions in Moral Theology: The Challenge of Being Human,</u> London: Geoffrey Chapman,1992.

Kraft, R. Wayne, <u>The Relevance of Teilhard</u>, R. Wayne Kraft, Fides Publishers, Inc., Notre Dame, Ind., 1968.

Leal, David, 'Respect for life in Germain Grisez's Moral Theology' in Nigel Biggar and Rufus Black, Eds., <u>The Revival of Natural Law: philosophical, theological and ethical responses to the Finnis-Grisez school</u>, Aldershot, England, Ashgate, 2000, pp. 203-221.

Lennox, James G., 'Nature' in Warren T. Reich, ed. <u>Encyclopedia of Bioethics</u>, Vol. 4, New York: Simon & Schuster, 1995, p. 1816 ff.

Locke, John, <u>A Letter on Toleration</u>, Edited by Raymond Klibansky, Translated from the Latin by J. W. Gough, Oxford: Clarendon Press, 1968.

Macnamara, Vincent, <u>The Truth in Love: Reflections on Christian Morality</u>, Dublin, Gill & Macmillan, 1988.

Marcel, Gabriel, <u>Creative Fidelity</u>, Trans. Robert Rosthal, New York: Crossroad, 1982.

McCabe, Helen, 'On Liberty: an Introduction', *Philosophy Now* Magazine, Issue 67, November/December 2009, pp. 7-8.

McCormick, Richard A., <u>Notes on Moral Theology 1965 - 1980</u>, Washington, D.C., University Press of America,1981.

McInerny, Ralph, 'Grisez and Thomism' in Biggar & Black, Eds., <u>The Revival of Natural Law: philosophical, theological and ethical responses to the Finnis-Grisez school</u>, Aldershot, England, Ashgate, 2000, pp. 53-72.

Mohler, Rev. Albert, Jr., 'Is Your Baby Gay? What If You Could Know? What If You Could Do Something About It?' at <u>www.AlbertMohler.com</u> posted Friday, March 2, 2007.

Mohler, Rev. Albert, 'Was it something I said? Continuing to think about Homosexuality', <u>http://www.albertmohler.com/blog</u>,16 March, 2007.

Mohr, Richard D., <u>Gay Ideas: Outing and Other Controversies</u>, Boston, Mass., Beacon Press, 1992.

Money, John and Lamacz, Margaret, <u>Vandalized Lovemaps: Paraphilic Outcome of Seven Cases in Pediatric Sexology</u>, New York, Prometheus Books, 1989.

Nelson, J. Robert, 'What is Life?', Christian Social Action, in <u>Biomedical Ethics</u>, Bender and Leone, Eds., 1991, p. 266.

Nelson, J. Robert, 'Genetic Research Broadens the Understanding of Humanness' in <u>What is Life?</u>, Christian Social Action, 1991.

Novak, David, 'Before Revelation: The Rabbis, Paul and Karl Barth,' *Journal of Religion* 71, January 1991.

Nugent, Robert, 'Homosexuality and Magisterial Teaching', *Irish Theological Quarterly* 53, 1987.

O'Neill, Terry, Ed., <u>Biomedical Ethics: Opposing Viewpoints Series</u>, San Diego, Greenhaven Press, 1994.

*Pastoral Constitution on the Church in the Modern World: Gaudium et Spes,* n. 16., Promulgated by Pope Paul VI on December 7, 1965.

Peters, Rev. Ted, <u>Playing God: Genetic Determinism and Human Freedom</u>, New York, Routledge, 1997.

Ramsay Colloquium, 'The Homosexual Movement: a Response', *The Month,* John McDade, Ed., July 1994, pp. 260-265.

Reiss M.J. and Straughan R., <u>Improving Nature?: The Science and Ethics of Genetic Engineering</u>, New York: Cambridge University Press, 1996.

Rifkin, Jeremy, <u>The Biotech Century: Harnessing the Gene and Remaking the World</u>, New York: Tarcher/Putnam, 1998.

Rose, Steven, Lewontin, R.C. and Kamin, Leon J., <u>Not in Our Genes: Biology, Ideology and Human Nature</u>, New York, Penguin Books, 1990.

Salzman, Todd A., 'The Basic Goods Theory and Revisionism: A Methodological Comparison on the Use of Reason and Experience as Sources of Moral Knowledge', *Heythrop Journal* XLII, 2001, pp. 423-450.

Sandel, Michael J. <u>The Case Against Perfection: Ethics in the Age of Genetic Engineering</u>, Cambridge Mass. & London, England: Belknap Press of Harvard University Press, 2007.

Savulescu, Julian, 'The BioRevolution and It's Ethical Implications', South Place Ethical Society, Sunday, 5 December, 2010.

Schmidt, Thomas E., <u>Straight and Narrow?: Compassion and Clarity in the Homosexuality Debate</u>, Leicester, England: Inter-Varsity Press, 1995.

Scroggs, Robin, <u>The New Testament and Homosexuality</u>, Philadelphia, PA, Fortress Press, 1983.

Smith, Tara, 'Rights, Wrongs, and Aristotelian Egoism: Illuminating the Rights/Care Dichotomy' in *The Journal of Social Philosophy*, Vol. 29 No. 2, Fall 1998.

Spargo, Tamsin, Postmodern Encounters: Foucault and Queer Theory, Duxford, Cambridge, Icon Books, 1999, p. 13.

Spayde, John, 'The Theory of Everything' in *Utne Reader*, August 98, No. 88, p. 96.

Stonestreet, Erica, 'On Individuality', *Philosophy Now*, Issue 76, Nov/Dec 2009, pp. 17-18.

Sullivan, Andrew, Virtually Normal: An Argument About Homosexuality, New York, Vintage Books, 1995.

Tatchell, Peter, 'Global Warning', *Pride Magazine*, London, 2004, pp. 77-78.

Teilhard de Chardin, Pierre, Human Energy, New York: Harcourt, Brace, Jovanovich, Inc., 1969.

Thielicke, Helmut, Theological Ethics, Foundations, Vol. 1, William H. Lazareth, Ed., Philadelphia: Fortress, 1966, pp. 420-430.

Weinreib, Lloyd L., *Natural Law and Justice*, Cambridge, Mass., Harvard University Press, 1987.

Wilson, Edward, O., Consilience: The Unity of Knowledge, New York, Knopf, Distributed by Random House, 1998.

Wilson, E. O. 'Reply to Fukuyama', *The National Interest*, no. 56, Spring 1999, pp. 35-37.

The Working Party of The Church of England, Homosexual Relations: A Contribution to Discussion, 1978.

Zimmerman, Burke E., 'Human Germ-Line Therapy: The Case for Its Development and Use', *Journal of Medicine and Philosophy*, December 1991.


Vatican Encyclicals:

Pope Leo XIII, *Rerum Novarum: Rights and Duties of Capital and Labor*, given at St. Peter's in Rome, May 15, 1891. Published online by Libreria Editrice Vaticana. Accessed 12 January, 2008. (See especially paragraph 12.)

Pope Paul VI, *Pastoral Constitution on the Church in the Modern World*: *Gaudium et Spes*, given at Rome, December 7, 1965 see esp. Part I, Chapter I, paragraph 16. And Part II, Chapter 1, paragraphs 48, 49 and 51. Accessed online on September 18, 2006.

Pope Paul VI, *Humanae Vitae*, given at St. Peter's, Rome, July 25, 1968. Accessed online on 20 January, 2007.

The Sacred Congregation for the Doctrine of the Faith, *Persona Humana: Declaration on Certain Questions Concerning Sexual Ethics*, Rome, 29 December, 1975. Accessed online on 7 October 2006. (See especially paragraph VIII.)

Congregation for the Doctrine of Faith, Joseph Cardinal Ratzinger, Prefect, *Letter to the Bishops of the Catholic Church on the Pastoral Care of Homosexual Persons*, given at Rome, October 1, 1986. Accessed online on 20 January, 2007.

The Sacred Congregation for the Doctrine of Faith, clarifying statement by Joaquin Navarro-Valls, Vatican Spokesman, *Some Considerations Concerning Legislative Proposals on the Non-Discrimination of Homosexual Persons*, 24 July, 1992. Accessed online on 7 October, 2006.

Joseph Cardinal Ratzinger, Prefect, _Considerations Regarding Proposals to Give Legal Recognition to Unions Between Homosexual Persons_, given at Rome, from the Offices of the Congregation for the Doctrine of the Faith, June 3, 2003. Accessed online on 24 February, 2006.

Lightning Source UK Ltd.
Milton Keynes UK
UKOW04f0718270815

257585UK00001B/77/P